Philosophy of the Encounter

Philosophy of the Encounter

Later Writings, 1978–87

LOUIS ALTHUSSER

Edited by
FRANÇOIS MATHERON and OLIVER CORPET

Translated with an Introduction by
G. M. GOSHGARIAN

VERSO
London • New York

First published by Verso 2006

The material in this collection was first published
in *Sur la philosophie* © Gallimard, 1993,
and *Écrits philosophiques et politiques*, Vol. 1, ed.
François Matheron © Stock/Imec, 1994.

1 3 5 7 9 10 8 6 4 2

This book is supported by the French Ministry for Foreign Affairs,
as part of the Burgess programme headed for the French Embassy
in London by the Institut Français du Royaume Uni.

Verso
UK: 6 Meard Street, London W1F 0EG
USA: 180 Varick Street, New York, NY 10014–4606
www.versobooks.com

Verso is the imprint of New Left Books

ISBN-10: 1-84467-069-4 (hardback)
ISBN-13: 978-1-84467-069-7 (hardback)

ISBN-10: 1-84467-553-X (paperback)
ISBN-13: 978-1-84467-553-1 (paperback)

British Library Cataloguing in Publication Data
A catalogue record for this book is available from the British Library

Library of Congress Cataloging-in-Publication Data
A catalog record for this book is available from the Library of Congress

Typeset in Monotype Baskerville by Andrea Stimpson
Printed by

Contents

Note on the French Texts **vii**

List of Abbreviations **ix**

Translator's Introduction **xiii**

Letter to Merab Mardashvili **1**

Marx in his Limits **7**

The Underground Current of the Materialism of the Encounter **163**

Correspondence about 'Philosophy and Marxism' **208**

Philosophy and Marxism **251**

Portrait of the Materialist Philosopher **290**

Index **293**

Note on the French Texts

The translation of 'Philosophy and Marxism' is based on the posthumously issued French edition ('Philosophie et marxisme', *Sur la philosophie*, Paris, 1993, pp. 29–79), an abridged version of the original French text, which first saw the light, unabridged, in Spanish translation (*Filosofía y marxismo: Entrevista a Louis Althusser por Fernanda Navarro*, Mexico City, 1988). The accompanying selections from Althusser's correspondence with Navarro first appeared in *Sur la philosophie*, pp. 81–137. The other translations are based on *Écrits philosophiques et politiques*, ed. François Matheron, vol. 1, Paris, 1994, pp. 341–582. For information on the origins and editorial history of the texts in this volume, see Matheron's and Olivier Corpet's presentations of them.

Illegible words, grammatically or syntactically extraneous words and phrases, and, in Althusser's correspondence with Navarro, certain passages mentioning third parties have been replaced with asterisks [***]. The footnotes are Althusser's, except for the explanatory material placed in square brackets. Endnotes added by the translator are followed by the abbreviation 'Trans.' in square brackets; all other endnotes are by François Matheron. The translator has silently corrected minor errors of transcription after comparing Matheron's editions of 'Marx in his Limits' and 'The Underground Current of the Materialism of the Encounter' with the manuscripts.

List of Abbreviations

Works by Althusser

Collections and Longer Texts

EI = *Essays in Ideology*, trans. Ben Brewster and Grahame Lock, London, 1984.

ESC = *Elements of Self-Criticism*, trans. Grahame Lock, London, 1976.

FM = *For Marx*, trans. Ben Brewster, London, 1996.

LC = *Livre sur le communisme*, A19-01 to A19-04.

LF = *Lettres à Franca*, Paris, 1998.

LI = *Livre sur l'impérialisme*, A21-01 to A21-03.

MRM = *Montesquieu, Rousseau, Marx: Politics and History*, trans. Ben Brewster, London, 1972.

MU = *Machiavelli and Us*, trans. Gregory Elliott, London, 1999.

POE = *Philosophy of the Encounter*.

PSPS = *Philosophy and the Spontaneous Philosophy of the Scientists and Other Essays*, ed. Gregory Elliott, trans. Ben Brewster *et al.*, London, 1990.

RC = *Reading Capital,* trans. Ben Brewster, London, 1997.

SH = *The Spectre of Hegel,* trans. G. M. Goshgarian, London, 1997.

SISS = *Socialisme idéologique et socialisme scientifique,* A8-02.01 to A8-02.04.

SM = *Solitude de Machiavel et autres textes,* ed. Yves Sintomer, Paris, 1998.

SR = *Sur la reproduction,* ed. Jacques Bidet, Paris, 1995.

THC = *The Humanist Controversy,* trans. G. M. Goshgarian, London, 2003.

VN = *Les Vaches noires,* A24-01 to A24-03.

WP = *Writings on Psychoanalysis: Freud and Lacan,* trans. Jeffrey Mehlman, New York, 1996.

Shorter texts

'CM' = 'The Crisis of Marxism', trans. Grahame Lock, *Marxism Today,* July 1978, pp. 215–20, 227.

'IISA' = 'Ideology and Ideological State Apparatuses: Notes towards an Investigation', *EI* 1–60.

'ISBMP?' = 'Is it Simple to Be a Marxist in Philosophy?', *PSPS* 203–40.

'LP' = 'Lenin and Philosophy', *PSPS* 169–202.

'MCTF' = 'Le marxisme comme théorie "finie"', *SR* 281–96.

'MPH' = 'Montesquieu: Politics and History', *MRM* 9–109.

'MT' = 'Marxism Today', *PSPS* 267–80.

'OMT' = 'The Only Materialist Tradition', trans. Ted Stolze, in

Stolze and Warren Montag, ed., *The New Spinoza*, Minneapolis, University of Minnesota Press, 1997, pp. 3–19.

'RTJL' = 'Reply to John Lewis', *EI* 61–139.

'THC' = 'The Humanist Controversy', *THC* 221–305.

'TN' = 'Three Notes on the Theory of Discourses', *THC* 33–84.

'TP' = 'The Transformation of Philosophy', *PSPS* 241–65.

Works by Marx, Engels and Lenin

C1 = Karl Marx, *Capital*, vol. 1, trans. Ben Fowkes, London, 1976.

C3 = Karl Marx, *Capital*, vol. 3, trans. David Fernbach, London, 1981.

LCW = V. I. Lenin, *Collected Works*, Moscow and London, 1960–1980.

MECW = Karl Marx and Friedrich Engels, *Collected Works*, London, 1970–2002.

'P' = Marx, Preface to *A Contribution to the Critique of Political Economy*, *MECW* 29: 261–5.

Works by others

E = Benedict Spinoza, *Ethics*. (A = Axiom, P = Proposition, S = Scholium. Example: *E* II, P 15, S 2 = Ethics, Book II, Proposition 15, Scholium 2).

L = Thomas Hobbes, *Leviathan*, ed. C. B. Macpherson, Harmondsworth, 1981.

P = Niccolò Machiavelli, *The Prince*, in Machiavelli, *The Chief Works and Others*, vol. 1, trans. Allan Gilbert, Durham, North Carolina, 1989.

'ROL' = Rousseau, 'Essay on the Origin of Languages', in Rousseau, *The Discourses and Other Early Political Writings*, trans. Victor Gourevitch, Cambridge, 1977, pp. 247–99.

'RSC' = Jean-Jacques Rousseau, 'The Social Contract', in *The Social Contract and Discourses*, trans. G. D. H. Cole, London, 1913, pp. 1–123.

'RSD' = Jean-Jacques Rousseau, 'Discourse on the Origin and the Foundations of Inequality among Men (Second Discourse)', in Rousseau, *The Discourses and Other Early Political Writings*, trans. Victor Gourevitch, Cambridge, 1977, pp. 113–222.

SPN = Antonio Gramsci, *Selections from the Prison Notebooks*, trans. Quintin Hoare and Geoffrey Nowell Smith, London, 1971.

TP = Benedict Spinoza, *Tractatus politicus*, followed by the number of the book and section cited. Example: *TP* V 7 = *Tractatus politicus*, Book 5, Section 7.

TTP = Benedict Spinoza, *Tractatus theologico-politicus*, trans. Samuel Shirley, New York, 1989.

Where the author of a text is not named, it is always Althusser.

Translator's Introduction

IN MEMORY OF CONSTANCE COINER, 1948–96

I

Philosophy of the Encounter collects nearly all the philosophical work that Louis Althusser produced from late 1977 to the year he stopped producing philosophy, 1987. The main texts in it, 'Marx in his Limits' and 'The Underground Current of the Materialism of the Encounter', date, respectively, from 1978–79 and 1982–83. Between them lies an abyss, in one sense – in 1980, overtaken by the psychosis that stalked him down to his death a decade later, Althusser killed his wife Hélène Rytman – and nothing, in another: 'The Underground Current' (rather, the amorphous manuscript out of which François Matheron has skilfully carved it) was the first piece of any note to come from Althusser's pen after he laid 'Marx in his Limits' aside.

A remark of Lenin's that Althusser last invoked in 1975 pinpoints the premise of his philosophical project until then: 'if Marx did not leave behind him a "Logic" (with a capital letter), he did leave behind him the *logic* of *Capital*.' Marxist philosophy's task was to retrieve this coherent logic, contained in the 'practical state' in Marx's *chef d'œuvre*, a model of 'conceptual rigour' and 'theoretical systematicity' marred only by an inconsequential flirt with Hegel. 'Marx in his Limits' revises the premise and subverts the project, for a reason encapsulated in another Leninist pronouncement that Althusser once dismissed as an enigmatic exclamation: 'it is impossible completely to understand Marx's *Capital*, and especially its first chapter, without having thoroughly studied and understood the *whole* of Hegel's *Logic*.' Althusser now contends, in sum, that Lenin was right about the relation between *Capital* and the *Logic*, and, therefore, wrong about the logic of *Capital*: Marx did not leave behind him *a* logic, but, rather, clashing idealist and materialist logics. Consciously, he espoused the former. *Capital* is 'an essentially Hegelian work' whose 'method of exposition … coincides with the speculative genesis of the concept'. It aspires to reducing the history of capitalism 'to the development, in the Hegelian sense', of the 'simple, primitive, original form' of value.[1]

One whole side of Marx's thought proceeds from this speculative geneticism. *Capital*'s Hegelianism has its pendant in a teleology of history exemplified by the 'famous comments' in *The Poverty of Philosophy* 'on the hand-mill, water-mill and steam-mill, which justify the reduction of the dialectic of history to the dialectic generating the successive *modes of* production, that is, in the last analysis, the different production *techniques*'. The 1859 Preface to *A Contribution to the Critique of Political Economy*, which draws from this principle of the primacy of the productive forces a universal theory of human history characterized by its avoidance of 'all mention of class struggle', thus attests, not a rare Marxian lapse into pre-Marxist idealism, but the centrality of a persistent idealist strain in Marx. As for his *magnum opus*, it is not a *purely* idealist work only because the simple form from which it would deduce all else proves, in theoretical practice, to *result* from the historical process supposed to proceed from it: Marx cannot account for capital without taking account of class struggle, which the deduction of history from the value-form, like that of each mode of production from its predecessor in a hierarchy, 'requires him to bracket out'. Whence Althusser's deconstructive solution to a classic problem: in the 'true heart' of *Capital*, its historical chapters, Marx's materialist logic exceeds the idealist ideo-logic of his overarching scheme, shattering the 'fictitious unity' of the whole. The book owes its success to its failure. A 1982 interview draws the general conclusion: 'one cannot be both a Marxist and coherent.'[2]

'The Underground Current' takes that conclusion as its premise. Rather than try to derive a philosophy from Marx's incoherency, Althusser now undertakes to produce a philosophy *for* Marx – that is, against the idealist Marx, and in the (aleatory) materialist's stead. He seeks the 'premises of Marx's materialism' where he noted, in 1975, that they lay buried: in a tradition binding 'Epicurus to Spinoza' and the Hegel to whom 'Marx was close', the reluctant Spinozist of a philosophical current that is 'hardly ever mentioned'. 'The Underground Current' reconstructs the history of this repressed 'materialism of the encounter' (renamed 'aleatory materialism' by 1986), ignoring Hegel while including Nietzsche, Heidegger, Derrida and others. His survey, Althusser announces near the end of it, is 'just a prelude' to what he 'wanted to call attention to in Marx'. He produces little more than the prelude. 'Marx in his Limits', however, has already distilled the essence of what he would have said if he had: 'that Marx's thought contains, on the question of historical necessity', both 'extremely original suggestions that have nothing to do with the mechanism of inevitability' – and just the opposite.[3]

It is not hard to show that Althusser's exposure of Marx's incoherencies exposes his own. Indeed, our summary of his 1978 indictment of the idealist Marx has done precisely that: it is a patchwork of indignant Althusserian *rebuttals* of the charge that Marx was a Hegelian.[4] From *For Marx* (1965) to the 1975 'Is it Simple to Be a Marxist in Philosophy?',[5] one finds dozens of similar earlier-Althusserian denials of Marx's Hegelianism, easily convertible, through negation of the negation in Freud's sense, not Hegel's, into later-Althusserian proofs of it. Manifestly, this is evidence of a startling reversal of position. The question is whether it does not also betray an underlying continuity.

The last substantial item in *Philosophy of the Encounter*, 'Philosophy and Marxism' (accompanied by extracts from Althusser's correspondence about the text), suggests – or embodies – an answer to this question. First published (without the correspondence) in Spanish translation in 1988, this primer of the philosophy of the encounter poses as an interview. But it is no such thing. As the 'interviewer',

Fernanda Navarro, has hinted by embedding, towards the end, a replica of the 'Portrait of the Materialist Philosopher' – Althusser's last philosophical text and the coda to the present volume – and, near the beginning, the portrait of the materialist philosopher that graces his 1965 introduction to *For Marx*, she has fashioned a picture of Althusser's thought out of passages or paraphrases of the writing he produced in between, pieced together with material from their conversations of the 1980s.[6] Far from diminishing the value of her 'pseudo-interview' (as Althusser unabashedly described her collage shortly before enthusiastically authorizing its publication),[7] this cut-and-paste work grounds it. For 'Philosophy and Marxism' proposes, by way of its form, a thesis its co-authors surely wanted us to consider: that Althusser's late work does not refute his earlier work, even when it contradicts it, but reveals patterns once invisible in it – not by repeating, but by transforming them.

II

Althusser presents the materialism of the encounter under another name in a March 1976 lecture, 'The Transformation of Philosophy'. Its subject is a 'new practice of philosophy', defined against that of the 'party of the state'. The philosophical practice of the party of the state consists in fictitiously unifying the whole range of social practices under its hegemonic Truth; it does so on behalf of a ruling ideology, thereby helping it to dominate the distinct ideology of the ruled. To bring out its commanding position in the philosophical tradition, Althusser calls this state philosophy simply 'philosophy'. He calls aleatory materialism 'non-philosophy', a term patterned after Engels' description of the proletarian state as a 'non-state'. Thus he introduces aleatory materialism (a term we shall use from now on to designate its Althusserian variant) as the non-philosophy of the dictatorship of the proletariat.

Between 'The Transformation of Philosophy' and what the composition of *Philosophy of the Encounter* suggests was a turn or *Kehre* (Antonio Negri)[8] – charted in the apparently prophetic letter placed at its head, initiated in 'Marx in his Limits', and negotiated in 'The Underground Current' – Althusser led a fight for working-class dictatorship, an idea the PCF was then retiring from its theoretical arsenal. 'Marx in his Limits' is a *summa* of his pleas for keeping it; this defence of the non-state leads on, in the present volume, to his plea for non-philosophy. The whole book can accordingly be read as the realization of the programme laid out in the 1976 lecture. In fact, Althusser's aleatory-materialist turn did not come with the passage from 'Marx in his Limits' to 'The Underground Current', which constitutes a record of the *Kehre* only in the sense that it stages a *re-enactment* of it. If Althusser's turn can be dated at all – that is, if his thought as a whole is not traversed by an aleatory-materialist current[9] countered by his own 'theoreticist' compromises with the philosophical party of the state – then it occurred not in 1983, but ten years before.

It was rung in by the 1969 manuscript *Sur la reproduction*, a theorization of the dictatorship of the bourgeoisie that is, unmistakably, a prototype of 'Marx in his Limits'. It was carried out in a pair of fragmentary unpublished books, *Livre sur le communisme* (1972) and *Livre sur l'impérialisme* (1973), which formulate basic concepts of the materialism of the encounter, and thus constitute a kind of prototype of 'The Underground Current'. When one adds that the 1972–73 manuscripts elaborate elements of a 'theory of the encounter' that Althusser sketched in 1966; that he undertook, around 1973, a study of the ancient atomists which soon saw them promoted to the rank of Marx's 'most important', albeit 'indirect', ancestors; and that he rehearsed his 1970s battle with the Party in the 1960s, it appears that the lesson of 'Philosophy and Marxism' can be transcribed in another, historical-philological key.[10] The late work is, in many respects, quite literally a transformation of Althusser's philosophy, a critical rewriting of earlier – often much earlier – work. To mistake the years in which aleatory materialism took provisionally final form for its only context is, therefore, to endow it with a fictive genealogy – one the late Althusser, to be sure, helped to invent.

As for the creative transformation of Althusser's philosophy wrought by the Anglophone consensus to the effect that he countenanced or even welcomed his Party's rejection of working-class dictatorship, it would be uncharitable not to ignore it. But the record should be set straight.

III

From the early 1960s on, the PCF's leadership was wedded to the thesis that the French road to socialism ran through the ballot box. Because the Party had, since the War, never polled more (or much less) than a quarter of the national vote, reason seemed to dictate that it had to forge electoral alliances with other Left parties; because it dwarfed them all, it could, the assumption ran, easily dominate its prospective allies. In 1965, this strategy spawned a Communist–Socialist electoral pact around the Socialist François Mitterrand's bid to unseat De Gaulle. Encouraged by his respectable showing, the PCF's leaders assiduously sought, in the years thereafter, to put the nascent Communist–Socialist 'Union of the Left' on the foundations of a common governmental programme. They succeeded in the aftermath of May 1968: the *Programme commun* was signed with the Socialists and another small party to their right in mid-1972.

Its history is a history of Socialist success at Communist expense. By 1977 at the latest, the cantankerous alliance had unmistakably turned to the advantage of the PCF's once junior partner; the Socialist Party was certain to emerge from the March 1978 parliamentary elections, which the Union of the Left was widely expected to carry, as the hegemonic Left force. Late in 1977, the PCF leadership therefore took a secret decision to sabotage the *Programme commun*, effectively handing the elections to the Right. For the millions who had been counting on them to ring in the final conflict with French capitalism, the defeat was traumatic. Moreover, it came at a time when Communist intellectuals and a section of the Party's mid-level leadership were in unprecedented revolt against the famously undemocratic methods of its ruling circle. For these and other reasons – among them the French mass media's timely 1975 discovery of the Gulag – the late 1970s saw thousands of voters desert the Party, initiating its precipitous twentieth-century decline. By 1981, when the Socialists swept the presidential and legislative elections, the PCF was already a distinctly minority force on the Left; the four secondary ministries it was allotted in Mitterrand's government reflected its subaltern place in the new political pecking order.

Althusser was theoretically in favour of a Communist–Socialist alliance, and ferociously opposed to paying the price at which he thought it would come: a swift retreat from class culminating in Communist rejection of the dictatorship of the proletariat (effectively accomplished in 1976). His verdict on the *Programme commun*, handed down in a 1973 conversation with a Communist potentate, Roland Leroy, reflected this opposition; the grail that, as Party leaders saw it, vindicated a decade of earnest questing was, he told Leroy, 'a lure, and a "paper" lure at that'.[11] They spoke a year after the agreement was reached. But Althusser had not waited until 1973 to decry his party's 1976 turn. In the first half of the 1960s, he and his co-thinkers had waged a preventive war against it, one the PCF's then 'official' philosopher quite rightly called a 'systematic attack on the Party's politics led by the group of philosophers influenced by Althusser'.[12]

Concretely, the Althusserians targeted the Marxist-humanist and Hegelian-Marxist philosophies that, by glossing over the themes of class struggle and revolutionary rupture, facilitated a Communist marriage with the Socialists on the Socialists' terms. The theoretical jousting escalated into a (carefully controlled) inner-Party organizational battle capped by a landmark 1966 Central Committee meeting at Argenteuil, where the Althusserians' 'left-wing anti-Stalinist positions' were lengthily debated and roundly rejected. The outcome of the clash convinced the principal loser that the PCF, like the CPSU, was 'objectively pursuing reformist, revisionist policies' and becoming a 'Social-Democratic' party, that it had 'ceased to be revolutionary' and was 'all but lost'.[13] The proof was that it must soon abandon the dictatorship of the proletariat.

Such, at any rate, was the burden of a set of texts that Althusser wrote in the wake of Argenteuil. The PCF had forgotten the lesson of Marx's 'Critique of the Gotha Programme', he warned in a 1966 letter that he resolved to hand to General Secretary Waldeck Rochet, and warned again in a 1967 polemic aimed at French Communism's Marxist-humanist intellectuals. 'For the sake of unity' with the party of reform, he complained, the PCF was preparing to strike an impossible 'compromise between Marxist theory and ideology'. But if the French Party was repeating the mistake the German Party had made at Gotha, its most prestigious theoretician was not about to repeat Marx's. To the PCF's re-edition of the Gotha Programme, he would oppose his re-edition of Marx's *Critique* – and, unlike his illustrious predecessor, see to its publication by the Party press before 1966 was out.[14] Intended for an audience of Communist activists, the projected book, *Socialisme idéologique et socialisme scientifique*, develops a point crucial to Marx's text as well: the idea that compromise on the question of working-class dictatorship inevitably saps the very foundations of revolutionary socialism.

The PCF's rejection of this 'key concept of Marxist theory', Althusser would argue in the 1976 text *Les Vaches noires* – a projected book on class dictatorship intended for the Party press and an audience of Communist activists – 'crown[ed] a long-standing tendency'. He meant, at one level, that the decision to retire the idea had been in the making for a decade and more, as its partisans were happy to agree.[15] But he also meant, as his 1966 evocation of Gotha indicates and *Socialisme idéologique* repeats, that it represented something like communism's original sin: an apparently congenital weakness for the deadly illusion that the state is above class, or could be or should be. Its susceptibility to this myth, according to *Socialisme idéologique*, stems ultimately from the inevitable immersion of the workers' movement in a sea of bourgeois and petty-bourgeois ideology, a situation that engenders the abiding temptation to transform the 'scientific notions of historical materialism' into their ideological travesties, and ensures that 'the struggle inside Marxist organizations' will 'last as long as the history of the workers' movement'. The 'decisive point at which this transformation makes itself felt', runs the decisive thesis of the projected book, 'is the class struggle and dictatorship of the proletariat', 'the critical point in the whole theoretical and political history of

Marxism'. What happens when socialism closes its eyes to it? The sleep of revolutionary reason breeds the reformist dream of a 'true, classless democracy', the idea that it is possible to define 'democracy without taking its class content into account'. That dream, in turn, encourages the substitution of a politics of 'class collaboration' for a politics of class struggle. Class collaboration is the practical consequence of the theoretical delusion that the exploited can 'reform society while avoiding revolution' – or 'put bourgeois society in parentheses in order to create the future in its midst'.[16]

Why can they not, at the price of a protracted war of position against their exploiters? Althusser's answer comes by way of his theorization of the ideological state apparatuses, proposed three years later in *Sur la reproduction.* The short form of it is that ideological state apparatuses are *state* apparatuses, and, as such, like courts, ministries, and death squads, part of the arsenal of the dictatorship *of the bourgeoisie.* The book contains, by the same token, his rebuttal of the PCF's developing argument for 'democratization' of the capitalist state, later erected into an alternative to working-class dictatorship on the basis of a notion of 'true democracy' that the Party mobilized in a feeble *defence* of class dictatorship at Argenteuil. We shall glance at the theoretical premises of *Sur la reproduction* in a bit more detail later. Its main practical conclusion, restated in 'Marx in his Limits', speaks for itself: 'If, one day in our future, the Communist Party and its allies find themselves in a position to win a majority in the legislative elections, they will need to bear in mind that … without *seizing state power,* without *dismantling the state's Repressive Apparatus* … without a long struggle to smash the bourgeois Ideological State Apparatuses, Revolution is unthinkable.'[17]

Althusser did not deliver his 1966 letter to the Party, or publish his other 1960s critiques of the developing Gallic Gotha Programme. The exception – the controversial 1970 paper on interpellation and the ideological state apparatuses culled from the otherwise posthumously released *Sur la reproduction* – was not really an exception, since the political intent of the book was lost on the vast audience of the paper, which seemed to most readers to plead the necessity of a long war of position inside the ISAs – that is, inside the capitalist state – not of smashing them along with the rest of it, in a long *post*-revolutionary struggle. Thus there was virtually no public record of Althusser's post-Argenteuil bid to forestall French Communism's seduction by the sirens of 'true, classless democracy'. In English, this remains the case.

Why did Althusser duck a crucial political-theoretical fight? He 'felt helpless in the face of realities like the Party'; he 'felt even more helpless in the face of certain ideological misunderstanding-effects' due to his status as 'a very prestigious personage'; and, not least, 'he was ill', he says in explanation of Marx's suppression of his *Critique* in 'Marx in his Limits' – which, like his previous decrials of his un-Marxist willingness to suppress his polemic, was also suppressed.[18] Yet the later Althusser cannot fairly be accused of continuing to follow Marx's bad example. Witness the second round of his fight for class dictatorship.

IV

In November 1977, a few months before the legislative elections that the French Communist Party and its allies were expected to carry, Althusser took the floor at a Venice conference organized by Il Manifesto, a far-Left group pushed out of the PCI in 1969, to proclaim that Marxism was in crisis. He made his provocative thesis still more provocative by echoing a charge that Italian Socialism's leading political philosopher, Norberto Bobbio, had been pressing the harder the closer the PCI and PCF came to power. Marxism did not 'have … a theory of the state, state power or the state apparatus', Althusser declared before an audience of socialists and union activists from across Europe and even the USSR, repeating something he had been saying in private for at least a decade. The lack was partly to blame for communism's 'tragic history'. One reason it had never been made good, he added, paraphrasing his abortive 1964 book on 'the personality cult', was that Stalin had murderously 'snuffed out' the theoretical crisis precipitated by his dogmatism, doing Marxist thought perhaps irreparable damage. Another was a baneful tendency to credit Marxism with a coherency and completeness simulated by *Capital*'s 'fictitious theoretical unity', but belied by the 'contradictions and gaps' that marked the book as they did the rest of Marx's work.[19]

This preview of 'Marx in his Limits' caused the predictable stir. The excitement was kept running at the desired pitch by a follow-up interview published in April in Il Manifesto's daily of the same name. From then until September and beyond, in the context of a controversy over the state that had been agitating the Western European Left since 1973, Italian, French, and German-speaking socialists replied to Althusser in *Il Manifesto* and elsewhere. The proceedings of the Venice conference appeared in Italian, French and English; the interview and most of the replies were collected in books published in Italy and West Berlin, while a similar debate ran in the French Communist journal *Dialectiques*. Thus 'Marx in his Limits', if published in its turn, would have come as Althusser's last word in a pan-European discussion kindled by a sampling of it and raging as he wrote it. In the event, his rejoinder was limited to a few pages on Marxism included in an Italian encyclopaedia in November 1978 – pages written before the fight had fairly begun.[20] Its embattled protagonist did not fully substantiate his 1977 charge about the rudimentary nature of the Marxist theory of the state until 'Marx in his Limits' appeared in 1994.

Althusser's defence of its rudiments, however, was better developed, and already in the public domain. Moreover, he continued, as it were, to press the defence while pursuing the attack – consistently, since both advanced the same struggle against the party of the state. The Marx he defended was the one for whom the sole alternative to capitalist dictatorship was working-class dictatorship, and the state a set of apparatuses that maintained one to the exclusion of the other. This was the Marx who knew that 'the vocation of a Communist Party is not to "participate" in government, but to overturn and destroy the power of the bourgeois state'; indeed, that 'the Party, for reasons of principle, should … keep out of the proletarian state as well'.[21] But there was also the Marx who authorized the teleological historiography of the primacy of the productive forces, and, with it, a Stalinist or Social-Democratic negation or attenuation of class struggle. Where was *this* Marx's theory of the state? It was in the blanks in the other's, the blanks that made his rudimentary theory rudimentary, the blanks partly filled in, notably, by those famous comments on the hand-mill, water-mill and steam-mill in *The Poverty of Philosophy*, the reductive treatment of the state in Volume Three of *Capital*, and the notorious 1859 Preface, but, above all, by the Marxian party of the state responsible for the tragic history of communism. It was materialized, no less, in the political practice of the putatively post-Stalinist Communist Parties, whose attempt to distance themselves from their tragic history were hobbled by the ties that firmly bound them to it. One, from Althusser's standpoint, mattered more than all the rest: their rejection of working-class dictatorship; in positive terms, their adhesion to the bourgeois ideology of the (at least potentially) class-neutral state, viceroy of His Apolitical Majesty, the Economy. It was from this 'hyper-Leninist' standpoint, as his Communist adversaries saw the matter, combined – in their view, paradoxically – with an 'anti-Party movementism' bordering on anarchism, that Althusser led the combat *for* Marx's position on the state which alone makes his denunciation of its limits intelligible.

Hostilities were opened with Georges Marchais's January 1976 public confession that, in his 'personal opinion', talk of class dictatorship was 'outmoded' in democracies such as modern France. The PCF soon discovered that it was of the same mind as its General Secretary: its February Twenty-Second Congress duly approved, by the usual unanimous vote, Marchais's recommendation that the Party statutes be purged of all mention of the idea. Formally, execution of the modification was left to the Twenty-Third Congress. In the event, this gave opponents three years in which to pursue a quixotic attempt to persuade the rank-and-file not to take the step. Althusser bent himself to the task. In 1976–77, he pled the case for the dictatorship of the proletariat not just in the open, but in the limelight, in France and abroad, orally and in print. By mid-1976, his opposition to the turn was public knowledge from Barcelona to Berlin. In Paris, it was *common* knowledge – and front-page news.[22]

The riposte to Marchais was launched, before the Twenty-Second Congress, by Étienne Balibar, acting, the opposing camp not unreasonably assumed, as the avant-garde of a small Althusserian-Communist army. Its presumed General unequivocally confirms, in *Les Vaches noires*, that he wholeheartedly approved of his younger colleague's forward defence. The public appearances that he began making shortly after the Twenty-Second Congress loudly broadcast the same message, captured in a quip with which he seems to have garnished all of them: disagreeing with the idea of class dictatorship, ran the one-liner borrowed from a stand-up comic, was like disagreeing with the law of gravity. The first of these talks, if we do not count his 1976 lecture on 'non-philosophy', delivered in Barcelona and Madrid, was given in Paris in April. Prevented by interference from the Party's upper echelons from speaking on the Twenty-Second Congress at the invitation of the Sorbonne's Communist Student Organization, the PCF's best-known philosopher capitalized on an invitation to its April book fair to present, along with his new book *Positions*, his stand on the dictatorship of the proletariat; he shared the podium with Lucien Sève, the Party's leading Eurocommunist philosopher and the leading proponent of its turn. A year later, at a presentation of *Les Communistes et l'État* – a semi-official apology for the PCF's move by Sève and two others – he presented it again, this time in a reply to the authors that he made from the floor, to wild cheering from a throng of young supporters. In the interim, in July 1976, he had returned to Barcelona and Madrid to deliver a long lecture on the theory of working-class dictatorship, inspiring a hostile Spanish commentator to reflect on the inordinate indulgence that the PCF was showing in not expelling him. He even managed, after stubborn effort, to deliver his Sorbonne lecture to the Communist Student Organization in December, despite the Party establishment's last-ditch effort to foil this 'veiled factional attack' by announcing its cancellation, and after braving a hail of leaflets unleashed by stalwarts of 'the line of the Twenty-Second Congress'.[23]

Althusser was a 'theoretical personage whose every word counted', as 'Marx in his Limits' says of Marx; the events just mentioned drew crowds thousands strong. The April 1976 lecture was reported in detail in the PCF's daily, which printed a surprisingly full, fair account of Althusser's argument to the effect that no socialist revolution could succeed without 'smashing the bourgeois state apparatus and replacing it with a revolutionary one'. (The book fair talk also provoked an oral assault by Marchais after Althusser had left – 'Do you want to abolish elections? Why cling to dogmas that are dead in our eyes?') A revised version of his Sorbonne lecture was issued as a short book in May 1977; more diplomatically worded than his other indictments of the Party's move – probably so as to seem a little less like a veiled factional attack – it, too, makes no secret of its author's conviction that the object of revolutionary politics is to seize state power and then 'democratize' its apparatuses by *dismantling* them. His July Madrid–Barcelona lecture, for its part, yielded a long text placed at the head of a 1978 Spanish collection of his writings; the main lines of Althusser's discussion of class dictatorship in 'Marx in his Limits', down to the concluding analysis of the antinomies of Gramsci's theory of hegemony, are all sketched in it.[24]

In a word, by the time he sat down to write 'Marx in his Limits', Althusser had said and published enough against the prevailing PCF line to convince observers such as the sociologist Alain Touraine that he had become 'the leader, perhaps despite himself, of a left opposition at the heart of the PCF'. He had *written* enough to justify the same judgement two years earlier. Had *Les Vaches noires* been published as planned – early in his campaign around the dictatorship of the proletariat – it would have sufficed to set Althusser up as what Touraine believed he had become towards the end of it: 'the source and potential leader of an "alternative" to the PCF's present politics'. So, at any rate, thought Balibar, who advised against the text's release on the grounds that it would thrust Althusser into an oppositional role which he lacked the 'means' and inner-Party support to sustain.[25] He might fairly have said the same thing about 'Marx in his Limits' – or, for that matter, *Socialisme idéologique*.

Every thesis is a counter-thesis, Althusser affirms, which suggests that, before we say a word about the positions he was defending in 'Marx in his Limits', we should touch on those he was defending them against. The better known require no summary. Denouncing the 'trick theatre' of the theorists of 'force, pure and alone', 'Marx in his Limits' is manifestly replying to a *certain* Foucault, and, especially, his protégés among the then newly prominent *nouveaux philosophes*. The thesis that the political apparatus of the bourgeois state should be the object, not the *terrain*, of working-class class struggle, is advanced against Nicos Poulantzas and a still closer comrade-in-theoretical arms, Balibar. The latter had by 1977 begun defending a version of the Poulantzian position that he had only recently been storming: the idea that the capitalist state can be democratized from within – even, as he puts it in a later summary of his nascent disagreement with Althusser, that the very 'existence of a social movement "outside the state" is a contradiction in terms', so that the 'development of democracy beyond its class frontiers' does *not* imply 'the dismantling of the state apparatus'. The closing critique of Gramsci calls for a longer gloss, since it names only one of its targets. The rest are the Italian Communist thinkers – who had, since the mid-1960s, been engaged in an attempt to present the Gramscian notion of hegemony as an alternative to class dictatorship – and their French disciples, notably Christine Buci-Glucksmann, who criticized Althusser in the light of the Italians' reinterpretation of Gramsci.[26]

The more obscure, and more central, polemic in 'Marx in his Limits' assumes a familiarity with odd debates on matters such as the revolutionary potential of the French anti-riot police, and now forgotten arguments that made their way from *Les Communistes et l'État* into the discussion documents for the PCF's May 1979 Twenty-Third Congress. Since Althusser did not consider such material too humble for extended, if scornful, notice in 'Marx in his Limits', we should review it briefly here.

V

The tendency that Althusser had fought in the PCF since the 1960s was common to most West European Communist Parties. By the mid-1970s it had acquired a new name, Eurocommunism. Eurocommunism's distinguishing feature was the one Althusser had labelled 'ideological socialism': rejection of the idea that a state was necessarily the lynchpin of the dictatorship of a particular class in favour of the claim that it was possible to change the class character of certain states. In particular, the proletariat and its allies could use certain parliamentary democratic states – notably those in which the biggest Eurocommunist Parties, the PCI and the PCF, hoped to help form governments – as tools for establishing truly democratic rule. It could then use those democratized states to replace capitalism with socialism.

The Eurocommunist argument rebutted throughout most of 'Marx in his Limits' was thus not that the existing French state was not a class state. Quite the contrary: according to a theory on which the PCF had put its imprimatur in the mid-1960s,[27] it was dominated by the boards of some thirty monopolistic firms that exploited most of the rest of the population in league with international capital. But, because these 'state monopoly capitalists' were numerically insignificant, they could be isolated by a 'Union of the French People', who shared an interest in chasing them from their state fiefdoms. This would be accomplished, after a Left victory at the polls, by 'pushing democracy to its limits' or transforming it into an 'advanced democracy' or a 'new democracy' (the formulas varied). There was no need to establish a violent class dictatorship to do so, or a power unrestrained by law: such forms had been mandated by specific historical conditions, notably those of the Russian Revolution, where only a minority had been for socialism and the Bolsheviks had confronted an armed dictatorship. Conditions in France were infinitely more auspicious. Thanks to a century and more of working-class struggle, representative democracy had imposed decisive legal constraints on state power. The monopolies respected them even under bourgeois democracy. Why should they respect them less under *advanced* democracy, where a large majority would see to their enforcement? Under such conditions, an absolute majority could be rallied to socialism before its construction began. There would then be no need to destroy the state of an already socialist populace; it could, rather, be continually democratized and 'revolutionized' from within, and thus transformed into an agent of the new order. Had Gramsci not shown that 'the conquest of state power is far rather the consequence than the cause of a class's dominant role'?[28]

'Marx in his Limits' takes particular issue with two corollaries of the idea of 'democratizing' the state. That the actually existing democratic state served special interests because it had been commandeered by monopoly capital suggested that, by nature, democracy had a universal vocation. The suggestion had its Communist *locus classicus*, for Althusser, in an 'openly Rightist, bourgeois' essay[29] by François Hincker later dissolved into *Les Communistes et l'État* and distilled back out in 'Marx in his Limits', where it does yeoman's service, anonymously, as the archetypal bad example. The French state, Hincker said, albeit 'bourgeois', was also 'social'. It exercised 'genuinely democratic functions', and, as such, had authentic 'universal content'; 'smashing' it was in fact a matter of liberating its universal social functions from their bourgeois prison. Witness the fact that it rendered services which, 'taken separately', possessed 'universal use-value'. It 'built schools, roads, and hospitals', and ran courts which, while they *tended* to favour the dominant, also 'ensured, like it or not, a certain security, order, and calm'. Moreover, if the state exercised a 'political class constraint', it did so, 'first of all, by law', which by no means necessarily implied the use of violence. As for the officials who applied this essentially non-violent constraint – civil servants, magistrates, court officers, police – they were increasingly troubled by the glaring, 'unbearable' 'class character' of their state, which thus harboured potential enemies in the 'very heart of its apparatus'. The last theme was a Eurocommunist shibboleth: the righteously indignant, even rebellious state agent, the riot policeman included, was a stock figure in the folklore of Eurocommunism, the short form of its argument against the orthodox Marxist thesis of the indivisibility of the class state. The space 'Marx in his Limits' devotes to minimizing it is an index of its popularity.[30]

For certain Italian Eurocommunist theorists, 'democratizing' the state meant saving it from itself. Pitting, on Gramsci's warrant, the idea of a gradual conquest of power against the thesis that a revolutionary class had to destroy the existing state, they argued that the Party had, in its quest for hegemony, to work 'profound strategic transformations' in its relation to it. In Biagio De Giovanni's version of the argument, to which 'Marx in his Limits' pays conspicuous if anonymous attention, the task of the 'proletariat's party of government' was no longer 'to detach major sections of the ruling class from the state', let alone to smash it; it was to 'build democracy on state terrain', *recomposing* the society and state which the dominant class's 'political forms' tended to '*disaggregate*'. It was *within* the new, recomposed state that a 'transformation of the relations between classes' would commence.[31] The passive support the PCI had already lent a Christian Democratic government was presumably proof that it already had.

VI

The reader will find Althusser's response to these arguments in 'Marx in his Limits'. Rather than summarize it, let us outline the principles that found it. They are the founding principles of aleatory materialism as well. For it is by virtue of Marx's discovery of the necessity of class dictatorship – his main contribution to knowledge, he wrote in 1852[32] – that he belongs, according to Althusser, to the 'undercurrent current'. Since Althusser's anti-teleological reconceptualization of it as the discovery of 'the necessity of contingency' grounds his own aleatory materialism, a glance at his thirty years' reflection on class dictatorship will provide us with the elements of an aleatory-materialist primer.

'The Underground Current' closes with a discussion of the two Marxian conceptions of the mode of production. The first, aleatory-materialist, has it that a mode of production originates in an 'aleatory encounter of independent elements'; it 'culminates in the theory of *primitive accumulation*'. The second, rooted in 'the necessity … of the accomplished fact', is 'totalitarian, teleological and philosophical'. This discussion breaks off after a few pages. It is pursued in Althusser's first book, the 1959 *Montesquieu: Politics and History*.

Politics and History claims that Montesquieu anticipated the materialist Marx. One reason is that he rejected 'the problem of origins as absurd', and thought 'history without attributing to it an end'. He was 'probably the first person to do so before Marx'. What was gained thereby is demonstrated in the book's conclusion, which applies Montesquieu's anti-teleological principles to Montesquieu.

The Marquis de la Brède did not work his 'theoretical revolution', says this lesson in aleatory-materialist historiography *avant la lettre*, because he was a prophet of the revolutionary bourgeoisie. Contrary to the usual claim, precisely the bourgeoisie's, he was a man 'who looked towards the past'. Indeed, there *was* no revolutionary bourgeoisie to which he *could* have looked. Althusser makes the last point in a passage about evading the 'appearances of retrospective history' that unmistakably anticipates a famous warning in *For Marx* about writing history in the future anterior. Just as unmistakably, it rehearses the conclusion to 'The Underground Current'.

The most 'delicate point' in *Politics and History*, says its author in a 1959 letter, bears on a 'singular encounter' of two ideas about the late feudal French bourgeoisie: that the 'primary conflict' of the day pitted it against the nobles; and that, in this conflict, the king 'sided with' it, or 'should have or could have'. We shall return to the king. Let us first consider the 'difficult problem of the nature … of the bourgeoisie'. It had to do with what Althusser calls, in 1983, the historiography of 'the accomplished fact', exemplified by the anachronistic tendency to think the early bourgeoisie as 'an *element predestined* to unify all the other elements of the mode of production'.

'The biggest danger', he goes on in 1959, 'is to project onto the "bourgeoisie" of this period the image of the later bourgeoisie.' One has to 'lend the *bourgeoisie* of absolute monarchy the traits of the later bourgeoisie in order to think it in this early period as a class radically antagonistic to the feudal class'. In reality, 'nothing is more doubtful' than that 'the mercantile economy' on which its 'most advanced elements' were 'essentially dependent' 'was foreign to feudal society in principle'. Not only was the mercantile bourgeoisie not alien to the feudal order, it was an integral part of it: 'the whole cycle of its economic activity … remain inscribed *in the limits and structures of the feudal State*'. The 1959 letter goes so far as to suggest that one cannot here 'speak of a bourgeois class' at all, at least 'as fundamentally antagonistic to the feudal class'. 'The mercantile economy on which its power and pretensions are based is not radically at odds with the economic category of feudal production in the period.'

Who sowed the illusion that it was? *Montesquieu* names accomplices; 'The Underground Current' unmasks their ringleader. It is the author of the discussion of the mercantile economy in *Capital*, where 'we encounter the great question of the *bourgeoisie*'. Here Marx forgets that he was the second person after Montesquieu to undertake to think history without attributing to it an end. He reverts to the ideology of the 1859 Preface, and, thus, the notion 'of a mythical "decay" of the feudal mode of production and the birth of the bourgeoisie out of the midst of this decay'. 'What proves', Althusser asks in 1983 as he does in 1959, that the feudal bourgeoisie 'was not a class of the feudal mode of production, a sign of the reinforcement rather than the decay of this mode? … What if the bourgeoisie, far from being the contrary product of the feudal class, was its … crowning perfection?'

The history lesson is also a lesson in politics. Feudal society, Montesquieu knows, obeys a 'necessity whose empire is so strict that it embraces not only bizarre institutions which last, but even the accident … contained in a momentary encounter'. He may even know why: the feudal constellation of institutions which lasts is crowned by one which ensures that it will *continue* to last, its 'limits and structures' intact, to the very moment of its dissolution. This guarantor of the necessity of feudal society's least contingencies is its 'State apparatus', embodied in the king.

Yet the king is not the state. The lonely hour of His Majesty never comes; the 'king is never alone'. The absolutist state, Montesquieu understands, is one in which 'eminences and ranks' prevail. The absolute monarch who forgets it comes up against the 'rock' of the aristocrats' idea of their aristocracy: their 'honour', on which the monarchy runs the way a motor 'runs on petrol'. Honour, for Althusser's Montesquieu, is an idea corresponding to a force 'above any laws, not just religious and moral … but also political'. Law is another translation of this force; the law of the realm preserves a force above the law from encroachment by the king, the people, or an alliance of the two. It preserves the king into the bargain, planting 'the rampart of the nobility' between him and the people. The people, the 'fourth *puissance*' banished to the other side of the twin ramparts of honour and law, is absent from the hierarchical alliance of their exploiters, and only allusively present in Montesquieu himself. Its absence is all but absolute: the fourth *puissance* 'haunt[s] the alliance of the other three as a memory does its loss: by its censorship'.

One sees, then, once the mirage of retrospective history is dispelled, why the encounter of the two received ideas about the late feudal period is dangerous. The idea that the conflict at its heart pitted bourgeoisie against nobility, and that, in this conflict, the king 'sided with' the former, breeds the illusion that the king played one off against the other in order 'to raise himself above' these 'two antagonistic classes' – or 'should have or could have'. That is, it encourages a 'notion of … the State' according to which 'a political power can be established outside classes and over them'. Marx, too, once entertained this illusion, writing in *The German Ideology* that in eighteenth-century France, where 'aristocracy and bourgeoisie [were] contending for domination', 'domination [was] shared'. But that, in Althusser's view, was the tribute he advanced to the un-Marxist myth of the state. Class domination, he saw soon thereafter, cannot be shared.

The reason lies in the very nature of domination. Grounded in exploitation, the 'force above the law' on which the state runs, says *Montesquieu*, is a *surplus* of force. This surplus measures the difference between the respective forces of 'power and poverty', between the violence of the exploiting classes, on the one hand, and that of the 'masses of the exploited' on the other. Transforming it into laws that 'maintain and perpetuate' the domination of the exploiters, the State apparatus necessarily excludes the exploited – the 'force' of the exploited – from the force crystallized in the state. They are similarly excluded, or, better, 'made … absent', by the force crystallized in the dominant ideology: for the ideology that provides the state's 'petrol' is *also* a realization of the excess violence that measures the ruling class's advantage in the struggle of the classes. This description, Althusser insists, applies to the feudal state as such, not, as might be imagined, to its more primitive forms alone. Absolute monarchy, according to *Montesquieu*, is the 'indispensable political apparatus' that the changing historical situation imposes on the underlying 'regime', a 'new political form required to maintain' the old 'regime of exploitation'. The regime itself would not change until the apparatus of domination that crowned it did – until 'certain *journées révolutionnaires*' smashed 'the limits and structures of the feudal State', shortening its royal representative by a head.

Whence the delicacy of the 'most delicate point' in *Politics and History*. It has to do with the '"bourgeois" contamination', Althusser says in his 1959 letter, 'of the Marxist idea of class relations'. Responsible for this contamination were the eighteenth century's 'reformists', the first to trade in the notion that 'absolute monarchy was set up *against the nobility*, and that the king relied on the *commoners* to balance the power of his feudal opponents'.[33] What these early representatives of the long-standing tendency failed to see (along with a certain Marx) was that feudal society was, from first to last, a dictatorship of the aristocracy.[34] What made their error delicate was the systematic transposition of it by their twentieth-century Communist heirs.

'Marx in his Limits' uses a term that Althusser introduced in a 1975 discussion of class struggle at the level of theory, 'conflictual difference', to name the concept that *Montesquieu* introduces, without the name, to think class struggle at the level of ideology and the state. It is the soul of Althusser's vision of class dictatorship or domination (the second word, the *Manifesto*'s, says 'Marx in his Limits', is 'a thousand times better' than the first, which Marx chose out of a 'taste for extremes');[35] it sums up, in a phrase, his quarrel with Eurocommunist visions of democratizing the state. Because the state results from the transformation of an *excess* of class force, the differential between the class struggle of the dominant class and all the others (friend or foe), it is by definition the preserve of the victors in the struggle. And it is such *whatever* the 'political form' through which the dominant exercise state domination: the dominion of the landed nobility persists under absolutism, that of the capitalist class is not necessarily diminished – the contrary generally holds – with the advent of parliamentary democracy. By the same token, dictatorship (in the usual political sense) and bourgeois democracy are both forms of capitalist 'dictatorship' (in Marx's). Reversing class domination is not a matter of changing such *forms*, but depends on securing a surplus of political, economic, and ideological force over a class adversary. Without that excess of force, there can be no question of springing 'structures and limits'.

An aleatory-materialist axiom affirms 'the primacy of the structure over its elements' 'once the encounter has been effected'.[36] *Montesquieu* illustrates it. It asserts, against the teleological Marx or his stand-ins, that the feudal bourgeoisie is thoroughly *feudal*, not an embryo of bourgeois society gestating in a late feudal womb, because it is a subordinate element of a structure constituted by a feudal class dictatorship. Whether or not the latter idea was, in 1959, an element of a structure of thought that could be called aleatory-materialist is a question we shall here suspend.

VII

If an encounter is to give rise to 'a world', 'The Underground Current' affirms, 'that encounter must last; it must be, not a "brief encounter", but a lasting encounter, which then becomes the basis for all reality, all necessity, all Meaning and all reason. But the encounter can also not last; then there is no world.' *Politics and History* considers, from the standpoint of its result, the lasting encounter, such as the ones that gave rise to the worlds of feudalism or capitalism. But Althusser's overriding concern is the brief encounter: concretely, the one that engendered Soviet society, shakily based on a 'socialist mode of production'. 'Socialism, too, can perish', he began warning in the mid-1960s, spelling out the thinly veiled thesis of his first books.[37] The most important of the genealogies of aleatory materialism begins with it.

The brief encounter is symptomatic. Hegel, the idealist Montesquieu's heir, cannot properly account for worlds which *last* for reasons suggested by the fact that, as Althusser flatly affirms in the 1962 'Contradiction and Overdetermination', the 'logic of supersession' cannot account for Stalin's (or his successors') USSR. The materialist dialectic, the Althusserian-Marxist logic of 'overdetermination', *can*, because, like the materialist Montesquieu's dialectic, it conceives the social whole as a combination of relatively autonomous levels, one of which is determinant 'in the last instance'. Hence it need no longer dismiss Soviet 'terror, repression and dogmatism' as contingent 'survivals' superseded by a higher necessity, or, on Engels' variant, as negligible accidents 'between which' an imperious necessity 'picks its sovereign way'. Overdetermination can account for the 'necessity of these accidents' themselves, explaining how the 'terribly positive and active structured reality' bred by the 'circumstances' of a peculiar 'national and international conjuncture' managed to 'cling tenaciously to life … after the Revolution and from then till now'.[38] For 'tenaciously', let us read 'tenuously', since they are synonyms in the context. Why was this constellation of terribly bizarre institutions which had clung to life for decades in imminent danger of perishing?

The answer Althusser proposed in 1962, elaborated in *Sur la reproduction*, and never abandoned, was that the socialist state was running on capitalist ideological 'petrol'. It was an answer dictated by Montesquieu. He apparently knew – albeit 'blindly', Althusser said in his 1976 Barcelona lecture on class dictatorship – even more than that the feudal state was 'class violence transformed into law'; he knew it was violence transformed into *ideology* as well. One cannot comprehend the state, on Althusser's 1959 summary of Montesquieu's argument, if one considers only its 'nature' – in other words, its constitutional form, that which answers the question: Who holds power and how is it exercised? One must also consider its 'principle', the question of the 'condition' on which it can exercise power 'by law'. That leads from formal considerations 'into life'. For men to be 'lastingly subject' to a government, they must have a 'disposition' to it (*Sur la reproduction* speaks of an 'attitude'). Such a disposition can be brought about only by a principle capable of maintaining 'the intersection of the *nature* of the government (its political form) with the real life of men' (*Sur la reproduction* says 'an imaginary relationship to men's real conditions of existence'). The state runs on this principle, and on it alone, 'the way some motors will run only on petrol', as 'Marx in his Limits' repeats after *Montesquieu* (and as Marx does not, for he ignores the issue: that is his main limit). In a word, Montesquieu's feudal dictatorship is a 'nature-principle totality', his version – or Althusser's – of Gramsci's 'expanded' state.[39]

Sur la reproduction adds that a state's ideological petrol fuels 'ideological state apparatuses' (ISAs), which 'realize' the 'state's ideology'; that such apparatuses and the fuel they run on are 'not materially grounded in the existence of the state', but in '*economic* class exploitation', which, crucially, also breeds class ideologies *outside* the state's; and that, under capitalism, the ISAs transform such economic 'conflictual difference' (the concept is present, the term is not) into means of dominating these other ideologies, *exterior* to bourgeois ideology. They do so for a reason that explains the existence of the (rest of the) state as well: in a class society, the inherently conflictual relation between exploiters and exploited which presides over the 'combination' of elements known as an economic mode of production cannot maintain itself by economic means of domination alone. 'Indispensable to the survival of this combination', says Althusser in *Reading Capital*, is 'a certain *political* configuration', 'imposed and maintained' 'by means of material force (that of the State) and of moral power (that of the ideologies)'. Economic class struggle accordingly obeys the logic of the supplement: the relations of production/exploitation that determine, in the last instance, the complex unity of the state depend for their survival on the state that derives from them, that is, on the supplementary political and ideological relations of domination which ensure their reproduction. Both *Sur la reproduction* and 'Marx in his Limits' call this the 'paradox' of the capitalist state. To end exploitation, it is first necessary to dismantle the state which, engendered by it, presides over it – the lynchpin of the dictatorship that sustains the capitalist economic regime.[40]

What enables an encounter of exploiters and exploited to last, then, is an economic, political, and ideological structure of domination that enables it to reproduce itself as a mode of production: a viable class dictatorship. Only after it has become capable of reproducing itself can it be said to *exist*. The same holds for its elements. As *Montesquieu* points out, the feudal bourgeoisie is not an element of capitalism that pre-exists capitalism; it comes into being *as* the capitalist bourgeoisie only with the production – that is, the reproduction – of the capitalist mode of production, which depends on the perpetuation of its victory in the class struggle. Class dictatorship is why history is not teleology.

The fact that the ISAs proceed from the 'conflictual difference' of economic class struggle is, from this point of view, essential. It does not preclude the possibility of a sometimes critically important struggle on their terrain. It does imply, however, that they remain, by definition, the terrain of the dominant, and thus that a struggle for 'hegemony' cannot be won until the class domination maintained by the state and all its apparatuses is reversed – that it is impossible to put a social formation 'in parentheses in order to create the future in its midst'. This is the kernel of the critique of Gramsci in 'Marx in his Limits'. But it by no means follows from it that, once domination is reversed, the battle to establish a new class dictatorship has been won; as a rule, it has just begun, because the ideologies and ideological apparatuses of the old order resist. Such is the lesson of the exemplary Althusserian example of the brief encounter.

It affirms, more concretely, that the failure of Soviet socialism represented the revenge of the pre-Revolutionary ISAs on the Revolution. That the conjunctural 'circumstances' surrounding the Russian Revolution did not just 'survive', but were 'reactivated' by a new structure that '*ensured* their survival' thus means that the pre-Revolutionary ISAs were incorporated into the Soviet state by a CPSU become a party of the state, when its chief task would have been to lead, as the party of working-class dictatorship, the long class struggle – 'without which Revolution is unthinkable' – to smash the bourgeois ISAs in a confrontation with the Soviet state itself. It follows that the failure of the Bolshevik Revolution, cause and effect of the poverty of an idealist philosophy which reduced the historical dialectic to a progressive sequence of modes of production generated by the expansion of the productive forces, stemmed from the attempt to build socialism after stifling, 'in the silences of the terror', the embryonic Soviet working-class dictatorship. The 'bastard or monstrous forms' that resulted, attributable in part to '"chance"', were still called 'socialism', declares 'Marx in his Limits', only because that had 'become routine, or in order to deceive the popular masses'.[41] Althusser had in fact long since come to the broader conclusion that socialism as such was a bastard form, not a mode of production in its own right. That thesis led on, in conjunction with his 1966–72 elaboration of the theory of the encounter first proposed in 'Contradiction and Overdetermination', to the materialism of the encounter.

VIII

'Marx's fundamental discovery, the topography', envisages a 'structure of domination' – a society structured by a class dictatorship – as a 'structure in dominance': an overdetermined combination of irreducibly distinct levels dominated by one of them and determined in the last instance by the economy. Conceived against Hegelian-Marxist theorizations of the social whole as an expressive totality, each part of which reflects the contradiction informing the whole, the topography is necessarily also conceived against the corresponding teleologies of history. Unsurprisingly, Althusser's alternative turns on explaining the constellation of the topography's distinct, autonomous levels as the effect of the contingent combination of their distinct, separately evolving *histories*. It is a short step to the conversion of the topography into an instrument for explaining, in non-teleological fashion, the irruption of anything new. Thus Althusser can declare in a 1966 letter on the emergence of the unconscious that defining a 'logic different from that of *genesis*', according to which a thing has to 'exist in some manner *before its own birth* in order to be born', 'amounts to the same thing as defining the specific forms of a materialist dialectic' – precisely what the topography was invented to do.[42]

The encounter was always, for Althusser, one of the specific forms of the materialist dialectic required by a topographical theory of the social structure. Moreover, he concluded, almost as soon as he had introduced his conception of the materialist dialectic in the 1962 'Contradiction and Overdetermination', that the theory of the encounter implied by the topography lent itself to explaining the emergence of things other than social formations, beginning with the theory of the encounter itself. In a 1963 letter, Althusser wryly makes his addressee declare 'Contingency, chance, or what Machiavelli calls *fortuna*', is 'the pre-Marxian concept that comes closest to what Lenin calls the encounter of the objective and subjective conditions of any practice whatsoever. … Knowledge, too, is only ever produced by an "exceptional" encounter … in other words, it is produced by a historical conjuncture in which *several distinct practices* intervene: I can sense, Louis, that you are going to develop … this point; I can already sense in your essay ['Contradiction and Overdetermination'] the imminence and, as it were, ineluctable necessity of this discovery.'[43] Like 'Marx in his Limits', *Reading Capital* pursues the programme sketched here, illustrating the theory of the '"exceptional" encounter' with respect to both the origins of capitalism and historical materialism.

'Marx's texts on primitive accumulation', Althusser declares at the end of his contribution to the book, 'constitute the material if not already the outline of … the theory of the transition [from feudalism to capitalism]'. This earnest of things to come serves as the bridge between his own illustration of 'the necessity of contingency', which bears on the 'combination' that produced Marxist theory, and Balibar's, about the 'encounter' that produced capitalism. A year later, Althusser drew up a balance sheet of these and related attempts to spell out, for Marx, the implications of Marx's fundamental discovery. They constituted, he said, a '*theory* of the encounter', in unpublished notes that assimilate the concept of the 'conjunction' to the Spinozist 'singular essence', and refer, in passing, to 'Epicurus, the clinamen, Cournot' and the 'theory of the swerve'.[44] A geneticist might be forgiven for concluding that, in the theory of the encounter, the *materialism* of the encounter existed, at least 'in some manner', before its own birth.

Nowhere are the affinities between the anti-finalism of earlier and later Althusserianism more striking than in the chapter on primitive accumulation in *Reading Capital.* In the transitional period between feudalism and capitalism, by Balibar's account of Marx's account of it, the 'unity of a conjuncture' throws up elements whose 'encounter', in the event of a happy 'find', coalesces in a structure that is both distinct from the one to which they previously belonged and, 'once [the new structure] has been constituted', determinant of them. It is thus 'necessary' with respect to these elements, once they come under its 'jurisdiction'. Its necessity is not, however, dictated by the old structure, which really 'dies out as such' when the new one is formed. Nor is it inscribed in the elements the new structure 'combines', which 'have different and independent origins'; they 'become its effects' only after their encounter imposes its necessity on their contingency. This contingency, finally, 'does not imply chance', a statement which seems to mean that the elements combined in the new structure are, not accidentally, combinable.[45]

A world comes about, in 'The Underground Current', when atoms falling parallel to one another in the void collide and pile up in consequence of an infinitesimal swerve called the clinamen. 'Swerve' engenders '*the form of order* and the *form of beings* whose birth is induced by this pile-up, determined as they are by the *structure* of the encounter; whence, once the encounter has been effected (but not before), the primacy of the structure over its elements; whence … what one must call an *affinity* and a complementarity of the elements that come into play in the encounter, their "readiness to collide-interlock"'. 'No determination of these elements can be assigned', Althusser adds, 'except by *working backwards* from the result to its becoming'.[46]

The geneticist error consists in assuming that this result came about before it did, or that it had to. Perpetrators of the error retrospectively obliterate the difference between the 'several distinct … elements engendered in the previous historical process by different *genealogies* that are independent of each other and can, moreover, be traced back to several possible "origins"', Althusser says in 1967. Only when atoms 'destined to encounter each other' combine or 'take hold', affirms 'The Underground Current', do they 'enter the realm of Being that they inaugurate [and] constitute *beings* … in short, there emerges in them a structure of Being or of the world that assigns each of its elements its place, meaning, and role, or, better, establishes them as "elements of."' Whence this 1966 warning about the perils of the retrospective illusion, a summary of Althusser's 1960–65 account of the emergence of Marxism as the 'surprise' of its prehistory, not its 'goal': 'In 1845, there appears something radically new … under the explosive impact of the combination of [its] diverse elements … the old *ideological* problematic was shattered, and a new, *scientific* problematic irrupted from its disintegration. … That certain concepts of the old ideological problematic took their place in the new one in no way affects our thesis: for we know that a concept is theoretical only as a function of the *theoretical* system in which it is inscribed, and which assigns it its place, function and meaning.'[47]

Does this warning about the transformative power of the combination apply to Althusser's early concept of the transformative power of the combination? Or does his 'late' concept of the encounter preserve the elements of its predecessor intact? *Reading Capital*, echoing *For Marx*, affirms that Marx's topography differs from idealist conceptions of the whole in that it is a *Verbindung* or 'structure which combines' autonomous levels constituting *Verbindungen* in their turn. 'The elements defined by Marx', Althusser writes in 1966, 'are "combined"; I prefer to say (to translate the term *Verbindung*) are "conjoined" in "taking hold" in a new structure. This structure can only be thought, in its irruption, as the effect of a conjunction.' 'Conjuncture means conjunction', explains his last book, 'that is, an aleatory encounter of elements.'[48] If the contingent or aleatory encounter is the defining concept of aleatory materialism then, it would seem to follow, late-Althusserianism had taken hold as the 'surprise' of its prehistory by 1962.

As for the metaphor of the 'take' (*prise* or *sur-prise*), introduced in 1965 by way of that pun, it might be said to have 'taken hold' in Althusser's 1966 'Three Notes on the Theory of Discourses' – if it were not that this text assimilates it to the topography proposed in *For Marx*. The unconscious, 'Three Notes' argues, is realized in articulation with ideology: when it comes together with ideological structures with which it has 'affinities', it abruptly 'takes hold' the way mayonnaise does (in French). This *prise* is said to 'call for a type of reflection … in every respect similar to the one by means of which Marx situates the different instances and thinks their articulation'. It is also similar to the one by means of which Althusser thinks their disarticulation: *For Marx*, where the mayonnaise is present in its absence, evokes the 'fusion' into 'a ruptural unity' of the 'circumstances' and 'currents' that crystallize in social revolutions. Ruptural unity or 'take': from the eggs' point of view, it is much the same thing.[49]

IX

But not every ruptural unity takes; there are, as it were, mis-takes, such as revolutions that fail to produce viable class dictatorships. And not every encounter fuses in the ruptural unity thanks to which it can take *place*; most encounters are virtual or utopian, that is, non-encounters. Althusser's long reflection on the first idea (the exemplary example of the 'swerve' which takes or not, in the 'late' terminology of 1966) was assigned a new place, meaning and role by the late theoretical system centred on the second (imaged as the rain of atoms falling side-by-side in the void, except when the clinamen induces a 'pile-up'). The transformation was catalyzed by an encounter with his own early thought as echoed in Gilles Deleuze's and Félix Guattari's Epicurean variation on Balibar's variation on the ur-Althusserian theme of the necessity of contingency.

'The encounter' that engendered capitalism, Deleuze and Guattari write in their 1972 *Anti-Oedipus*, generously quoting Balibar's study of primitive accumulation in Marx, 'might not have taken place, with the free workers and money–capital existing "virtually" side-by-side'.

The proof is that 'great accidents were necessary, and amazing encounters that could have happened elsewhere, or before, or might never have happened … to … fashion a new machine bearing the determinations of the capitalist socius'.[50] This Deleuzian conclusion was scarcely the surprise of its Althusserian prehistory; the surprising thing is that Althusser did not state it first. Hardly was it stated for him than he formulated its premises in *Livre sur le communisme* and *Livre sur l'impérialisme*. We shall sketch the most important in closing. Readers of 'The Underground Current' will decide whether and to what extent these premises underpin the materialism of the encounter.

They are bound up with the question of the USSR. 'Ensuring the survival' of the pre-Revolutionary ISAs, Stalin's party and state had, on Althusser's analysis, ensured the demise of Soviet working-class dictatorship; yet he maintained, through *Sur la reproduction* and beyond, that Soviet society was based on a 'socialist mode of production'. The problematic implication was that a mode of production could be reproduced by a state apparatus inimical to it. By 1973, the problem has disappeared. 'There is no such thing', *Livre sur l'impérialisme* contends, 'as a socialist mode of production'; socialism is a contest between co-existing elements of the capitalist and Communist modes of production. The argument is elaborated by way of another about the transition from feudalism to capitalism. The heart of it is the Deleuzian-Althusserian claim that capitalism might not have happened. The stake of it is the idea that communism might never happen.

We treat the victory of capitalism as inevitable, according to *Livre sur l'impérialisme*, because, confronted with its results, we approach them as the historian does: 'we always reason on the basis of the accomplished fact'. Yet history itself gives the lie to this 'fetishism of the *fait accompli*'. Regarded with an eye to its uncertain unfolding, it shows, rather, that a mode of production 'can fail to exist, come into existence but perish as soon as it appears, or, on the contrary, grow stronger and pursue its historical destiny'. Thus 'the capitalist mode of production died several times before "taking hold" on the feudal (or other) modes of production', as in the thirteenth-century Po Valley. Whence a first, methodological principle: the object of materialist history should be, not the accomplished fact, but its *accomplishment.* 'How', asks *Livre sur l'impérialisme,* 'did the accomplished fact become one'?

Everything that is is accomplished fact: '*Die Welt ist alles, was der Fall ist* ... everything that comes about, everything that is the case, everything that falls.' More exactly, the world is everything that succeeds in reproducing itself, since 'existence is self-reproduction'; and everything that happens is part of the history of the world. Yet not everything that happens is 'historic', and, 'paradoxically, history itself' judges what is. Its judgements take the form of 'the results of the class struggle', that is, the 'victory of the dominant class'. Historic are events which give rise to such victories. Better, such events give rise to what counts as historic, for there is no measure for them outside themselves: 'the measure of the event is measureless', says *Livre sur le communisme,* after Lenin. This means, in particular, that they give rise to their own elements, beginning with the victorious and defeated class. Whence a second key principle, simultaneously political and theoretical. The class struggle, *Livre sur l'impérialisme* repeats after the 1972–73 'Reply to John Lewis', has primacy over the contending classes. It is because exploitation 'is the case' that there is a dominant class, whose class struggle commences with, and essentially consists in, the fact that it exploits. Similarly, exploitation engenders the exploited classes, whose usually defensive class struggles originate in their resistance to it. 'The Underground Current' talks, more cryptically, about the 'priority of the occurrence, of the *Fall,* over all its forms', and 'the primacy of the encounter over the forms to which it gives birth'. The contingent encounter which combines 'atoms' in a 'world', it adds, 'confers their reality upon the atoms themselves'; before the encounter, there is only 'the non-world that is merely [their] *unreal* existence'.[51]

How, then, did the accomplished fact of capitalism become an accomplished fact? 'In a certain sense', Althusser affirms in 1973, 'the encounter of the owners of money ... and free labourers ... is sufficient response to the question.' In another, as we have seen, it is not, for a reason stated in *Sur la reproduction*: 'the "duration" of a given social formation dominated by a given mode of production … depends … on the "duration" of the class state'.[52] Both ideas beg translation into the language of the aleatory-materialist encounter which lasts, or fails to – if they are not the original of which aleatory materialism is the translation.

What Althusser learnt from *Anti-Oedipus* bore, however, less on the accomplishment of accomplished facts than on the non-accomplishment of what has failed to come about. 'The existence of a thing is a result,' *Livre sur le communisme* proclaims, 'and this result is not preformed in the state of affairs preceding the existence of the thing.' So ran the alternative proposed by the 'theory of the encounter' to the geneticist logic which has it that a thing has somehow to exist '*before its own birth* in order to be born'. But the anti-geneticism of the theory of the encounter, if it did not quite reason on the basis of accomplished facts, nevertheless sets out from the fact of their existence – as Balibar's Marx writes, the history of the process that produced capitalism on the 'basis of knowledge of [its] result'. The materialism of the encounter, for which *die Welt ist alles, was der Fall ist*, also reasons backwards from the '*Faktum*', the 'that is just how it is' of existence. It does so, however, in the awareness that every *Fall* stems from a 'fall' that endows a thing with an existence comprising an exception to the rule of its non-existence – as capitalism is, in *Anti-Oedipus*, an 'amazing' exception to the state of affairs in which free workers and money–capital exist 'virtually' side-by-side, in a void defined by their non-encounter. Non-existence, in other words, is, for the Althusser of 1973, the state in which a thing is normally held, so that its existence must be conceived as a result of the always exceptional encounter of elements whose surprising fusion fails to prevent it from appearing. *Livre sur l'impérialisme* introduces this lesson in more familiar terms: 'In socialism, the conditions for the non-existence of communism are all met, and there for all to see … they are the still existing elements of the capitalist mode of production. … As for those who think that the game has already been won….' Althusser's conclusion, formulated, as it happens, on 26 August 1973, might be taken to mark the moment of his turn to aleatory materialism proper: 'The secret of the historical existence of existent modes of production … is to be sought less in the accomplished fact of the conditions of their existence than in the annulled, because non-accomplished fact of the conditions of non-existence of the same modes of production (for these conditions have sometimes been the death of them).'[53]

It was about the same time that he declared that the *Programme commun* was a lure. That is, perhaps, reason enough not to read the first half of the present volume first. When all the evidence is in, the conclusion may well be that the battle for working-class dictatorship chronicled in it was fought from aleatory-materialist positions fully explained only in the second.

Notes

1 'ISBMP?' 213; *LCW* 38: 319, 380; *SISS* 4; *THC* 170; *FM* 200; *POE* 36ff., 54 ff.

2 'Conversation avec Richard Hyland', A46–05.04, p. 5.

3 'ISBMP?' 215–6; *POE* 188, 93.

4 *RC* 125–6; *FM* 108; *SR* 244–7.

5 *FM* 197–8; 'ISBMP?' 215.

6 Besides 'The Underground Current', *FM*, and Althusser's correspondence with Navarro, 'Philosophy and Marxism' ventriloquizes 'LP', *ESC*, 'Au lecteur latino-américain' (A30–02), *Initiation à la philosophie*, *Introduction à la philosophie* (A25–03 ff.), and 'TP'. The Spanish version of the text, unlike the published French version translated below, also incorporates an unexcelled summary of Althusser's critique of historicism, taken from 'Entretien donné à Gretzky, 20 janvier 1973' (A46–02.04).

7 Letter of 25 December 1985 to Fernanda Navarro.

8 Antonio Negri, 'Notes on the Evolution of the Thought of the Later Althusser', trans. Olga Vasile, *Postmodern Materialism and the Future of Marxist Theory*, eds. Antonio Callari and David F. Ruccio, Hanover, New Hampshire, 1996, pp. 51–68.

9 Gregory Elliott, 'Ghostlier Demarcations', *Radical Philosophy*, no. 90, 1998, p. 28.

10 *POE* 33; 'Notes sur Lucrèce', A58–02.16 (notes on Francis Wolff's master's thesis on Lucretius).

11 Letter of 19 July 1973 to Étienne Balibar.

12 Roger Garaudy, letter of 14 February 1966 to Rochet, PCF Archives. See my Introduction to *THC*, pp. xxiv–xxxi.

13 'La conjoncture, 4 mai 1967', A11–03.01, p. 2; *LF* 693–4.

14 'Lettre aux camarades du Comité central d'Argenteuil', A42–04.01, p. 20 (forthcoming in *Historical Materialism* in William Lewis's English translation); 'THC' 297–8; letter of 12 July 1966 to Guy Besse.

15 *VN* 55, 36.

16 *SISS* 5, 12–19, 25–8.

17 Waldeck Rochet, *Le marxisme et les chemins de l'avenir*, Paris, 1966, pp. 20–7; *SR* 139.

18 *POE* 31ff., 50 ff.

19 Letter of 14 August 1966 to Michel Verret; Norberto Bobbio, 'Is There a Marxist Doctrine of the State?' [1975], *Which Socialism?*, ed. Richard Bellamy, trans. Roger Griffin, Cambridge, 1986, p. 51; 'CM' 216–20; 'Aliénation et culte de la personnalité', A3–04.01, pp. 17, 23. Bobbio lost no time launching the ongoing campaign to represent Althusser's position as a post-Marxist defence of the 'autonomy of politics' ('Marxism and Socialism' [February 1978], *Which Socialism?*, p. 173).

20 *Il Manifesto*, ed., *Power and Opposition in Post-Revolutionary Societies*, London, 1979; 'MCTF'; 'MT'.

21 'Extracts from Althusser's "Note on the ISAs"' (1976), trans. Jeremy Leaman, *Economy and Society*, 12, 1983, p. 431; 'MCTF' 290.

22 Thierry Pfister, 'L'abandon de la dictature du prolétariat est critiqué au sein même du P.C.F.', *Le Monde*, 25–26 April 1976, p. 1. A German newspaper not known for its excessive interest in Gallic Communism took the trouble to warn its readers that the philosopher might be conspiring with KGB chief Yuri Andropov. Harry Hamm, 'Kritik aus der Partei an Marchais?', *Frankfurter Allgemeine Zeitung*, 28 April 1976, p. 4.

23 *VN* 55; Alain Wasmes, 'Les Communistes et l'État', *l'Humanité*, 1 April 1977, p. 4; Claude Prévost, 'Quelques impressions (fugitives) sur un débat', *l'Humanité*, 2 April 1977, p. 3; 'Projet d'intervention à un débat', A23–02.02; Manuel Vazquez Montalban, 'Althusser y *El Correo*', *Triunfo*, no. 703, 17 July 1976, p. 12; Étienne Balibar, letter [December 1976?] to the Secretary of the History–Philosophy Cell of the Communist Student Organization's Sorbonne Branch; Gérard Molina and Yves Vargas, *Dialogue à l'intérieur du PCF*, Paris, 1978, p. 34.

24 *POE* 53; Georges Bouvard, 'Débat sur la philosophie', *l'Humanité*, 24 April 1976, p. 3; Thierry Pfister, 'M. Louis Althusser met en garde contre "le risque de déferlement droitier"', *Le Monde*, 25–26 April 1976, p. 7; 'On the Twenty-Second Congress of the French Communist Party', *New Left Review*, no. 104, July–August 1977, pp. 3–22; 'Algunas cuestiones de la crisis de la teoría marxista', *Nuevos Escritos*, Barcelona, 1978, pp. 9–54.

25 Alain Touraine, 'Les dangereuses illusions de Louis Althusser', *Nouvel Observateur*, no. 706, 22 May 1978, p. 56. The remark was partly inspired by

an Althusserian denunciation of the Party's resemblance to the 'bourgeois state and military apparatus', itself inspired by a harsher denunciation in *VN*. See Althusser, [Étienne Balibar and Jean-Pierre Lefebvre], 'What Must Change in the Party', trans. Patrick Camiller, *New Left Review*, no. 109, May–June 1978; Étienne Balibar, letter of 20 September 1976 to Althusser.

26 Nicos Poulantzas, *State, Power, Socialism*, London, 1978; Étienne Balibar, 'The Infinite Contradiction', *Yale French Studies*, no. 88, 1995, p. 157; Christine Buci-Glucksmann, *Gramsci and the State* (1975), trans. David Fernbach, London, 1980, ch. 2; Biagio De Giovanni et al., *Egemonia, Stato, Partito in Gramsci*, Rome, 1977; *POE* 144.

27 For example, Rochet, *Le marxisme et les chemins de l'avenir*, pp. 58–61.

28 Fabre et al., *Les Communistes et l'État*, Paris, 1971, p. 71 and *passim*.

29 *VN* 65.

30 Hincker, 'Pour une assimilation critique de la théorie', *La nouvelle critique*, no. 93, April 1976, pp. 5–9.

31 De Giovanni, Remarks, *Egemonia, Stato, Partito in Gramsci*, pp. 269–72.

32 *POE* 19–20.

33 *POE* 197ff.; 'MPH' 20–9, 45–53, 72–3, 99–104, translation modified; letter of 4 May 1959 to Michel Verret.

34 Perry Anderson notes the persistence of Marx's and Engels' view of 'shared domination' under absolutism in *Lineages of the Absolutist State*, London, 1974, pp. 15–6.

35 'ISBMP?' 205, translation modified; *POE* 109, 89.

36 *POE* 191.

37 *POE* 169; letter of 14 August 1966 to Michel Verret.

38 *FM* 103, 113–9; 'MPH' 53.

39 'Algunas cuestiones', p. 34; 'MPH' 45–7; 'IISA' 36, 41.

40 *SR* 113–7, 156–7; 'IISA' 59–60; *RC* 177–8; *POE* 77.

41 *RC* 198; *POE* 93.

42 *SISS* 84; *FM* 205–6; *WP* 57, 59.

43 Unposted letter of 24 November 1963 to Lucien Sève.

44 *RC* 45, 197, 281, translation modified; 'Diverses notes', A11–02.05, p. 1. For other early Althusserian discussions of the encounter, see *SISS*, *WP*, 'THC', and 'TN'.

45 *RC* 279–83, translation modified.

46 *POE* 191–3; *RC* 279.

47 'THC' 296; *POE* 192; *RC* 45; 'Théorie et pratique', A8–01.01, p. 34.

48 *RC* 41; 'Sur la genèse', A11–02.01, p. 1; *POE* 264.

49 *POE* 196 note 61; 'TN' 56–9; *FM* 99.

50 Gilles Deleuze and Félix Guattari, *Anti-Oedipus*, trans. Robert Hurley et al., Minneapolis, 1983, pp. 225n., 140.

51 *LI* A21–02.04, pp. 1, 23, 3; A21–03.01, p. 3; A21–03.03, pp. 3, 9; A21–03.02, pp. 11–12; *LC* A19–02.04, p. 3; 'RTJL' 82; *POE* 190, 170.

52 *SR* 181.

53 *LC* A19–02.01, second folder; *POE* 177; *LI* A21–03.01, p. 5.

Letter to Merab Mardashvili

Briefly mentioned in The Future Lasts a Long Time,[1] *the Georgian philosopher Merab Mardashvili was an old friend of Althusser's who carried on a regular correspondence with him beginning in 1968. A specialist in Western philosophy, Mardashvili taught first in Moscow, and then, from 1985 on, in Tbilisi; his work focused on the theory of consciousness. A book of interviews with him has been published in French (Annie Epelboin, ed.,* La Pensée empêchée, *Paris, 1991). He died in 1990.*

Dated 16 January 1978, Althusser's letter to Mardashvili pursues, from a different angle, the analysis of the crisis of Marxism he was developing in his theoretical writings of the period. But this letter is perhaps said to be more than just a theoretical balance sheet of the kind one finds in Althusser's other texts. 'The day of reckoning *has come', he says here: that is something rather more than a balance sheet.*

16 January 1978

My dear Merab,

Your note and the marvellous little coin necklace arrived in the mail today. I'm deeply touched. There was your call, and then the news about you passed on by various people, including Annie, whom I saw once after I don't know how long (she's still rushing around with the best of them, but in other parts), and, in general, I was told that you were doing 'well'. I don't believe everything I hear when word filters through third parties, but I know you're pretty tough, so I said to myself that what I'd been hearing was perhaps true, even if all the signs were pointing the other way, and even if all your friends were leaving, as I imagine they are. This time I have the truth in your own hand. Of course I'd like to see you and hear you, but I can pretty well imagine, given what I glimpsed *una volta*, what things around you must be like. As in the past, you know, 'elephants are contagious';[2] today everything communicates with everything else, curtains can't stop that; all that changes is the forms, which can be important, since they let things in with comparative ease, or relentlessly block them. Often, very often, I've thought about a remark you once made: 'I'm staying put, because it's here that one sees things bare, and right to the bottom.' A duty of the intellect, but one that must come at a high price. Not staying comes at a high price as well, to judge by those I've seen who have left. A high price – but of a different sort. And few resist the general assault, launched with a view to exhibiting them like the 'wolf-children' who can tell us a thing or two about the woods! You may have heard about a 'conference' organized by *Il Manifesto* in Venice on the situation in the 'post-revolutionary' countries:[3] they had to find the right word! I went 'in order to take part in the discussion', and since there was nothing but a series of interventions, led off by *émigrés* who were followed by trade-unionists and politicians, I eventually had to speak, because I was there and people knew it (the plague of being 'famous'; you know Heine's quip about one of his enemies: 'X … who is well known for being famous'), so I delivered pretty much the little exhortation that I attach to this note. It might be called, cynically, 'the moral of the story [*histoire*]; *or*, the morale of history [*histoire*]'. I'll let you judge the moral by the morale. Of course, there are 'effects' of the conjuncture and style (for and by those who exploit it), and it's well known that conjunctures are like storks – they come and go, even when they don't get too high off the ground (unlike storks) – but a bit more's at stake, after all: the day of *reckoning* has come. It doesn't much matter who draws up the bill, it can even be nobody at all, but eventually a day comes when the little debts that one had avoided totalling show up on a long list: and, in general, it's not the big spenders who have to pay the tab, but poor slobs like you and me (and how many others who are still more confused). Since bills are always wrong or rigged, one has to check them, but first one has to agree to pay them: all this in a political and theoretical cesspool without precedent (barring worse), the sole advantage of which is that there's no avoiding it. At all events, one has to pay for oneself (which is understandable) and also for the others – and what Others!

That's roughly what I tried to say between the lines of my 'masked' intervention in Venice – which was improvised, so that there was no rigorous argument to it – in order to dyke up the waters somewhat. The dykes that Machiavelli mentions – but he had rivers in front of him; as for us, who can say if it's rivers or what it is. I have the impression that this is something no one has ever seen before. Variations in the conjuncture we know about; this isn't the first time an accumulation of little mistakes has ended up changing the very face of things, arriving insensibly, taking a long time to make up its mind, and then, all of a sudden, it seems, one is no longer breathing the same air. But this time, although the facts are abundant and even recurrent, the guideposts are gone. Another impression: that of having struggled for a very long time on a front, only to discover that it's melting away, that there's no more front, but that the battle (or whatever is standing in for it!) is everywhere, and, to begin with, behind your back. One would have to be Kutuzov, and know how to sleep on one's horse for the grand retreat in the cold. But there are no horses (at least not in our part of the world; and, without a horse, how does one go about sleeping on one?).

It's here that one can perceive one's limits or insanities – not in the consciousness that has always been haunted by their existence, but in the perspective afforded by the passage of time. I see clear as day that what I did fifteen years ago was to fabricate a little, typically French justification, in a neat little rationalism bolstered with a few references (Cavaillès, Bachelard, Canguilhem, and, behind them, a bit of the Spinoza–Hegel tradition), for Marxism's (historical materialism's) pretension to being a science. Ultimately, this is (or, rather, was, because I've changed a little since) in the good old tradition of any philosophical enterprise conceived as a guarantee or a warrant. I also see that, things being what they were, the claims and counter-claims being what they were, and I being what I was, it couldn't have happened any differently; my counterattack was, as it were, natural, as natural as Spinoza's storms and hail. I only half believed in it, like anyone of 'sound mind', but the doubtful half had to be there so that the other half could write. This scaffolding doubtless rendered people a service, allowing them to climb up on to the roof of the house; who knows what they've gone and done with the roof and the house! And with the view of the landscape that climbing up there afforded them! Matters are fairly complicated, after all. Besides, I've become certain of another thing: that one text follows another by a logic such that, if you simply recognize, in a general way, the necessity of it because you have at least a modicum of the philosopher about you, it can't be 'rectified' all that easily. Rectify as much as you like; something of it will *always* remain.... The prison of the persona remains, even if the 'persona' who is imprudent enough to drop his mask in a text decides to announce that he has changed. Which reminds me of the famous precept: never write the works of your youth! Never write your first book!

Not everything about this adventure was vain or worthless, for the logic of the game of making assertions is not the logic of the assertions themselves. But the question is how to 'manage' this presumed or presumptive past in a situation like the one we're saddled with today. The only answer I can find for the moment is silence. And, despite all the differences, I understand your silence, which has many other motives, just as I understand the temptation and the expediency of a withdrawal into the 'metaphysical depths', which have the advantage of fighting solitude. A silence that can become permanent – why not? Or a step back in order to publish a few little things after all, on Machiavelli, Gramsci and company, or a few impudent remarks on philosophy – an old idea that I've been carrying around with me for some time, as you'll recall, but one that I'll have to revise considerably, in the light of experience, since we took our walks through the meadows – or, who knows, something on the Epicurean tradition. It's not much in a day and age in which one ought to be armed with enough concrete knowledge to be able to discuss matters such as the state, the economic crisis, organizations, the 'socialist' countries, and so on. But I don't have that knowledge. Like Marx in 1852, I would have to 'begin again from the very beginning'; but it's very late, given my age, fatigue, lassitude and, also, my isolation.

Of course, there's also the possibility of returning to *Capital*, now that we can pretty well see what doesn't work in its reasoning: something that has to do with, not the Idea of the undertaking, but its arguments. Still, there too, if we want to be logical, it wouldn't be enough to take the mechanism apart;[4] one would have to 'put it back together again'. But that requires that one have other parts, and something altogether different from the limited philosophical culture that I possess.

You speak of 'disgust': I hear the word around me, in the mouths of the best people. Yet the situation here is not like the one in your country; still, it's the same word. It's the word that says right out loud that one can no longer find one's place in this cesspool, and that there's no use looking for it, because all the places have been swept away by the crazy course of events. One can no longer bathe in a river at all, unless one is a post planted in the stream, holding on in silence. Holding fast to a little patch of firm ground. It's all a question of finding that little patch of ground underwater. After all, it is the 'trembling of the world' evoked by Montaigne, who, when it comes to conjunctures, saw all kinds, and then some. But the book has already been written. One needs to find something else.

If you can write to me, I'd be happy to hear about your 'metaphysical depths': out of curiosity and to see how you manage; and to guess, from the answers you're looking for, the questions that are troubling you.

I had a very hard summer, but now I've found a certain equilibrium again; I can read a little bit and am capable of waiting. It's incredible the way the world's problems get tangled up with personal fantasies, incredible and merciless: I've experienced that. But I've also experienced the beginnings of a resolution of this business, which has given me a little courage and a kind of 'informed' serenity. That doesn't in any way change the shambles the world is in, but it does change the obsessions of the soul … it's a start, and, let's say, encouraging, after all. From which it follows that one ought to change the order of one's thoughts rather than the order of the world....

Forgive me for confiding in you at such length, Merab. Here I keep all this to myself; with you, it's another matter.

You're in my thoughts. With all my affection,

Louis

Notes

1 Althusser, *The Future Lasts a Long Time*, in *The Future Lasts a Long Time* and *The Facts*, trans. Richard Veasey, London, 1994.

2 A quip of André Breton's.

3 For the proceedings, see *Il Manifesto*, ed., *Power and Opposition in Post-Revolutionary Societies*, trans. Patrick Camiller and Jon Rothschild, London, 1979. Among those who spoke at the conference were Leonid Plyusch, Jiri Pelikan, Charles Bettelheim, Bruno Trentin, Rossana Rossanda and Krysztof Pomian.

4 The text reads *il ne suffirait pas de démontrer* (it would not be enough to demonstrate), no doubt a mistake for *il ne suffirait pas de démonter*, the reading adopted here. [*Trans.*]

Marx in his Limits

Althusser wrote 'Marx in his Limits' in summer 1978, shortly after publishing, in the daily Le Monde, *a four-part article bearing the eloquent title 'What Must Change in the Party'* [Ce qui ne peut plus durer dans le Parti communiste français].[1] *In this text, he attempts to draw up a balance sheet of the achievements of Marxist theory, something he had already begun to do in his February 1977 foreword to Gérard Duménil's* Le Concept de loi économique dans *Le Capital (Paris, 1978), in a paper, 'The Crisis of Marxism', that he read at a November 1977 conference organized by the group* Il Manifesto *in Venice, and in an article entitled 'Marxism Today', published in Italian in the* Encyclopedia Garzanti *in 1978.*[2] *'Marx in his Limits' is not one of the unpublished texts which Althusser circulated widely; indications are that only a few close friends had ever seen it before its posthumous publication in 1994.*

1. At Last, The Crisis of Marxism![3]

All the events that we have been living through for years on end, if not for decades on end, have today come to a head in what must forthrightly be called the crisis of Marxism.

Let us take Marxism in the broadest sense, in which it means not only Marxist theory, but also the organizations and practices inspired by Marxist theory, which, after a long and difficult history, led to the Russian and Chinese revolutions, and so on, only to culminate not just in the split within the *international workers' movement* after the October

Revolution and the *Union sacrée* of the Social Democratic parties, but also, following the dissolution of the Third International, in a *split within the international Communist movement itself*: an open split between the USSR and China, and a veiled split between the so-called 'Eurocommunist' parties and the CPSU.

Earlier, before 'the collapse of the Second International',[4] the international workers' movement successfully took its inspiration from Marxist theory in order to forge its unity, at a time when the blows were coming overtly from the bourgeoisie. Since the Sino–Soviet split, very serious[5] conflicts have come into the open in the socialist and Marxist camp itself, naturally calling into question *both* the interpretation of history offered by Marxism and the various Marxist movements, and the interpretation of Marxist theory itself.

The Twentieth Congress of the Soviet Party[6] suddenly exposed a terrible reality that had, for more than twenty years, been concealed from rank-and-file Party activists, who had to struggle to lend cover to the justifications with which Stalin had legitimized his practices, particularly the monstrous trials staged in 1937–38 in the USSR and in 1949–52 in the 'People's Democracies'. Things had come to such a pass that even Khrushchev's revelations of the massacres, the mass deportations and the horrors of the camps were not enough to redress the situation, which, in the USSR and the Western parties, would for a long time continue to be dominated, and in large measure still is, by the very practices being denounced. This plainly showed that the crisis which was emerging into broad daylight *in this form* was even deeper than had been admitted. At stake was not the effects of what was branded the 'personality cult', nor mere 'violations of socialist legality',[7] but a whole theoretical and practical system capable of surviving the most shocking revelations.

What spawned all these horrors? A good deal of time has passed: twenty-eight years have gone by. True, China has broken with the USSR,[8] criticizing, among other things, Stalin's economistic politics and international practices; true, it has, under Mao, tried to rectify the worst failings of Stalinism with the Cultural Revolution, albeit largely unsuccessfully;[9] true, the Western parties have taken a considerable distance from the Soviet Union and are now denouncing the oppressive regime still in place there, as well as the USSR's armed interventions beyond its borders. But no Communist party – neither the CPSU, nor even the Western parties – has had the elementary political courage to attempt to analyse the causes of a history some of whose effects these parties have denounced. Obviously, the truth about this past is not the sort of thing one is supposed to talk about. Indeed, it may well be intolerable, or impossible to face. The result is that the Marxists who call themselves Communists have proved incapable of accounting for their own history.

The political crisis of Marxism thus points to what must clearly be called its *theoretical* crisis, malaise or disarray. How could a history made in the name of Marxism – the theory of Marx and Lenin – remain obscure for Marxism itself? And if it is in fact obscure (consider, a few exceptions aside, the weakness of the studies that have been devoted to this problem, limited, when what is involved is not sheer political and theoretical inanity, to scholarly chronicles devoid of political or theoretical interest and a handful of still hazardous hypotheses), then we have to ask ourselves a broader question: why has the Communist movement been incapable of writing its own history in convincing fashion: not just Stalin's history, but also that of the Third International and everything that preceded it, from *The Communist Manifesto* on?

This question is not only political; it is theoretical as well. And it compels us to ask one last question. Is it not *in Marxist theory itself*, as conceived by its founder and interpreted by his successors in the most widely varying conjunctures, which ought to have served as theoretical experiments, that we must *also* seek the means with which to account, in part, for the facts that remain obscure for Marxist theory? I think that this, too, is clearly the case, and that, today, we must forthrightly talk in terms of the *crisis of Marxist theory*,[10] with the crucial reservation that this crisis has lasted for a very long time, yet took, in the 1930s, with 'Stalinism', a particular form, which blocked any possible resolution of the crisis itself and prevented it from being formulated in questions, something that would have made it possible to undertake the task of political and theoretical research, and, thus, rectification as well.

Today we are not only in a crisis that has lasted a long time, one for which we have paid the price (Stalin's favourite victims, as is well known, were Communists, from the highest leader to the humblest Party activist). We are also – thanks to the mass movement itself, which sharpens contradictions and ultimately drags them into the light, the broad light of day, and puts them on the agenda – in a novel situation. It allows us to declare that *the crisis has at last come to a head! It has at last become obvious to one and all! And it is at last possible to begin with the work of rectification and revision!*

Taking this as our starting point, we can get down to work, utilizing not just our experience, but also the carefully considered attempts of all those who, long isolated and excluded, were the first eyewitnesses to this crisis, and, often, victims of their determination to speak out. These are the people who interest us, not those who can be relied on to object, 'But why have you waited until today?' If their surprise is sincere, that is because they do not know or have forgotten what things were like in the PCF only ten years ago, and what they are still like today. As for the dyed-in-the-wool anti-Communists, for whom Marx's theory was a species of religion wrapped up in an economic metaphysics, and the currently fashionable anti-Marxists, who waltz down the pavements of the great capitals and through the Conferences where it is the fashion to sport Gulag buttons in one's lapel,[11] if they should by chance have anything serious to say (but if they did, we would have found out a long time ago), we will consider it; if not, they will just have to resign themselves to playing the role of media stars.

As for our comrades, who have not only had to endure this history, whether they managed to stay in the Party or were compelled to leave it (how many fall into the second category!), they should bear something in mind. Every revolutionary knows or feels that it can be a delicate or even dangerous business to utter the phrase 'crisis of Marxism', for the simple reason that words tend to take their own course, and that a crisis generally leads to a collapse [*faillite*] (Lenin spoke of 'the collapse' of the Second International), while a collapse generally leads to liquidation or death. But a crisis can also open out on to 'a crisis of liberation', even 'of growth'. Let these comrades judge on the evidence, then; let them decide if the reflections that follow are more likely to bring about a collapse or a renaissance.

If they fear, as may be legitimate, that our adversaries will pounce on the word 'crisis' as if it were a 'confession', twisting it as is their wont in order to throw it back in our faces, they should bear something else in mind, something I must say with a certain solemnity. *We would be prolonging one of the effects of the crisis of Marxism, in one of its worst aspects, if we consented to close our eyes to reality* and continued to accept a blindness which, until only very recently, was obligatory for anyone who wished to be accepted as a Communist. *We would be prolonging one of the effects, one of the worst aspects, of the crisis of Marxism, if we deprived ourselves of the right to call the reality that has beset and bedevilled us for a very long time by its real name, right out loud,* on the pretext that the first bourgeois journalist or ideologue who comes along is going to turn the expression against us.

For a very long time now, from the end of the nineteenth century on, the ideologues of the bourgeoisie have been proclaiming, and always in the same terms, *the crisis, collapse and death of Marxism*, which they have publicly and sarcastically buried beneath their arguments. Philosophers from Weber through Croce to Aron and Popper have 'proved' that 'Marx's philosophy' was impossible or metaphysical, like the philosophies that Marx criticized. 'Scientific' economists have 'proved' that the theory of value was a fairy tale, and the theory of surplus-value worthless, because it was 'not operational', mathematically speaking. Monastics, moralists, sociologists and 'political scientists' have all 'proved' that the theory of the class struggle was an invention of Marx's and that the Marxists subjected the world to its laws, whereas the world could very well have done without it – indeed, had everything to gain from doing without it. All of them have long since pronounced Marx dead; worse, stillborn. And those who have tried to 'save Marx' have turned him into a revolutionary by moral indignation, humanism or religion; they too have buried him, but beneath their high praise and ideological exploitation.

If, today, we talk about the 'crisis of Marxism', we are not providing our adversaries with a single weapon that they themselves have not already used a hundred times over. Nor shall we talk about it as they do, in order to supply them with fresh arguments, but, rather, in order to wrest from them arguments currently at their disposal as a result of our own political and theoretical weakness. Here, too, let our comrades judge on the evidence. It is not even a question of talking about the crisis of Marxism the way one might sound an alarm. Today, thanks to the strength of the labour movement and the popular movements in the world – *yes, thanks to their strength*, and despite their very serious contradictions – we are able to speak, positively and with sang-froid, of the crisis of Marxism, in order to free ourselves at last of its known causes; or, at least, in order to begin to know them in order to free ourselves of them. *The crisis of Marxism, for perhaps the first time in its history, can today become the beginning of its liberation, hence of its rebirth and transformation.*

There is no act of faith in these words, but a political act pointing to a real possibility, *already on its way to being realized* in our own world. Indeed, we have reached a point such that it depends on us, on our political and theoretical lucidity, whether the crisis in which Marxism has very nearly perished culminates not just in its survival, but in nothing less than its liberation and rebirth. If it is to do so, however, all our Communist comrades will have to become actively involved: whatever post they occupy in the class struggle, they can, with the exception of those who have given up or turned their coats, contribute to the rebirth of Marxism. It would appear that 'everyone counts for one';[12] well, then, let 'everyone count on his own strength',[13] and, all together, we can help the Party overcome the crisis of Marxism, which is also, today, across the globe, the crisis of the Communist parties: their internal crisis.

2. The Theoretical Crisis of Marxism

It is 1978. It was 130 years ago that there appeared a little pamphlet which went virtually unnoticed in the revolutions of 1848 in Europe: *The Communist Manifesto*, by Marx and Engels. It was 110 years ago that the first volume of Marx's *Capital* appeared; this text did attract some notice, but it was years before it had any effect, and it was interpreted in the spirit of the day, then dominated by the evolutionism of the German Social Democratic movement.

Since these grand, silent dates, any number of things have taken place in the Marxist universe, dominated only by *The Manifesto* (and the core chapters of *Anti-Dühring* as well as Lenin's great texts, etc.), and scarcely at all by *Capital* (except in Germany and the USSR). Marxism has weathered the worst ordeals; when it seemed moribund in Western Europe because of the *Union sacrée*, it was being revived in Russia, before moving on to China. The worst ordeals and, as well, the worst dramas and tragedies.

Here we propose to confine ourselves to the theoretical aspects of this history and its ordeals (without, of course, ignoring political events in the history of Marxism), because the theory is accessible to us, whereas the history is slumbering in the sealed archives of the USSR, and also because a Marxism squarely in the tradition of Marx, Lenin, Gramsci and Mao attaches great importance to the *quality of its theory*.

Is it possible, then, in 1978, to sketch a sort of balance sheet of the history of Marxist theory, particularly of some of its historically significant contradictions, while taking into account the fact that it has been, and still is, deeply engaged in the practical struggles – open or clandestine, clear or obscure – of the international workers' and mass movements, down to the splits that have punctuated its history? Yes, we can try to do this, for we have not only the advantage of historical, and therefore comparative, perspective, but also the long experience of history, of the victories, defeats and tragedies of Marxism. We can, no doubt, proceed with greater assurance because we have now begun to live under the law of the open crisis of Marxism (no Communist Party has promulgated it … but we are used to these well-known, perpetual 'lags',[14] which make up an integral part of this crisis), a crisis so radical and profound that it seems capable, all on its own, of dispelling a number of carefully cultivated illusions, and forcing sincere Communists to face up, at last, to the pitiless, healthy test of reality. We can do so with still greater assurance because, as Mao rightly said, 'the main tendency is towards revolution',[15] and because the mass movement, down to its worst contradictions, demands and meets the test of reality.

I shall therefore ask the limit-question (the hardest question is always the best). What can we retain of Marx today as being truly essential to his thought, even if it has perhaps not (indeed, has surely not) always been well understood?

To begin at the beginning, I would say: we can retain the following few facts, which I shall first set out and then comment on as best I can.

3. Was Marx a 'Marxist'?

We can begin by retaining the following simple fact, which does not seem to amount to anything at all, yet is of crucial importance.

Marx said, on at least one occasion, 'I am not a Marxist.'[16] The quip is well known. It has been taken for a *bon mot* from someone with a free, modest, caustic mind. But matters are not that simple. For elsewhere, in the Preface to *Capital*, Marx urges his reader to 'think for himself', fleshing out his demand as follows: 'I welcome every opinion based on scientific criticism. As to the prejudices of so-called public opinion, to which I have never made concessions, now, as ever, my maxim is that of the great Florentine: "*segui il tuo corso, e lascia dir le genti*".'[17]

The matter was becoming serious: to think for oneself, to think freely, to scoff at 'the prejudices of public opinion,' did not mean *to think just anything*, but, quite the contrary, *to speak the truth*, in the name of which every 'scientific' critique is said to be welcome.

The truth of the matter is that Marx was profoundly convinced – let us, rather, say absolutely convinced, without the least inner hesitation – that he had inaugurated a new form of knowledge, pitted, as the only true one, against all the others that had been advanced in this domain: *the knowledge of the conditions, forms and effects of the class struggle*, at least in the capitalist mode of production. It is not that the history of 'pre-capitalist forms' did not exist for Marx; in 1857–58, he devoted a rather short study to them (which went unpublished for a long time),[18] making frequent use of it in the text of *Capital* itself. But the centre of all his attention and certainty was the capitalist mode of production; elsewhere, when other modes of production were in question, things were less sure (we are beginning to realize this today). And, in his time and terminology (there is nothing shameful about registering this fact), Marx did not hesitate to say that he had been the first to produce a work of 'science' [*Wissenschaft*] in the field that he was in the process of *discovering*. The word must be taken in the strong sense: *to discover* means, in Marx's case, to free or strip capitalist society of all the ideological constructions that had *covered it up* in order to mask, and thus ensure, the domination of the bourgeoisie. Understand by this that Marx was convinced that he was 'producing', bringing out, revealing and explaining, *for the first time*, clearly and systematically, objective knowledge, hence the kind of knowledge that could contribute to, and guide, a revolutionary movement, about which he simultaneously demonstrated that it really existed in the working masses, and that everything tended to endow it with the strength and means to abolish the class struggle and classes.

In this respect, *Marx was well and truly a 'Marxist'*; he believed in his work, which, from first to last, he unhesitatingly called 'scientific' – not ideological or 'philosophical'. This was, perhaps, a science unlike all the others, given that Marx called *Capital* 'the most terrible missile that has yet been hurled at the heads of the bourgeoisie',[19] and therefore an 'explosive', scandalous, 'revolutionary'[a] science – but it was a 'science' none the less.

However, in affirming that he was 'not a Marxist', Marx was protesting in advance against any interpretation of his work as a philosophical or ideological system or vision, and, in particular, as a reworking of the 'philosophies of History'. He was protesting, *above all*, against the idea that he had at last discovered the 'science' of the 'object' which, in the bourgeois culture of the time, bore the name Political Economy. Marx was thereby protesting in advance against the idea that his thought could lay claim not only to presenting but also to possessing a *total* or *totalizing* unity, constituting a body of thought that could then be labelled 'Marxism', and that this 'unified' *œuvre* could have been produced by 'an' author: by himself, Karl Marx, an intellectual of bourgeois origins – and, 'naturally', a Jew.

a A 'new' philosopher, that is, a rancid philosopher who has ideas only on condition that he can distort them to produce a sensation, has seen fit to indict this word on suspicion of mischief. We shall let him sort the matter out for himself.

Thus Marx warned us against this claim *by refusing to affirm that* Capital *was the 'science' of Political Economy*; he called it, instead, a '*critique of Political Economy*' (the subtitle of *Capital*). Here, too, 'critique' or 'criticism' must be taken in the strong sense which Marx gives it: as criticism of all the idealist philosophical presuppositions according to which Political Economy was an exhaustive, distinct [*propre*] theory of a supposed 'object' defined by distinct 'ideological'[b] categories, such as subject, need, labour, distribution, consumption, contract, and so on, all of them related, *as if to their origin, to the subject of need, labour and exchange*; according to which, again, it was possible to found a 'science' of the 'object' defined by these dubious but by no means innocent concepts.

Marx made no blanket rejection of the works of the Economists; he rejected *the ideal* of the kind of Political Economy that had been imposed on them by the dominant bourgeois ideology and established on the basis of the concepts of which I have just given a partial list. Marx thought that there were scientific elements in the works of the Physiocrats, Smith, Ricardo, Hodgskin,[c] and so on, elements of objective knowledge, but that, in order to perceive and make use of them, it was necessary to overturn the existing system of categories, shift to new ground, and therefore radically criticize *both* Political Economy *and* its supposed 'object' (the satisfaction of needs, or the production of the 'Wealth of Nations', and so on). Hence it was necessary radically to criticize its claim to be the 'science' of the object that it thought it was talking about. Political Economy spoke well, but about something else, namely, the political 'values' of bourgeois ideology; that is, among other things, about bourgeois (economic) policy disguised as 'Political Economy' for ideological and political reasons.

But Marx thereby modified (perhaps without clearly perceiving the fact) the traditional meaning of the expression 'critique of …', and, consequently, the meaning *of the concept of critique.*

b Obviously, a category taken by itself is not ideological, but becomes ideological by virtue of the system to which it is subordinated.

c See Jean-Pierre Osier's remarkable little book *Thomas Hodgskin: Une critique prolétarienne de l'économie politique*, Paris, 1976. It contains treasures on Smith and his heirs.

The old notion of criticism or critique, which a whole century, from Bayle to Kant, had invested with philosophical dignity, had been charged by the entire rationalist tradition with distinguishing the false from the true, with delivering the true from the false (from errors, 'prejudices' and illusions); or again, and more boldly still, with denouncing error (as Voltaire did at a number of famous trials) in the name of Truth, whenever Truth was ridiculed or assailed by error. In his early work, Marx was largely pursuing this rationalist tradition in order to denounce the 'irrationality' of Reason's conditions of existence (for example: the state is, in itself, Reason, yet exists in unreasonable or irrational forms; it is necessary to denounce this contradiction and the insult proffered to the State-Reason – by means of critique, with a view to re-establishing the truth and condemning error). At the level of *Capital*, however, Marx confers an altogether different meaning and function on the word 'critique'. As the intelligent Russian critic cited in the Postface to the second German edition of *Capital* was to write, critique is not, for Marx, the judgement which the (true) Idea pronounces on the defective or contradictory real; critique is critique of existing reality by existing reality (either by another reality, or by the contradiction internal to reality).[20] *For Marx, critique is the real criticizing itself*, casting off its own detritus itself, in order to liberate and laboriously realize its dominant tendency, which is active within it. It is in this materialist sense that Marx's critique could, as early as 1845, treat communism as the very opposite of the 'ideal', the deepest tendency of the 'real movement'.[21]

But Marx did not content himself with this still abstract notion of critique. For which 'reality' is in question here? Until one knows *which 'reality' is in question*, everything can be real or be called real – everything, which is to say anything at all. Marx tied critique to that which, in the real movement, grounded critique: for him, in the last instance, the class struggle of the exploited, which could objectively overcome the domination of the bourgeois class because and only because of the specific nature of the existing forms of their exploitation: the forms of capitalist exploitation. That is why, taking an astonishing short-cut that proves the acuity of his vision, Marx wrote, in the Postface to the second German edition of *Capital*:

> The peculiar historical development of German society therefore excluded any development of 'bourgeois' economics there, but did not exclude its critique. In so far as such a critique represents [*vertreten*] a class, it can only represent the class whose historical task [*Beruf*] is the overthrow of the capitalist mode of production and the final abolition of all classes – the proletariat.[22]

If we carry this to its logical conclusion, it becomes clear that, by way of this conception of critique, Marx was rejecting (without explicitly saying so, to be sure, and therefore without drawing all the consequences) the idea, 'obvious' to everyone at the time, that he, the individual Marx, the intellectual Marx, could be *the* intellectual or even political author (as the absolute origin or creator) of such a critique. For it was the real – the workers' class struggle – which acted as the true author (the agent) of the real's critique of itself. In his own fashion and style, with all of his intellectual culture turned upside down by the experience he had acquired and was still acquiring, with his acute sense of the conflicts of his time, the individual named Marx 'wrote' on behalf of this 'author', infinitely greater than he was – on its behalf but, first of all, *by its agency and at its urging.*

4. Marxist Theory is Internal, Not External, to the Workers' Movement[23]

This, however, abruptly draws our attention to *another* fact.

It was because Marx played a direct and personal part, for several years, in the practices and struggles of the workers' movement that his thought was able to establish itself 'on new foundations' (the line from the 'Internationale' is on the mark), becoming 'critical and revolutionary' (*kritisch-revolutionär*).[24]

When I say the workers' movement, I mean the workers' movement of pre-revolutionary and revolutionary Europe (1835–48). This movement was extremely variegated at the time. In some cases, as in England, it had come together under a radical workers' party (Chartism, both a political movement and also one that fought for better wages and working conditions); elsewhere it was dispersed, or even, in France, divided up into utopian sects and 'socialist' movements of petty-bourgeois communitarian inspiration (Louis Blanc, Proudhon himself). (Marx and Engels, who knew Proudhon, Fourier, the Saint-Simonians, etc., showed and would always continue to show the greatest political respect for them, and their theory and activity in this period.)

Yet Marx and Engels joined, not these utopian sects, but the radical groups of worker-artisans, mainly of German origin, which brought together political *émigrés* in groups calling themselves 'communist' (Cabet[25] represented this current for France, Weitling[26] for Germany). After the historic defeat of Chartism in England, these very active, astonishingly lucid little groups represented the communist avant-garde of the European workers' movement. It was their life and their struggles that Marx and Engels shared. And it was their membership in these groups that led them to put their thought 'on new foundations', making a radical shift to new positions tied to the proletariat [*rattachées au prolétariat*] in both philosophy and the theory of class struggle.[27]

This thesis is not merely a matter of observable fact, a matter that is best left to 'the history of ideas' (an uncertain and superficial discipline, at least as far as most of its avowed pretensions go). In the history of the workers' movement, this thesis has been an object of intense political and ideological debate, from Marx's day on. For example, when Marx wrote, in a famous 1852 letter to Joseph Weydemeyer,

> as for myself, I do not claim to have discovered either the existence of classes in modern society or the struggle between them. Long before me, bourgeois historians had described the historical development of this struggle between the classes, as had bourgeois economists their economic anatomy,

it was in order to add:

> my own contribution was 1. to show that the *existence of classes* is merely bound up with *certain historical phases in the development of production*; 2. that

> the class struggle necessarily leads to the *dictatorship of the proletariat*; 3. that this dictatorship itself constitutes no more than a transition to the *abolition of all classes* and to a *classless society*. Ignorant louts such as Heinzen, who deny not only the struggle but the very existence of classes, only demonstrate that, for all their bloodthirsty, mock-humanist yelping, they regard the social conditions in which the bourgeoisie is dominant as the final product, the *non plus ultra* of history.[28]

With this, *as early as 1852*, Marx declared that he had not been the first to talk about social classes and class struggles, since bourgeois historians and economists had already discussed both (he might also have mentioned the philosophers and politicians who had discussed the subject beginning in the earliest period of classical Antiquity: see Plato, Thucydides, Aristotle, Tacitus, Machiavelli, Spinoza, Locke and others). Yet Marx maintains that he treats this subject in an entirely different way – that is, puts it on an entirely different foundation, at once philosophical and theoretical. This different philosophical foundation is the materialism defended from the *Theses on Feuerbach* on, and then the dialectic, consciously taken over from Hegel, but said to be 'demystified', starting with the 1857–58 *Notebooks* (the *Grundrisse*) and, subsequently, the 1859 *Contribution*. I think I have rightly characterized this different theoretical foundation by showing that, at least with respect to the capitalist mode of production, it takes the form of the *primacy of* class *struggle* over *classes*.[d] Only an understanding of this primacy (or the primacy of contradiction over the opposed terms) makes it possible to understand *Capital* – both what it says and what it does not, or cannot, say.

What Marx merely suggests here, he says very clearly elsewhere: in the 1859 Preface, in which, discussing *The German Ideology*, he affirms that he and Engels felt the need, as a result of their own experience, to 'settle accounts with [their] former philosophical conscience'.[29] Marx's thought was thus established on new foundations under the impact of an experience of the struggles of the workers' movement in which, together with Engels, he had been personally involved.

d See 'RTJL' [*EI* 82].

This simple question was to become the stake of very intense ideological-political debates that have been pursued down to our own day. We will have a better sense of them if we recall that it was Kautsky who gave canonical form to the 'reformist' interpretation of this crucial question, which involved a great deal more than the personalities of Marx and Engels. In the triumphant period of German Social Democracy, whose inevitable electoral victory Engels himself had predicted a few years earlier, Kautsky wrote:

> In this connection socialist consciousness appears to be a necessary and direct result of the proletarian class struggle. But this is absolutely untrue. Of course, socialism, as a doctrine, has its roots in modern economic relationships just as the class struggle of the proletariat has, and, like the latter, emerges from the struggle against the capitalist-created poverty and misery of the masses. But socialism and the class struggle arise side by side and not one out of the other; each arises under different conditions. Modern socialist consciousness can arise only on the basis of profound scientific knowledge. Indeed, modern economic science [*sic*][30] is as much a condition for socialist production as, say, modern technology, and the proletariat can create neither the one nor the other, no matter how much it may desire to do so; both arise out of the modern social process. The vehicle of science is not the proletariat, but the *bourgeois intelligentsia* [Kautsky's emphasis]: it was in the minds of individual members of this stratum that modern socialism originated, and it was they who communicated it to the more intellectually developed proletarians who, in their turn, introduce it into the proletarian class struggle where conditions allow that to be done. Thus, socialist consciousness is something introduced into the proletarian class struggle from without [*von außen Hineingetragenes*] and not something that arose within it spontaneously [*urwüchsig*].[31]

If this were not the case, Kautsky adds, it would be impossible to understand why England, the country in which 'capitalism is the most highly developed', is the country in which 'this socialist consciousness is the most remote'.

It is well known that, only a few months after this text appeared in *Die Neue Zeit* (the theoretical review of German Social Democracy), Lenin would, in *What Is To Be Done?*, cite Kautsky's very words in support of his struggle against economistic spontaneism (against those who believed in the omnipotence of the economic class struggle and spurned political struggle); he took them over without changing so much as a comma. Lenin, however, did not usually put the emphasis, as Kautsky did, on the idea that 'intellectuals were the sole guardians of science,' and that 'economic science' and (revolutionary) socialist consciousness were identical. He had other objectives in mind. They emerge clearly in *What Is To Be Done?*: the absolute necessity for revolutionary theory and a revolutionary political party – more precisely, a party of 'professional revolutionaries' capable of coping with the problems of clandestine action. He repeatedly explained his position on this question later, in reply to those who accused him of wanting to subordinate the workers' consciousness, hence socialist consciousness, to the 'science' of intellectuals who, by their very nature, were external to the proletariat. His adversaries accused him, consequently, of wanting to sanction the omnipotence of intellectual leaders over party activists and the masses themselves. This polemic took the form of a discussion of the conception of the party and the relations between the party and the trade unions. Lenin's reply to his critics is encapsulated in a few words that I have taken from his 1907 Preface to the Collection *Twelve Years*:

> *What Is To Be Done?* is a controversial correction of Economist [spontaneist] distortions and it would be *wrong to regard the pamphlet in any other light*. … The basic mistake made by those who now [1907] criticise *What Is To Be Done?* [1902] is to treat the pamphlet apart from its connection with the concrete historical situation of a definite, and now long past, period in the development of our Party…. To maintain today that *Iskra*[32] exaggerated (*in 1901 and 1902!*) the idea of an organisation of professional revolutionaries, is like reproaching the Japanese, *after* the Russo–Japanese War,[33] for having exaggerated the strength of Russia's armed forces…. To win victory the Japanese had to marshal all their forces against the probable maximum of Russian forces.

> *Unfortunately, many of those who judge our Party are outsiders, who do not know the subject*, who do not realise that *today* the idea of an organisation of professional revolutionaries has *already* scored a complete victory. That victory would have been impossible if this idea had not been pushed to the *forefront* at the time, if we had not '*exaggerated*' so as to drive it home to people who were trying to prevent it from being realised.... Nor at the Second Congress *did I have any intention* of elevating my own formulations [on spontaneity and consciousness, on the party, etc.] as given in *What Is To Be Done?*, to the 'programmatic' level, constituting special principles. On the contrary, the expression I used – and it has since been frequently quoted – was that of 'bending the stick". *What Is To Be Done?*, I said, straightens out the stick bent by the Economists (cf. the minutes of the Second R.S.D.L.P. Congress in 1903, Geneva, 1904). I emphasised that precisely because we were so vigorously straightening out the stick, our line of action would always be the straightest.[e] [34]

It would be extremely interesting to ask why, notwithstanding this unambiguous interpretation of *What Is To Be Done?*, the book continues to elicit ambiguous interpretations that are fiercely hostile to Lenin's own. No doubt it is the course of the class struggle that has decided the matter: the letter of Lenin's formulations, however, has undeniably encouraged this counter-interpretation. Lenin did in fact take over [Kautsky's][35] formulations. Written or rewritten by Lenin himself, they have been ascribed to Lenin, who has been berated for them right down to our own day: it would seem that one cannot [***] bend the stick in the other direction if, as a materialist, one wants to straighten it out, for this counter-bending also leaves traces which, thanks to the ideological struggle, are deeper than the one that was corrected by the counter-bending, and is no longer topical. The fact is that a formula produced by an author in a position of authority survives the objective meaning that his use of it had in a given conjuncture, in which it was not at all ambiguous; it can then be turned against the person who, earlier, made legitimate use of it. Circumstances come and go, but words remain, and can serve to

e My emphases, L. A.

support or even entrench an ambiguous or hostile interpretation or even tendency. Marxists – by which I mean politicians or others who, in their internal debates, appeal to the authority of Marx and Lenin – have unfortunately paid insufficient attention to this phenomenon of the survival and revival of formulas beyond the conjuncture that called them into existence: they prefer to tear each other to shreds rather than make the effort required to understand the auxiliary laws (for these laws are never fundamental, except perhaps in extreme cases of closely balanced conflicts) governing the relationship of their formulas to variations in the conjuncture.

The truth is, I might add, that Lenin, too, failed to consider the problem of the political repercussions of the letter of what he himself wrote or quoted. To my knowledge, he never posed the problem explicitly and theoretically (although, as a rule, he resolved it as if by 'instinct', taking into account, at the practical level, the 'echoes' which some of his formulas might have). Moreover, his 'explanation' in terms of the historical context, far from making up for the 'gaffe' he had inadvertently committed, simply made it worse. For, if we examine the matter closely, it appears that the 'then topical' problem with which Lenin was confronted in 1902 really had very little to do with Kautsky's problem, and could perfectly well have been resolved with formulas provided by Lenin himself, which would have been wholly adequate for his purposes at the time. Why, then, did Lenin take the liberty of including this lengthy quotation from Kautsky in his text, condemning himself – for all his 'explanations' are just denials that reinforce the effect they are supposed to counteract – to drag this heavy burden around with him? Doubtless he needed to appeal to an 'authority' (Kautsky's), but there is nothing innocent about this, unless we assume that, in spite of everything he said later, Lenin truly subscribed to Kautsky's theses, either temporarily (Kautsky's text had just appeared), because he was intimidated by them, or over a longer period (but this is very much open to question, especially if we recall what Lenin would later say about intellectuals …). In any event, there is a blind spot here, of which the theory of the stick bent in the other direction serves as an index; but it is also the index of a shortcoming or slip, since Lenin uses a very different stick when he 'throws Kautsky into the battle' in a text in which he really has no place.[36]

Let us generalize. When, in the case of phenomena of this kind (ambiguous quotations from, or ambiguous formulas by, an author considered 'authoritative'), one tendency repeats the very formulas of an older tendency as powerful as itself, then all intelligent scruples about the phenomenon (why this repetition? etc.) are banished by the self-evidence of the thing. In fact, leaving aside the passage cited by Lenin on the question of the production of Marxist theory by bourgeois intellectuals external to the workers' movement, and its introduction into the workers' movement from without, the idealist-mechanistic tendency was clearly already present in Kautsky; it was in perfect harmony with his conception of Marxism and his practice as a leader of the Second International. Moreover, it survived him, as did his adversaries, who, since they were sometimes – or above all – Lenin's adversaries as well, seized the occasion to direct their fire at him, too, imputing Kautsky's theses to him in order to condemn them in Lenin. It must be conceded that they were also able to find other real or subjective appearances in Lenin that tended in the same direction. But here, too, Lenin appealed, or would have appealed, to the 'conjuncture' ….

However that may be, beneath the general conception, under the Second International of the early twentieth century, of a theory – that of a '*science produced by bourgeois intellectuals*' and '*introduced from without into the workers' movement*' – there clearly appeared the outlines of an idealist, voluntarist representation of the relation between theory and practice, between the Party and the mass movement, hence between the Party and the masses, and, finally, between the Party leaders (who were intellectuals; whether they were of working-class background is immaterial) [and rank-and-file activists]. In the last instance, this representation could not but reproduce bourgeois forms of knowledge, that is, forms of the production and possession of this knowledge on the one hand, and, on the other, bourgeois forms of the possession and exercise of power, all these forms being dominated by a *separation* between knowledge and non-knowledge, between the informed and the ignorant, between the leaders, the guardians of knowledge, and the led, reduced to receiving it from without and from on high because they were naturally ignorant of it.

Let us now turn back to Marx and Engels. There is no question that they were bourgeois 'intellectuals' with a traditional university education. One has to be born somewhere:[37] they were born, in the one case, a scion of the relatively modest *Bildungsbürgertum*, and of the industrial bourgeoisie in the other. But birth is not necessarily destiny. The real destiny that defined Marx and Engels in their historical role as new intellectuals, as 'organic' intellectuals of the working class (to borrow Gramsci's convenient, if hardly unequivocal, terminology), was played out in their *encounter* with – that is to say, their direct and practical, or, in a word, personal, experience of – the exploitation of the working class. Engels, immersed in the colossal struggles of the Chartist movement, acquired this experience in England (see *The Condition of the Working-Class in England*, 1845); Marx acquired it in France, owing to his participation in the political class struggle of the socialist and communist organizations. As Auguste Cornu has clearly shown,[38] Marx became a communist in France, in 1843–44, whereas Engels, who followed the same trajectory, did so by studying, first-hand, the conditions of exploitation of the English working class and the methods of exploitation used by the industrial bourgeois class (he was well placed to do so: he had an important management position in an industrial firm controlled by his family, and lived with Mary, 'an Irish immigrant worker' employed in the same factory).

As Marx himself has noted, it was in Brussels, in 1845, that the two men realized that their personal trajectories and individual experiences, albeit different, had brought them to the same conclusion. It is well known that Marx, whom Engels would proclaim to be by far 'the more accomplished of the two of us', declared at the time that Engels's 'brilliant essay'[39] (on *Nationalökonomie* or Political Economy[40]) had put him on the path which led him to an understanding of the mechanisms of the capitalist mode of production. For those who want to find an author at all costs, here we have two, each giving credit to the other, and for good reason, since both had learnt what they discovered from the only 'author' there was in this domain: the class struggle of the exploited.

The first-hand experience of the bourgeois and workers' class struggle acquired by Marx and Engels leaves its traces in the astonishing stages of their 'Early Works', in the 'objects' treated in these works, in the 'problematics' they adopted in order to treat them, and in the contradictory results they produced – results which led to incessant displacements, substitutions of one object for another, modifications of the problematic, and so forth. And I maintain, *pace* all those who have a stake in making the 'tree' that disturbs them disappear in the universal forest of a continuist history, whether it be the forest of the here and now, uninterrupted genesis, a reassuring continuity, or the 'spatio-temporal' – *pace* all those who have produced an incredible literature in order to provide their bad conscience with reading matter capable of salving it: I maintain, I say, that we can track, text by text, from 1841 to 1845 (and beyond, of course), the different stages of this astonishing political-theoretical experience, in which it is political consciousness, the emergence of a political class-consciousness, that serves as the motor, and theoretical consciousness which follows, registers, develops, anticipates, compares premisses to conclusions, modifies the premisses, and so on.

Not only can we track the different stages of this experience, but we can even pinpoint (here we are again: at the point which I had the imprudence to call an epistemological 'break' or 'rupture'[41]) the 'moment' when there suddenly emerges, in the 'consciousness' of Marx and Engels, the need to question, not partially but totally and radically, the theoretical principles that they learnt at university, the need to think in an altogether different way, to 'shift ground' or change elements (to echo Themistocles addressing the Athenians: change elements – instead of fighting on land, fight at sea!). This moment 'blossoms' after the dramatic confrontation with the Feuerbachian philosophy of alienation, that 'unprecedented theoretical revolution', and with the concepts of bourgeois Political Economy, which had initially been taken up uncritically; it occurs after the *1844 Manuscripts*, which Marx never tried to publish (but which of our critics, who are ready to make the most of any text Marx ever wrote, even if it is one that he must have considered it unwise to publish, since he left it in his files – which of our critics respects this desire in the least, or even takes it into account?), and which are theoretically untenable, because they set out to attain the real by marrying an idealist, Hegelianized–Feuerbachian philosophy of alienation[42] to the mythical ideology of a Political Economy adopted without a critique!

This moment, having become 'consciousness' (that, apparently, is how one must put it), comprises both the encounter in Brussels, the basic agreement acknowledged by these two explorers and fighters of the battles of the working class, and the declaration that the time has come to finish with 'our philosophical consciousness as we formerly [*ehemalige*] professed it', to 'settle accounts with' it or 'liquidate' it [*abrechnen*].

Not for nothing did Marx talk about his 'philosophical consciousness', and hence about philosophy, if it is true that philosophy sustains or props up, in the last instance, every theory and every problematic. Not for nothing did Marx talk about philosophy, if the philosophy he means is, in the final analysis, a kind of 'precipitate' of the theoretical principles of the dominant ideology, considered in its basic antagonism with the ideologies that are said to be dominated.

Marx was born a bourgeois and became a bourgeois intellectual. It was none of his doing, except in so far as he became aware that capitalist society obscured the class exploitation on which it lived, hiding this exploitation under the complex effects of the play of ideological elements that the state and its apparatuses strive to unify in a dominant ideology. It was none of his doing, except in so far as he understood, after an experience that he had been honest enough to go through with his eyes wide open, that the Truth uttered by the major prophets of the dominant Ideology – Locke, Smith, Kant, Hegel and others – was maintained only in order to occult the class exploitation on which capitalist society lived, under the watchful eye of its state, about which Hegel said that it should rely on the wisdom of its professors of philosophy so as not to go astray or founder. It was none of his doing, except in so far as he understood that this whole construct had to be swept away, and that philosophy had to be established on new foundations, so that one could at last understand *both* this world of exploitation and oppression, *and* the mechanisms that transformed the reality of this exploitation and of class struggle into the Philosophy of History, Political Economy, and so on. Marx made no mistake: one had to start with philosophy, demand that it give an account of itself, and dismiss its impostures – not in order to abolish it, but in order to put it on new philosophical foundations. That it was, and has been, more difficult to make this fundamental philosophical change than Marx thought is shown by the texts of the 'break'. The 'Theses on Feuerbach' sketch out, very vaguely, something like a subjectivist historicism or even a Fichtean or pre-phenomenological historicism of 'praxis'. Six to ten months later, *The German Ideology* offers us a historicist positivism that tosses all philosophy on to the scrapheap, in order, as it turns out, briefly to relapse into a 'materialist' philosophy of history (a 'materialist' philosophy of the individual). But this relapse hardly matters. Something decisive has taken place, something that is irreversible.

Yes, there is plainly something like a 'rupture' or 'break', hence a 'moment' that does not resemble the preceding ones. Marx no doubt believed that he had reached his goal, so self-confident does he seem – if not in the 'Theses on Feuerbach' (yet another text that he did not publish), then at least in *The German Ideology*, which blithely announces the end of philosophy and a return to 'things themselves',[f] to factual, visible, tangible things, to individuals (but not to persons!), even while confecting a hallucinatory, albeit interesting, materialist philosophy of history. Marx thought that he had reached his goal; who can fail to understand him? Yet his labours were just beginning.

And, once again, labour, the silent work of theory upon itself, with philosophy attempting to formulate itself in the wake of the discoveries made in the Critique of that illusory Political Economy. These discoveries, for their part, were proceeding apace, beginning with *The Poverty of Philosophy* (1847), in which Proudhon is dismissed, although Marx had only recently treated him (in *The Holy Family*) as if he were the sole guardian of the 'science of the proletariat'(!).[43] Marx now puts in place the first concepts which make it possible to think that it is on condition that they are related to the class struggle that the 'categories' assembled under the imposture of Political Economy can, in conjunction with these new concepts, acquire their true meaning.

f *Zu den Sachen selbst* [back to things themselves]: long before Husserl, Feuerbach made this his watchword.

But this theoretical labour is inseparable from political struggles: *The Communist Manifesto*, written late in 1847, appears in 1848, just before the revolutions.

Marx had been commissioned to write the *Manifesto*, hurriedly, by the Communist League. They really were 'in a rush': the revolutions were knocking at the door. And Marx threw himself, with Engels, into the bitter revolutionary struggles of the Rhineland. He became a political journalist, a party leader, a leader in a political and a civil war, and then reflected at length, in the refuge provided by the silence and poverty of his London years, during this endless 'time in the wilderness', *both* on the reasons for the 1848 defeat, *and* on the capitalist mode of production – plagued by sickness and hunger, with Engels helping as best he could, but from afar, where he worked to put bread on the table for two. Unremitting study at the British Museum went hand in hand with political correspondence and political struggle: the aim was to rally the dispersed troops while waiting for better days. The years 1857 and 1858 were years of intense labour, when Marx wrote the manuscript (it went unpublished: and how well anyone who has read it both understands and regrets that Marx failed to publish it!) known as the *Grundrisse* (he himself did not choose this title for his notebooks, and for good reason). The year 1859 saw the publication of *A Contribution to the Critique of Political Economy*. *Zur Kritik* .... Critique is the essence of the matter, already, always. A laborious text. Once again – but from the great distance Marx had taken since 1850, when he declared that he had 'to start again from the very beginning',[44] from scratch, after the dead-end of *The German Ideology* and the failure of the 1848 revolutions, he may well have believed that he had reached his goal; yet we know (thanks to the unfinished notes called the *Introduction*,[45] certain chapters of which are very strange indeed) that he doubted it after all: and he had good reason to, given the approximate character, bordering on caricature, of his mediocre Preface.

In the same period, Marx worked for newspapers in order to make some money: American, English and German papers. This work, done to scrape a living, transformed him into a chronicler and political analyst of all the events of contemporary world history. In analysing political and economic events in a number of countries across the globe, alert to everything from stagnation in India to the cyclical English crises – the cotton crisis, and so on – Marx applied, verified and revised his conception of things. Increasingly, he tightened the link between class struggle and what he called its material and social conditions and 'economic' and ideological effects – and their often paradoxical 'dialectic'. Here, too, the *Kritik* of Political Economy was at work – in the light, naturally, of class struggle.

Then, in 1864, came the foundation of the International, in which Marx was soon playing the leading role that would be his down to the Commune and 1872, the date the International was dissolved. This was when his time in the wilderness at last came to an end: 1867 saw the publication of Volume One of *Capital.* The first section (the section containing the 'flirt' with Hegel) was rewritten a good dozen times, because Marx felt the need for a 'scientific' beginning, and had a 'certain' idea as to what such a beginning should look like. It was a rather unhappy idea, unhappily for us, unless we have the courage and also the means to say that this Idea of the beginning is untenable, and even prevents *Capital* from producing all the effects it might be expected to. Marx was overjoyed at seeing intelligent bourgeois and, especially, 'the most advanced circles of the working class'[46] take an interest in his book.

Volumes Two and Three – which remained unfinished, although they were written before Volume One – would be published by Engels, and, after Engels's death, by Kautsky. Strange. There is a whole history of *Capital* waiting to be written. This work, produced over the long term – only the first volume appeared in Marx's lifetime – has played a curious role, one hopelessly overshadowed by the *Manifesto* and even Engels's *Anti-Dühring,* and also, of course, by *Zur Kritik* (the famous Preface!). This book, which Engels, laying it on rather thick, called 'the Bible of the working class',[47] made significant headway only in Germany, and, later, in Russia. It has been making its way in France and Italy for … all of twenty years!

There followed the great silence of the last years, when Marx was overwhelmed by his political duties and illness, before the sudden burst of energy represented by the 'Critique (yet another critique!) of the Gotha Programme'. Here Marx took up his pen from a position outside the German Social Democratic Party (Engels: 'the only reason that Marx and I ever intervened in the Party was to rectify theoretical errors ...') in order to pulverize these stupid formulas, foreign to the spirit of communism – only to discover, without getting overly upset about it, (1) that the leadership of the 'Party'[g] refused to publish his pamphlet (Engels managed to do so fifteen years later,[48] but only at the price of trickery and blackmail); (2) that the public, bourgeois journalists, and even workers, had taken these platitudes, foreign to the spirit of communism, for ... communist declarations! It is unfortunate that Marx did not pursue his analysis of these two strange, apparently minor, but in fact immensely important events.

All this took place four years after the Commune, in a mind enlightened by the Commune. Surprised by the Parisians' revolt, Marx had, in his enthusiasm, promptly extended them his support and counsel, in the form of the brilliant addresses collected in *The Civil War in France* (1871).

It was necessary to recall these facts and dates, as well as the political background to these writings, in order to show how closely Marx's theoretical thinking is bound up with his political thinking, and his political thinking with his concrete activity and political struggle, conducted, from start to finish, in the interests of the international working class. We can, then, affirm that in his theoretical work, as well as in his political battles, *Marx never once, from his initial commitment of 1843 on, left the terrain of working-class struggle.* Thus it is not particularly difficult not only to reject Kautsky's formulas, unfortunately repeated verbatim by Lenin (whose defence based on 'the context' is not, when it comes down to it, tenable: he really had no need to quote Kautsky, but could have spoken in his own name, and differently), but also to propose a thesis that reflects the historical and political reality of the matter more closely than Lenin's does.

We may, then, say roughly the following: *Marx's thought was formed and developed not outside the workers' movement, but within the existing workers'*

g Lasalleans + Marxists, unified at Gotha = the Social Democratic Party. It was considered important 'not to undermine the unity of the Party'. Mireille Bertrand's phrase was used against Marx by the Party leadership in 1875! [Bertrand sat on the Political Bureau of the PCF when Althusser was writing 'Marx in his Limits'.]

movement, on the political basis provided by that movement and its rectified theoretical positions. That this basis and these positions were not laid down in advance – better, that they had to be constantly modified – is abundantly clear to anyone who has even a nodding acquaintance with the history of Marx's thought. This theory was by no means 'introduced into the workers' movement from without'. It expanded *from within the workers' movement,* from the first Marxist circles – at the price of great struggles and contradictions – to the big mass parties.

If this thesis is admissible, then all the literature about the 'bourgeois intellectuals who are the guardians of the science' that 'is introduced into the Workers' Movement from without' – this literature initiated by Kautsky and exploited by Marx's and Lenin's critics, a literature which delights the vicious little lapdogs everybody knows all too well – loses all relevance. To be sure, bourgeois intellectuals exist, and can even be found holding posts at all echelons in the Communist parties, where they ply their trade, in their capacity as leaders, in an organization that endures them, tolerates [them], flatters them, or makes them to measure. But Marx – who, thank God, was not alone – was not one of this breed. He loved arguing too much (as Brecht says, he loved 'nothing so much as a good argument') not to consign the bourgeois intellectual and his soul to perdition, once he had seen the reality of the working class and its struggle close up. As to whether he was an 'organic intellectual' of the working class, we will have to throw some light on what this rather-too-transparent phrase of Gramsci's means before making up our minds.

5. Is Marxism a River Fed by Three Sources?

Since we are talking about the legacies of ambiguities, let us note that we find the same 'fuzziness' (to leave it at that) in Engels's famous thesis on 'the three sources of Marxism'. It is systematized by Kautsky in a pamphlet to which it gives its title, and is evoked by Lenin, who is very 'classical' here too.[49] This is another way of thinking about the history of Marx's thought – this time with regard to its origins.

Of course, Marxist thought did not come from nothing; it has ancestors, and direct ancestors. (It is, be it said in passing, by no means certain that the direct ancestors are the most important; but that is another matter, which would call into question certain certitudes of the ideology of the 'sources' of any body of thought.) Of course, as a result of their academic training and, in addition, the culture then dominant in Western Europe, Marx and Engels were intellectuals schooled in 'German philosophy', 'English political economy' and 'French socialism': for those are our 'three sources', which we can hardly help but rediscover, and they are the sources of a river at that. Let us note that 'French socialism' is rather vague, unless we detect in this term echoes of the class struggles of the French Revolution, which Marx studied with passionate interest, and of the radical revolutionary tendencies which grew out of Babeuf and came into their own with Blanqui. But that doesn't matter much. What does matter is the theoretical and historical pretension that consists in reducing Marx's thought to the vague confluence, at once necessary (to complete the 'picture') and imprecise, of these three currents, and thus 'accounting for' it. To do so is openly to affirm a reassuring principle that doubtless provides the requisite moral assurances about Marx's identity and claims to legitimacy (son of Hegel, and of Smith–Ricardo and Saint-Simon and Proudhon … or of Babeuf and Blanqui?). By the same token, however, it is to lapse into the superficiality of the commonplaces inherited from the biblical genealogies (Abraham, son of Isaac, son of Jacob, etc. [*sic*], *ergo* Abraham himself, in person), or, at best, into a history of ideas. One accordingly finds oneself incapable of thinking the socio-politico-theoretical base which necessitated the encounter of the Big Three constituent currents that flowed from these Three Sources into a particular body of thought: that of Karl Marx and company. Above all, one finds oneself at a loss to transform this 'encounter' into a 'revolutionary critique' of its own constituent elements.

No one denies that Hegel (and, behind Hegel, German philosophy), Ricardo (and, behind Ricardo, Smith and the Physiocrats, who were themselves strikingly in advance of Smith and Ricardo, because they were theorists of reproduction) and Proudhon (and, behind Proudhon, Saint-Simon? but there are others who are much more interesting when it comes to understanding Marx) formed Marx's historical horizon. They represented the culture he had to acquire, the culture from which every intellectual of his sort who was keen to understand his times had to begin, the raw material upon which he was obliged to work, and so on. However, *nothing in this reassuring list compelled Marx to go past the ideological façade and overturn its principles* in order to perceive what Hegel called (in discussing self-consciousness) its 'back', 'rear', 'or 'hidden backside'[50] – in a word, the occluded reality of the matter. Yet to go past the façade was precisely to 'shift ground' and adopt an entirely different position, a 'critical and revolutionary' position, the famous 'critique that ... represents the proletariat'.

To reduce the history of this revolution in Marx's thought to a mere geographico-fluvial confluence of 'Three Sources' was thus, ultimately, to treat Marx as an 'author' who succeeded (his 'genius'!) in skilfully combining the elements whose point of convergence he happened (but why? how?) to be.

Thus it was that – outside the communist tradition, to be sure, but sometimes in it as well – people repeatedly affirmed that Marx was nothing but 'Hegel applied to Ricardo', with the result that Political Economy was transformed into a 'metaphysics' (Croce, Aron, *et al.*). Thus it was that, in the Marxist tradition, beginning with Marx's own formulas, people chose to believe that the revolution to which Marx subjected the authors of his 'Three Sources' was a materialist 'inversion' of *each element*, a revolution which, it followed, put philosophy, political economy and utopian socialism 'back on their feet', while leaving the structures of each of these elements intact: in order to constitute, by this miracle, Political Economy as a *science*, *philosophy* as *dialectical materialism*, and the visions of *French socialism* as *a philosophy of history*, or – the practical version of its messianism – as 'scientific socialism'.[h]

It is common knowledge that the phrases just quoted are not to be found, in this definitive form, in Marx. But we find almost all of them in Engels, in texts produced while Marx was still alive and, according to Engels, under his supervision .... Moreover, they belong to the

h This phrase is the only thing in Marx that the Twenty-Third Congress of the PCF has retained, on the grounds, let us say, that it provides the best possible summary of his work. The phrase is, however, nowhere to be found in Marx.

history of Marxism, in which, from the Second International on, they have stood as the official definition of Marxism, set out in three moments: 'dialectical materialism', historical materialism, and scientific socialism. The 'finishing touches' were put on later, in the 1930s, under the direct political impetus of Stalin, who came up with the solution that consisted in declaring that 'historical materialism was an integral part of dialectical materialism'.[51] That way, the exits were well guarded!

6. Marx Still a Prisoner of Idealism

I know we can find things in Marx which justify some of these formulas and seem to justify others. We emphatically do find in Marx the one-hundred-per-cent Feuerbachian theme of 'inversion', which is a watchword rather than a true concept, for, if it is mistaken for a concept, it condemns every reader who 'thinks for himself' to theoretical contortions: for example, the 'inversion' of the Hegelian dialectic, which has to be inverted because it is idealist (Engels doubles the dose, affirming that idealism results from a first inversion, that of materialism, which is said to be, by rights, primary...[52]).

We also find in Marx – increasingly subject to criticism, yet always present just beneath the surface – the idea of a philosophy of history, of an Origin and an End: in short, of a Meaning [*Sens*, which also means direction] of history. It is embodied in the sequence of 'epochs marking progress' represented by determinate modes of production (see the Preface to the 1859 *Contribution*). This sequence culminates in the transparency of communism (see *The German Ideology*, 1845; the *Grundrisse*, 1857–58; and even the famous line in *Capital*, in 1867, about the supposed transition 'from necessity to freedom'), a transparency embodied in communism, the myth of a community of labouring men (who ultimately, amid abundance, hardly work at all but, rather, give themselves over body and soul to the 'development of their personality' – or, according to Lafargue's controversial satire, to laziness).[53]

Yes, we find in Marx a latent idea of the perfect transparency of social relations under communism, the idea that these social relations are 'human relations', that is, crystal-clear relations between nothing but individuals (ultimately, all individuals) in the conquest and realization of the 'free development of their personality'. Yes, from *The German Ideology*, which expiates on this theme at length, down to *Capital*, the first volume of which describes states of social transparency, from Robinson and the family based on patriarchal production to the free association of communism, Marx never manages to relinquish this mythical idea of communism as a mode of production *without relations of production*; in communism, the free development of individuals takes the place of social relations in the mode of production. And this is very easy to understand, since productive relations will become, under communism, as superfluous as the state, commodity relations, money, politics, political parties, democracy, the division of labour among men, the split between manual and intellectual labour, between city and country, between the sexes, between parents and children, mothers-in-law and sons-in-law, and so on.

It is true that Marx discusses communism in less idealistic terms in 'Critique of the Gotha Programme' (1875); and especially in his final text, the lovely 'Notes on Wagner' (1882),[54] we can clearly sense that he has kept almost nothing, or even nothing at all, of this whole idealist myth, which came to him straight from the utopian socialists (compare Fourier: communism is the reign, organized as rationally as possible, of the development of the passions of individuals – meaning, first and foremost, the erotic passions). He adopted it in *The German Ideology* before all but abandoning it in *The Communist Manifesto*, only to rediscover it again later, more tenacious than ever, in the *Grundrisse*. It is still present, albeit in a limited way, in *Capital*.

The latent or manifest idealism of these themes haunts [***] the 'materialist' philosophy of history expounded in *The German Ideology* (this manuscript, too, went unpublished and was left 'to the gnawing criticism of the mice', although Marx and Engels meant to have it brought out in 1845; they were, however, taken unawares by the revolutions of 1848, and, in the end, the thing was done only much later, prompting Engels to remark that this text proved 'how incomplete' their 'knowledge of economic history still was at that time'[55]). But it also haunts the 1859 Preface. The modes of production are lined up there in a continuous list and a mandatory order that is, moreover, 'progressive' – rather as the early-nineteenth-century Ideologues, in the wake of Rousseau and the Natural Law philosophers, affirmed that there had been first savages, then barbarians, then 'civilization'. Similarly, it was in the form of a 'progressive' series that Marx presented the ordered sequence 'primitive communism, slavery, feudalism, capitalism, communism'. Apparently no society was capable of 'catching a moving train'; each had to go through the mandatory series of the prescribed modes of production. It is well known that Marx changed his mind about this in connection with the 'Asiatic mode of production', and – to cite no other examples – the paradoxical case of India, whose archaic structures scandalously resisted English colonial capitalism, although the latter was more 'progressive'.[i]

All too often, it was in the same revolutioneering, idealist spirit that Marx conceived of the problem of the 'transition', that is, the question as to the conditions under which the transition from one mode of production to another (to the *next in line* …) could come about. It was in this context that Marx made the hallowed pronouncements that so delighted Gramsci, uttering those grand phrases which, supposed to say everything, ended up meaning nothing, except that they expressed very clearly Marx's 'desire' to see real history unfold as he liked or would have liked. For example: 'No social order [*formation*] is ever destroyed [!] before all the productive forces for which it is sufficient have been developed.' Now just what might that mean? For example: 'Mankind [!] thus inevitably sets itself only such tasks as it is able to solve.'[56]

But the same idealism haunts *Capital* itself, in an infinitely more subtle form. For some of us were forced to recognize, at the price of a long, painstaking analysis carried out in the face of the ideas prevailing in this domain, that something about Marx's 'order of exposition' did not work. However impressive the unity of the mode of exposition in *Capital* might be, we came to see it for what it was: *fictitious*. But

i It is common knowledge that, once it struck out in this direction, the Second International adopted the thesis that imperialist colonialism was of course, from the standpoint of Universal History, a good thing, because it gave the natives capitalism, the obligatory access route to socialism….

what was the reason for this fictitious unity? It was that Marx *believed that he was duty-bound*, as a good 'semi-Hegelian' – that is to say, a Hegelian 'inverted' into the materialist he was – to broach, in a discipline of a scientific nature, the purely *philosophical* problem of the *beginning* of a philosophical work. A misconception of this sort is understandable.

It is no accident that Marx rewrote Book I, Section I, the beginning of *Capital*, a dozen times or more; that he was determined to begin with that which was 'simplest' and with the 'abstract', namely, the commodity, and therefore with value; that he therefore set himself the task of beginning with *the abstraction of value*, something that lent his demonstrations impressive force, but, at the same time, situated them in the 'framework' of a theoretical field that proved problematic as soon as it was a question of 'deducing' money, capitalist exploitation, and the rest. Not to mention that which is presupposed by the abstraction of value, 'abstract labour', namely, the existence of a homogeneous field ruled by – because it has *already* triumphed – the equivalence of socially necessary labour-times in any equation of value whatsoever (x commodity A = y commodity B). For this equivalence is in reality *merely tendential*, whereas, in order to reason in the rigorous form that he adopted, or had to adopt, Marx sets out from it as if it were a *given*: not the result of a terribly complicated historical process, but, as it were, the 'simplest' original state. Not to mention, finally, the fact that this 'order of exposition' necessarily leaves out something that Marx must of course discuss – but outside the order of exposition – in order to be able to propose a theory of exploitation, which is irreducible to the theory of surplus-value (regarded as a difference in values). For, paradoxically, in order to propose such a theory, he has to take into account what the *order of exposition* requires him *to bracket out*: the productivity of labour in all its forms; labour-power as something other than a simple commodity; and, quite simply, the history of the conditions under which capitalism arose, which necessitates, among other things, reference to primitive accumulation. Whence the very long chapters on the working day, the labour process, manufacture and big industry, and the extraordinary chapter on primitive accumulation.

These chapters[j] stand *outside* 'the order of exposition'. They have confronted commentators with a formidable problem: why this leap from theory to history, from abstraction to the concrete, without the least justification? And, ultimately: what is Marx's real object? 'The capitalist mode of production and exchange in its ideal average', as *Capital* incessantly repeats, or the concrete history of the conditions of class struggle that precipitated the Western bourgeoisie into capitalism? But if it is the latter, then we are at the very heart of 'the concrete', for primitive accumulation and the expropriation of (rural and urban) workers' means of production and conditions of reproduction, which produced the capitalist mode of production, have nothing to do with any abstraction or 'ideal average' whatsoever. How, then, are we to hold together the discordant elements of a body of thought which itself never ceases to proclaim its unity, and to impose this unity by way of *Capital*'s supposed order of exposition?

Better: what are we to think of a theory which sets itself the goal of demonstrating the production of the prices of production starting out from value, and succeeds only at the price of a mistake, by leaving something out of the calculation? Sraffa, Gramsci's old friend, who emigrated to England – Sraffa and his school must be given credit for closely checking Marx's demonstration of this point, and discovering, to their amazement, that the demonstration was erroneous. The error has deep roots: it is rooted, precisely, in the principle that it is necessary to begin with the simplest element, the first, namely, the commodity or value, whereas this simple form is in fact neither simple nor the simplest. The mistake is *also* rooted in the principle that it is necessary to begin *in an 'analytical' mode*, the mission of analysis being to discover, in the simple form, its essence and the effects of this essence, effects such that we ultimately again find, by synthetic deduction, the concrete itself. Yet Marx himself ignores this exigency not only in the concrete chapters that he injects into the order of exposition of *Capital*, *but also through the*

j Marx himself advised Kugelmann's wife to read *only* these chapters; she did not have to read the others to understand the essence of the matter, which 'even a child could grasp'. [Marx, Letter of 30 November 1867 to Ludwig Kugelmann, trans. Christopher Upward, *MECW* 42: 489. Althusser's translation is inaccurate. Compare Marx's letter of 11 July 1868 to Kugelmann.]

injection of the abstract concepts that he is continually injecting into the theoretical field of the abstract order of exposition *in order to broaden it.* He thereby shows that he is – thank God – as un-Hegelian as can be.

We must therefore ask why the question of the beginning represented the exigency and the 'sticking-point' that it did for Marx: 'beginnings are always difficult in all sciences', he writes in the opening pages of *Capital.*[57] Why did Marx *think that he had to begin with the ultimate abstraction of value*? No doubt we have, at some point – if we have understood Marx properly – to proceed by way of something that has to do with 'value'. Nothing, however, requires that we start out from it, unless the aim is to overcharge this concept with meanings that are difficult to keep under control. Actually, it seems clear that all these requirements, and the problems they entailed, were imposed on Marx by a *certain Idea of science* [*Wissenschaft*] (nobody ever avoids this in any period, although the idea involved varies): of, that is, the immutable formal conditions with which every Thought-Process [*Denkprozess*] must comply *in order to be 'True'.*

The text in which we can see the contents of this Idea at work very clearly is the one devoted [to the subject] in the Introduction to the 1858 *Contribution* (another text that Marx did not publish!): 'The Method of Political Economy'.[58] Here Marx develops, first and foremost, the idea that true – that is, materialist – Thought-Processes necessarily begin *with abstraction,* contrary to the reigning prejudice. True thought, science, proceeds not from the concrete to the abstract, but from the abstract to the concrete: it must therefore begin with abstraction, that is, the simplest or the simple (the most general, etc.). Why this exigency? Marx states this principle, of which his work (*Capital*) is to provide the proof, since method does not exist outside its realization, that is, outside the knowledge produced when it is put to use.[k] However, because *Capital* (as we have just noted) does not really provide this proof, but provides proof of its own confusion instead, it is incumbent on us to ask: *why did Marx have this Idea of the Process of True Thought, and subject that process to these precise requirements*?

k Here we are brought back to the remark found in the [Preface to *A Contribution to the Critique of Political Economy*]: expounding the method before demonstrating the results can be 'confusing'.

Marx most assuredly had his eyes trained on the natural sciences; he generally [took] his examples from analytical chemistry, but also appealed to physics and even mathematics (where analysis consists in presupposing that a problem has been solved and 'analysing' the conditions, which can then be discovered, for solving it). Behind these purely scientific references, however, there can be no doubt that Marx was guided, right down to his way of interpreting them for the purposes of his demonstrations, by an Idea of Truth inherited from Hegel and much earlier thinkers. In fact Hegel's *Logic*, and the whole 'dialectical' deduction of Nature and Spirit, plainly suggest that it is necessary to 'begin' – but *in philosophy, not in the 'sciences'* – with pure abstraction, which in Hegel is at the same time not determinate abstraction (as Della Volpe clearly saw),[59] but *indeterminate abstraction.* This crucial difference aside, we can affirm that, in Hegel as well, the Idea of Science [*Wissenschaft*] requires that one begin with abstraction, and that the thought-process proceed from the abstract to the concrete, from the more abstract to the more concrete. We can also affirm that this Idea requires that one analyse each content (Being, Nothingness, becoming, etc.) in order to discover the emergence of the next.

Yet, in his actual practice in *Capital*, in the chapters which stand outside the order of exposition, and especially when he was injecting concepts into the theoretical space conquered by analysis, Marx in fact broke with the Hegelian idea of Science, hence of method, hence of dialectic. At the same time, however, he remained sufficiently attached to this Idea to consider himself obliged to begin with value, to regard the 'inverted' Hegelian dialectic as his own, and to think what he had discovered within the impressive but *fictitious unity* of the (in principle) one and only order of exposition in *Capital.*

That Hegel – whom Marx had known in his youth, later forgot or combated, and then rediscovered in 1858 thanks to a chance encounter with a book (the 'Greater Logic') bequeathed him by Bakunin[60] – is present in Marx's thought, *Capital* included, and that Feuerbach's philosophy of alienation is also active there once Hegel has been injected into this philosophy, is something that we can now confidently and also serenely affirm, because these questions have played a not insignificant part in animating the debates of the 'Marxologists' over the past twenty years (the same phenomenon appeared throughout Europe from 1920 to 1930). But we should go on to draw from this the kind of conclusions that permit a better understanding of *Capital* and Marx's political intentions. Yes, Marx – how could it have been otherwise? – was subject to the limits that the dominant ideas of his own time imposed on him, despite his determination to break with them. The surprising thing is not that he was subject to them, but that, despite their weight and despite these limits, he opened up for us the knowledge of a reality that no one else – or almost no one else – had glimpsed before him.

On this condition, we may turn back to *Capital*. We will readily see the effects that the still-idealist philosophical conception of the Process of True Thought had on Marx's thinking: for example, what appears to be the purely arithmetical presentation [*Darstellung*] of surplus-value[1] (but this is only a matter of appearances: it is not a question of prices, but of values) as the difference between the value of labour-power and the value created by labour. *Imposed in this form* by the order of exposition and its conceptual deduction, this presentation can lead to an 'economistic' interpretation of exploitation. For, in reality – Marx is very clear on this point – exploitation cannot be reduced to the extraction of a surplus of value; it can be understood only if the whole set of its concrete forms and conditions is treated as determinant. The whole set of these concrete forms does indeed include the extraction of value, but it also includes the implacable constraints of the labour process embedded in the process of production and, therefore, exploitation: the socio-technical division and organization of labour; the length of the 'working-day', a notion peculiar to the capitalist system, and therefore nowhere to be found before it; speed-up; compartmentalization; the material conditions of the centralization of labour (the factory, the workshop); work-related accidents and illnesses; the practice of forcing people to take jobs below or above their level of competence; and so on. And the process of production must

1 Jean-Pierre Lefebvre and Étienne Balibar have recently proposed, rightly, to translate *Mehrwert* as *sur-valeur*. See Lefebvre and Balibar, 'Plus-value ou survaleur?', *La Pensée*, no. 197, 1978, pp. 32–42.

in turn (lest one remain abstract) be conceived as a decisive moment in the process of reproduction: the reproduction of the means of production, but also the reproduction of labour-power (family, housing, children, child-rearing, schooling, health, problems faced by the couple, by young people, etc.) – to say nothing of the other moment of the process of reproduction of labour-power, which brings the state and its apparatuses (repressive, ideological, etc.) into play.

Marx discusses these questions – which the simple equation for surplus-value must obviously *bracket out* in order to show that exploitation consists in the retention of value – in the famous 'concrete' chapters of *Capital*; they are at odds with the book's abstract order of exposition. The result is that the theory of exploitation is indeed to be found in *Capital*, but 'expounded' in several places: not only in the theory of surplus-value, in an apparently purely arithmetical form, but also as explained in the chapters on the working day (absolute surplus-value) and the capitalist transformation of the labour process (relative surplus-value), to say nothing of the chapter on primitive accumulation. This division of a key question into its abstract 'exposition' and concrete explanations is not without theoretical consequences, which begin to come into view in the shortcomings of the theory of labour-power or even wages, as well as in various other questions: for example, today, the question of the transformation of the working class by the 'technical' forms of the imperialist class struggle on a global scale (immigrant labour, the reorganization of tasks, the new competition facing labour-power due to the investment 'policy' ['*politique*'] of the multinationals, and so on).

It would be possible to cite many other examples of difficulties and contradictions in which Marx gets caught up because he feels he is *under an obligation* to begin with the abstraction of value. For example, the thorny question of the 'transference' of the value (which value, precisely?) of the means of production through 'utilization' by labour-power, and the famous limit-case that Marx introduces to test his reasoning, by setting C, constant capital minus means of production, to zero.[61] For example, the transformation of value into prices of production, where Marx has been caught pursuing a flawed line of reasoning, and so on.

Thus the obvious need to 'shift ground' or adopt a position 'representing the proletariat', however keenly Marx was aware of it (there is an interval of thirty-two years between the two formulas!), clearly did not suffice, in and of itself and from the outset, 'to settle accounts0' with Marx's former philosophical consciousness. The materialism that he professed applies to him as well: his consciousness could not exhaust his practice, his consciousness could not even exhaust his thought in its real forms, and his thought, which was still subject to the most subtle of the dominant philosophical and ideological forms, could not take charge of, and resolve, the contradictions in which it became entangled as a result. A materialist will conclude from this that there was more in Marx's practice, thought, and the contradictions of his problematic than in his consciousness. *He will also conclude that the limits of Marx's thought were not without effect on his acts or those of others.*

We might note, as a sign of this unavoidable disparity, the fact that apart from the brief, enigmatic declarations of the 'Theses on Feuerbach', Marx would never clarify his new positions – that is to say, ultimately, his philosophy, the one he must have espoused after breaking with his former philosophical consciousness. Marx vaguely promised Engels twenty pages on the dialectic, if he could 'find the time'. He never wrote them. Was it because he did not have the time? And he dropped the 1857 Introduction – the most fully elaborated statement of his position from a philosophical point of view (especially the chapter on the method of Political Economy, which has fascinated countless Marxists, yet is, in the final analysis, both gripping and highly dubious). 'It seems to me confusing', he said, 'to anticipate results which still have to be substantiated.'[62] True enough; but how are we to explain Marx's silence *thereafter*?

This is not to say that Marx did not wrestle, endlessly, with philosophy, with the task of giving shape and substance to the new philosophy that informed his thinking from the 'moment' he clearly saw that he had to break with the old one, which was too deeply committed to 'glorify[ing] what exists',[63] too closely tied to the ideological and political interests of the dominant class. The fact is that this whole process of self-criticism and rectification took place within Marx's work itself –

in his political and theoretical practice, and at the price of what difficulties! – so that he could arrive at a somewhat clearer vision of things. It took place in his scientific work, as is more than obvious, but also, and above all, in his struggle to reconstruct the workers' movement in the terrible years that stretched from the defeat of the 1848 revolutions [through] the foundation of the First International to the Commune. An interminable struggle, amid contradictions, amid contradiction, to insure the new positions against the return and revenge of the old – a battle whose outcome was always in doubt, even when it seemed won: a battle to find words and concepts that did not yet exist in order to think what had, until then, been occluded by all-powerful words and concepts. For – as goes without saying – the battle is also a battle over concepts and even words, whenever they sum up the stakes of great conflicts, great uncertainties, or silent, obscure contradictions. Witness the most profound hesitations in *Capital*, in which the word, theme, notion, or even concept of alienation continues to haunt not only the theory (which is one-hundred-per-cent Feuerbachian) of fetishism, but also the theatrical opposition between dead and living labour, the domination of working conditions over the worker, and the figure of communism, that free association of 'individuals' who have no social relations other than their freedom – alienation, an old word, an old idealist concept that can be put to any use you like (including that of making felt what is still inadequately thought) and is manifestly there to think something else: something which is unthought, and has remained so.

Why has it remained so? We must seek the answer both in the history of the workers' class struggle, in its 'limits', and in Marx's philosophical conception of the order of exposition that one had to follow to think the true.

7. The 'Omnipotence of Ideas'?

Here is another example of how history, being a good materialist, surprised and overtook Marx's thinking.

Marx is distinguished from all idealist political philosophy (in this, he is in agreement with only one thinker, Machiavelli) by the fact that he never entertained any illusions about the 'omnipotence of ideas', including his own. It was Lenin who, in the heat and the pitiless give-and-take of polemic, unwisely wrote that 'Marx's ideas are omnipotent because they are true'.[64] Of course they are true, but they are not 'omnipotent', for no idea is 'omnipotent' simply by virtue of the fact that it is a true idea. From the *Manifesto* onwards, Marx's position is clear and was never to change: not communist ideas, but the general movement of the proletariat's class struggle against the capitalists is paving the way, and will continue to pave the way, for communism, which is a 'real movement'. The influence of ideas makes itself felt only under ideological and political conditions that express a given balance of class forces: it is this balance of forces, and its political and ideological effects, which determine the efficacy of 'ideas' 'in the last instance'.

The extraordinary thing is that Marx, consistent with his own theses, takes his own theory into account by politically *posing* and *exposing his own ideas* – that is to say, by situating them within the scheme [*dispositif*] of society! This is clear in the *Manifesto* as well as in the 1859 Preface. Here the presentation of the major theoretical principles takes the form of a 'topography', a figure laid out in a space in which places (*topoi*) and their relations are defined in order to 'make visible' relations of relative externality, determination, and so on, and thus of efficacy between 'instances': the infrastructure (production/exploitation, hence 'economic' class struggle) and the elements (Law, the State, ideologies) of the 'superstructure'. This means – here is the crucial point – that Marx adopts a *topographical* arrangement in order to present his own theoretical ideas twice, and in two different forms or 'places' in the same space.

Marx first presents his theoretical ideas as principles of analysis of *the whole of his object*, whether this object is a pre-revolutionary political conjuncture considered against the backdrop of class struggle between capitalists and those they exploit (the *Manifesto*) or the structure of a social formation in general (the 1859 Preface). Thus, Marx's theoretical ideas are present everywhere; they occupy the whole space (and therefore the place) of this object as well, because the aim is to mobilize them to provide an understanding of this object as a whole.

Simultaneously, however, Marx arranges for the same theoretical ideas to appear *a second time*, but by situating them in a determinate, extremely limited 'place' within the space occupied by the same global reality. Let us say – to repeat the formula of the 1859 Preface – that Marx now situates his own theoretical ideas among the 'ideological forms in which men become conscious of [class] conflict and fight it out'.[65] In thus situating his ideas a second time, in a place defined simultaneously by class relations and their ideological effects (in the 'superstructure', alongside the state), Marx treats and presents his theoretical ideas not as principles of explanation of the given whole, but solely in terms of their possible effect in the ideological, and therefore political, class struggle commanding this 'whole': such-and-such a social formation, such-and-such a conjuncture, and so forth. In fact, when they change their place (and function), the theoretical ideas change their form: they shift from the 'theoretical form' to the 'ideological form'.

The measure of Marx's materialism, which Lenin called 'consistent', lies not only in the dissipation of all illusions before the objectivity of actually existing reality and the knowledge of this reality, but also, and simultaneously, in the acute, practical consciousness of the conditions, forms and limits within which his own ideas *can become* active. Hence their double inscription in the topography. Hence the distance (which is considerable at first) between the 'truth' of the ideas that cover the whole of their object, and *the efficacy* of these ideas, which are situated in a small part of the 'space' of their 'object'. Hence the essential thesis that ideas, even if they are true and have been formally and materially proven, can never be historically active in person, as pure theoretical ideas, but can become active only in and through *ideological forms – mass ideological forms*, it must be added, for that is fundamental – caught up in the class struggle and its development.

Yet, by a stupefying historical irony, which has been, for working-class activists, an experience – and what an experience! – etched into their very flesh, Marx was not in a position to conceive, or was unable to foresee, the possibility that his own thought might be perverted into playing the role of the all-too-real, albeit only alleged, 'omnipotence of ideas', and, in the guise of his 'doctrine', pressed into the service of the politics of those who would one day cloak themselves in the prestige of his name in order to falsify his ideas. The whole history of the deviations (beginning with the Second International) and splits in the international Marxist movement, followed by the history of its 'evolution' in the post-revolutionary countries, can be summoned to bear witness at this proceeding. There is a great deal to answer for. There can, of course, be no question of arraigning Marx here, and 'judging' him on the basis of something other than his own political and theoretical history; first, we owe it to him to arrive at an understanding of the import and limits of that history. There can, of course, be no question of attributing to Marx insights that were not his, or of criticizing him for lacking insight into experiments he never saw. Due allowance made, that would be like criticizing Newton for not being Einstein.

Unless we wish to scapegoat the past for our problems or our demonstrations, the only real targets of our criticism, those who truly have to answer for what they have or have not made of Marx's thought, are those to whom these questions *have posed themselves* or upon whom they *have ultimately imposed themselves*, those who can and want to (or neither can nor want to) confront them: above all, the Communist parties. But these parties maintain a stubborn, stupid silence on these questions, or reluctantly drop a few niggardly, sententious remarks that are not even self-critical (other people are always to blame!), and are always made 'belatedly' – inevitably so, because the Communist parties *deliberately spend their time ducking these questions, which are too embarrassing for them.* The necessary answers will therefore have to be provided, in the Parties' stead, by rank-and-file revolutionary activists, whether they are members of these parties or not.

It must, however, be acknowledged that Marx's theoretical shortcomings have occasionally, quite as much as his merits, been accompanied by strange silences. I shall mention only two by way of illustration.

The astonishing collection that Marx published under the title *The Civil War in France* (the Commune) provides an ongoing analysis of the political history of the Commune, a history internal to the movement of the Commune itself, and, simultaneously, a theorization of the popular political inventions that we owe to the Commune, in which Marx immediately recognized the active force of the dictatorship of the proletariat. It is a matter of common knowledge that he initially opposed the revolt, yet unstintingly offered enthusiastic, lucid help once the movement had begun. Yet there is something in his analysis of the Commune that leaves us unsatisfied: his virtual silence when it comes to analysing the balance of class forces in France, and, especially, the forms and conditions *of the bourgeois class struggle*, hence the class conditions surrounding the Communards' defeat.

Let us make this more precise. It can be argued that Marx had already settled this question in *The Class Struggles in France*, even if the France of 1871 was no longer the France of 1850; in twenty years, the country had undergone extensive economic development and seen the triumph of the industrial and financial bourgeoisie over the big landowners, as well as the growth of the proletariat. Let that pass. The question nevertheless remains as to why Marx was unable to exploit this experience, which was extraordinary as such experiences go, to provide a better analysis of the functioning of *the bourgeois state* and *bourgeois ideology*, and to mine it for ideas richer than the inadequate notions he had already put forward in 1852. And how is it that Marx also made no attempt to understand what was happening *on the ideological plane in the Communards' case*, and on the plane of *politics*, which was transformed by their innovations? *The Civil War in France* offers a prodigious, dramatic, detailed chronicle of events, and a theorization, which was to prove its pertinence, of the political forms of the dictatorship of the proletariat. Yet it contributes nothing to our knowledge of the bourgeois state, ideology (that of the bourgeoisie and the Communards), or the conflicting politics of the two sides. On these subjects – the state, ideology, politics – it is quite as if Marx felt no need to take a closer look: either because these were, so to speak, obvious matters for him, or because he saw no particular mystery in them.

I would like to come back to the episode surrounding the 'Critique of the Gotha Programme', that strange affair. Let me point out, first of all, that Marx was not really an active party militant at the time; and, secondly, that he drew no conclusions from his misadventure.

The Gotha Congress that unified the Marxist and Lasallean parties was convened, and it approved a programme. Stupefied, Marx ruthlessly criticized its main theses: they have nothing to do with communism, and he proved it, brilliantly.

Apprised of his reaction, the leadership of the new, unified party, the Marxist leaders among them, ordered Marx not to publish his critique! Marx waited for a while, and then discovered, to his stupefaction, that 'the jackasses on the bourgeois papers', and even 'the workers', had 'read into' the Gotha Programme things that were not there. Whereas they had been served up reformist theses, they 'believed' that they were being given communism! Marx and Engels leave us in no doubt on this matter: *Marx chose not to defy* the (unified) Social Democratic Party and *not to publish his critique* 'solely because … the jackasses on the bourgeois papers' and even 'the workers', found things in the Gotha programme that were not actually there.[66] The upshot was that Marx held his tongue. Although he had often written that 'the interests of the future of the workers' movement must not be sacrificed to its immediate interests', and that to do so was opportunism, he gave no thought to the future; he did not ask himself whether, in a few months or years, the formulas of the Congress would have had their effects, and the irreparable damage have been done. Seventeen years later, by blackmailing the leadership of the German Social Democratic Party, Engels finally saw to it that the 'Critique' saw the light. Why so late? And to what end? Did Marx's critique merit publication after all? Marx had since died; but he had done nothing to make his critique known while he was still alive.

An odd sentence of Engels's comes to mind here: '[Marx and I] have hardly ever interfered in internal party affairs, and then only in an attempt to make good … *theoretical* blunders.'[67] Perhaps. But it is by no means easy to respect this distinction. And it would appear that the 'Critique' banned by the leadership of the Party, which Marx left unpublished 'solely because of the circumstance that …', *did* have something to do with the theoretical 'blunders' of the Gotha Programme, after all.

A Party and its leadership, with Marx's closest friends at the head of it; a radical critique of a Programme, muzzled 'so as not to undermine the unity of the Party' (Party leaders keep making the same argument, from 1875 to 1978); Marx's stupefaction over the emergence of a fantastic misunderstanding of the text of the Programme, one that united 'the jackasses on the bourgeois papers', and even 'the workers', in the (mistaken) conviction that this Programme contained communist theses; the fact that Marx was consoled by this misunderstanding, and therefore said nothing – all this is, after all, food for thought, as are the closing words of the 'Critique': '*dixi et salvavi animam meam*'.[68] In fact, for perhaps the first time in his life, Marx found himself confronting a Party which he belonged to but did not lead; thus he was in a rather neutral position, that of a rank-and-file Party activist or semi-activist. And we know what this Party did. And Marx contented himself with the very meagre consolation that 'the jackasses on the bourgeois papers', and even 'the workers', discerned, in the Programme, things that were not there. What an experiment this was – involving the Party, its way of conducting itself in the political and theoretical domain, and the ideological illusion produced by a reformist text. Marx held his tongue. To be sure, he was ill. It was as if he had been disarmed and helpless, and had seized the next best excuse to bow to the Party leadership's diktat, asking himself no questions about the nature of the Party, the strange nature of these Theses that had bred such misunderstandings, his own willingness to withdraw his critique in exchange for an illusion, or his own debate with himself, trapped as he was in a situation whose stakes were, all at once, the Party and its strivings for unity, and so for compromise (but on condition that Marx hold his tongue), the reformist ideology that triumphed in the Programme, and the ideology in the heads of 'the jackasses on the bourgeois papers' and 'the workers', which led them to take the moon for green cheese. Marx accepted all this without the least thought for the future. For he washed his hands of the matter like a Beautiful Soul: '*dixi et salvavi animam meam*'....

That Marx held his tongue is one thing. Because he was who he was, he could speak out, and could therefore also hold his tongue.[68] Other activists doubtless criticized the Gotha Programme inside the Party. However, as they did not wield Marx's authority, they had to fall back into line, and their protests disappeared into the Party leadership's files. That in all this – as, indeed, in all other circumstances – Marx gave no thought *to the fact of his own persona*, is, after all, rather surprising. He washed his hands of the matter with a show of modesty ('I am not a Marxist', etc.), which was also a way of 'saving his soul'; he pretended, to himself, that he was not what he objectively was, whatever his scruples – a very prestigious personage, and, still more important, a *theoretical* personage whose every word counted, whose formulas and phrases were taken for gospel, and taken seriously, with all the ambiguity which assimilates – or very nearly so – political seriousness to religious or religiose submission. But the 'theoretical-personage effect' is, beyond any doubt, an important political and ideological effect – not only in the history of the bourgeoisie, but also in that of the workers' movement, the Marxist workers' movement included. Marx, who found Bakunin's or Lassalle's 'persona' unbearable, although he had no choice but to take it into account, was keenly aware of this. Yet it seems that, in his own case, he did not care to know anything about it. And because he was not alone in this business, in which the leading personalities of the Party (Liebknecht, Bebel, etc.) were also involved, as were both the Party and the leaders who ordered him not to publish his critique, as was all the ideology contained in the Gotha Programme (and, behind it, that of the two parties), plus the ideology of the 'journalists … and even the workers', the only possible conclusion would seem to be that the whole thing was just too complicated, or that Marx believed that the Party, after these episodes, would recover its 'essence', or that, in any case, it was a matter of no particular importance, so that it was enough for him to write to 'save his soul' … buried in the files ….[70]

Here, too, we are reduced to making negative hypotheses, but only after duly noting that Marx felt helpless in the face of realities like the *Party*, with its structure, mechanism, effects and decisions, and that he may have felt even more helpless in the face of certain *ideological misunderstanding-effects* – above all, in the face of the *ideological status of his own theoretical persona*, and so on.

The state, ideology, politics, the Party, the theoretical and political persona in the workers' movement: these are all among Marx's 'absolute limits', which we have to assess if we are to think seriously about them.

8. An Absolute Limit: The Superstructure

We must, then, draw up an inventory, with the perspective we have gained thanks to careful reflection and the passage of time. We need to evaluate, as precisely as possible, what Marx has bequeathed us by way of 'theoretical' indications about the nature of 'the superstructure and the ideologies'. On this point, after carefully weighing everything up, it must be said that while the indications Marx has left us are from a political standpoint, important, even crucial, *they are, from a theoretical standpoint, unsatisfactory.*

Let us return to the 1859 Preface, which has served generations of communists as a reference, and which Lenin and Gramsci took as the basis for their thinking. What does Marx say there? Looking back at his own history, he declares:

> A general introduction, which I had drafted, is omitted, since on further consideration it seems to me confusing to anticipate results which still have to be substantiated. A few brief remarks regarding the course of my study of political economy may, however, be appropriate here.
>
> Although I studied jurisprudence, I pursued it as a subject subordinated to philosophy and history. In the year 1842–43, as editor of the *Rheinische Zeitung*, I first found myself in the embarrassing position of having to discuss what is known as material interests. The deliberations of the Rhenish Landtag on forest thefts and the division of landed property; the official polemic started by Herr von Schaper, then Oberpräsident of the Rhine Province, against the *Rheinische Zeitung* about the condition of the Moselle peasantry, and finally the debates on free trade and protective tariffs caused me in the first instance to turn my attention to economic questions. On the other hand, at that time when good intentions 'to push forward' often took the place of factual knowledge, an echo of French socialism and communism, slightly tinged by philosophy, was noticeable in the *Rheinische Zeitung*.

I objected to this dilettantism, but at the same time frankly admitted in a controversy with the *Allgemeine Augsburger Zeitung* that my previous studies did not allow me to express any opinion on the content of the French theories. When the publishers of the *Rheinische Zeitung* conceived the illusion that by a more compliant policy on the part of the paper it might be possible to secure the abrogation of the death sentence passed upon it, I eagerly grasped the opportunity to withdraw from the public stage to my study.

The first work which I undertook to dispel the doubts assailing me was a critical re-examination of the Hegelian philosophy of law; the introduction to this work being published in the *Deutsch-Französische Jahrbücher* issued in Paris in 1844. My inquiry led me to the conclusion that neither legal relations [*Rechtsverhältnisse*] nor political forms could be comprehended whether by themselves [*aus sich selbst zu begreifen sind*] or on the basis of a so-called general development of the human mind, but that on the contrary they originate [*würzeln*] in the material conditions of life [*Lebensverhältnisse*], the totality of which Hegel, following the example of English and French thinkers of the eighteenth century, embraces within the term 'civil society' [*bürgerliche Gesellschaft*]; that the anatomy of this civil society, however, has to be sought in political economy. The study [*Erfahrung*][71] of this, which I began in Paris, I continued in Brussels, where I moved owing to an expulsion order issued by M. Guizot. The general conclusion at which I arrived and which, once reached, became the guiding principle of my studies can be summarised as follows.

In the social production of their existence, men [*die Menschen*] inevitably enter into definite relations [*Verhältnisse*], which are independent of their will, namely relations of production [*Produktionsverhältnisse*] appropriate to [*entsprechen*] a given stage in the development of their material forces of production [*Produktionskräfte*]. The totality [*Gesamtheit*] of these relations of production constitutes the economic structure [*Struktur*] of society, the real foundation [*Basis*], on which arises [*erhebt*] a legal and political superstructure [*Überbau*] and to which correspond definite forms of social consciousness [*gesellschaftliche Bewußtseinsformen*]. The mode of production [*Produktionsweise*] of material life conditions [*bedingt*] the general process of social, political and intellectual [*geistig*] life. It is not the consciousness of men that determines their existence, but their social existence that determines their consciousness. At a certain stage of development, the material productive forces of society come into conflict [*Widerspruch*] with the existing relations of production or – this merely expresses the same thing in legal terms – with the property relations [*Eigentumsverhältnisse*] within the framework of which they have operated hitherto. From forms of development of the productive forces these relations turn into their fetters. Then begins an era of social revolution. The changes in the economic foundation [*Grundlage*] lead sooner or later to the transformation of the whole immense [*ungeheure*] superstructure. In studying such transformations [*Umwälzungen*] it is always necessary to distinguish between the material transformation of the economic conditions of production, which can be determined with the precision of natural science, and the legal, political, religious, artistic or philosophic – in short, ideological forms [*ideologische Formen*] in which [*worin*] men become conscious of this conflict [*Konflikt*] and fight it out [*ausfechten*]. Just as one does not judge an individual by what he thinks about himself, so one cannot judge such a period of transformation by its consciousness, but, on the contrary, this consciousness must be explained from the contradictions of material life, from the conflict [*Konflikt*] existing between the social forces of production and the relations of production. No social order [*Gesellschaftsformation*] is ever destroyed before all the productive forces for which it is sufficient have been developed, and new superior [*höhere*] relations of production never replace older ones before the material conditions for their existence have matured within the framework of the old society. Mankind thus inevitably sets itself only such tasks as it is able to solve, since closer examination will always show that the problem [*Aufgabe*] itself arises only when the material conditions for its solution [*Lösung*] are already present or at least in the course of formation. In broad outline, the Asiatic, ancient, feudal and modern bourgeois modes of production may be designated as epochs marking progress [*progressive Epochen*] in the economic development of society. The bourgeois mode of production is the last antagonistic form of the social process of production – antagonistic not in the sense of individual antagonism but of an antagonism that emanates from the individuals' social conditions of

> existence – but the productive forces developing within bourgeois society create also the material conditions for a solution of this antagonism. The prehistory of human society accordingly closes with this social formation.[72]

From this famous text – which I have tried to translate as closely as possible,[73] more faithfully than the available translations – it can be seen that, in general, Marx conceives a 'social formation' as intelligible on the basis of its mode of production, a concept that essentially turns on the distinction between relations of production and productive forces. I shall go no further into the analysis of the elements included in the forces of production and the relations of production. Marx explained the matter at length in *Capital* with regard to the capitalist mode of production, and about this 'domain', that is, the 'domain' which he terms *Struktur* or *Basis*, a term translated as *infrastructure*, *base*, or again, if more rarely, *structure* – about this domain, which is that, not of 'civil society', but of production and exploitation, we have at our disposal, besides the substantial analyses in *Capital*, all the reflections to be found in the *Grundrisse* and *Theories of Surplus-Value* (which was to comprise the fourth volume of *Capital*).

But it can also be seen from the text I have just translated that the relations obtaining between the relations of production and the forces of production (relations that are internal to the 'infrastructure') can take two extreme forms: that of *correspondence* [*entsprechend*] or *antagonism*. It can also be seen that the driving element [*l'élément moteur*] behind the variation of these and all intermediate forms are the productive forces. In the 'dialectic' productive forces/relations of production, it is the productive forces which are determinant: when they exceed the 'capacities' of the relations of production, the relations of production are shattered, leading to social revolution, an *Umwälzung* that rocks the whole edifice: not only the infrastructure, but also the whole 'immense superstructure', which eventually gives way – 'more or less rapidly'.

Several remarks suggest themselves here.

Let us first note that, in the extremely general presentation of the Preface – which sketches the 'progressive process' of universal history, since it seems to list *all* the modes of production that have existed in history – the dialectic of correspondence or antagonism is presented as if it were *universal*, that is, valid for *all* modes of production. Yet Marx really devoted his efforts only to the capitalist mode of production.

Let us also note that, in any case, *it is the productive forces which are the motor of the upheaval*: they need only develop until they have not only 'filled' the capacities of the relations of production, but exceeded them, causing the carapace to split open and new relations of production, ready and waiting in the old society, to take their place.

Finally, let us note that, given all the connotations just pointed out, the 'historical dialectic' presented here unfolds without a hitch, because humanity (= human history) sets itself only such tasks as it is able to solve [*lösen*]; that the fact that a task proposes and imposes itself is a sign that the solution has already ripened or is ripening in the old society; and, finally, that the productive forces are always stronger than the relations of production, since they always have sufficient capacity to 'fill' and exceed them, thus inducing the transformation known as a social revolution.

Here there is no question of a difference between the capitalist mode of production, with reproduction on an extended scale, and other modes of production, with simple reproduction or, possibly, an increasingly limited reproduction that eventually induces their disappearance. Hence there is no question *of the death of modes of production*, by which I mean their death pure and simple, not only in consequence of an invasion by conquerors who are more powerful and better armed, but in consequence (let us stick to Marx's terms) of the tendential weakness or decrepitude of the productive forces, or contradictions between the relations of production and the productive forces *with no available alternative solution*.

Granted, this is a very general text which in fact only indicates *a direction for research* into the capitalist mode of production. But, after all, the rhetoric is lofty, and somewhat too categorical not to have elicited a goodly quantity of inanities from the commentators, who have come a bit too readily to the conclusion that they were in the presence of a 'global', exhaustive text, or a sacred text, and so drawn from it the well-known mechanistic and economistic conclusions about the primacy of the productive forces, and, within the productive forces, about the primacy of the means of production over labour-power. (I say nothing of the purely idealist inanities of those who ecstatically repeat the lines about 'mankind inevitably setting itself only such tasks as it is able to solve …' and then go prospecting in them for the foundations of a historicist philosophy that they imprudently attribute to Marx.)

The fact of the matter is that, except in these passages and a few others, Marx never upheld the primacy of the productive forces over the relations of production, any more than he upheld the primacy of the labour process over the process of production. He simply upheld the thesis of the primacy, 'in the last instance', of the infrastructure (the base) over the superstructure. As for the infrastructure, he in fact upheld, as far as the capitalist mode of production is concerned, in addition to the idea of the unity of the relations of production and the productive forces, that of the primacy of the relations of production (which are, at the same time, relations of exploitation) over the productive forces. Moreover, he showed that labour-power is one of the 'elements' making up the productive forces, and that the primacy of the relations of production means only one thing: it invites the conclusion that exploitation is class struggle, and that, in the capitalist mode of production, technical and technological questions are questions which form an integral part of, yet are subordinate to, class struggle.

But I shall say no more on this point, which, by now, is rather widely acknowledged. It should nevertheless be noted that it was not always acknowledged. Not only Stalin, but, before him, the 'Marxism' of the Second International bowed down before the productive forces, in the sense of the means of production, hence technique and technology. Moreover, there prevails, in our own day, the holy, blessed religion of the 'scientific and technological revolution', which is charged with miraculously resolving the 'minor' problems of the class struggle neglected by our leaders.

I turn now to the superstructure. In the topographical metaphor of the edifice (base and superstructure), the superstructure occupies the upper storey; it arises [*erhebt sich*] on the base. Furthermore, Marx speaks of a 'legal and political superstructure', which thus includes both law [*le droit*] and the state. Note that Marx, who makes constant use of the term correspondence, *by no means says that the superstructure corresponds to* [*entspricht*] *the base.* He reserves the term 'correspondence' for two and only two cases: the correspondence between the relations of production and the productive forces, and the correspondence between the superstructure (law and the state) and the 'forms of ideological consciousness that correspond to them'. This is a sign of prudence.

It is a sign of prudence, but also embarrassment, and is therefore, to some extent, of confession. Doubtless Marx, and Lenin after him, were to stress the fact that all class societies are exploitative societies, and that the dominant classes express their political and historical complicity through the transmission of the means of domination – law and, above all, the state, which one dominant class accommodatingly bequeaths to the next, in a historical heritage that survives these classes' own disappearance or historical assimilation. Thus the bourgeoisie inherited Roman law and a venerable state machinery that had been 'perfected' in the course of millennia of class struggle; it has gone on to 'perfect' it still further, the better to subjugate those it exploits. Thus there emerges a transhistorical International of the solidarity of the exploiting classes; it takes recognizable form in the law and, especially, the state. Yet, as a rule, the appeal to history is often merely a way of eluding the theoretical problem.

Hence the malaise subsists. *Why* (and neither *Capital* nor Lenin abandons this strange cautiousness) *this theoretical lacuna concerning the nature of the relation between the base on the one hand and the superstructure on the other?* The concepts by means of which Marx expresses the relations between the relations of Production and the Productive Forces (at the extremes, correspondence and antagonism), as well as those between Law and the State on the one hand and ideological forms on the other (correspondence again: here, apparently, there is no mention of antagonism), vanish when it is a question of thinking the relations between infrastructure and superstructure. All that Marx says about this is that *the superstructure arises* [*erhebt sich*] *on the base*.... Quite an advance: this is, as it were, Hegel 'inverted', with the small semantic difference that Marx, as a good materialist, talks about *Erhebung* rather than *Aufhebung*; the erection or, as one would say today, the abduction [*l'élèvement ou, comme on dirait aujourd'hui, l'enlèvement*] of Law and the State. Law and the State are a concrete construction; and they arise concretely on the base. They therefore constitute a world utterly different from the base – not the base 'conserved–superseded' in its 'supersession'. This is important; conceptually, however, it is not much at all.

9. In What Sense is the State an Instrument, and 'Separate'?

As everyone knows, Marx did not leave it at that, but drew very powerful political conclusions from the concrete distinction between the state and the base. Theoretically, however, he never got very far. What is said in the Preface has to do with a basic theme of Marxist thinking about the state: the state is not only distinct from the base, but *separate* [*séparé*].[74] This time, the break is clear and explicit.

This theme of the 'separation' of the state has a long history both in Marx and before him; it is inseparable from the question of Law. The whole problematic opened up by the philosophy of Natural Law, from Grotius through Hobbes, Locke and Rousseau to Kant, was based on an incredible imposture, or, if you like, an obligatory 'self-evident truth' (obligatory owing to the dominant ideology that then ruled supreme, or sought to: bourgeois ideology). This imposture consisted in the idea that one had to *resolve questions of public* (or political) *law in terms of private law*.

Hegel, after Spinoza, had understood this rather well, [as he showed] when he criticized the philosophers of natural law for their 'atomistic' conception of the subject. It was easy for him to prove to them that they had struck out on the wrong path, since it is never, quite simply never, possible to derive political law – for example, the state – from private law, which mobilizes atomized subjects of law. How are you going to reconstitute the whole, if you set out from the atomistic element, the individual human subject? What contract –

which, however shrewdly formulated, is necessarily concluded between individuals – will ever allow you to reconstitute the primary, inaccessible Reality known as the state? Thus Hegel gave Hobbes his due for being intelligent enough[75] to conceive of a subordinate contract between everyman and everyman ('a covenant from one with another'[76]) pledging 'to agree not to offer resistance' to the Sovereign, an absurd contract between the contracting individuals and the Sovereign, since the Sovereign was not bound by any contract [*était hors contrat*]; they conceded everything to him without getting anything in return!

A brief review of the history of this conception suffices to show that the Natural Law philosophers did nothing other than to try to solve [the same problem]: apologetically, and each in his own way, in accordance with the shifting balance of power and what could and could not be said (in their day, political writings were nothing to sneeze at). They tried to find, *in mercantile law* (the reality behind what the jurists call private law), the means with which to think both public law (the state) *and* the establishment of mercantile law itself under the protection of the state. Prisoners of the self-evident truths of mercantile practice, which got along quite well with mercantile law *alone*, and wishing to create a state that would guarantee this mercantile law while respecting it in its own political practice, the Natural Law philosophers imagined that it was possible to found the state on mercantile law, and spent all their energy trying to accomplish this absurd task, whose political benefits were by no means negligible. Obviously, they did not envision the separation of the state. Quite the contrary: they wanted, at all costs, a state that was not separate, but founded on mercantile law itself, on the law of the proprietor who is the proprietor of his goods: who can, that is, consume them, sell them, or use them to buy labour-power and thus acquire more goods, and so on – but on condition that his proprietary rights be guaranteed. Guaranteed by whom? What a question: by the state, of course!

The proprietor, in order to obtain from the state the guarantee that it would not behave arbitrarily – would not only not deprive him of the benefits of mercantile law, but would guarantee them for him – had, in the seventeenth century, Grotius [***] and then Locke, men whose work as ideologues consisted in publicly (their writings circulated furiously, which means that they were read) founding the state on private law, mercantile law, and the freedom of the human subject. What a scandal it was when Rousseau, with his radical way of posing problems and attacking problematics and other flags of convenience from behind, undertook to demonstrate, in the *Social Contract*, that the state was not only everything, but a totality [*non seulement tout, mais le tout*]. It was the totality of the sum of particular wills expressing, by means of an astonishing system, a general will that never went wrong; it was one and indivisible, one and coercive ('we shall compel him to be free').

Kant wriggled out of the problem by evoking the distant horizon of morality and the reconciliation of human history, Nature and Freedom in the Idea. In the meantime, he stuck to a rather materialist conception of the law as 'constraint'. Hegel replied with a theory of the state as the supreme ethical reality; all the anticipations, mired in their finitude, of abstract law and morality, and also of the family and 'civil society' (the system of needs = political economy), aspired to this ethical state. Thus the state was elevated above everything – above morality (the Kantian solution) and the subjectivist atomism of Natural Law philosophy. It was the End and Meaning of all the rest. But it was not 'separate', for what is separate smacks of the understanding in Hegel, and the understanding is 'that's just how it is' and 'no good'. Hegel proceeded as ecumenically as one could wish. Thus he resolved the problem of Natural Law itself by showing that it was enough to 'invert' things, and to refuse to set out from the free subject to think the state in order to set out from the state to think the free subject, abstract (mercantile) law, and so on. For Hegel, the End holds the meaning of the beginning and all the stages in between.

Marx on the state sets out from Hegel. The state is Reason; nothing that exists is as rational as the state or superior to the state. In the state, we have the reign of the universal. The proof is the citizen, a member of the state: he is free, equal to all the others (the Sovereign included), and decides freely in all that concerns both himself and the constitution and delegation of the general will. As a citizen, he ceases to be the pitiful shoemaker reduced to his shop and his shabby shoes, his problems with his wife, and his worries about his children: he dwells in the universal, which (at least in theory) he decrees, or, rather, concretizes [*décrète ou plutôt concrète*].

Taking this powerful assurance as his starting point, Marx very soon had occasion to discover, under Friedrich-Wilhelm IV – in private, a very liberal Prussian prince who turned out to be a tyrant in the public sphere – that the state, which was Reason in itself, led a sadly unreasonable existence – even, factually speaking, an irrational one. He extricated himself from the problem, temporarily, with the ingenuous notion that 'there is always Reason, but not always in its rational form'. In sum, it was enough to wait.

He was still waiting when Feuerbach made his entry on to the German philosophical scene. This man, who stunned all his contemporaries with a veritable revelation, had had the simple idea to wonder: 'but, if so, why does Reason *necessarily exist in irrational forms*?' It was the recognition of this *necessity* which changed everything. Earlier, the state had been irrational by accident. The subtitle of *The Essence of Christianity* (since, in the Germany of Feuerbach's day, everything turned on the displaced question of religion) was *Critique of Pure Unreason.*[77] Held up against Kant's *Critique of Pure Reason*, this was a real provocation.

Feuerbach's main thesis is well known (all the others depend on it). It is owing to the alienation of Reason that Reason necessarily exists in the form of pure Unreason (or impure Unreason: but, ultimately, there is no impurity in Feuerbach; everything is pure, transparent: opacity and the night do not exist). Alienation of what? Alienation of Man's Essence, which is the alpha and omega not of all existence (a dragonfly and a star are not the alienation of Man's Essence) but of all *signification*, including that of the dragonfly (man's extreme freedom) and the star (the light of contemplation). However, of all existing significations, some are exclusively cultural-historical, produced in their entirety (unlike the dragonfly and the star) by labour, struggle, desire and all the human passions. These are the significations which fill the annals of human history: individual significations (Feuerbach wrote extraordinary philosophical love letters to his porcelain-ware fiancée[78]), but, above all, collective cultural and social significations – in short, generic significations, the ones in which the human genus[79] (of which every individual representative is 'abstract') recognizes itself, because it is expressed there. These grand generic human significations are, first and foremost, religion and then philosophy, followed by the state. The list ends with trade as well as craft and industrial production.

Religion offers the purest instance of the alienation of the human Essence. In God, men worship, love and fear their own infinite generic essence, which is omnipotent, omniscient, infinitely good and has the power to save (for Feuerbach, all these attributes are the attributes not of an imaginary human genus, but of flesh-and-blood humanity: he 'proves' it). The human genus contemplates itself, sees itself (physically), touches itself, smells itself, and loves itself, its own power and its infinite knowledge, in God. That is because it has projected and alienated its own essence in God; it has made this Double, which it worships and to which it prays, out of its own flesh and soul, without realizing that He is the human genus. Thus a gigantic illusion has created God, who is not the image, but the essence of man. And the distance between the little individual that I am and the human Genus whose infinite limits I do not know is so great that it is no wonder I am crushed by the omnipotence of the Genus (= God), its infinite knowledge, infinite love, and boundless goodness and mercy. The abyss is so great that the little individual will never realize that he – not as a limited individual 'with a snub nose' [*sic*],[80] but as a member of the human Genus – is himself the God he worships.

How were things arranged at the outset? How did alienation make its entrance on to the historical scene? It did so owing to a first abyss, which lay between little men and omnipotent, terrifying nature (which is, at the same time, generous enough to ensure their survival). Men identified their nature with the nature of Nature; then, with the emergence of history, they transformed their God in line with the historical modifications of their history (contrary to what we read in Marx,[81] who needed this mistake, *history is terribly real for Feuerbach* – a history of a very Feuerbachian kind, of course). There was the God of the Jews, that 'practical' people ('practical' = selfish: see the Fifth Thesis on Feuerbach[82]); there was the God of the New Testament; there were other Gods as well. All reflected its own speculary Essence back upon the historically determined (and limited) human Genus. Then came philosophy, a by-product of theology, which was itself a by-product of religion (with one exception: the Greeks, who were materialists – they worshipped their own Essence in the beauty of the cosmos, the body of the star-spangled universe, and the body of their beloved – and also philosophers, who made philosophy their religion). Then came the state, a substantial form of alienation, since the state is the secular, terrestrial God. Then came the great scientific discoveries and the great technological, scientific revolution of modern times (already!), the French Revolution, during which the human Genus recognized itself in Reason, worshipped as such and within easy reach. The long birth pangs of history, industry, the steam engine, the great crisis of the Restoration after the French Revolution, the religious crisis – everything indicates that we now have a way out, that the time is ripe, that religion has been challenged and shaken, that it is in crisis and on the verge of yielding up its secret, and that the moment has come in which a man will at last be able to utter the Truth. The Truth bears a name: 'Man'. The man who utters the truth bears a name: 'Man' is a handsome, bearded, forty-year-old philosopher who lives in the countryside in a small porcelain manufactory, whose daughter he has married. Engels – once the great Feuerbachian passion had passed, once it had been discovered that the great man didn't lift a finger in 1848 – was to write: look what happens to a great mind when he lives in the country!

Marx took one thing from Feuerbach: the idea that 'the root of man is Man', and that the unreason of the state is the effect of man's alienation. He added (in 1843) that the reasons for alienation had to be sought elsewhere than in the difference between the individual and the species – in the alienated conditions of life in society; then in the alienated conditions of the workers; and finally – before he dropped this frenzied exploitation of the theme of alienation (which he never completely abandoned, at least not in *Capital*) – in 'alienated labour' (the *1844 Manuscripts*).

Marx applied the schema of alienation to the state exactly as Feuerbach had applied it to God. It was here that the notion of *separation* first came into play. Like religious man in Feuerbach, man leads a double life. He contemplates his generic, universal life in the state, which is Reason and the Good. He leads his private, personal life in his practical activities. As a citizen, he has a right to live the life of the species, the life of Reason. As a private individual, he has a right to wealth or poverty – to nothing resembling his other life. Man is *separated* into two parts, and that is why the state is *separated* from men. This gives us the celebrated passages in *On the Jewish Question* and the (manuscript) *Contribution to the Critique of Hegel's Philosophy of Law*[83] on 'the rights of man', the contradiction between formal rights ('the state is the heaven of political life') and the real 'rights' that are nonexistent or altogether different, without relation to these formal rights (the Earth of private life, where egoism and the competitive struggle reign supreme). Conclusion: alienation and alienated labour must be abolished here below, on the Earth of need and competition, so that, once man has at last recovered the heaven of his essence, the *separation* between men and the state, between men and politics, will disappear, along with, at the same stroke, the separation between men and nature (which in Feuerbach, let us not forget, is the origin of everything). After that, fully developed '*naturalism*' will be nothing other than fully developed '*humanism*', and vice versa. These are Marx's very words in 1844.

They were meant to be strong words (Marx chose not to publish the *1844 Manuscripts* that contains them, and, once again, we can understand him), but they prove their own theoretical weakness in the confusion of their conclusion. Marx was to drop the conclusion, but he retained the idea that the *separation* (alienation) of the state stems from the alienation of men, of the men at the centre of production: the workers. To arrive at this conclusion, however, he needed something other than the path, blazed in 1844, which led to 'alienated labour'. Alienation is merely a word, quite incapable of explaining itself. What Marx needed was a long detour through the critique of Political Economy and, before that, the accumulated experience of the 1848 revolutions.

Read *The Eighteenth Brumaire*: it contains not a trace of the themes of 1844. The state is plainly still 'separate', but now it has become a 'machine' or an 'apparatus', and there is no longer any question of accounting for it in terms of alienation. Thus the 'separation' of the state no longer means that the state is identical to the political life, nor, *a fortiori*, that it is the generic life of the human species. The 'separate' state now acquires a different theoretical status, mechanistic-materialist enough to shake to their roots *both* all the humanism of Feuerbach and his epigones (the 'German socialists' or other moralizing sects) *and* all the 'Hegelian' dialectics that Marx had profoundly compromised in the *1844 Manuscripts* by 'injecting' Hegel into Feuerbach. The best of the 'Eurocommunist' intelligentsia is still shaking. What, then, is the theoretical status of the separation of the state? The state is separate because it is, in Marx's words, an 'instrument' (Lenin was even to call it 'a bludgeon') that the dominant class uses to perpetuate its class domination.

It is on this basis, not another – on this sole basis, but, alas for us, solely on this basis – that what is imprudently called 'the Marxist theory of the state' (when one should, rather, say elements[84] of a theory of the state) has been erected. I repeat something I said earlier: although these were nothing more than the elements of a theory, they at least had *a crucial political signification.*

Let us sum up. The state is separate. The political is not reducible to the state – far from it (thank God). The state is a 'machine', an 'apparatus' destined (?) to be used in the class struggle of the dominant class, and to perpetuate it. Lenin would later say: the state has not always existed. This is only to be expected: if the state is an instrument of class domination, there can be a state only in class society, not before. The state perpetuates itself. Why? In the Western world, the instrument took its initial form in Early Antiquity, and the dominant classes that foundered and disappeared handed it down to their successors, who 'perfected' it. A disarmingly simple explanation: the state perpetuates itself because … there is a need for it. There we have all that is certain; and there we have all that is ever said. Of course, Engels would later attempt, in *The Origins of the Family, Private Property and the State*, to sketch a theory of the emergence of the state, but his book is a work of compilation that is not very persuasive. Matters would be left at that.

The *political* import and consequences of these simple theses are nevertheless crucial. The stake of the class struggle (economic, 'political' and 'ideological') is the state: the dominant classes struggle to conserve and strengthen the state, which has become a gigantic 'instrument'; the revolutionary classes struggle to win state power. (Why 'power'? – because we need to distinguish the machine from the power needed to run the machine: if one seizes control of the machine without being able to make it run, one has struck a blow for nothing.) The working class will have to take state power, not because the state is the universal in action, or the whole, nor because it is 'determinant in the last instance', but because it is the instrument, 'machine' or 'apparatus' on which everything depends whenever it is a question of changing the economico-social bases of society, that is, the relations of production. Once the bourgeois state has been conquered, it will be necessary to 'destroy' it (Marx, Lenin) and build 'a state which is a non-state', an altogether different revolutionary state, different in structure from the present 'machine', and so designed that it tends not to grow stronger, but to wither away. This is the moment of entry into the phase of the 'dictatorship of the proletariat', about which Marx said, in 1852, that it was a discovery for which he deserved the credit, and the main thesis he had developed.

All this terminology – I say terminology – calls for explanation. For we are so used to the words by now that we *no longer know*, or, worse, *no longer care to know*, what they mean or might still mean – by virtue of which it would appear that the 'Eurocommunist' parties have – either in solemn Congress, or on the quick, or both – 'abandoned' the dictatorship of the proletariat, by virtue of which we are in the process of contenting ourselves with 'democratizing' the state so as not to have to 'destroy' it (France), or of 'recomposing' it by might and main so as no longer to have to put up with its 'decomposition', 'separation', and so on (Italy).[85]

Let us first say a word about the term 'instrument'. Yes, the state is an 'instrument' in the hands, and at the service, of the dominant class. The term is not well thought of in our day (read the glosses by our authors, who hold it at a distance that would move mountains). But to say '*instrument*' is to say '*separate*'. Every instrument, such as the musician's instrument and the policeman's 'bludgeon', is manifestly separate from its agent. Separate from what? That is the whole question. 'Separate from society'? That is a truism, a platitude, even if it was Engels who uttered it; what is more, it rehabilitates the old opposition between the state and 'civil society', which Marx excluded from the text of the Preface, a profoundly theoretical text (even if it contains dubious phrases). Thus the state would be 'separate' from what is not the state, from the *remainder*, or civil society (production, etc.). And when Gramsci, in order to restore (not without certain intentions, which are not without consequences) the symmetrical balance between the terms, declares that civil society is separate from 'political society', he doesn't change much of anything (except that he has his own peculiar definition of 'civil society' up his sleeve). Are we to assume that the state is separate from the dominant class? That is unthinkable. I shall [ignore] the intermediate solutions, and go straight to the main point.

I think we must say that if the state is 'separate' for Marx and Lenin, it is in the narrow sense of '*separate from class struggle*'. Now there is something that will give the shivers to all our theoreticians of the full 'traversal' [*traversée*] of the state by the class struggle; all those who, because they have taken up arms against the idea of the 'separation' of the state, and are aware that the class struggle is, in a certain way which is difficult to conceive, at stake here, quite as ardently reject the idea that the state is an 'instrument'. Pooh! You will not find *us* among those vulgar Marxists who accept this crude 'mechanism'.... This time (and at certain other times, as we shall see) we must give due credit, not to vulgar Marxism (which one should seek where it is to be found), but to Marx, Lenin and Mao, who, in a situation of theoretical penury, at least kept a firm grip on this decisive 'end of the chain'. Of course *the state is separate from class struggle, since that is what it is made for*; that is why it is an instrument. Can you imagine an instrument used by the dominant class that would not be 'separate' from class struggle? It would be in danger of exploding in the hands of this class at the first opportunity! And I am not only talking about the 'traversal' of the state by the class struggle *of the masses* (I imagine that that is what is meant by our *non-vulgar* Marxists, who are so fond of cruises), a mass struggle that has doubtless 'traversed' the state in history only to culminate in bourgeois politics (as in 1968). I am talking, above all, about the bourgeois class struggle itself. If the big state apparatuses were at the mercy of the 'traversal' of the state by the bourgeois class struggle, the upshot might well be the end of bourgeois domination.... It almost came to that during the Dreyfus affair and the war in Algeria, to cite no other examples.

If I affirm that the state is separate from the class struggle (which unfolds in the realm of production–exploitation, in the political apparatuses and the ideological apparatuses) because that is *what it is made for*, made *to be separate from the class struggle*, that is because the state needs this 'separation' in order to be able to intervene in the class struggle 'on all fronts' – not just to [***] intervene in the struggle of the working class in order to maintain the system of exploitation and general oppression of the exploited classes by the bourgeois class, but also to intervene, should the need arise, in the class struggle within the dominant class, with a view to overcoming its divisions, which can seriously jeopardize this class if the struggle of the working class and the masses is powerful.

I would like to take an extreme example to illustrate this: the situation of the French bourgeoisie under Pétain in 1940, after the defeat. The Popular Front and the Spanish Civil War had so frightened the French bourgeoisie that it silently made its choice even before the World War began: 'better Hitler than the Popular Front'. This choice inspired France's military policy, the 'phoney war'. As for the defeat, it was welcomed by the 'possessing classes' as a 'divine surprise', to cite Maurras's quip. The consequence was Pétain and the politics of collaboration. But the consequence was also, under terribly difficult conditions, the refusal to accept defeat and the rejection of German Nazism and Pétain's Fascist corporatism by the people of our country, under the leadership of those who were politically the best educated [*formé*]. For several months, the leadership of the French Communist Party tried to convince the occupying forces to 'legalize' the organization; it sacrificed the best Party militants to this attempt, calling on them to resume their public activities as a way of backing up its request. These militants ended up dying before Nazi firing squads, beginning with [Jean-Pierre] Timbaud and [Charles] Michels at Châteaubriant, and how many others elsewhere.[86] But many other

Communists who were cut off from the leadership spontaneously took up the struggle (see the eyewitness account by Charles Tillon, leader of the FTP[87]). At the same time, an army general, a patriot of aristocratic extraction, De Gaulle, called on the French to join him in London. In this extreme situation, it became possible to see just what the state was.

For the fact is that the French bourgeoisie was divided. In its immense majority, whether because it was 'apolitical' or by implacable political design, it supported Pétain. A small minority of the bourgeoisie and, especially, the petty bourgeoisie followed De Gaulle. His first appeal[88] played on people's refusal to accept humiliation and defeat, and on their patriotism as well. He further demanded that all patriotic officers and soldiers 'do their duty', and join him in London in order to form the backbone of a military force. A general, and a great bourgeois politician to boot, De Gaulle proclaimed that he embodied the resistance of the nation and provided the nation with its legitimate state, Pétain's being nothing but an instrument under German control.

De Gaulle's politics, during the war and afterwards, the subsequent 'Algerian business' included (yet another war that divided the bourgeoisie), consisted in imposing on a divided bourgeoisie which, in its majority, had compromised itself with Pétain, an alternative (and more 'intelligent') bourgeois politics, come hell or high water. De Gaulle had the (bourgeois) intelligence to understand that the bourgeoisie as a class risked not being able to resist the movement of popular resistance (which could not fail to grow) unless it was itself represented in the Résistance and could endow itself, in the interim, with a state capable of taking over from Pétain's fascist puppet state. We have to start out from the conscious class position adopted by De Gaulle in order to understand the tumultuous history of his relations with the forces of the domestic resistance, which obviously did not wait for orders from him to go into action. We have to set out from the class position adopted by De Gaulle, who represented the class interests of the bourgeoisie as a whole – even if only small sections of the armed forces and volunteers from the ranks of the bourgeoisie followed his lead – in order to understand his attitude towards both

Pétain and the officers and immense majority of the bourgeoisie who had rallied to Pétain's cause. De Gaulle's aim was to restore the unity of the bourgeois class after its division during the War. In this undertaking, he was able to reap the maximum benefit from the legitimacy of the state in whose name he spoke and with which he identified.

After serious conflicts and a long period in which his fortunes waxed and waned, De Gaulle succeeded in obtaining Allied recognition of his 'government'. On this basis, he authorized the Free French Forces to undertake armed actions. He had managed to rally these forces, drawn from the ranks of the existing French military, by appealing to the patriotism of officers and men and calling on their sense of 'duty'. In London, and, later, Algiers, he built up, not without difficulty, a whole state apparatus geared to controlling the domestic resistance movements. In the conflicts that grew out of this 'encounter' imposed by military and political events, the policies advocated by the popular movement clashed with those animating De Gaulle's embryonic state. Whereas the whole history of the Résistance resounded with powerful historical echoes of the class struggle, whereas political plans for change and sometimes even social revolution took shape in the struggle itself, De Gaulle always acted in the name of principles which called for sharply subordinating patriotism to the 'national interest', 'considerations of state' [*le sens de l'État*], 'duty', discipline and obedience to the orders issued by the head of state, who represented the 'general interests' of the nation. Having taken a forthright political stand, De Gaulle could hardly order others not to 'engage in political activity' within the resistance organizations. Yet there was a great deal less political activity in the Free French Forces, where it was possible to cultivate the sentiment that one was acting not only to 'liberate the fatherland', but also out of a sense of duty or discipline. Moreover, in the rear of the theatre of battles over which he had little or no control, and by means of these battles, De Gaulle established the elements of a state apparatus that was supposed to take over, at the right moment, from the state apparatus that had remained in France. More precisely, it was supposed to supervise this apparatus, redeeming it, its most prominent leaders aside, for the purpose of serving the interests of the bourgeoisie as a class.

As everyone knows, De Gaulle's plans worked out very much as he had wished. He was able to conduct negotiations with the political parties; the Communists were tractable, hobbled as they were by the Thorez affair (the 'desertion' of a man who had not wanted to leave France, but gave in to Stalin, who all but sequestered him, as if he were a hostage).[89] He rammed through a policy of sending political commissars to France, and, after the Normandy landing – thanks to the political weakness of the resistance movements, the power of the agents of the state apparatus who had remained in France, and, ultimately, the overt political support of the Allies – eliminated the political problems posed by the organizations and military units of the domestic resistance. He decreed the amalgamation [of the different resistance groups], brought the domestic resistance to 'turn in its arms', and threw the resistance fighters into the regular army's struggle against Germany.

It is more than obvious that the state, the state apparatus – not merely the embryonic state apparatus created in London and then in Algiers, but also the state apparatus that had stayed behind in France and carried out collaborationist policies – played a crucial part in De Gaulle's political scheme for saving the bourgeois class as a class. It is more than clear that the mechanisms of these apparatuses, which were identical in London and Vichy, facilitated matters. That De Gaulle succeeded in realizing his plan only by playing on the traditional 'values' of the state apparatus, that is to say (besides, and over and above, patriotism, which inevitably sowed division), duty, discipline, obedience to the state and its representatives, hierarchy, 'service to the nation' and 'public service' – in other words, by *separating*, as far as possible, the state apparatus from the most pressing problems of the class struggle; and that De Gaulle successfully brought off this separation by relying not only on the 'structural effects' [*effets de structure*] of the state apparatus, but also on the ideology of the state with which he inculcated his agents in London, an ideology skilfully combined with patriotic demands – I do not think there can be any denying this. One can no more deny it than one can deny that the restoration of the unity of the bourgeois class, perilously divided and vulnerable to the struggle of the popular forces, was achieved thanks both to an 'intelligent' politics capable of looking far into the future and declaring that losing a battle did not mean losing the war, and also to adroit manipulation of a state apparatus which, for several years, had a peculiar feature: some of its agents were in London, while others were in France.

I would doubtless have to go into greater detail to make a more convincing argument. However, I believe that, in the light of this historic episode, which is a limit-case, we may affirm that the state apparatus, if it is to perform its function as an instrument in the service of the dominant class, must, even in the direst circumstances, *be separate from the class struggle* as fully as possible, must be as far removed from it as it can be, so that it can intervene against not just threats of popular class struggle, but also threats embodied in the forms that class struggle can take within the dominant class itself (and against a combination of both).

What makes the state the state – this is just how it is – is the fact that the state is made in order to be, as far as possible, separate from the class struggle, and in order to serve as an instrument in the hands of those who hold state power. The fact that the state 'is made for this purpose' is inscribed *in its structure*, in the state hierarchy, and in the obedience (as well as the mandatory reserve) required of all civil servants, whatever their post. This explains the exceptional situation imposed on state personnel in the military, police forces and civil service administration. Members of the army or those who exercise leading political functions have no unions and do not have the right to strike; they face draconian punishment if they do. There now exist, and have existed for some time, unions in the police and, as of recently, the judiciary; and, as of very recently, there are unions in the CRS[90] as well. But there are no unions in the 'hard core' of the state, the armed forces, the gendarmery, the anti-riot police, and so on – the repressive forces *par excellence*. And if the police have the right to strike (in exceptional circumstances), there have never been strikes in the army, the CRS, or the gendarmery. At most, there has been 'unrest', as in the days of the Résistance, in 1968, or in a few other cases in which the forces responsible for maintaining public order concluded that they had been unwisely sent into dubious battle or into conflicts too costly for them (in exceptional, extremely rare cases, the 'unrest' was a protest against orders to carry out violent actions contrary to their conception of 'keeping the peace'). Of course, since the 1946 Constitution, civil servants have enjoyed the right to strike. However, this right does not extend to those civil servants who [in the words of the Constitution] 'exercise authority', and includes neither the army nor the forces responsible for maintaining public order (the CRS, anti-riot police and gendarmery, which, incidentally, is part of the army). Moreover, when a magistrates' union takes a progressive initiative, it is very rudely rebuffed not only by the responsible minister, but also by the high-ranking civil servants of the judiciary, who impose disciplinary measures on the 'offenders' for not respecting the 'reserve' that is mandatory for all civil servants. In difficult conjunctures, this makes it possible to apply virtually any sanction that is deemed desirable.

We have trouble imagining the 'exceptional situation' imposed on the state and its agents. For we tend to cast a veil over the 'duties' of soldiers, the CRS, the gendarmes, magistrates and high-ranking civil servants said to 'exercise authority' – that is, the 'hard core' of the state, the kernel that possesses and contains [*détient et contient*] the physical force that the state can mobilize in its interventions, as well as its 'political' force – in order to consider only secondary phenomena, those that come into play in the strikes and demonstrations of civil servants employed in the 'public service' sector, from teachers to postmen, railway workers and others with 'civil service' jobs. Moreover, we tend to take the demonstrations staged by certain magistrates, teachers, and so on as open forms of class struggle, when we should, at the very least, question the tendency and effects of some of these demonstrations.

I am thinking here of what Marx says about the factory inspectors, who were much more 'advanced' than our modern labour inspectors (I have in mind modern labour inspectors in general, not the remarkable individual cases), and of their denunciations of the length of the working day, which was inhuman at the time. Their efforts were crowned with success when the bourgeois English state established the ten-hour day in 1850. This measure, a result of the workers' class struggle, met with fierce resistance from a section of the English industrial bourgeoisie, and was imposed by the bourgeois English state. Yet Marx showed that it actually served the interests of the English capitalist bourgeoisie by protecting its workforce – that is, the health and reproduction of its labour-power. And, after the passage of this measure, regarded as scandalous by most capitalists, there appeared bourgeois studies (quoted by Marx) which proved that, in ten hours of work, workers employed full-time *produced more* than they had in twelve or fifteen hours, since fatigue had diminished their total output to a level lower than that attained in a ten-hour day.[91]

That is what the state is: an apparatus capable of taking measures against the will of a part or even a majority of the bourgeoisie in order to defend the bourgeoisie's 'general interests' as the dominant class. And that is why the state must be separate. It was by mobilizing the nature of the state, its separation, and the values that underwrote this separation (above all, 'public service' and refraining from political activity) that the English bourgeois state was able to impose the law on the ten-hour day, or that De Gaulle was able to rally – in the name of State, Nation and Fatherland – a state military force strong enough to gain him Allied recognition as President of the Provisional Government of the French Republic (= of the French Republican State), and that he was able to milk his legitimacy for all it was worth, in every field and on every question.[92]

But this confronts us with a strange paradox. How are we to think the fact that the state is an instrument, hence 'separate', yet is simultaneously the instrument which the dominant class uses to ensure and perpetuate its domination? To ensure it: the state must be powerful. To perpetuate it: the state must endure so that the conditions of exploitation will endure as well.

There is no contradiction here – or, rather, there would be no contradiction if the state were purely and simply an instrument completely isolated from the class struggle. But if it is 'separate' from the class struggle, that is precisely because this 'separation' does not go without saying and is not brought about without effort, the proof being the whole set of measures that the state has to take with regard to the various categories of its agents – politicians, members of the armed forces, police, magistrates and others – in order to guarantee this 'separation'. These include all the measures of compartmentalization of tasks, and all the measures of hierarchization – which, moreover, vary from apparatus to apparatus, but always have one thing in common, a strict definition of responsibility – as well as all the measures pertaining to duties, service, mandatory reserve, and so on.

It is by no means certain, as I have just shown, that all these measures are intended merely to 'separate' the state from the effects or contagion of the struggle of the working class and the masses (it should never be forgotten that the great majority of civil servants, including those in the 'forces responsible for keeping the peace', are of peasant, working-class, or popular origin, as Gramsci very clearly pointed out). These measures may also be intended to 'separate' the state from the forms of division that can arise within the dominant class, from the intrigues of certain groups, or even from practices completely foreign to 'the spirit of public service' that is supposed to hold sway among the agents of the state, and usually does, notwithstanding a few scandals (which are rare in France and more frequent elsewhere; consider the Lockheed scandals[93] that have occurred throughout the Western world).

If, however, we take all these facts into account, it is clear that the 'state instrument', 'state apparatus', or state *tout court* is not neutral, but terribly biased in favour of the ruling class. Officially, to be sure, it 'does not engage in politics', as the bourgeois ideology of the state proclaims. The state does not engage in politics, for, we are told, it is not partisan; it stands 'above the classes' and merely attends to the nation's business, everyone's business, objectively and fairly. Or, if you like, it has a politics, but it is the politics of 'public service'. It is precisely this ideology with which the state inculcates its agents, whatever post they hold.

Marx was the first to expose this mystification: *the state is indeed 'separate', but so that it can be a class state* that best serves the interests of the dominant class. In fact, all its higher-ranking agents are avowed, tried-and-tested champions of the interests of the dominant class. The head of state maintains the unity of the state and steers state policy [*politique*]. He is part of the political apparatus of the state, with the government and his ministries, which like to shelter behind the technical nature of the issues and their own technical competence in order to mask the politics that they implement, and serve the higher interests of the dominant class. The vast majority of higher-ranking civil servants, whether politicians, military men, or police officials, belong to the big bourgeoisie by background or career. Moreover, even if hierarchy and responsibility, state secret and state reserve are the principles of the functioning of the state, it is so complex today that by the time we arrive at a counter at the post office, national railway or national health service, we have long since lost sight of *the class politics* that govern all our administrative apparatuses from afar, yet imperiously. We may well have the impression that we are dealing with 'formalities', which are, it is true, complicated, but which could be simplified, and are 'natural'.

What could be more natural than buying a book of bus tickets or a monthly Underground pass? A protest movement has sprung up, precisely, around the Underground pass; it contests the reasons given for raising its price. Moreover, because money is at stake, one does not have any impression at all that one is dealing with a 'natural formality' when one finds oneself at the tax office, any more than when one has to bear the brunt of the terrible indirect taxes that tap the surplus-value in the wallets of the lower classes (the rate is 17.5 per cent in France!), with the result that the heaviest tax burden falls on the most disadvantaged. They do not, after being exploited at work, find it 'natural' to have to pay, in addition to their income taxes (on which a minister can pretend to make a few concessions in favour of the old and the poor), a draconian tax on bread and milk, to say nothing of clothes and popular consumer goods.

The state is a class state by virtue of its policies [*politique*], as anyone can understand. But it is tied to the dominant class by way of its high-ranking and middle-ranking civil servants – directly tied to it, for these agents of the state are either big bourgeois or are bourgeois by conviction. And since these high-ranking civil servants have the others in their grip, thanks to the hierarchical state system, the whole system of responsibility and reserve, the whole system of exceptions that supposedly put matters 'above class struggle' – constitutionally, at least, and in actual fact in decisive instances (the army, the police, the CRS, the gendarmery, the Secret Services, the prisons, etc.) – we may legitimately affirm that the state is 'separate from the class struggle' in order the better to intervene in it.

There are contradictions in the state apparatus. The army does not work the way the police do: in some countries, it has political opinions and can translate them into acts; in others, it is the police, official or unofficial, who control everything. In still others – France, for example – the Finance Ministry occupies an exorbitant position and exercises exorbitant control. All this is 'in the order of things'. A state is complex. As everyone knows, its contradictions can serve as a springboard for the intentions or ambitions of certain fractions of the bourgeoisie; there have even been studies of this. Finally, it is more than obvious that these contradictions can be exacerbated by the class struggle in general – even, and above all (this is what interests us here), the class struggle of the workers and the broad masses, and by its contagiousness, which can help to touch off strikes in certain civil service administrations, and, of course, in industries or companies in the public sector. But no one has ever seriously claimed that the structure and unity of the state apparatus – even if this apparatus has, in certain sectors, wobbled, as it were (especially during the psychodramatic absence of De Gaulle, when he went to see Massu, who 'didn't engage in politics') – were ever, even in 1968, seriously undermined. The police, CRS, anti-riot police and gendarmery held firm, very firm indeed, as those who demonstrated on the barricades can testify; they did not fire a single shot (see the Memoirs of Police Chief Grimaud).[94] As for the army, it left its tanks parked under the trees of Rambouillet Forest, not making a show of force the better to quell the rioting.

To leap from this to the conclusion that the state 'is by definition traversed by class struggle' is to engage in wishful thinking. It is to take certain effects – profound effects, to be sure – or certain traces of the class struggle (bourgeois and proletarian) for the class struggle itself. But I maintain, precisely, that the state, the core of the state – which comprises its physical, political, police and administrative forces of intervention – is, so far as possible, constructed in such a way as not to be affected, or even 'traversed', by the class struggle. That it manages not to be, and manages very well indeed, not only in France, but also in Italy – where, since Gramsci, people have been happily developing a theory of the weakness or non-existence of the state, which seems to me to be a mistake[95] – is all too obvious. That this costs it an effort is sometimes perceptible. The fact is, however, that it succeeds, as much in the Western countries [*chez nous*] as in the USSR, and by employing, in both cases, much the same means.[96] From time to time, some (not all) agents of the state apparatus strike; but it is never those at the physical core of the state, and we can almost treat these manifestations of discontent as safety-valves or a warning system enabling a self-regulating adjustment that culminates in slogans such as 'public servants should be paid higher salaries', or 'administrative services must be upgraded so as to improve relations with the public, and administrative formalities must be simplified'. [Valéry] Giscard [d'Estaing] himself, the head of state, excels at producing these soothing phrases, which, whatever one may say, have their effect.

All this is a way of repeating that *Marx's and Lenin's formula to the effect that the state is an 'instrument', and is therefore separate from the class struggle the better to serve the interests of the dominant class, is a powerful formula.* There can be no question of abandoning it.

The same goes – since we are still dealing with terminology – for the expression 'apparatus' or 'machine'.

10. But Why is the State a Machine?

In his Sverdlov University lecture on the state,[97] Lenin employs, with extraordinary insistence, just two terms. He does not say 'institution', 'organization' or 'body'; he says *apparatus* and *machine.* And he insists even more stubbornly on the fact that this 'machine' is 'special' and that this 'apparatus' is 'special', without, however, spelling out in what sense they are 'special'. We shall therefore have to try to interpret these terms, which must have a precise meaning, because Lenin, who does not succeed in stating it (any more than Marx before him), clings to them as if they were the last possible word on the subject of the state.

We would not be betraying Lenin if we said that if the state is a '*special*' apparatus and a '*special*' machine, then they are unique entities, and therefore *unlike the others*: that is, unlike what we find in the rest of 'society' or of 'civil society'. Thus they are not simple institutions, like the Council of State [*Conseil d'État*];[98] they are not associations, like the Parent–Teacher Association; they are not Leagues, like the League for Human Rights; they are not organizations, like the political parties or the churches; nor are they bodies [*organismes*], a term which is still more vague. The state is a special machine in the sense that it is made of a different metal. That is to say (since all thinking about the modern state is also haunted by the metal of tanks, machine guns and submachine guns), the state has a different structure, is made of different 'stuff', has an altogether different texture. We are thus led back to what we said a moment ago in order to show that the state is indeed 'separate' and an 'instrument'.

There remain the terms 'apparatus' and 'machine'.

If I dwell on the terminology, it is because Marx and Engels did too, with incredible obstinacy, as if certain words which they used for the state, and only for the state, were *indices of a concept* that they were unable to formulate in any other way, but wanted at all costs to point out. 'Apparatus' and 'machine' are essentially (to the best of my knowledge of Marx's terminology, at any rate) reserved for the state, something that is itself surprising: thus Marx never – absolutely never – talks about the 'machine of production' or the productive apparatus, terms that today are in general use (and, what is more, rather neutral). What is significant, over and above this exception, is, in view of this exception, the pair of terms *apparatus–machine*. What does it, if not mean, then at least indicate?

'Apparatus' [*appareil*], which gestures in the direction of 'pomp' [*apparat*] (the outward display of a thing, with all its trappings), means, according to the dictionary, 'an ensemble of elements which work together to the same end, forming a whole'. The state apparatus may well display a diversity of apparatuses (repressive, political and ideological); what defines them as state apparatuses is the fact that they all work together to 'the same end'. This holds for the state whenever it is defined as an instrument. An instrument (which can comprise different elements) exists by virtue of an end: in the present case, maintaining the power of the dominant class. But the dictionary definition also says that, in the 'ensemble of elements', none is *superfluous.* On the contrary, all are perfectly well adapted to their end, in so far as all are parts of the articulated whole designated as the 'apparatus': here, the state. This therefore presupposes a sort of mechanism in which all the parts, all the wheels and cogs, work together to the same end, which is obviously external to the apparatus; if it were not, the apparatus would not be 'separate'. This externality seems pronounced when we think of expressions such as 'apparatus of torture,' or even 'artificial limb' [*appareil de prothèse*].

Does the idea of *mechanism* [*mécanique*], which is suggested by the fact that all the parts work to achieve a single (external) end, not simply evoke the idea of a machine – or, to cite another of Marx's terms, of machinery? (Here it should be noted that the German *Maschinerie* does not have exactly the same sense as the French word.) I do not think so, and would like to advance a hypothesis.

Let us first note that Marx and Lenin carefully avoid two words. Not only do they never discuss the state in terms of a *body*; they also never discuss it in terms of a *mechanism.* 'Machine', then, wins out over 'mechanism'. Did Marx and Lenin mean by this that the state is an enormous machine, but one so complicated that, although we can see the political effect produced by it, we are unable to grasp its intricate mechanisms? Perhaps. Did Marx and Lenin mean to say, when they described the state as a 'machine', that it works all by itself, as some machines do (for example, the steam engine)? But as anyone who lived in the age of the steam engine and Fourier's or Carnot's laws knew, no machine works all by itself. Anyone who said so was using a metaphor to insist on the 'autonomous' or 'automotive' nature of the state. We know enough about the state, however, to be able to say that the separation of the state has nothing to do with autonomy. Marx and Lenin never talk about the autonomy of the state.

In the seventeenth century – in, for example, Bossuet – we also find the expression 'great machine of the state', although this language is obviously marked by the state of the knowledge of Bossuet's time: pomp and splendour are associated here with the idea of mechanical movement, akin to that of the 'mechanical' machines of the period. Again, ballistic and other types of 'war machines' have existed since

Antiquity. Machine: '*a system of component parts* [*corps*] *that transform one form of work into another*', whether manpower or gravity. In the seventeenth century, a machine transformed a particular form of motion into another; one was always in the realm of motion, the motive force being that of a man or an animal, or else of gravity. But what of the nineteenth century, during which, beginning in 1824 (when Marx was twelve),[99] Carnot studied 'caloric-engines' [*machines à feu*] and made some surprising discoveries about the 'steam-engines, that is, caloric-engines' on which all English capitalism was based?

Marx discusses the steam engine, the machine *tout court*, and the machine tool in the chapter on relative surplus-value in Volume One of *Capital*. He had closely read Babbage, a competent technician who, however, did not have a theoretical turn of mind. Babbage wrote, in 1832: 'the union of all these simple instruments, set in motion by a single motor, constitutes a machine'.[100] Marx repeatedly affirms that it is not the steam engine but the machine tool that revolutionized production: the machine which sets a whole series of tools in rapid motion, whereas the human hand can manipulate only one, and slowly at that.

Marx is so thoroughly haunted by the relation '*motor–transmission* and *working machine*' that he gives short shrift to motors: 'The motor mechanism acts as the driving force of the mechanism as a whole. *It either generates its own motive power*, like the steam-engine, the caloric-engine, the electro-magnetic machine, etc., or it receives its impulse from some already existing natural force ... the transmitting mechanism ... regulates the motion, changes its form where necessary, as for instance from linear to circular, and distributes it among the working machines'.[101]

Since, thereafter, it is simply a question of transmitting and transforming this motion, everything depends on the motor of the new 'machine' known as the caloric- (or heat-) engine. The dictionary says, implacably: 'machine: a usually complex manufactured object designed to transform energy and to utilize this transformation ("machine" is, in principle, distinguished from "apparatus" and "tool", which only utilize energy)'.

If this is indeed the pertinent distinction, 'machine' adds something essential to 'apparatus': to the idea of the simple utilization of a given amount of energy, it adds that of the *transformation of energy* (of one type of energy into another: for example, of caloric into kinetic energy). In the case of an apparatus, one kind of energy is sufficient; *in the case of a machine, we have to do with at least two types of energy, and, above all, the transformation of one into the other.*

Unless the state is more than just a 'bludgeon', and cannot be appropriately defined as an 'instrument', either – a term that is not false, but too general – I do not see why, for a whole century, Marx and Lenin would have gone to such lengths to talk not just about an apparatus, but also about a 'machine'. Something of the basic meaning of the term must be at stake in their truly ferocious insistence on it (which they left unexplained). When one seizes, in this fashion, on one or two words, both of which, in the case to hand, tend in the same direction, the second enriching the first by adding a crucial stipulation – when one clings to them without being able to say why, this is because one has touched on a point that is both vital and obscure.

To my knowledge, there is only one other instance of this kind of ferocious, and, at the same time, partially blind terminological insistence in Marx and Lenin: the word 'dictatorship' in the expression 'dictatorship of the proletariat'. In the latter case, however, it is easier to find the explanation in Marx and Lenin, albeit often between the lines, so that we have to put the text to work upon itself to bring out its meaning.

11. Why the Dictatorship of the Proletariat?

I think that it must forthrightly be said – now that, provisionally, the guns seem to have fallen silent on the question of the dictatorship of the proletariat,[102] [***] its solemn 'abandonment' by the PCF and the PCE, [and] its surreptitious abandonment by the PCI, and so on – that Marx and Lenin are not always clear on this point, and that the ambiguities which they have bequeathed to us have had an extremely important role to play, in view of the prestige of their authors and the religious devotion of their successors (when what was in question was not simply their sordid, unspoken material interests). We therefore need to discuss this ambiguity.

Marx manifestly inherited the expression 'dictatorship of the proletariat' and the corresponding idea (I do not say concept, because the matter is not clear) from Blanqui. He borrowed it after the failure of the European revolutions of 1848, after the June massacres in France. We have already seen a trace of it in the 1852 letter in which he affirmed that his basic accomplishment was to have conceived of the necessity of the dictatorship of the proletariat (not the discovery of the classes and their struggle). A borrowing is just a borrowing: incorporated into a new context, it should normally shed the connotations conferred on it by the old one, and take on a fixed, unambiguous meaning. Unfortunately for us, this was not quite how things happened.

Marx, and then, in particular, Lenin (but Lenin had the excuse of having to lead a day-to-day struggle under appalling conditions) knew what they were after when they used the word 'dictatorship': they wanted to catch people's attention with a provocative term that was on a par with their discoveries and their thought. To say 'dictatorship', as Lenin often repeated, is to evoke a state of affairs that is beyond all legality, irreducible to the laws, and, in a certain sense, even more powerful than the laws. (Let us take 'laws' to mean, in the most natural sense, the existing civil and political right [*droit*]: the constitution, and, if it is parliamentary, the parliamentary constitution in a given country.) The fact is that the vocabulary of the day contained no word that captures, in all its force, what Marx and Lenin were trying to express.

Now the whole question and the whole ambiguity can be summed up as follows: what is this 'beyond the laws' that is irreducible to the laws and, at the same time, more powerful than the laws, which it encompasses? Is it a *political* form, a form of government over men of the kind that has been seen in history, such as the 'Roman dictatorship' (a provisional dictatorship, the eventuality of which had been provided for), the dictatorship of the Convention (legally provided for as a state of emergency), or the many political dictatorships familiar to us, born of the violence, peaceful or bloody, of a successful *coup d'état*? In many cases, it must be admitted, *Lenin himself identified the dictatorship of the proletariat with violent government* by the representatives of the proletariat, or, quite simply, the leaders of the Party and the Party itself, implementing political measures that violated or suspended the established laws.

I do not say this in order to criticize the statesman Lenin for dissolving the Constituent Assembly without due process of law, for outlawing and prosecuting the Social Revolutionaries, or for banning all political parties except the Bolshevik Party, and so on. Lenin suspended the constitution and governed by decree rather than by voted laws, but he had serious reasons for doing so in a period in which the power of the soviets was under attack from foreign powers that were, inside the borders of the USSR itself, aiding and abetting the forces of the far Right, who had cast all restraint to the winds and were perpetrating unspeakable barbarities. In this case, anyone who fails to opt for the extreme course of suspending the political laws in order to save the revolutionary state, and of taking all the radical measures that the situation calls for, himself falls victim to barbarity and chooses defeat: not only his own, but also that of the revolutionary masses as a whole. For, as far as I know, there was nothing 'legal' about the 'Allied' interventions on Soviet soil and the military operations of the counterrevolutionaries. Lenin simply responded to the illegal horror of the invaders with the only weapons he had: not just by suspending the laws, but also by mobilizing the people to save the state of the soviets.

My question lies elsewhere. *The question has to do with Lenin's definition of the dictatorship of the proletariat* when he discussed it, and he discussed it often, very often: for he thought – and he was right – that this business was at the heart of the drama of the Russian Revolution. But Lenin – like Marx before him, although this is infinitely clearer in Lenin – plainly wavered between two conceptions: a first conception, which seems to me to be correct and should be recognized as such; and a second conception, towards which he usually, and, under the pressure of events, increasingly inclined. The second conception seems to me to be wrong.

In a word, the incorrect definition of the dictatorship of the proletariat consists in taking the word 'dictatorship' in the *political* sense – to be very precise, in the sense of a *political regime*, that is, a political government over men that operates 'outside the limits of the law' and thus puts itself 'above the law', imposing a violent and arbitrary will. Contempt for the law and the exercise of arbitrary violence against individuals (even if it is in the interests of a class or party): that is what the dictatorship of the proletariat would come down to. Following the violence of the revolution (which is also above the law), the violence of a dictatorial political government, exercised in the name of the proletariat, thus seems to be on a continuum with violent revolution, and, therefore, to be natural. Since revolution can be carried out only in violation of the established laws (which serve the bourgeois class), and, consequently, can be achieved only by violence, the government that issues from the revolution, which sets out to destroy the bourgeois state and install a revolutionary state, is, naturally, the direct heir to this violence, and must be, if it is to smash the order of the bourgeois state and found the revolutionary state. Such is the 'logic' of the propositions that follow one from the next in this conception. But they stand up on only one condition: *that we construe the word 'dictatorship' to mean a regime of violent political government*, governing by decrees and by coercion, outside the limits of any established law.

Lenin gave in to this 'logic' in many different passages of his writings and speeches. The fact that the situation required him to fall back, in actual practice, on a regime of 'political' dictatorship, to suspend the laws, to govern by decree and resort to the use of force, certainly did inflect his thinking – or, at all events, his terminology – in a direction that was, at the time, clear to everyone: dictatorship = political government by coercion, with the suspension, if not of all law, then, at least, of many laws. Let us imagine that Lenin had had the time, a few years later, to review the harsh texts of this terrible period: he would doubtless have said: 'but it is impossible to take them out of context! but, at the time, I had to *exaggerate*, to bend the stick in the other direction in order to straighten it out…'. He would once again have held, as he in fact often did in the actual practice of these texts, that one word (a very weak one: an appeal to the political context) could explain and excuse another; and he would have paid no attention to the weight carried by words uttered by someone with his authority. As everyone knows, Lenin suffered from that type of blindness. The fact is – and there is no excuse when it comes to theory, or, in any case, no excuse of this sort – that he pushed the ambiguity we have evoked in the direction of the wrong meaning.

Yet the means required to conceive of another interpretation of dictatorship were to be found in Marx and Engels, and even in Lenin himself: for what is in question here is *the dictatorship, not of a government or regime, but of a class.* In Marx's thought, the dictatorship of a class has nothing to do with political dictatorship or a dictatorial form of government. There is another word in our authors – not hegemony, which has been contaminated by Gramsci and his authority, but class *domination* – that is a thousand times better than 'dictatorship'. It occurs in the *Manifesto*, which says that the proletariat should 'raise itself to the position of the dominant class'. Domination, dominant class, dominant instrument: 'domination' is an excellent term. Why did Marx drop it and replace it with class dictatorship? Was it under Blanqui's influence after the major defeats of 1848? That is a rather thin explanation. Was it that he wanted to set himself apart from the crowd by using as strong an expression as he could? That is more likely. Marx had a taste for extremes, even for provocation. The fact is [that] '*class domination*' *was replaced by* '*class dictatorship*'. This did not hold across the board, incidentally, but it did hold for the proletariat.

If we agree to use the term 'class domination', we find ourselves on firmer ground. In a class society such as capitalist society, there exist dominant classes (the big landowners and the bourgeoisie) and dominated classes. What is class domination? It is not restricted to political government over men, which can take different forms: monarchy by divine right, Cæsarism, constitutional monarchy, the parliamentary republic, or, later, fascist dictatorship. Class domination encompasses the whole set of economic, political and ideological forms of domination – that is to say, of class exploitation and oppression. Within this set, the political forms represent a subset of variable size which is, however, always subordinate to the whole set of forms. The state then becomes the apparatus or machine that serves as an instrument for class domination and its perpetuation.

The expression 'dictatorship of the proletariat' or 'class domination of the proletariat' now acquires its full meaning. If we say that every class society presupposes class domination in the sense just stated, then the revolution that is the tendency of capitalist society will modify the relationship of class domination in the sense of an inversion (although matters will be more complicated in actual fact): the domination of the bourgeois class will necessarily give way to that of the working class and its allies. But, here again, proletarian class domination cannot be reduced to the exercise of dictatorial political power by, say, a party representing the new class or a coalition representing the working class and its allies. *The class domination of the proletariat can only designate the whole set of economic, political and ideological forms by means of which the proletariat has to impose its politics on the old dominant, exploiting class.* It is perfectly possible that this will come about non-violently, if the exploiting classes consent to what amounts, ultimately, to a restructuring of social relations. Moreover, if the former exploiters overstep the new laws or circumvent them, they can be compelled to respect these new laws not by force, but by law. Obviously, if they succeed in precipitating a foreign intervention in order to put themselves back in the saddle, or in exploiting discontent to tendentious ends in a difficult period, going so far as to provoke acts of armed violence, the revolutionary authorities will clearly be obliged to resist by employing force, as a last resort, after exhausting all other arguments; but, in any event, this by no means settles the question of the 'dictatorship of the proletariat', or of the class domination of the proletariat. If it is to exist, this domination must exist *in the forms of production* (nationalizations combined with a more or less extensive market sector, self-management, workers' control over production, and so on), *in political forms* (councils, represented in a National Council by their delegates) and *in ideological forms* (what Lenin called cultural revolution).

In all this, the question of violence – if the word is taken to mean physical violence, the intervention of the armed forces to settle political and economic problems, and so on – occupies a subordinate and always transitory place. This is so clearly the case that Marx and Engels, and even Lenin, always allowed for the possibility of a 'peaceful' and 'legal' transition to socialism by electoral means. It is common knowledge that Engels expected the German Social Democracy to realize this possibility. It is all a matter of the balance of power, and therefore of the conjuncture. This has never happened to date: so what? New conjunctures can suddenly emerge. Moreover, even if the revolution should be accomplished, in an extremely tense situation, with a degree of violence or, quite simply, by violent means, this does not predetermine the sequel, unless violent revolution is taken to entail a definite commitment to violence.

The working class and its allies must [*doivent*] become the dominant class, and, in order to do so, must become the dominant class across the whole set of economic, political and ideological forms. This is not a moral 'duty' [*devoir*], but a tendency inscribed in class relations.[103] If the revolutionary coalition fails to become master of these forms of domination, it will find itself in a very precarious position; it will be at the mercy of a revolt, or else compelled to take arbitrary measures that will send it hurtling headlong towards social forms that may be new and unprecedented, but have very little in common with socialist perspectives. Lenin understood this very well: he contrasted the dictatorship of the bourgeoisie, as the dictatorship of the few, with the dictatorship of the proletariat, that of the immense majority of the people, arguing *that the political form which corresponded to this dictatorship (or domination) was mass democracy* (by no means dictatorship). In the repetitive weave of the words imposed by the tradition and constantly revived by its greatest representatives, so that these words are taken at face value by almost everybody, one always surprises one's interlocutors when one says that, for Lenin, the dictatorship of the proletariat is democracy in the broadest sense, that is, mass democracy 'taken to the limit'. They do not understand. And it must be granted that they are not altogether in the wrong.

For *one cannot say, without further ado, that the dictatorship of the proletariat is the broadest possible democracy.* This expression is incorrect, because the sequence of words in it (dictatorship … is democracy) sows confusion; so abrupt a short cut is unacceptable. It is as if one were to say: Continental Europe is the most radiant Greece! In the formula 'the dictatorship of the proletariat is the broadest possible democracy', critically important words are omitted; their absence drives meaning and acts (yes, acts) down a catastrophic short cut, or into a dangerous cul-de-sac. One must say, rather: 'the dictatorship of the proletariat includes among its forms of domination – and thus takes as its objective – the broadest possible democracy'. Or: 'the political form of the dictatorship of the proletariat must be the broadest possible democracy'. The second of these two formulations assigns the political form its proper place; it does not reduce all forms of domination (what takes place in production is, let us recall, determinant in the last instance) to the political form alone. What is more, it by no means decrees in advance that the form of political domination must be the naked force of dictatorship.

It will be objected that in formulas such as: 'the dictatorship of the proletariat *must* take, as its political form, the broadest possible mass democracy', class dictatorship or class domination is defined in terms of a 'must' [*devoir*, which also means 'duty'] that in no sense judges the facts in advance, and can even be a way of excusing them on the plea that 'the circumstances' prevented the realization of this 'must'. For example – and we have never been loath to use such arguments – the 'backwardness of the USSR', the excessive 'power' of the Soviet state and 'gelatinous' nature of Soviet civil society (Gramsci), the absence of a 'democratic tradition' in Russia, and so on. But it is playing on words to believe that the matter comes down to establishing what the class domination of the proletariat 'must' be, as if what were at stake were a moral obligation. In fact, the word 'must' designates what Marx and Lenin always considered to be *the form of existence of a dominant tendency*. Like any tendency in Marx, it is internally 'countered' by causes that tend to thwart its realization and call for the presence, inscribed in its very conditions of existence, of a force capable of fostering its realization: the organization of the political class struggle of the working class, the Party. (We are putting all this in the singular for the sake of convenience, although we should in fact speak of organization*s* in the plural, and mention the popular allies of the working class.)

Clearly, for Marx, Lenin and Mao, what is known as 'subjective' (that is, both theoretical and organizational) capacity, the quality of the organization, of its theory and line, *is therefore determinant* when it comes to judiciously combating the 'causes that counter' the dominant tendency of the process of class struggle, and facilitating the realization of this 'tendency'. It follows that no fatality presides over the term of the process. Quite the opposite is true. Whether the tendency is realized, or, on the contrary, whether some 'monstrous' result results from a struggle conducted without regard for 'the causes that counter' the development of the tendency, depends on the theoretical, organizational and political capacities *of the Party*, even in its most insignificant practices. These causes lie first and foremost with the bourgeois class struggle, but they can also lie with the Party – with its poor organization, absence of theoretical vision, failure to produce a concrete analysis of the concrete situation, unsatisfactory political practices, inability to seize the 'decisive link' (whether 'the weakest' or 'the strongest'), and so on.

When the 'causes that counter the objective tendency' prevail, and they can prevail as a result of the weaknesses of the Party itself, then all is lost – not, perhaps, for ever, but for a very long time, during which there can reign unprecedented, virtually unclassifiable societal forms which, while continuing to invoke 'socialism' because that has become routine, or in order to deceive the popular masses, are simply bastard or monstrous forms. Aristotle, whom Marx held in such high esteem, wrote, among other things, a treatise on monsters – biological monsters, of course. Marx himself suggests, in the closing lines of the 1859 Preface, that history can give birth to monstrous historical forms, and that 'chance' plays a role here. All this is consonant with the logic of a body of thought that has nothing to do – the famous lines in the same Preface notwithstanding – with a 'must' [*devoir*] which, if it is plainly not a moral duty, is none the less defined in function of an End, a model of the mode of production that is to be attained, and 'normally' must or should be attained, in the 'progressive' succession of modes of production that are complacently and rather too facilely listed by Marx.

We have to come to see, once and for all, that Marx's thought contains, on the question of historical necessity, extremely original suggestions that have nothing to do with the mechanism of inevitability, or with the inevitability of destiny or the hierarchical order of the modes of production. We made a first approach to this idea in our discussion of the way Marx exposes his ideas twice, in a 'topographical' spatial arrangement, in order to indicate both the extremely broad range of their theoretical validity and the extremely narrow conditions of their politico-historical efficacy. This idea is reinforced when we observe the way he thinks, with respect to the definition of the class domination of the proletariat and its allies, the 'necessity' of the seizure of power and its future: *in terms of a dialectic of the tendency*, necessarily entangled 'with countervailing causes' (spawned, first and foremost, by the tendency itself), in which it is both possible and necessary to intervene politically in order to make possible the realization of this tendency. *Without this 'intervention', the tendency will never be automatically realized.* If this 'intervention' is inept, the worst is to be feared: the mediocrity of a 'historical compromise' whose variants can be infinite, and which can culminate in horrors. All that is required is that the situation of imperialism lend a helping hand.

Let us sum up. If we untangle all the theoretical, political, semantic and other difficulties in the texts of Marx and, especially, Lenin – difficulties that all too often encumber these texts and turn them against the 'general line' of a body of thought which has to be given its coherence if we are to *think* what it *designates* – we discover, precisely, a coherent body of thought.

The famous expression 'dictatorship of the proletariat' helped Marx, overwhelmed by the bloody defeat of the 1848 revolutions throughout Europe, to think an undeniable reality: that of the *class dictatorship* which is inevitable in any class society. It helped him to think another reality as well: that any working-class and mass revolution, however convincing, will end in disaster if the proletariat and its allies are incapable of ensuring the absolute condition for its survival: class domination over the old classes by the new classes grouped around the proletariat. This domination, in order to be precisely *this domination*, must be a domination exercised in the forms of production, politics and ideology taken together. *The political forms* of this domination cannot – barring exceptional cases, and even then only provisionally – have anything at all in common with the forms of a government which is 'above the law' and 'knows no law', and is therefore violent and dictatorial. The forms are 'normally' the forms of the broadest possible mass democracy, in which democracy 'is taken to the limit'. All this constitutes a coherent whole, and is, moreover, clear. But then why were matters not always as clearly stated? It was not easy to state them this clearly from the outset. Gripping, lapidary formulas were required to gain a hearing and ensure understanding. And – let us not hesitate to add – neither Marx nor Lenin had a well-controlled conception of the semantic effects of the expressions he used, expressions uttered by individuals who held positions of authority over the movement and the organization.

12. Back to the Machine of the State

Be that as it may, we shall soon be convinced that this long detour through the dictatorship of the proletariat was absolutely necessary in order to clarify the key terms in Marx's and Lenin's definition of the state, especially the term 'machine'.

A long sentence of Marx's, tucked away at the end of Volume Three of *Capital* ['The Genesis of Capitalist Ground-Rent'], will put us on the right path, and show us his *absolute limit.*

Marx is investigating the presuppositions for capitalist ground rent. He pauses over an examination of the conditions under which 'the self-sustaining labourer' can earn a surplus over his necessary means of subsistence; can, in other words, produce what will become 'profit' in the capitalist mode of production. This 'self-sustaining labourer' is, as often in Marx, a purely hypothetical entity that can take a number of different forms: here, that of the serf and then the peasant community. What is decisive, however, is the fact that Marx, from the outset, mobilizes the category of 'reproduction', which Volume One usually brackets out in order to focus on the theory of value and surplus-value. Here Marx reveals the core of his thinking:

> That the serf's product must be sufficient in this case to replace his conditions of labour as well as his subsistence is a condition that remains the same in all modes of production, since it is not the result of this specific form but a natural condition of all continuing and reproductive labour in general, of any continuing production, which is always also reproduction, i.e. also reproduction of its own conditions of operation.[104]

Reproduction is thus the condition for all 'continuing' production, hence for the persistence through time of any mode of production. Marx remarks:

> It is clear, *too*, that in all forms where the actual worker himself remains the 'possessor' of the means of production and the conditions of labour needed for the production of his own means of subsistence, the property relationship must *appear* at the same time [Althusser's translation reads *doit fatalement se manifester*] as a direct relationship of domination and servitude,[105]

which is the 'embryo' of a political relationship. It is curious that Marx says 'too', which would ultimately not matter much if it were not that he says nothing more *about reproduction* in this sentence (which immediately follows the one quoted a moment ago). The political relation then appears – both in principle and in its embryonic form – as a more or less direct manifestation of the property relation, which is assimilated to the productive relation. This is not, to be sure, false, but it is striking that, in this definition, Marx makes nothing of what he has just said about *reproduction*. And he maintains his silence throughout the famous passage that occurs a page later:

> The specific economic form in which unpaid surplus labour is pumped out of the direct producers determines the relationship of domination and servitude, as this grows directly out of production itself and reacts back on it in turn, as a determinant element. On this is based the entire configuration of the *economic community arising* from the actual relations of production, and hence also its *specific political form*. It is in each case the *direct relationship* of the owners of the conditions of production to the immediate producers – a relation whose particular form *always corresponds* [Althusser's translation reads *correspond naturellement*] *to a certain level of development of the type and manner of labour*, and hence *to its social productive power* – in which we find the innermost secret, the hidden basis of the *entire* social edifice, and hence also *the political form of the relationship of sovereignty and dependence*, in short, the *specific form of state* in each case. This does not prevent the same economic basis – the same in its

> main conditions – from displaying endless variations and gradations in its appearance as the result of innumerable different empirical circumstances, natural conditions, racial relations, historical influences acting from outside, etc., and these can be understood by analysing these empirically given circumstances.[106]

Thus Marx defends the fundamental thesis that the secret of the state, 'the *hidden* basis of the *entire* social edifice', is to be sought in the '*direct relationship* of the owners of the conditions of production to the immediate producers', hence in the relation of production or exploitation. He insists: the state is the political form taken by every form of dependence and domination, and is itself merely a *manifestation* of the relation of production. He insists: this 'secret' is hidden beneath and in society.

Let us leave two questions aside: that of the 'correspondence' between such-and-such a form of dependence, hence such-and-such a political form, and the 'level of social productive power', a formula that may seem to echo those of the 1859 Preface; and that of the variations which concern not, as one might expect, the *forms of the state* (passed over in silence), but the *forms of the base,* that is, the mode of production, whose 'variations' are subject to countless natural and social influences. Let us note, to begin with, that Marx says the '*specific* form of state', giving us to understand that each mode of production has its own peculiar state; in other words, that the state as such is a specific reality – a 'special' reality, as Lenin will say, frequently repeating the word.

In any event, what we have here is an outline of a theory of the state that puts the state in virtually 'direct' relation (the adjective is Marx's) with the property *relation,* hence (here too, we have an equation) with the *productive* relation characteristic of a given mode of production: and Marx means not just the existence of the state, but its form as well. The existence of the state is, indeed, merely a *manifestation* of the relation between lord and serf, which is itself the manifestation of the relation of production via the (immediate!) mediation of the 'property relation'. *This implies that the state issues directly from the relation of production, as its manifestation.* Marx adds that the same relation *also* defines the political form of the state. Let us leave aside the intermediate level, the lord/serf relationship, which is a manifestation of the relation of production, and is accordingly that of which the state is the 'political form'. Here Marx gets into trouble, in view of what he says about its direct nature, on the one hand, and, on the other, the 'mediation' of a property relation that has no effect whatsoever on the immediacy of the relation between the Relation of Production and the State. But Marx left this text in the form of a draft, after all; it was Engels who published it. In any event, this passage presents a very simple theory of the state: *the state is the 'direct' manifestation of the relation of production*, which is its 'secret'. This theory is very simple but very important, since Marx here shows that the state is rooted in the relation of exploitation, thereby demonstrating its class character. At the same time, however, this very simple and very important suggestion leaves us unsatisfied, for two reasons.

The first is that Marx says nothing here (which does not rule out his saying something elsewhere) about either the specific 'forms' of this manifestation or the 'element' in which the productive relation is manifested in the political form of the state. Thus what we have here is a theoretical deduction or theoretical genealogy in the guise of an instantaneous short cut which assumes that we know not only what the relation of production is (most of *Capital* is devoted to that question), but also what the state is. Now we have a rather good idea of[106] what the state is if we have read, say, *The Eighteenth Brumaire* – but then it becomes very hard to see how the complexity of the state and its powerful role can be reduced to this 'direct' deduction from the productive relation. The deduction of the state that Marx gives us in these few lines is rather reminiscent of the foreshortened, schematic 'deduction' of the modes of production in *The Poverty of Philosophy*, where he imprudently affirms that with the windmill you have the [***] and with the water-mill the [***].[108]

The second reason is more troubling. Marx, who has just discussed, very clearly and consciously, the crucial category of reproduction, begins speaking a new language, *regressing to a level anterior to reproduction in order to discuss the state.* I believe that this may be called one of the '*absolute limits*' which the 'Marxist theory of the state' comes up against, before coming to a dead stop. *Neither in Marx nor in Lenin do we find*, to my knowledge – at least not in their explicit discussions of the state – *any mention of the state's function in reproduction.* Marx does discuss the role of the state in primitive accumulation and the emission of money; he also discusses the intervention of the English state in the law limiting the working day to ten hours: but *he does not envisage the state from the standpoint of the reproduction of the social (and even material) conditions of production*, hence in its relation to the continuity or perpetuation, the 'eternal nature' or 'reproduction' of the relations of production. It is easy to understand, if we do not go beyond this disappointing conception, why the theory of the State-as-Instrument should have irritated Gramsci and his modern commentators as a theory that is, taken literally, unacceptable. But the paradox is that Gramsci criticizes this theory of the state with respect to its *effects* (economism), without contributing anything at all noteworthy to it, for he, too, remains at a level anterior to reproduction. In Marx's formulas, the dimension of reproduction and the functions of the state are reduced, in derisory fashion, to those of intervention, and, ultimately, brute force.

Yet it is by taking the path of reproduction, it seems, that we can pull Marx's and Lenin's thought out of the rut in which it has been stuck for so long, and so move it beyond its 'absolute limits'. It was in following this path that I put forward certain propositions in a 1969 essay entitled 'Ideology and Ideological State Apparatuses'.[108] We shall see whether they need to be rectified and whether they can be extended. In any case, it is from this standpoint that I would like to present my hypothesis as to why Marx and Lenin held so firmly to the terms *apparatus* and, especially, *machine* in their discussions of the state.

13. Why is the State a 'Special' Machine?

Let us review the conclusions reached thus far. The state is a 'special apparatus', a 'special machine', which constitutes an 'instrument' for the dominant class in the class struggle. This 'instrument' must necessarily be 'separate' not only 'from society', not only 'from civil society', but from the class struggle, *so that* it can intervene, as fully as possible, as an 'instrument': that is, so that it can best serve, without rebelling, the class interests of the dominant class taken as a whole, while being protected, as far as possible, from the vicissitudes of the class struggle, that of the dominant class no less than that of the dominated classes. The state is thus a class state, brought to bear in the class struggle by the dominant class, in order to dominate those it exploits and perpetuate its domination, the conditions of exploitation and oppression. If all this is true, then the question so far left in abeyance, the question that now arises, *the* question, is the question of the adjective '*special*', which Lenin repeats at least ten times in his famous 1919 lecture at Sverdlov University.[110] The state is a 'special' apparatus, a 'special machine'. What does this prodigiously insistent adjective, repeated so often that it is impossible to miss, indicate (not think, but indicate)?

To begin with, it indicates that the state is made of *a completely different metal* from all the other institutions, organizations or bodies in society – from the rest of society, in short – and that it alone has been forged out of this 'special' metal. It indicates, further, that it has a completely different function from the other social institutions or organizations.

The state does not 'produce' anything (except when there are royal manufactories or a public sector, but it is not this productive function which defines the state in that case), and has no hand in the circulation of goods (with the exception of trading societies in the public sector), although it mints the money without which there would be no circulation of goods. Yet the state, although it produces nothing, nevertheless levies taxes, with which it pays soldiers, policemen and civil servants, covers its 'public' expenditures, finances the aid that it gives the trusts, and so on; it produces nothing, but spends an enormous amount of money for which the productive masses and others are tapped through direct and, especially, indirect taxes. Furthermore, the state dispenses 'justice': it has its gendarmes, police, magistrates and prisons. It 'administers' and manages foreign policy. Thus it most definitely has a very 'special' function, a function unlike all the others. This can be demonstrated: for those who are fond of organization charts, or for the more serious, it can be demonstrated that *the state does not function like a private enterprise*, or *a Church*, or *a Party*, although a party, for its part, can 'function' like a 'state' or like 'the state', and so forth.

It must therefore be granted that, between the 'special metal' out of which the 'body of the state'[111] is made, and the very 'special', but *very precise* [way] in which this state functions, there exists a very 'special', but also *very precise* relation.

The 'body' of the state is made up of a number of apparatuses which, it will readily be agreed, do not all take the same form. To simplify, let us distinguish:

1. the apparatus of public force[112] [*l'appareil de force publique*] (or repressive apparatus), comprising the 'hard core' of the state, its forces for internal or (and) external armed intervention: the army, the various police forces, the gendarmery, the CRS and the anti-riot police, to which we may add the agents of the judiciary, the prisons with their agents, and a long list of disciplinary or paradisciplinary institutions, on the frontiers of psychiatry, medicine, psychology, teaching, and so on.
2. Next, *the political apparatus*, comprising the head of state, the governmental corps, the prefectural corps, and all the big civil service administrations, which, although they claim to provide 'public service', are merely agents for the execution of state policy [*politique*], hence a class politics [*politique*].
3. Finally, what I have proposed to call *Ideological State Apparatuses,* to which I shall return.

A list of this sort, even if it distinguishes three typical forms within the state as Apparatuses or Machines, does not make it clear why such apparatuses are 'special'. We need to examine the matter more closely, in 'areas' that Marx and Lenin left unexplored.

The first reason to be noted – already quite clearly perceived by certain sociologists and, long ago, Max Weber – is that the 'special' nature of the 'body of the state' turns on relations of a very particular kind imposed from on high by the system that obtains between hierarchical superiors and their subordinates. The principle governing these relations is that of a hierarchical centralization taken to the furthest possible extreme. Everything comes down from above; no civil servant can take an initiative unless he knows that he will be 'covered' by his superior. It will perhaps be objected that the same principle prevails in a productive enterprise, but this is inaccurate: the latitude for initiative is infinitely greater there, and, what is more, initiative can be punished by dismissal or internal sanctions. It has even been argued that the tenure system for civil servants, which seemed to liberate them, actually helped to reinforce the forms of hierarchy and, accordingly, administrative submission. High-ranking civil servants, who take their orders directly from ministers or prefects, see themselves as expert technicians charged with applying a policy that they usually approve of, but in any case apply, under cover of an ideology of 'public service' or 'technique'. Orders come down hierarchically, with all the slowness characteristic of the 'administration', and the inevitable complications due to interferences arising from the association of several ministries or *grands corps*[113] charged with handling the same item of business. Many of these worlds are in fact nearly self-contained, and are sworn to secrecy: the army, the police force or forces, the gendarmery, the CRS and the anti-riot police, but also the judiciary, attorneys, teachers,[114] and so on. Moreover, each corps tends to work in its prescribed domain, in order to avoid all conflict with the others, in line with an ideology that thoroughly deserves the name 'esprit de corps'. There is an 'esprit de corps' almost everywhere – even among teachers, who are themselves divided, and in the 'judiciary'. An incredibly strict division of labour prevails there (some people may be surprised to learn that attorneys who practise private law are completely cut off from their colleagues in public and administrative law). Thus we are dealing with *a very 'special' corps* indeed, made up of 'special', self-contained corps divided by discipline and a desire to uphold their honour that is part of the 'esprit de corps'. Indeed, the state is not clearly separate from the class struggle unless it is separated or divided by internal separations, those of its corps and their 'esprit de corps'.

But that is not the essential reason [for the special nature of the state]. To discover the essential reason, we need to consider the state's 'armed forces', its physical might, which is only partly visible. If the state is a 'special apparatus', that is because, unlike any other social organization, it '*runs on public force*'. To be sure, a big capitalist firm may have its private militia, and a trade union or political organization may have its 'security forces', but the comparison cannot be seriously sustained: these forces are 'private', weak, and not always 'legal'. The state, in contrast, maintains hundreds of thousands of armed men who either train while waiting for the moment to intervene, or intervene daily in social life, both public and private. The immense majority of them receive physical combat training, and if, in 'normal times', they use their weapons as little as possible, the fact remains that they are there, in large numbers, disciplined and *armed.* Let us recall Lenin's symptomatic insistence on the fact that 'the state consists of groups of armed men'. Usually, a part of these forces remains out of sight: the army. But all the others may be seen daily, and intervene constantly. The police intervene every day, as do gendarmes, prison guards, nurses in certain psychiatric wards, and so on; the CRS and anti-riot police, however, intervene only when demonstrations threaten. And if we think of the immense network of control, sanctions and surveillance spread over the whole country and all its activities, we may well conclude that we have underestimated the role played by the physical force of the state.

That, in the final analysis, is no doubt what makes for the very 'special' character of the apparatus known as the state: everything that operates in it and in its name, whether the political apparatus or the ideological apparatuses, *is silently buttressed by the existence and presence of this public, armed physical force.* That it is not fully visible or actively employed, that it very often intervenes only intermittently, or remains hidden and invisible – all this is simply one further form of its existence and action. Lyautey[115] liked to repeat that one had to make a show of one's force so as not to have to make use of it; he meant that his experience showed that it sufficed to deploy one's (military) force to achieve, by intimidation, results that would normally have been achieved by sending it into action. We may go further, and say that *one can also not make a show of one's force so as not to have to make use of it.* When threats of brute force, or the force of law, subject the actors in a given situation to obvious pressure, there is no longer any need to make a show of this force; there may be more to be gained from hiding it. The army tanks that were stationed under the trees of Rambouillet

Forest in May 1968 are an example. They played, *by virtue of their absence*, a decisive role in quelling the 1968 riots in Paris. Read Police Chief Grimaud;[116] he says this in so many words. For to send in the tanks would have been risky for the bourgeoisie: the rebellion of some of those called up to serve in Algeria had not been forgotten.

Thus if what leads Lenin to say that the state is a 'special apparatus' or 'special machine' is *both* the mechanism of the hierarchical relations governing civil servants or state employees *and* the inevitable presence of a public, armed physical force which has its place at the heart of the state and makes itself felt in all state activities, this explanation perhaps settles the question of the *special* nature of the state-machine. It does not, however, explain why Marx and Lenin make such insistent use of the terms *apparatus* and, especially, *machine*.[m]

I propose – and I do not think that I am forcing the language of my texts, even if I am obviously making them say things that they authorize but do not overtly affirm – the following *hypothesis*, which I state

m It should be noted that the English historian Perry Anderson has very clearly understood and illustrated this point of theory and politics. In a brilliant essay on what he calls Gramsci's antinomies ['The Antinomies of Antonio Gramsci', *New Left Review* 100, November–December 1976, esp. p. 43], Anderson likens the presence-absence – a presence rendered effective by its very absence – of the state's armed forces to the monetary gold reserves of the Central Banks. These stocks of gold can fluctuate somewhat, but, overall, the total stock in the world remains constant. Occasionally, national monetary policy (that adopted by one or another state) or international monetary policy (that of the dominant form of imperialism) does employ gold in its transactions, either by selling off some of its reserves or by buying gold to build them up. However, general circulation in all its forms (which are practically infinite) takes place independently of the presence of the gold stocks on the market. *Yet such circulation would be impossible if these reserves did not exist* (the decision to abandon the gold standard has by no means eliminated them). As the phrase goes, they 'impinge on the market' simply because they make *this* market (this market and no other) possible, in exactly the same way as the invisible (should I say 'repressed'? – that is indeed the right term as far as most people are concerned, since they 'do not care to know' that these reserves exist and play a determinant role) presence of the police or armed forces impinges on a situation, simply because they make that situation or order (that *particular* order, not, obviously, another) possible for, obviously, the dominant class; and, therefore, because they make that order necessary for the dominated classes. All this, because it is done 'gently', produces the admirable effects of consensus attributable to an armed force which impinges so heavily on the established order that, ultimately, it need (almost) not intervene in it – that is, can leave this task to the unarmed forces of the state.... Among these forces – sometimes the first among them – are the ideological convictions of the 'citizens', who consider it preferable, all things considered, to stay at home and peacefully cultivate their gardens.

directly in positive terms, as if it had already been verified, although it obviously has not been. *The state is a machine in the full, precise sense of that term*, as established in the nineteenth century [***] after the discovery of the steam engine, the electro-magnetic machine, and so on: that is to say, in the sense of a *man-made device* [*dispositif*] comprising a *motor* driven by an energy 1, plus a *transmission* system, the purpose of the whole being to transform a specific kind of energy (A) into another specific kind of energy (B).

A machine of this sort constitutes, first of all, an artificial *body* [*corps*] comprising the *motor*, the *transmission* system, and the organs of *execution* or application of the energy that is transformed by the machine. In the case of machine tools (or machine instruments), *this body is material*, consisting of different parts, made of a 'special' metal, which ensure that energy A will be transformed into energy B and applied by the tools (of which there are usually a great number) to the raw material worked on by those tools.

It is easy to generalize this into the statement that *any machine*, which is a site and a means of the transformation of energy, *comprises a special material 'body'* made of a special 'metal', and that *the body of the machine*, albeit the condition for the transformation of this energy, is, *as a body, 'separate'* from the function of energetic transformation that it accomplishes. In actual fact – in, say, the steam engine – the metallic 'body' of the machine is perfectly distinct, hence 'separate', from the coal, which transforms water into steam and steam into first horizontal and then circular motion; it is also 'separate' from the tools and the 'work' they perform on the raw material (cotton, etc.). The '*separation*' of the *material body of the machine* from the fuel it consumes in order to transform it is the absolute precondition for the existence of the machine and its functioning. Of course, energy is also required to produce the body of the machine (the different parts, made of different metals), but the machine exists only if this preliminary energy has already done its work and been crystallized in the body of the machine. This earlier energy no longer intervenes as energy *in* the operation of the machine, for it has disappeared in its product: in heat, the pistons, the transmission belts, shafts and wheels by means of which the transformation of energy comes about.

We may now turn back to the machine of the state, in order to understand better why Marx talks about a machine, why this machine *has a body, and, above all, what kind of energy the machine transforms into what other kind of energy.*

We have already seen that the state has a material 'body'. This was brought out in our discussion of the idea that the state is an apparatus, and that this apparatus is 'separate'. This confers a new meaning upon the 'separation' of the state. The state is 'separate' because it necessarily has a body, so constructed as to produce a transformation of energy. We can, furthermore, understand why this material body should be '*special*', that is, *not just any body*, but either a body 'which is not like the others', made out of a 'special metal', about which we were able to form an idea by examining the 'special' nature of the body made up of the agents of the state: members of the armed forces, the forces responsible for maintaining public order, the police, as well as the other civil servants employed by the various administrations. But we are still faced with the key question of the transformation of energy, and the nature of the energy B resulting from the transformation of energy A by the state-machine.

As I see it, the state can, from this standpoint, be defined in one of two ways. First, we might say that it is a power machine [*une machine à pouvoir*], in the sense in which we talk about a drilling machine or a rotative machine.[117] In this case, the machine is defined *by the type or form of energy (B) that it produces as a result of the transformation of the initial energy (A).*

In this case, we would put the emphasis on the result of the energetic transformation, and we would clearly say that the state is a *machine for producing power.* In principle, it produces *legal power* – not for reasons involving the moral privilege of legality, but because, even when the state is despotic, and 'dictatorial' to boot, it always has an interest, practically speaking, in basing itself on laws; if necessary, laws of exception, even, if necessary, in order then to violate or 'arbitrarily' suspend them. This is safer from the state's point of view, for laws are also a means of controlling its own repressive apparatus. As we all know, to our consternation, the most tyrannical and fanatical, the most horrible states *gave themselves laws*, endowed their regimes of terror and extermination with laws: Hitler promulgated laws concerning the Jews and the extermination of the Jews. We also know that no state on earth is more punctilious about its own laws than the USSR, where there rages a form of repression that is legally selective and thus protected, since it is required by law. *The state*, in this respect, *is a machine for producing legal power*. In fact, the whole political apparatus, like the whole state administration, spends its time producing legal power, hence laws, as well as decrees and ordinances that are said to be, at the limit, decrees and ordinances 'of application', whenever the power produced by the state-machine comes into direct relation with concrete reality. I said a moment ago that the state produces nothing: as far as the production of material goods is concerned, this is correct. But *the greater part of the state's activity consists in producing legal power, that is, laws, decrees and ordinances. The rest of it consists in monitoring their application* by the agents of the state themselves, subject in their turn to the monitoring of inspectorates beginning with the Court of Auditors [*Court des comptes*]; and, of course, by[118] the citizens subject to the laws.

It is not sufficient, however, to define the state as a power machine, for energy B (power) tells us nothing about the energy that is transformed (A) so that power may be produced as its result. What, then, is this energy A that is transformed into (legal) power by the state-machine? It is hard to find a name for it, because matters are very complex here, and, what is more, very complicated at the empirical level. To give some sense of what this energy is, I shall again resort to a comparison: the state is, from this second standpoint, that is, with respect to the energy transformed by it (the energy that 'functions' in its motor and makes it run in order to ensure its transformation into energy B), a force machine or violence machine, in the sense in which we talk about a steam engine or petrol engine.

A word about the steam engine. Carnot's use of the term caloric-engine or, rather, engines [*machine à feu*, literally, 'fire machine'] instead of steam engine was insightful. For energy A, the energy constituting the 'motor' of the subsequent transformations, is 'fire', heat, or 'caloric' energy, not steam. It is heat which, by transforming water into steam and harnessing the steam's kinetic energy, sets the piston in motion and 'makes the machine go'. From the kinetic energy of the gases to the 'motion' of the piston, we do not have, properly speaking, a shift from one order to another. One and the same kind of energy, *kinetic energy*, simply changes form. The leap, and the energetic transformation, intervenes between the coal in the stable state and the burning coal.

Recall the passage in which Marx discusses machines, quoted above.[119] In this passage, Marx's interest is focused almost exclusively on the machine tool, that is, on the *final* stages of the energetic transformation. To be more precise, he is interested only in the *transformations of motion, of kinetic energy*, which are observable at the end of the process, when the motion is transmitted to the tools, multiplying human hands in the guise of the machine tool. The fact is that Marx *is not interested in the motor as such*; he says that 'it generates its own motive power' (!), noting that it is a matter of indifference whether the energy of the motor is 'external' to the machine or 'internal' to it. A human being, exactly like a waterfall, merely drives the machine tool from without. When the motor is 'internal', as in the steam engine, there is no change of register for Marx. He does not wonder what goes on in this motor, serenely remarking – and not without reason – that, from the standpoint of productive technology, it was not the steam engine but the machine tool which revolutionized production. The real question, however, lies elsewhere.

For what failed to interest Marx in the case of the machine tool did perhaps (?) interest him in the case of the state-machine, although he was probably not alert to a comparison that he was practising for good reasons of which he was unaware.

In the case of the state-machine, if the state-machine is a power machine, that is because it transforms one form of already existing energy, that of Force or Violence, into another, the energy of Power. What, then, is this energy A, which we are here calling Force or Violence? It is, quite simply, the force or Violence of class struggle, the Force or Violence that has 'not yet' been transformed into Power, that has not been transformed into laws and right [*droit*].

Let us note straight away, to avoid all temptation to invoke metaphysical Powers here (the 'Will' dear to Schopenhauer, or the 'Will to power' that has, in Nietzsche, a meaning very different from the one that interests us, etc.), that Force and Violence are relative, not absolute concepts; that Force designates *the Force of the one who has the greater force*, and Violence, the *Violence of the one who is the more violent*; and that Force and Violence consequently designate a *conflictual difference*,[120] where, amid difference and conflict, it is the one who possesses the greater force who represents Force, and is therefore Force, and the one who is the more violent who represents Violence, and is therefore Violence. Some people would like to see, in the trick theatre that they have themselves rigged up, Force, pure and alone, and Violence, pure and alone, produce the effects of fascination that suit their purposes. But what we mean here is something else entirely: class struggle, where one class is powerful and violent only because it is the dominant class, in other words, exercises its force and violence upon another class (which is also a force) that it must, in a never-ending struggle, hold in check if it is to maintain the upper hand over it. The relatively stable resultant (reproduced in its stability by the state) of this *confrontation* of forces (*balance* of forces is an accountant's notion, because it is static) is that *what counts is the dynamic excess of force* maintained by the dominant class in the class struggle. It is *this excess of conflictual force, real or potential, which constitutes energy A*, which is subsequently transformed into power by the state-machine: *transformed into right, laws and norms.*

Just as Marx said that 'the tailor disappears in the costume' (the tailor and all the energy that he expended cutting and sewing), so the whole hinterworld of the confrontation of forces and violence, *the worst forms of violence of class struggle, disappear in their one and only resultant: the Force of the dominant class, which does not even appear as what it is – the excess of its own force over the force of the dominated classes – but as Force tout court.* And it is *this* Force or Violence which is subsequently transformed into power by the state-machine.

This shows us the new sense in which the state [can be called] a '*separate*' machine. For class domination does indeed find itself sanctioned in and by the state, in that *only the Force of the dominant class enters into it and is recognized there.* What is more, this Force is the sole 'motor' of the state, the only energy to be transformed into power, right, laws and norms in the state. Emphatically, only the Force of the dominant class enters into the state and is recognized there, through the violent 'separation' that is responsible for the fact that this entry into the state is simultaneously a radical rejection and negation of the class struggle from which this separation has nevertheless issued: as its resultant but also, let us clearly say, as its condition. That the whole state is constituted in order to act as a support for this absolute, violent rejection, that its own body [*corps*] is 'made for that purpose', is something we have already said, but descriptively. Only now can we see the theoretical reasons for the effects that unsettled us and yet commanded our attention.

Furthermore, it is not only *the body* of the state that is *made for the purpose* of rejecting that 'hinterworld' of class struggle from which alone the Force of the dominant class emerges, in order to repress, necessarily, all the rest. *The ideology which the state professes* is *also made for that purpose* – an ideology which, in a thousand guises, denies the existence of class struggle and the class functioning of the state, in order to stammer, out of the convinced mouths of its agents (or the political parties that have vested interests here, or are complicit in this illusion), the litany of the virtues of 'public service', of the public-service state, on the pretext that it maintains the post office, railways and hospitals, as well as the shops that sell stamps and cigarettes! What we have here is a *prodigious operation of annulment, amnesia and political repression.* It is this operation which seals and guarantees *the* 'separation' of the state, *the one which* the dominant class needs the most, not only in its ideology, but in its very practice, in order to guarantee the perpetuation of its hegemony. The reasons for which *only* Force (= the excess of force) or Violence (= excess of violence) is represented in the state and transformed into power by it, in short, the reason that the dominant class alone has access to the state for the purpose of transforming its own force into power – *these reasons, which are class reasons* concealed by the (alas, effective) inanity of the ideology of 'public service' – are so deeply ingrained in the very nature of the body of the state that they manage, despite their obviousness, to remain 'secret', as Marx says, 'hidden' beneath the whole social edifice. This is a 'fetishism' which – hardly by accident – Marx failed to detect!

14. On the Body of the State

I shall again be discussing the *body* of the state. This is necessary. For, unlike the caloric-engine, in which the energy source (say, the coal or wood) bears *no relation* to the *metal* of which the boiler, pistons, and so on are made, in the case of the state, however 'separate' it may be – and this is yet another reason to strive for its 'separation', which is so hard to realize – *the body of the state is, naturally, not unrelated to the energy that it has to transform.*

What is the body of the state, considered from this angle? It is men, weapons, techniques and practices, buildings and land as well, and all the instruments required to ensure their functioning. But, *first and foremost, it is men*, the majority of whom come from the classes exploited by the class that dominates the exploited classes and holds state power.

A paradox! The personnel of the body of the state, in its overwhelming majority, is made up of the children of peasants and workers, together with the children of white-collar workers (in the army, CRS, gendarmery, police and civil service administration). As Gramsci repeatedly stressed, not only do army soldiers come from the popular classes (we do not have a professional army in our countries, but one that is subject to renewal thanks to a steady influx of recruits, who are supervised by a large number of career officers); so do policemen and other members of the forces responsible for maintaining public order, priests, and other state or Church intellectuals. Doubtless the mere fact of being a state agent represents 'social advancement' for the vast majority of these men from the popular classes, but the state takes many precautions besides mere social advancement to 'separate' them from their brothers of the same background and class, and it succeeds in effecting the 'separation' which is crucial to imposing the 'discipline' of their function on them. It is these men who make up the great majority of the state apparatuses charged with the maintenance of public order. Most other civil servants are of the same background. Of course, they are directed, trained, and subjected to extraordinarily restrictive rules and regulations, as we have seen. There is nevertheless a strong temptation to think that, all in all, the state differs from the 'caloric-engine' in that its 'body' is not passive, like a boiler's, or made of quite different stuff than fuel and fire, but consists, rather, of men like those it rules – and, moreover, of men from the social classes that the dominant class holds in check with the force of a state essentially represented *by* these men.

This enters into both the perceived and the ideal conditions for ensuring that the revolution takes place. If the armed core of the state were to revert to its origins, if the army and police were to go over to the side of the people, then, barring foreign intervention, the people could take state power. 'Brave soldiers of the 17th regiment' – you who refused to 'fire upon your brothers' during the revolt of southern French winegrowers facing famine because of the mildew – you live on in the popular memory which sings of your fame.[121] Yet this noble deed did not produce the revolution. At the very least, the question must be political, and national in scope.

It is true that, in 1917, the Tsar's army, weakened by defeat and demoralization, and utterly disorganized by the war itself, heeded the appeal of the Bolshevik militants: to these hunger-stricken peasants in rags, treated like animals by their officers, the Bolsheviks promised peace and, later, land as well. They were listened to; but so were the Social Revolutionaries, who had closer ties to the peasantry. And the revolution took place. Yet, elsewhere, how many sons of peasants and workers in arms, despite the Party militants and their propaganda, 'did their duty', firing on their fellow workers – from the Germany of 1919–21 through countless other examples to, finally, Chile, which, it appears, frightened Berlinguer and inspired his project for the 'historic compromise'.[122] If we consider only the social origins of the 'personnel' of the public forces (and the state administrations), we see that exceptional circumstances (which should not be ruled out a priori) are required to bring the body of the public armed forces to break with the 'separation' imposed on them by the state.

This truth allows us to judge the highly dubious value of a whole series of contemporary speculations on the supposed 'crisis of the state'. They reflect a subjective wish rather than a reality, in so far as the expectation is that the crisis will be sparked by movements that have affected certain state employees; thus the state is reputed to be 'traversed by the class struggle'.[n] I think that this is a utopian notion based on an unwarranted extrapolation. That there are stirrings of discontent in the judiciary and the police forces (the uniformed police forces, at any rate), that this discontent is fuelled by the mood of our day, in which demands are expressed through strikes, and that strikes are, to some extent, forms of class struggle – none of this is wrong; yet the reasoning is sloppy. For it must also be borne in mind that not all strikes are forms of the workers' class struggle. Some are forms of petty-bourgeois or corporatist class struggle. They can also be forms of conservative or even reactionary class struggle; and, in any case, it is not just movement that allows us to define a movement but, in addition, the tendency of this movement, and therefore its limits. Moreover, to judge this tendency, one must know whether it is revolutionary or progressive, assess the modifications affecting the body of the state itself, and determine whether these strikes are, in part, reasonably enlightened reactions to these modifications, or, rather, tend in the same direction as the modifications themselves, and so on.

All the foregoing considerations have only one objective: to refocus our attention on the paradox that the 'body of the state' is made up of men who, in their great majority, come from the popular classes, and thus on the paradox that the dominant class manages to utilize the state to mould its agents in such a way that their class origin is repressed or neutralized. Thus they become obedient 'subjects' who, even if they call a strike, will never call into question – let us say, never seriously call into question – their 'service', whose security they ensure. Training, ideological inculcation, strict discipline, a 'service' ethic, guaranteed employment, a pension, the right to strike for civil servants (except for the forces responsible for preserving public order): the state (and behind it, in it, the dominant class) succeeds, by exploiting and skilfully combining these means (including the various conventions that apply to civil servants – in France, the perquisites of those who are employed by the Ministry of Finance or belong to one of the '*grands corps* of the state', for example), in forging itself a 'body'

n In reality, the 'theory' of this state crisis is nothing but an apologetic illustration of prevailing illusions about a certain political line.

that is indeed separate from class struggle and made of a special 'human metal'.[123] One need only glance at the history of strikes in the French or even Italian 'civil service' in order to understand that the net result has been quite meagre, quite disappointing as far as politics, and, *a fortiori*, revolutionary politics go. One really has to conjure up altogether exceptional circumstances in order to imagine that this 'body' could crack and fall apart. Such circumstances ought not to be ruled out a priori, but the least one can say is that they are not on the horizon.

15. On the Destruction of the State

The state then, has a special, separate body. The transformation of Force-energy into power-energy takes place through it and in it. When Lenin talked about the destruction of the state, he had in mind, very precisely, *the body of the state*, which is inseparable from its conservative or reactionary ideology. When he said that the bourgeois state must be *destroyed*, employing, for the occasion, a word as powerful as the idea he meant to express (although this word as well was doubtless too powerful not to frighten his contemporaries and his readers), he had in mind, above all, the body of the state, which shows that he was aware of the importance of the body of the state for the definition of the function of the state (something that Marx had already demonstrated, taking the Paris Commune as his example, but unfortunately without thoroughly studying the social and political reasons for this adventure and its failure).

The many different passages in Lenin on the destruction of the state are doubtless the most advanced that Marxism has bequeathed us on the question of the state. They bring out *the organic unity existing between the 'metal' of this body and its functions.* Here, too, the state appears as a very 'special' 'apparatus', precisely in that its body is so well adapted to its functions that its functions seem to be a natural extension of its organs. Here Lenin has, above all, two things in mind: (1) the domination of the state by the upper echelons of the military, police and political administrations, the absolute domination (guaranteed by the upper crust of the dominant class in person) which a tentacular caste maintains over the masses of agents in the various corps or agencies; and (2) the division of state labour among the various corps or agencies of the state.

Lenin did not by any means think that *the 'whole state' had to be destroyed*, a formula that makes no sense, unless it means that all agents of the state are to be exterminated and all existing state services abolished. He did, however, believe that it was necessary to *destroy the forms of domination and subordination* in all state apparatuses, and, simultaneously, *the forms of the division of labour between the various apparatuses.* His view of the matter – and it is a profound one – was that the separation of the state was not only produced but also reproduced[o] by the hierarchical system obtaining between the base of the civil service and the summit, and also by the division of labour between the distinct 'corps' of the state or its various agencies. It is indeed patent, once one has perceived the ideological role which the 'esprit de corps' can play in the state, that this 'esprit de corps' serves above all to maintain a division of labour in the state: a division of labour which may well have been in gestation for a long time, but was, in the end, established very firmly indeed, and relatively quickly at that, in order to ensure that the class state would have as effective an instrument as possible at its disposal. The state knows that one must 'divide' in order to 'rule', and applies this famous maxim to itself first. If the summits of the state are to 'rule' over their subordinates, their subordinates have to be divided, which means that the 'corps' or 'agencies' have to be divided as a function of the division of their functions.

All this seems *natural.* But what defines and establishes the functions of the state, if not the class domination and the nature of the dominant class? The major shake-up in the definition of these functions of which the Paris Commune dared to give a bad example, launching the dangerous idea that such redefinition was possible, plainly showed, like the experience of the soviets in 1905, that these functions are not 'natural' or self-evident, hence that the divisions between them are not either, hence that the apparatuses destined to

o The question of the reproduction of the forms, agents, practices and ideology of the state apparatus is crucial. It is closely bound up with the theme of the 'separation' of the state.

ensure the performance of these functions are not either. Lenin expected that modifying the division of labour between the different state apparatuses would, among other things, abolish the separation of the state, or would in any case be a step towards abolishing the separation of the state, or towards the withering away of the state. The destruction of the bourgeois forms of the state was to be nothing more than the inaugural moment of this process.

Seeking to put an end to the 'separation' of the state, the number one instrument of any state of a dominant class, Lenin attempted to carry out two different types of action. Starting from below, *from the soviets*, he sought to abolish, from below, the separation of the state from the workers – whence the idea of a state of soviets. At the same time, however, starting from above, and targeting the body of the state, he sought to destroy, in this body, the forms of the division of labour between the different 'functions' that Tsarist policy [*politique*] had assigned the state.

No one text by Lenin discusses this question systematically and theoretically. Practically, however, he never stops discussing it. That force and power should be one and the same thing in the state, that the body of the state should be, not 'special', but made of the same human stuff as the workers and the peasants: this is what he sought to realize with the slogan 'all power to the soviets!' and the formula 'the state of the soviets'. However, in order that the forms of this state not be marked by, determined by, and entrenched in a division of labour based on the division of functions considered desirable by the dominant class, Lenin went to work on these forms themselves. Hence he sought to *destroy – yes, destroy* – the division of labour prevailing within the state. He sought to abolish, for example, the separation of powers, the separation between education and work, culture and politics, manual and mental labour, and so on. I am using his very words, which should sometimes be employed with caution. His intention, however, is unmistakable, and it is lucid.

It is based on the idea that if one leaves the body of the state intact, if one does not alter its metal, then one can try as much as one likes to impose different policies or personnel on it; the end effect of the system by which the state reproduces itself (its personnel, as well as the criteria used to measure the 'competence' to command or obey), and the end effect of the separation of powers, apparatuses and agencies, is that *this policy [will] ultimately be neutralized by the body of the state*, which will consent to produce laws, but not the corresponding decrees, or decrees, but not the directives calling for their application, and so on – in short, will boycott and sabotage the official policies of the revolution. Lenin soon learnt this by painful experience. It is not enough to put workers in the posts formerly held by bourgeois, or to give revolutionary orders to ensure that they are executed. The body of the state, for as long as *its organization* – that is, its ostensible natural *functions* together with their ostensible 'natural' *division* – is not called into question, will end up absorbing all the orders and transforming them into red tape in which even revolutionaries and the revolution will end up drowning. 'We have a state that is suffering from a grave defect. It is the state of the soviets, but it is suffering from a serious bureaucratic disease' (1919). By the end of his life, Lenin had quite simply sunk into despair: he had to make up his mind to create a 'reliable apparatus', a hardline apparatus, the Workers' and Peasants' Control commission, for the purpose of monitoring a bureaucratic state. Experience was to show that this was not a measure, but a failure. Those seeking the causes of Stalinism are not wrong to focus on the terrible adventure of the relations between the state and the Revolution. Nor are they wrong when they say that while we can deduce this handful of propositions from Lenin, he never clearly collected or stated them. Doubtless the reason, quite apart from the lack of time, was his failure to arrive at a sufficiently clear idea of the state.[124]

When one has ground to a halt before the 'absolute limit' represented by certain formulas that are extraordinarily accurate in and of themselves, but stated so enigmatically and peremptorily as to be intimidating and to block all research beyond the theoretical space that they delimit, it is no wonder that the most striking, dramatic experiences remain in the passive state of experience. They lack the liberty they would need to become experiments from which the actors of history can learn what is genuinely new about what they contain. If we fail to recognize the existence of these phenomena, which combine insight with blindness to what has been understood, precisely because of the enigmatic intensity of the formulas in which a 'certain portion of truth' is captured, then we fail to grasp, cannot grasp, the 'limits' in which not only 'the Marxist theory of the state' – or, rather, the 'elements' of a theory that stand in for it – but also the historical actors found themselves trapped. For they were obliged, like Lenin, to innovate and cast about for ways of meeting terrible exigencies, despite the urgency of the situation and because of this urgency. 'Beyond this limit, your ticket is no longer valid.' The memory of this formula in its enamelled letters stayed with me for a long time; it had caught my eye when, in 1945, I took the Paris Underground. It had not appeared on the barbed wire of the POW camps from which I was returning to France: the barbed wire had taken its place. I often recalled it in later years while reading Marx and Lenin, struck by their astonishing reactions of blockage. These authors certainly provided us with 'tickets', and very valuable ones at that. But 'beyond' certain 'limits', whose contours one had to discover in their works and their struggles, the 'tickets' were 'no longer valid'. Matters have remained at this point, without budging, for many years. It may be that they will change now, and that the old enamelled signs will at last disappear from Marxism just as, today, they have disappeared from the Paris Underground.[125]

16. The Great Mystification of the State

Once we begin prospecting in the vicinity of the aforementioned 'limits' of the 'Marxist theory' of the superstructure and, especially, the state (for this point commands everything else in that 'theory'), we cannot get away with adding a few new stipulations, however emphatic. It is enough to lift the 'barriers' ever so slightly to discover a landscape made up of an infinite number of questions that we can, at least, try to pose. Providing concrete answers would require painstakingly concrete analyses, which it is not possible to essay here.

Take the simple point of the 'separation' of the state, which, as we have seen, is 'separate', as far as possible, from class struggle, but only so that it can intervene in it reliably, and 'from all sides at once', in order to maintain and perpetuate the class domination of the dominant class. This is the first meaning of the separation of the state, found in Engels as well, in a passage in which the state is said to be 'above the classes'. It is 'above the classes', and therefore above class struggle, *only* in order to intervene the more effectively in both, in the interests of the dominant class.

Yet this formula, if it is isolated from its explanation, can breed illusions. It can even come perilously close to the definition of the state always given by the ideology of the dominant classes. That the state is 'above classes' would thus mean that it bears no relation, either by nature or by function, to any of the classes in the struggle. Quite the contrary: it is a Neutral Institution that stands 'above the classes', like a Referee who, because he is above the match between two teams, or two classes, limits their struggle and their excesses in such a way as to guarantee that the 'common interest', or the 'general' or 'public' interest, will prevail.

On this hypothesis, the body of the state is made up of neutral civil servants (the best and the most 'cultivated', in Hegel's view, recruited by means of objective examinations that are in their turn subject to the control of an objective jury under the supervision of a neutral president). And these civil servants have only one goal: 'public service'. There might be the occasional lapse, but, overall, the system works. The notion of the 'civil servant' effacing himself before his service is held in such high regard that even the German philosopher Husserl defined himself by way of his definition of philosophers as the 'civil servants of humanity'. It is also well known that the French philosopher Brunschvicg (who, as a Jew, was stripped of his post by Pétain and persecuted) declared one day that since the policeman's function was to maintain respect for public order, and since the same respect [for the] same public order constituted [one] of the functions of Reason, nothing was more respectable and reassuring than a policeman.... Brunschvicg was a pure, Kantian soul, but he was unable to 'anticipate' certain 'perceptions'.

This version of the thesis of the 'separation' of the state can – as is clearly shown by the interpretations prevailing in the Communist Parties of, for example, France and Italy – mobilize a massive argument that never fails to impress, since it is rooted not only in 'obvious empirical realities' (just open your eyes!), but also in certain formulas taken from Engels, which, at the very least, have been misinterpreted.[126] Yes, the basic argument runs, the state does provide essential public services – water, gas, electricity, the post, transport, health, education, and so on and so forth. Yes, the state does play a role in investment (in France and Italy, it is the biggest financial power). Yes, it does play a role in maintaining the value of labour-power, and as an 'arbiter' between the two sides (employers and workers), and so on. In all these cases, it 'decides', on its own, in the 'general interest', or 'arbitrates' between two different or contradictory interests. And it can take on and fulfil this role of arbiter only because, charged with carrying out *objective* 'public' tasks, it is truly, in a sense, 'above classes'. Think of those amazing societies of the ancient Middle East, endowed with what is called an 'Asiatic' or, by others, a 'hydraulic'[127] mode of production. In order that the peasant communities, virtually the only producers, could live and work, these societies had to construct huge systems of dams, reservoirs and irrigation ditches to ensure the circulation and distribution of water. This was beyond the capacities of any individual or group, or of any class (if there were classes), just like the construction of the pyramids in Egypt or Mexico, and so on. Only the state, which was 'above the communities' or 'above classes', had agents and soldiers enough to levy enough taxes in kind and mobilize masses of men, compelling them to carry out these mammoth tasks. Public service.

It is here that we see the superficiality (and therefore sterility) of a descriptive conception of the state that is content to affirm that the state is 'separate' and 'above classes'. Such a conception is 'ripe' and ready to fall into the bourgeois theory of the state as the objective arbiter of class conflict. In reality, to shed some light on this question, *we need to bring reproduction into play.* The state is 'separate' and 'above classes' only in order to ensure the reproduction of the conditions of domination by the dominant class. This reproduction does not consist solely in the reproduction of the conditions of 'social relations' and, ultimately, the 'productive relation'; it also includes the reproduction of the *material conditions* of the relations of production and exploitation.

Exploitation does not take place in the realm of 'intersubjective relations'[128] or ethereal 'social relations'. It takes place *in material conditions* that are by no means arbitrary, but are, rather, the material conditions required and produced by the existing mode of production. To give an example which could be multiplied *ad infinitum*: those who imagine that the major roads, built by the state since time immemorial – the Roman roads or, in our countries,[p] the highways – were built in order to facilitate pleasure trips are telling themselves fairy tales. The major roads have always been constructed – just as the railways, and so on, later were – in accordance with plans and directions (and also *in* directions) whose objectives were military or economic, and closely bound up with contemporaneous forms of domination, and therefore also exploitation. That, over and above everything else, these roads are also used by people on holiday, and that these highways, now that their military utilization has been more or less suspended, are also, and today primarily, used *both* by heavy-goods vehicles *and* for holiday travel, now a capitalist enterprise in its own right, not only does not exclude the purpose they were really designed for but, on the contrary, reinforces it with an unforeseen supplement (those very 'holidays' which help to reproduce labour-power). It would be interesting to demonstrate this with respect to the railways, even if they have been 'nationalized' in France, and almost everywhere else, both for reasons having to do with the class struggle, but also (this is, moreover, in part the same thing) for reasons deriving from the needs of 'modern industry', that is, the classical material form (there are other forms!) of capitalist exploitation. The fierce competition between trains, lorries and aeroplanes, the politics of differential price schemes (low rates for the big companies, high ones for individuals), the systematic closing of routes said to be of 'secondary interest'), and so on, would enable us to make a more accurate estimate of the stakes of the economico-political conflicts over 'transport policy'. This might seem to be a purely 'technical' matter; yet the high-ranking civil servants who work for the French National Railway

p It makes little difference whether they are (as in France) constructed and managed by 'private' firms, to which they are leased by the state.

company (or for *Gaz de France*, or the electrical and nuclear power industry), as well as those who assist the ministers and government in coming to a decision that is ultimately taken by all the political personnel of the state, make no bones about the fact that several different 'technical solutions' exist, but that a political choice always comes into play, so that only one solution wins out. It is then justified by bogus 'technical' arguments, notwithstanding its profoundly political nature. (What is more, this class politics is increasingly an international class politics.)

Those Communists who (for unavowed reasons) can think the state only by moving towards a definition of it as a public service in the public domain are perhaps telling *themselves* fairy tales. It does not much matter whether, in order publicly to defend the theses they defend, they feel the need to believe in them (thc function creates the organ!). In any event, they display (I am not talking about their bad faith or visionary mystifications here) stubborn ignorance of the nature of the Marxist theory of exploitation. Class struggle does not take place in the sky. It begins with exploitation, and by far the most exploitation takes place in production, hence *in matter*: the matter of factory buildings, machines, energy, raw materials, the 'working day', the assembly line, work rhythms, and so on. Moreover, to assemble all these things in the same place, the materiality of the means of transport, the processing of financial and technical information, and so on, is required. That all this ultimately presents itself in the form of railways and ground, air or sea transport; that all this also ultimately presents itself in the form of the postal service and post-office counters (with, here too, special sliding rates unavailable to the 'general public'), or in the form of a switch that one flips to bring the current leaping to light up one's house; that all this also takes the form of the 'modern' material conditions of private life, that is, *private life considered from the standpoint of its mass distribution, as so many conditions for the reproduction of labour-power* (children, the school system – also a 'public service', is it not?; the national health service – also a 'public service', is it not?; the Church and sports – also 'public services', are they not?; and the telephone, but watch out for taps, and the telly – also 'public services', are they not?, even if they are at the beck and call of adroit or inept ministers), *is not only not surprising, but necessary and inevitable.*

Public 'service' is the form taken by the gigantic mystification of the so-called 'public services' of the state, which *has been compelled to provide and multiply public service* in order to cope with the modern forms of class struggle. And if one invokes the tendential fall in the rate of profit here, in order to explain, as Boccara[129] does, that it is owing to the 'devalorization of capital' (too much capital for the existing workforce to exploit) that the state has had to take charge of such-and-such a loss-making 'sector' in order to operate it as a loss-making public service, one sharply reduces the import of the Marxist theory of the tendential fall in the rate of profit, which is in fact a *theory of the tendential rise in the class struggle.* One makes it a question of financial performance, even operating results, whereas it is in fact a profoundly political question. One has to be singularly blinded by the putatively theoretical arguments which serve only as theoretical window-dressing for political convictions received from the higher echelons in order to suggest or maintain that, because the 'state' must increasingly take responsibility for sectors which only yesterday were nonexistent, or left to the private sector, it is, owing to its 'expansion', becoming increasingly 'socialized', or soon will; or that – to repeat an unfortunate phrase of Lenin's (but consider the context: this was under Kerensky, and 'disaster' was 'imminent'!)[130] – the state of so-called State Monopoly Capitalism is the antechamber of the socialist state. But let us say no more about these inanities, which exist only in the state of *Wunscherfüllung*, as Feuerbach said first[131] and Freud repeated after him. They were both talking about dreams.

17. The Pseudo-Circle of the State

But if we take the concept of reproduction seriously; if we take seriously the requirement which 'even a child would understand' (Marx) – namely that, in order to exist, every 'society' has to reproduce the conditions of its own production, and that every class society has to perpetuate the relation of exploitation and of production that sustains it; if we conclude from this that the state plays, in this reproduction, a 'special' role, on condition that it is 'separated' from the class struggle in order to be able to intervene dependably in the service of the dominant class (a dependable servant has to be cast in a special metal and mentality); if, finally, the state can play a role only as a machine, then we are still not at the end of our labours.

For the attentive reader will certainly have noticed a curious sort of 'play' in our explanations.

Even if we admit the principle of the transformation of energy ensured by the state-machine, which – reproducing the result of class struggle – transforms the excess of Force of the dominant class into legal power *tout court* (the classes having been conjured away during this transmutation), the fact remains that we confront a situation which is hard to think.

If the state-machine serves to transform class Force or Violence into Power, and to transform this Power into right, laws and norms, *it would seem that there is a before and an after*, in the following order: *before*, there was the Force that is an excess of the Force of a dominant class over the dominated classes; this Force enters into the state-machine or the power-machine not as an excess of force, but as Force *tout court*; afterwards, at the other end of the machine, this Force emerges in the form of Power and its juridical, legal and normative forms (the way the pig comes out the other end of the meat-mincer as pâté and sausages). Yet this is not quite how things happen, unless we are to trace the state back to its *origin* (which it is difficult to pinpoint), as Engels tried to do in his famous book[132] (but without examining this Machine in detail). As for us, we are not only not in a position to reason about the origin; *the origin, even if it could be pinned down, would be of absolutely no use to us*. For what functions in the state today has nothing to do with the origin; it has to do with *the forms of reproduction* of *both* class society *and* the state-machine itself.

To put it another way: the Force that enters the mechanisms of the state-machine in order to emerge from them as Power (right, political laws, ideological norms) does not enter as pure Force, for the very good reason that *the world from which it issues is itself already subject to the power of the state*, hence to the power of right, laws and norms. This is as might be expected, since, in attempting to understand the class domination which requires a state for its defence and perpetuation, we invoked 'the ensemble of the forms of class domination, in production, politics and ideology'. But the existence of the ensemble of these forms presupposes the existence of the state, right, political and other laws, and ideological norms. Thus there is no breaking out of *the circle of the state, which has nothing of a vicious circle about it, because it simply reflects the fact that the reproduction of the material and social conditions* encompasses, and implies the reproduction of, the state and its forms *as well*, while the state and its forms contribute, but in a 'special' way, to ensuring the reproduction of existing class society. The 'special function' of the reproduction of the state is the reproduction of the 'special' forms (those of the state) required to control the class conflicts that are, at the limit, capable of undoing the existing regime of exploitation. Gramsci mocked the Mancunian formula that made the state a 'night watchman', and he was right: for even when Mancunian capitalism was at its peak, it was absurd to conceive of the state as guarding society only at night, when everyone is asleep. The state is indeed a watchman, but it is a permanent watchman, on duty night and day, and it sees to it that, in Engels's euphemism, 'society' is not 'destroyed' as a result of the struggle of its antagonistic classes. I would say, rather, that it sees to it that class struggle – that is, exploitation – is *not abolished, but, rather, preserved, maintained, and reinforced*, for the benefit, naturally, of the dominant class; hence that it sees to it that the conditions of this exploitation are conserved and reinforced. To that end, it also 'keeps an eye out for' explosions, which are always possible, as in 1848 and 1871 – there the result was bloodbaths – or in May 1968, when it was tear gas and the violence of street confrontations.

Lenin was right a thousand times over to emphasize, in his Sverdlov lecture on the state, that the state is 'complex', terribly complex, and to add that class struggle is the cause of its complexity. But he was wrong to reduce class struggle to certain of its ideological effects: above all, to the bourgeois ideologues who 'confuse and complicate everything'[133] – that is to say, do so consciously and by design, so that the popular masses will misunderstand the state and lend credence instead to the 'self-evident truths' of what Plato, in his time, called the

Noble Lies required for the exercise of state power. This is a bit too simple; this judgement proves that Lenin, in the tradition of the founders of Marxism, overestimated the powers of the conscious ideology of his class adversaries. The truth of the matter is that bourgeois ideologues lie as easily as they do, and trap the popular masses in their Noble Lies as easily as they do, only because 'the lying goes on all by itself' [*ça ment tout seul*],[134] because the reality of the separation of the state, of the special character of the state-machine and the disconcertingly simple forms of the reproduction of the state on the basis of its own effects, constitute a system with extraordinarily complicated mechanisms. At every moment, this system objectively masks its functions behind its apparatus, its apparatus behind its functions, its reproduction behind its interventions, and so on.

If I may be allowed to charge the term 'circle' with the weight of everything I have just said, then it is '*the circle of the reproduction of the state in its functions as an instrument for the reproduction of the conditions of production, hence of exploitation, hence of the conditions of existence of the domination of the exploiting class' which constitutes, in and of itself*, the *supreme objective mystification.* The bourgeois ideologues whose misdeeds Lenin evokes simply extend the effects of the supreme mystification in the classic apologies of their writings or pamphlets. They do not have a clear understanding of matters, for all that; we give them much too much credit if we believe that they are aware of a truth that they falsify for class reasons. It must therefore be said – *pace* Lenin – that if the question of the state is indeed terribly complex, the 'credit' does not, in the last instance, go to the falsifications of the bourgeois ideologues, but to the complex nature of the mechanism which reproduces the state-machine as a 'separate, special machine' in a class society.

18. On Fetishism

Let us note something in passing: because *Capital* (which becomes one-hundred-per-cent Feuerbachian in Chapter 1, Section 4) offers us a theory of objective mystification, the theory of fetishism, what we have just said about the state may enable us to settle – at least in part, because there is no controlling the destiny of words – the vexed, endlessly rehashed question of fetishism in *Capital*.

Everyone knows that the few visionary pages that Marx devotes to fetishism, which are too self-evident for what they pretend to be, have spawned an enormous literature that continues to proliferate and 'is laid on a little thicker' with each new round. The reasons are easy to see. In these pages (rather too often regarded as homogeneous, and therefore always right), all those Marxists who refuse to enter into the logic of the 'mechanistic economism' of certain of Marx's formulas seek the means with which to defend positions that are, let us say, 'workerist' in the noble sense of the term; the means with which to defend the human resources represented by the workers' rebelliousness, or by their 'straight talk'. These Marxists refuse to be intimidated by the fact that the theory of fetishism also provides a springboard for all the 'humanist', or even 'religious', interpreters of Marx's thought.

In a text of this importance, situated where it is in *Capital*'s order of exposition, several different 'meanings' come into play. The fact is that Marx plays on this multiplicity of possible meanings; it is not even impossible that it helps him make his demonstration, which, near the beginning, evokes religion: 'to find an analogy, we must take flight into the misty realms of religion'.[135] The counter-proof appears at the end, where we learn that Christianity is 'the most fitting form of religion' for a society based on commodity production. Held fast in the religious model, exalting the simplicity and transparency of the *relations* between the man Robinson Crusoe and *things*, Marx can advance his thesis: 'To the producers … the social relations between their private labours appear as what they are, i.e. they do not appear as direct social relations between persons in their work, but rather as … social relations between things.'[136] This sentence (I have picked out the one that gives fetishism its best theoretical chance) actually states the reality of fetishism rather well.[137]

Here Marx plays on the term 'social relations', which are sometimes relations between 'persons' [*personnes*] and sometimes relations between things. When he evokes the immediate social relations of 'persons' in their work itself, he in fact evokes a double transparency, founded in each instance on *immediacy*: (1) every subject's relation to the product of its labour (a thing) is transparent; and (2) the reciprocal relation between subjects in their collective (social) labour process is transparent. These relations are transparent because they are immediate. But this is to take a purely philosophical postulate for granted (a subject's relation to 'its' object is transparent because it is immediate), unless one traces this transparency-by-virtue-of-immediacy back to the domain where it rules supreme: mercantile law, or, rather, the ideology of the law [*du droit*].

In mercantile law, the relation of a subject of law to a thing in its possession, of which it is also the legal owner, is indeed transparent-because-immediate. Juridical ideology even affirms that, because all commodity relations are founded on the immediacy of the possession of things by each subject of the law, this transparency extends to all juridical relations. Finally, it affirms that the relation of the subject of the law to things is simultaneously, since it is a proprietary relation, a relation which entails the right to alienate, and therefore to buy and sell 'things' (commodities). This makes the immediate, transparent relation of the subject to the thing appear to be a social relation. Thus the law recognizes that the social relations between men [are] identical to the social relations between commodities (things), since they are merely the other side [*l'envers*] of these relations.

The paradox is that Marx opposes relations between men to relations between things, whereas the reality of the law itself describes these relations in their unity. Actually, if we examine Marx's text closely, we see that his quarrel is less with this unity than with the fact that it is *apparent*: the relations between men *appear* to them to be relations between things. Yet this appearance – Marx observes that it continues to exist after being deconstructed at the theoretical level – is as much a part of the reality of social relations as is the other appearance, that of the immediacy and transparency of the relations between men and 'their things' or 'their products'.

For as long as we remain the prisoners of a conceptual system based on the opposition person/thing, the two basic categories of law and juridical ideology, we can just as easily defend Marx's position as its opposite, or adopt both positions, or even reject both. In any case, we remain trapped in the categories of the law or in the notions of juridical ideology.

In reality, the theory of fetishism in Marx is merely a kind of parable whose ulterior motives appear clearly in the rest of the text. When they do, however, they destroy the effect of 'demonstration' that the brilliant paragraphs which precede lead one to expect.

Marx first offers us a series of examples of 'societies' in which 'the social relations between persons' reign supreme in their immediacy and transparency – and not, as in commodity-producing society, *while appearing* to be social relations between things (commodities). For example: Robinson Crusoe, the man who stands in a perfectly transparent relation to things, including those he produces in order to reproduce on his island, for himself, the world of the 'objects' of a civilized society based on commodity production. For example: feudal society, in which the relations between men do not wear the appearance of relations between things, since these relations unfold between persons, in direct, crystal-clear fashion (for example: corvées, bastinadoes, and so on). For example: a patriarchal family. One final example: the society of freely associated producers, in which everything unfolds amid the transparency of consciousness and the planning to which all give their voluntary consent.

Taken literally, Marx's ostensible proofs have no general meaning. For, every time Marx uses the terms 'person' and 'thing', he assigns them the meaning that fits his 'demonstration': the rabbit is always-already in the hat. If, on the other hand, we have ears to hear the parable, it means that the commodity relations in which we live and which, like all established social relations – whether Robinsonian (Robinson Crusoe's relation with himself is a social relation), feudal or patriarchal – always have the 'transparency' of their 'obviousness' going for them; it means that these commodity relations have not always existed, that they are not foreordained and immutable, and that communism will abolish them. In that case, we understand. But we do not understand why Marx had to entangle himself in this parable.

Marx, however, goes on to offer us a series of examples that are far more convincing. This time, it is a question of more or less ideological 'theories': those of the Mercantilists, who held that all wealth (value) resided in the qualities of one or another metal (gold or silver); of the Physiocrats, who held that the soil alone was productive; of the penny-a-dozen ideologues who hold that capital consists of 'things' (means of production), and so on. Here Marx calls his adversaries by their real names, denouncing 'the degree to which some economists are misled by the fetishism attached to the world of commodities, *or by the material appearance* of the social attributes of labour'.[138] Yet he simultaneously admits something that is perhaps not without importance: that fetishism is here identified with the 'illusions' of the 'economists', ideologues doing their job as ideologues. The short circuit thanks to which Marx relates these 'illusions' of the 'economists' to the 'fetishism inherent in the world of commodities' is overhasty, to say the least; it is a way (which ought to be justified) of relieving them of their theoretical responsibility by pinning it on 'the world of commodities'.

What is more, Marx is obliged to 'lay it on' very thick indeed, for he does not hesitate to say '*the material appearance of the social characteristics [attributs] of labour*', a phrase that undeniably designates everything that is material: the material conditions of labour, including raw materials and the means of production, currency, and so on. What, then, is this 'labour', this Substance which is thus endowed from the outset with Social Attributes (the means of production), and whose material reality is, in its entirety, nothing but '*appearance*'? If we recall a memorable little phrase from the 'Critique of the Gotha Programme' in which, discussing 'labour' and a thesis in the Programme to the effect that all value comes from it (in sum, from Labour-Substance),[139] Marx vigorously denounces the bourgeois ideologues' belief in the 'omnipotence of labour', then we have reason to be astonished by the words 'the material appearance of the social characteristics of labour', which here found the whole theory of fetishism.

It is only too clear that Marx intended in this passage, which paves the way for the chapter on money, to fit himself out in advance with the means for an easy refutation of the theory of the Mercantilists (who think that the value of gold derives from its 'nature'). It is only too obvious that he also intended to discuss commodity relations (note that he talks about 'private labours', a curious notion) while pursuing the trajectory dictated by his unfortunate order of exposition, based on the decision to begin *Capital* with the simple (and transparent) abstraction of value. It is understandable that he should discuss commodity relations in order to clear a path for the idea that social relations are not necessarily commodity relations. But his reasoning is quite weak, and simply points back, here as in every other passage in which he is weak, to his first weakness, into which he throws all his strength. It comes from beginning *Capital* the way he did.

These reflections do not constitute a digression. For if we leave fetishism to one side as the theory of a certain appearance that is necessary in general – a theory that is here based, hardly by accident, on the abstraction of value and its commodity form – what remains in this text, what is serious about it, is what it says by way of what it does not say. For the one thing which is certain, out of all the examples that Marx cites, is the case of the 'illusions of most economists', that is, the theoretical constructions (which are illusory, at least as far as some of their affirmations are concerned) that have served as economic thought not for a 'world of commodities', but for an already advanced 'capitalist world': a world in which there existed not only commodities and a gold-based currency, but also wage labour, hence capitalist exploitation, and the state. In deducing things from the simplest abstraction, value, Marx has no choice but to bracket these realities, which are of fundamental importance for understanding not only Robinson Crusoe, but also the 'illusions of the economists'. He cannot bring them into play in order to account for 'commodity fetishism', since, at this point, he has not got beyond the deduction of the concept of the commodity.

Thus we see Marx make the stupendous attempt to derive the necessity of the 'illusions of most economists' – the economists whom he will have to refute in order to introduce his deduction of money, the economists who dwelt in a world altogether different from that rooted in the relation between value and the value-form, not to speak of the concrete relations of this world, which [made] it a world rather than a chapter in a book – by setting out from a wholly improvised, imaginary theory of 'commodity fetishism'!! It is the commodity all by itself, its 'division' into use value (the thing) and value (a social relation between men), which will provide, all by itself, an explanation for the sensational misunderstanding that bamboozles you into conferring upon the 'Social Attributes of Labour' (coal, ore, blast furnaces, etc.) a '*material appearance*'!

We can deduce two things from this. First, that Marx, who was in a rush, wanted to indicate, at this early point, the end he had in mind (communism, a 'mode of production' without commodity relations). Second, that from the moment he '*began*' with the simple, transparent abstraction of value, he had the wherewithal to confect this theory[140] of 'fetishism', since it depends on juridical categories and the notions of the corresponding juridical ideology in whose terms, precisely, he has to think in order to 'begin' with the beginning of his *magnum opus*, *Capital.* Basically, Marx was 'itching' to produce this theory (which depends on a theory of alienation) from the very first words of *Capital.* He had everything he needed to produce it, and, as soon as he had derived the commodity form, as if urged on by his impatience, he delivered the goods, just before turning to the 'illusions of the economists' about money.

This is not a digression, because what is missing in this text, what prevents us from grasping such reality as it contains, is – besides everything that Marx will say later about the process of capitalist production and the process of its reproduction – everything that law [*droit*], the state and the ideologies contribute to producing the 'illusions of the economists'. As soon as we bring up law, we are talking about the state. Marx clearly tried, in the unpublished essays entitled *A Contribution to the Critique of Political Economy*, to 'derive' mercantile law [*le droit marchand*] from ... commodity relations [*des rapports marchands*]; but, unless we are to endorse the notion of a providential self-regulation of these commodity relations, we cannot understand how they could function without money minted by the state, transactions registered by state agencies, and courts capable of settling possible disputes. Moreover, since the commodity relations in question here are not those of an imaginary society in which, by guesswork or some other method, 'private' individual producers compare the time they will spend on their respective private labours in order to determine the value of the products which they set out to produce long before they actually produce them (for these private producers believe, not in the 'material appearance' of the celebrated 'Social Attributes of Labour', but in the material conditions of their own labour); and as the commodity relations in question here are those of an already quite advanced capitalist society, these 'commodity relations' are established as commodity relations the way they always have been: between, not 'private' individuals, but social groups – here, social classes – of which one owns the 'Social Attributes of Labour', while the other owns, not the 'Substance of Labour', but its own raw labour-power. Moreover, in this capitalist class society, the state and law [*droit*] adamantly continue to exist – not just private, mercantile law, but also public, political law, which is, despite the term 'common law', of an altogether different sort; and there are also the ideologies, which the ideology of the dominant class strives to unify in the dominant ideology.

That the law and juridical ideology are at the heart of the (tendentially) dominant ideology known as bourgeois ideology no doubt has something to do with the 'illusions of most economists', who lapse into the 'fetishism' of believing that the social relations between men take on 'the appearance of relations between things'. These worthies believe that the value of gold stems from the matter it is made of, from the quality of this matter. They are vulgar materialists. But that this law and this juridical ideology are at the heart of the (tendentially dominant) ideology known as bourgeois ideology no doubt also has something to do with the 'illusions' of the 'omnipotence of labour' that found the 'illusions' of a 'theory of the fetishism *of the* commodity' of a philosopher named Marx. Here he pays the price, for the first but not the last time, for having set off on an analysis of the capitalist mode of production (*Capital*) with a certain idea of the order of exposition that compelled him to 'begin' with the prescribed beginning: the simplest abstraction, value.

Let us note this point carefully. For, on the first occasion on which Marx risks a discussion of 'illusory', and *necessarily* 'illusory', discourses – and therefore, in the case to hand, risks coming face-to-face with law, the state and also the reality of what is conventionally called (for lack of a better term) 'ideologies' – he goes very wide of the mark. And he does so because he has been wide of the mark from the first. The most serious reason for this is not, as he himself believed, that he 'flirted' with Hegelian terminology, but, rather, that in his way of broaching the subject of value, and in his insistence on broaching it from the outset in order to derive everything else from it, he got entangled in the notions of bourgeois juridical ideology concerning, precisely, value itself, without as yet being able to extricate himself from them. I talked, somewhat earlier, about the 'absolute limits' of every author, including Marx. This is an example of what I meant.

I do not think that it makes any sense at all to talk about the fetishism of the commodity, as if the commodity could be the source [*l'auteur*] 'of' fetishism. No doubt it does make some sense to use the term fetishism, but only on condition that we bring fetishism into relation with what actually causes it, without telling ourselves the fairy tales that Marx inflicts on us in order to fabricate the evidence he needs. Moreover, it is not certain that fetishism, which comes down to considering that that which appears natural is only 'natural', can take us very far towards an 'explanation' of these illusions: for the essence of any 'illusion' is to appear as if it went without saying, that is, as if it were natural.[141] More than this mark of self-evidence, what matters is the explanation of the mechanism that produces it. But the mechanism, or, rather, the 'twofold character' [*double face*] of value, surreptitiously transmogrified into its 'division' in the interests of a dubious theoretical cause, is only a pseudo-explanation of fetishism, a reduplication of the concepts (person, thing) by means of which Marx has already thought value. In contrast, at the level of Marx's concrete examples (the 'illusions' of the Mercantilists, Physiocrats, *et al.*), the explanation calls up different realities: the existence of capitalist production, law, money, the state and the ideologies which bourgeois ideology, with juridical ideology at its core, 'works on' in order to become dominant.

There are fetishisms and fetishisms: when considering 'illusions', it would be far more fruitful to examine those that owe their existence to the state, which, according to Engels, was 'the first ideological power' on earth.[142] We have said enough about the state's political-economical-ideological function as a machine for transforming the force that emanates from class struggle into power, and enough about the conditions for the reproduction of the state, to warrant the suspicion that this very complicated reality may be at the origin of massive mystifications that go well beyond the illusion that consists, or is said to consist, in taking the social relations between men for social relations between things.

19. The 'Absolute Limits' of Marx on Ideology

While still on the subject of Marx's 'absolute limits', I would like to mention the conception of ideology that he arrived at very early, and, as far as I know, never gave up.

Marx, who borrowed the term 'ideology' from the Ideologues while considerably altering its original meaning, basically always conceived of it as something related to the consciousness-form, as an 'object' of consciousness. He conceived consciousness, in turn, in very traditional fashion, as the subject's capacity to be present to sense perceptions, emotions and ideas that come to it from without or within: an external sense and an internal sense, with the internal sense capable of perception, reflection, retention (memory), protention (anticipation), judgement, and so on.

On this basis, which not only takes up the 'classic' (= bourgeois) philosophical theme of consciousness, but also situates the self-conscious act at the summit of the hierarchy of the subject's acts, Marx made a significant contribution by considering the possibility that the ideologies are *systems of ideas and representations* in which the reality of the subject itself is represented, although it is distorted and usually inverted; and also by defending the thesis that the ideologies are social (Lenin would talk about 'ideological social relations'), and have a function in the class struggle.

Of course, he applied this notion to class struggle and the social classes themselves. Thus he distinguishes, in *The Poverty of Philosophy*, the social class 'in itself' from the social class 'for itself'[143] (that is, endowed with self-consciousness). He also attaches extreme importance to political consciousness: not to the simple subjective consciousness that can produce rebellious or embittered subjects, but to the objective consciousness (or 'theory') that can attain knowledge of the objective conditions of social life, exploitation and struggle. Slogans about 'raising the consciousness' of political activists and endowing them with 'true class-consciousness' derive from this terminological tradition. In the Preface to *A Contribution*, Marx goes so far as to talk about ideologies '*in which* men become conscious of [class] conflict and fight it out'. In this formula, ideology is no longer considered to be the sum of individual ideas, but is, rather, regarded as a supra-individual 'mental' reality that imposes itself on individuals. This is the sense that eventually prevails in Marx; although he keeps the term 'ideology', he ceases to conceive of it as the distorted individual representation of a subject, conceiving instead of an objective reality 'in which' men – here, classes, but also the individuals in these classes – 'become conscious' of their class conflict 'and fight it out'.

But this collective reality, to which Marx begins to refer very early on (the concept of a dominant ideology associated with the dominant class appears as early as *The German Ideology*), was something he never attempted *to think*. No doubt, he believed that he had, in principle, acquitted himself of that task with his 'theory of fetishism', which has indeed served generations of Marxists as a theory of ideologies. Confronted with this theoretical vacuum filled by a fictitious theory (that of fetishism–alienation), those who have undertaken to produce an explanation of this ideal [*idéal*] social reality have produced very disappointing statements. Thus we find ideology explained in psycho-sociological terms in Plekhanov. The explanation is altogether disarming, because it is redundant: to explain the social nature of ideology, Plekhanov contents himself with the term 'social mentality' [*conscience sociale*], regarded as a godsend by sociologists, those with a Marxist bent not excepted.[144] Gramsci – at least in my opinion – has not contributed much of importance on the question; he is content to emphasize that the function of ideology is to serve a social group as a 'unifying "cement"' (something that Durkheim and others had already said), and happily replaces the question of ideology with that of 'culture'. In this way, Gramsci pulls Marx's innovations 'back into line', back on to the well-trodden paths of the philosophy of his day, which revived a theme that had been previously 'worked up' by Hegel and all of German Idealism, from Kant to Goethe, Fichte and Schelling.

It may safely be said that Marx basically never abandoned the conviction that *ideology consists of ideas*, and that, to understand an ideology, it suffices to have three absolute terms of reference: first, *consciousness* (which Marx was careful not to call 'social'), and then *ideas*, with the whole – as is, of course, fitting for a good materialist – brought into relation to, and compared with, the '*real*': the real conditions of the existing subject, whether it is an individual, a class, or even a 'society'. Whence the materialist precept that no individual, class, society or historical period should be judged by its 'self-consciousness'.

This recommendation implies the primacy of the real over consciousness, of 'social being over social' (and individual) 'consciousness'. It further implies that one can distinguish consciousness from being, and thus presupposes a certain conception of ideological distortion, as either simple distortion or inversion (the way the image is inverted on the retina or by the *camera obscura*). But 'distortion' and 'inversion' (typical of the ideological relation for Marx) did not give rise, any more than 'commodity fetishism' did, to any theoretical explanation at all, except for the appeal to alienation, which was conceived of in terms that were borrowed directly from Feuerbach, and were vague or precise, depending on the case. It is no accident that so many Marxists have fallen back on fetishism to account for ideological alienation: this is consistent with the logic of the 'operation' that Marx attempted in order to think these two 'material appearances' in terms, precisely, of an idealist philosophical 'operation'.

At any event, the real was real, and the ideas of ideology were *merely ideas*. To the transparency of consciousness, therefore, there corresponded the transparency of ideas. Despite all the difficulties with which concrete history confronted Marx – as he realized, for example, in *The Eighteenth Brumaire* – and despite all the problems thrown up by the existence of the 'illusions', not only of 'most economists', but of most politicians and ordinary people as well,[q] Marx never felt any

q The 'illusions' sustained by the Gotha Programme provide an example.

need to quit the philosophical domain from which he drew *both* consciousness *and* ideas, skilfully combining them in order to obtain the effect of distortion he was after. Although he manifestly believed that the ideologies bear a relation to practice, or 'the interests' of groups or classes, Marx never crossed 'the absolute limit' of the material existence of ideologies, of their material existence in the materiality of the class struggle. He did not say the contrary; rather, he said nothing at all about the material existence of ideology. He remained on the hither side of this 'limit', which, as one of the falsely 'self-evident truths' that he accepted, was, in his view, not a limit at all.

By suggesting that the ideologies could find this *material existence* in apparatuses that are tendentially linked to the state, I attempted – in a text that is already old and, in many respects, inept[145] – to cross this 'limit'. In the face of ideas that seemed very obvious at the time, I risked the suggestion that one could and should, if not systematically, then at least tendentially, approach ideologies *in terms of Ideological State Apparatuses.*

This suggestion was criticized on the grounds that it might be functionalism. Yet the 1970 notes to my essay[146] flagged that danger, and what I then saw as the means of avoiding it (thinking and affirming the primacy of class struggle over the ISAs). As a rule, readers eliminated all mention of the state from my formula (I*S*A), retaining only the term 'ideological apparatus', for obvious political reasons. My critics did not want to compromise, by association with the class values of the state, the 'values' at stake in the 'family', the 'school system', 'health care', 'architecture', the constitutional order, the news services, the press, culture, the Churches, the parties, the trade unions, and so on.

Moreover, it seemed that what I was suggesting had already been said, and said much better, by Gramsci (who did indeed raise the question of the '*material* infrastructure of the ideologies', but provided a rather mechanistic and economistic answer to it). The general assumption was that I was discussing the same thing in the same register.

It seems to me that Gramsci does not, in fact, have the same object in view as I did in making my remarks. Gramsci *never* talks about *Ideological State Apparatuses*; his term is 'hegemonic apparatuses'. This leaves a question hanging in midair: what produces, in Gramsci's apparatuses, Gramsci's hegemony-effect? Gramsci, in sum, defines his apparatuses in terms of their effect or result, *hegemony*, which is also poorly conceived. I, for my part, was attempting to define the ISAs in terms of their 'motor cause': ideology. Furthermore, Gramsci affirms that the hegemonic apparatuses are part of 'civil society' (which is nothing but *the whole set of them*, unlike traditional civil society, which is all of society *minus the state*), on the pretext that they are 'private'. Thinking, as he does, in terms of the distinction between public (the state) and private (civil society), Gramsci nevertheless does eventually come round, in one of those stupefying reversals that make one dizzy because they contradict, word for word, a formula he defends in the same breath, to saying that 'civil society … is the State' [*l'Etat … est la société civile*].[147] When one thinks in this perspective, one embarks on the adventures of, not the dialectic (Gramsci had plenty of them, and to spare – adventurous verbal manipulations, at any rate), but *hegemony*.

20. Hegemony According to Gramsci

It is not easy to understand the question of hegemony in Gramsci: to begin with, because one has to make out – behind his vocabulary and, especially, the varied, contradictory examples which he complacently adduces – what he is driving at and, not very convincingly, trying to say. It is not easy, again, because of Gramsci's *terminology*; on the question of the state, he owes almost nothing to Marx and Lenin (apart from the word 'hegemony'), but a great deal to Croce, Gentile and Mosca,[148] whom he naturally utilizes after his own fashion. It is even harder today, since Togliatti,[149] beginning in 1947, made Gramsci the official theoretician of the PCI, and now that countless philosophers, politicians, historians, Party leaders, and so on have tried to add something of their own to Gramsci's terminology, which has become something very much like the terminology of the Tower of Babel – with the proviso that the tower in question is under the control of another, the one from which the PCI's political watchmen keep a vigilant eye on these linguistic deviations. With all these reservations, and on condition that the reader consents to tolerate a few deviations from what has become a consecrated, hallowed vocabulary, I shall try to explain why Gramsci's way of attempting to cross the 'absolute limit' of Marx on Ideology and the State (the two problems are closely connected), at the price of profound hesitations and contradictions, is not the best.

To understand this, however, we have to go where Gramsci unexpectedly summons us, in order to subject us to an astonishingly simple problematic.[150] He has read Machiavelli (I shall discuss this at length elsewhere[151]) and learnt from him that a Prince (a true, classic Prince, or the Communist Party, the 'modern Prince' ...) is simultaneously 'man and beast', like the centaur which, in Greek mythology, educates the men who have to rule men. The Prince is, then, both man and lion; he is, then, Force (the lion) and morals or ethics (Gramsci, who knows Hegel by way of [***][152] and, above all, Croce and Gentile, loves to talk about ethics). It is on this basis that, after contradictions that Perry Anderson has analysed extremely well (in his *New Left Review* essay),[153] Gramsci invites us into his problematic on the state.

He is not holding too many cards. He has the state, with its two 'moments' or 'elements': namely, Force, and hegemony or consensus. He has 'civil society', which, for him, comprises the whole set of 'hegemonic apparatuses'; we do not know what they run on (a petrol engine runs on petrol; an Ideological State Apparatus runs on ideology; but what does a hegemonic apparatus run on?). And that is all! That is all; for Gramsci, who cannot be unaware of the existence of the 'infrastructure', hence of production and the state-determined [*étatique*] conditions of production (law, currency and control over the reproduction of social relations, hence of the class struggle, in the interests of the dominant class), does not discuss them. For him, obviously – apart from, after all, a certain echo of the class struggle in the simple evocation of Force and hegemony – the infrastructure and the state-determined conditions of exploitation and the reproduction of social relations have been put in brackets, so that the question of the state can and must be decided *for itself*, on the basis of the four concepts at his disposal, and without bringing the infrastructure into play. Gramsci is reluctant to refer to the infrastructure, for the Marxist distinction between infrastructure and superstructure seems to him to be, fundamentally, a mechanistic-economistic error on Marx's part.

We must be aware of this reservation[154] if we are to understand what will be played out between the state, hegemony, the hegemonic apparatuses and civil society. I shall not go into the details of the little game of swapping words and places in this match with four players; I shall go straight to the point.

The point is that, *in Gramsci, the 'moment' of Force is ultimately swallowed up by the moment of hegemony.* Gramsci offers us a long series of equivalents for force: coercion, violence and, of course, dictatorship (it is here that, in the Gramscian tradition of the Italian Party, the sleight of hand that Gerratana clearly perceived is brought off[155]), a dictatorship which has nothing to do, at this point in Gramsci's manipulations, with class dictatorship or class domination, but, rather, characterizes one of the 'moments' of the state, which has two. Similarly, Gramsci proposes a long series of equivalents for Hegemony: consensus, agreement, voluntary consent and non-violent leadership, with all the possible variants (active, passive, and so on). What is the reason for all this 'labour' on concepts that have been adopted arbitrarily, and taken more from the political scientist Mosca than from Marx and Lenin? The answer is that Gramsci hopes to arrive at a strategy for the workers' movement after the great failures represented, in his view, by the 'dictatorial' political form dominant in the USSR, *and* the success of fascism in Italy, Germany and Japan, *and* Roosevelt's New Deal policies in America.

Thus what presents itself, in Gramsci, as a 'theory of the state' (or, rather, what has been taken for a theory of the state for precisely identifiable political reasons) seems to me more closely akin to *a political examination of the 'nature', hence of the 'composition' or internal arrangement [dispositif] of the states of the day, undertaken with a view to defining a political strategy for the workers' movement* after all hope that the schema of 1917 would be repeated had faded, and after these states had been marked by the transformation inflicted on them by the development of imperialism – by, that is, industrial and financial concentration.

Within the framework of this political 'in-depth study' [*auscultation*], the investigations carried out by Gramsci – who constantly alters his terminology, blithely contradicts himself, and *eventually comes to think everything in terms of the category of Hegemony* – may make some sense at the political level; although this is not always certain[156] in view of their abstraction, which is such that they can always be filled with pious contents. In any case, the real reasons commanding the definition of 'civil society' and its private hegemonic apparatuses; the distinction between, and subsequent identification of, 'political society' (the state) and 'civil society'; and, finally, the absorption of political and civil society by the single category of 'Hegemony' – and, consequently, the reasons commanding these strange theoretical concepts that cannot be distinctly defined without inconsistency – are to be sought in the famous theory of the war of movement (frontal attacks, as on the Winter Palace in 1917 Russia) and of position (in which one conquers, inch by inch, and over the long term, the trenches and fortifications of 'civil society', which protect the state from a great distance).[157]

As has often been pointed out, to reduce the extraordinary complexity of the events of 1917 in Russia, or to describe the Tsarist state as being 'too powerful' for a 'gelatinous' civil society,[158] involves outrageous simplifications that are difficult to defend. But Gramsci needed this excess (accompanied by all the classic inanities about the backwardness of both Russian society and the Russian state) as a foil. It enabled him to propose another 'political line', that of the war of position, a long-term war which involves conquering, step by step, the 'fortifications and trenches' constituting the glacis of any proper, normal state, governed by 'the proper balance' between Force and hegemony – that is, of a state in which 'hegemony [is] armoured with coercion'.[159]

The idea that a strategy of long-term struggle is required to ensure the hegemony of the workers' movement over its allies (this is the sense in which Lenin uses the term 'hegemony') – that is to say, over social elements that belong not just to the working class, but include rural workers as well as members of the productive or salaried petty bourgeoisie – is a classical thesis of the Marxist tradition. The idea that this struggle therefore takes as its objective the conquest of positions in *both* the infrastructure *and* the superstructure, or even of the 'associations' that Gramsci restrictively designates as 'civil society', contains nothing that is genuinely new. The novelty that Gramsci introduces is, rather, the idea that Hegemony can, as it were, *be representative of the whole constituted by* (1) *'civil society'* (which is its domain); (2) *the state as Force or coercion;* and (3) *the effect, also called Hegemony, that results from the functioning of the state as a whole*, comprising, be it recalled, Force and Hegemony.

In other words, hegemony is inscribed twice, or even three times, in the Gramscian scheme. The initial hegemony is that of the private 'hegemonic apparatuses' (the school system, Church, trade unions, and so on) which induce acceptance, without violence, of the power of the state, and, behind it, of the dominant class. This initial Hegemony (H1) is, let us recall, one of the two moments of the state, the one that coexists with Force. The second hegemony (H2) is the effect of the hegemony of the state itself considered in its entirety – that is to say, the effect of the 'well-balanced' union, in a proper state, of Force and Hegemony (H1). Force has not disappeared from this conception of hegemony, but it is so well 'enveloped' by hegemony, integrated in hegemony (H2), that, ultimately, there is no need for it to be displayed or exercised. There we have the beautiful state, the ethical state, which functions like a beautiful organism, whose 'organic intellectuals' see to it that the hegemonic apparatuses of 'civil society' operate smoothly. Yet there is a third form of Hegemony: that of the party of the working class, which ensures that the Party can lead, without the use of force, both its members and its allies, and, without using any force at all, extend its influence beyond its limits, and, ultimately, over … the whole of 'civil society', and even 'political society'. If we carry this line of reasoning to its logical conclusion, we will conclude that *everything can be played out at the level of Hegemony*: first, the Hegemony of the working class, its party, and its allies; second, the Hegemony exercised by the dominant class by means of the state; and, finally, the Hegemony-effect that the dominant class derives from the unity of Force and Hegemony in its state ('civil society'). In this case, it would be legitimate to speak in terms of a '*conflict of Hegemony*'; or – to go even further, since the two Hegemonies are united in One[160] – it would be necessary to speak in terms of a '*crisis of Hegemony*', as if Hegemony were an entity that absorbed within itself, and summed up in itself, all the conflicts and contradictions of 'society'. In this perspective it is readily understandable that, throughout the class struggle, we are, in the last instance, never dealing with anything *other than a contradiction internal to Hegemony*, and that this ultimate contradiction, which sums up all other struggles, can undergo a radical reversal [*basculer*] purely as a result of its crisis.

It is all too obvious that this ingenious, ambiguous 'montage' can be construed to mean that Gramsci is talking about class struggle, so that, at this level, the term 'Hegemony' clearly designates class domination, that is to say, what Marx and Lenin called class dictatorship, either bourgeois or proletarian. This 'reading' would consequently authorize a 'left' reading of Gramsci, a Leninist interpretation of him. But it would come at the very high cost of a strange silence about the reality of the economic, political and ideological class struggles. They are represented in this scheme in the form of a Hegemony-effect alone, and at the price of the absolute idealism of *a Hegemony lacking a material basis*, with no explanation of the Coercive Apparatuses which nevertheless play an active part in engendering the Hegemony-effect.

In reality, this ambiguity has pushed most of Gramsci's commentators into making 'right-wing interpretations', which are, moreover, authorized by the fact that Gramsci almost completely hides the infrastructure behind the arbitrary concept of a private 'civil society', and therefore also hides both reproduction and the class struggle, with its different levels and its stake, the state. The Force of the state is accordingly regarded as virtually nil, since it is fully integrated into the Hegemony-effect. Hence everything in this fluid model is played out within the abstraction of 'Hegemony'. It is not only the supreme effect, but also the supreme cause, since it is the cause of itself and, simultaneously, the effect of itself; for we are told nothing about what causes it. Moreover, it has extraordinary power, since it needs only go into crisis (or is it always in crisis?) for the domination of the dominant class to begin to totter and then collapse.

To be realistic, we have to say that Gramsci's reasoning in all his celebrated texts is not, in fact, that of someone who is ignorant either of *Capital* or of Marx's and Lenin's theses on the state; it is the reasoning of a politician who thinks that everything which occurs in the infrastructure, reproduction and the class struggle *can be bracketed out*, i.e., that these realities may be treated as *constants*. The pathetic little tag to the effect that 'hegemony is born in the factory'[161] is hardly sufficient to counterbalance this conclusion, for, even if we give Gramsci's 'repetitive discourse' on the state the benefit of the doubt, it is clear that the Hegemony he discusses begins nowhere, for it has no 'beginning'.

The idea that it might be not merely possible, but actually necessary, *to decipher everything that happens* not just in the infrastructure, reproduction and the class struggle, but also in law and the state (Force + Hegemony), *exclusively at the level of what Gramsci calls Hegemony* in his discussion of the 'crisis of Hegemony'; the idea that it is possible to decipher everything about the terribly material nature of production and exploitation (hence of the class struggle in production) and the terribly material nature of the constraints and practices of the law, of the political and ideological class struggles, by referring exclusively to the reality that Gramsci christens Hegemony (without telling us just what the word might mean!) is an astoundingly idealist notion.[162]

This impression is redoubled when we ask just what the specific meaning of the term 'Hegemony' might be. The root of the word signifies a form of 'leadership' [*direction*] that is not dictatorship, coercion or domination. It suggests the idea of an effect of voluntary consensus. Let us put to one side the fact that this effect of voluntary consensus can just as easily be produced – to repeat the Aristotelian and Hegelian distinctions that constantly peek through Gramsci's writing and thought – by a good state (the 'ethical state') as by a bad one (brute Force + gelatinous civil society). The fact remains that this consensus can as readily be produced by naked Force, Force cloaked in beguiling discourse, or elegant rhetoric or elegant sophistry, as by a truth that is voluntarily set out and voluntarily consented to for the reason of its truth. Rousseau long ago said, of a brigand at the edge of a wood, that 'the pistol he holds is also a power'[163] – of dissuasion, of conviction, and thus of consensus. He added that the sophistic discourse of the philosophers of his day produced the same effect of deceptive consensus. But it would be too easy to have it out with Gramsci at this level of argument.

We must trace matters further back: to the old Hegelian idea, adopted by Croce and Gentile, that the *state is, by its nature, an educator*,[164] and that men become men, that is to say, are educated, only under constraint – an argument that can be defended; but also that mass education [*Bildung*] is the ideal which humanity sets itself as its ultimate task. With this, we begin to understand Gramsci's strange fondness for the idealist phrase in the Preface to the *Contribution* to the effect that 'mankind inevitably sets itself only such tasks as it is able to solve' – in Gramsci's case, as in that of all idealists, one would have to say 'as it *must* [*doit*] solve'. However surprising it may seem, Gramsci has not got beyond the Hegeliano–Crocean conception of culture as the ultimate End of Humanity, and therefore the ultimate task of Humanity. Moreover, as in Hegel or Croce, the state is plainly the 'instrument' foreordained to accomplish this task and this End. Hence we can understand the *process of the sublimation of the state into Hegemony* that unfolds before our very eyes in so many of Gramsci's texts, along with his catchphrases about the state. No doubt some constraint is required – fundamentally, a *measure* of constraint in general [*de la contrainte*] – in order to transform 'uneducated' men – whether improperly educated, or poorly educated – into educated men, endowed with *Bildung*. That is why Force figures in the state, even if Gramsci never feels the need to show us where it is lodged, what it is made of, and how it is exercised. Force, however, is as discreet as it is only because there are better things to do than to use or display it: Hegemony (H1) is far superior, since it obtains the same result of 'training' (Gramsci's word) as Force, at lower cost, and, what is more, simultaneously anticipates the results of 'culture' itself. In hegemony (that of the 'apparatuses of civil society'), one learns without violence and solely by virtue of one's recognition of … the truth. It is this nostalgic notion that Gramsci has literally sublimated in the notion of Hegemony (in the second sense), by granting himself a conception of the state as the kind of educator that realizes the ideal of a *universal self-cultivation*. It cannot, to be sure, come about without the 'mediations' indispensable to any teleological system, but it is essentially achieved 'without violence', if not without 'pain'. In this self-cultivation (*Selbstbildung*: self-training, self-education, and so on) is realized the supersession, in the Hegelian sense [*Aufhebung*], of all Force. Hence it is all too clear that Force disappears from the ultimate 'definition' of the state as the 'unity of the state and civil society', of the state as Hegemony, and, finally, of Hegemony all by itself (since the state itself has been 'superseded'). Thus Gramsci confesses his profoundest idea. Fortunately for us, it is contradicted by other views of his.

There is no need to linger over the conception of the working-class political party that Gramsci goes on to develop. The End and Task of this 'modern Prince' is the 'regulated society' (!) known as communism. But it will not attain it unless it plays, as a party, its pre-state role, by educating its members and the masses over whom it extends its 'leadership', its 'hegemony'. Just like the state, the Party has to educate men, with a view, once the revolution has been made and 'the party has become the state',[165] to ensuring the triumph of the End of humanity in this regulated society in which Hegemony, its Hegemony, will continue to rule, until it vanishes before the end result of universal cultivation become self-cultivation: the infinite development of free individuals in free association.

To espouse these views of Gramsci's is not without consequences. I shall mention only three.

The first consists in making the specific problems of the state quite literally disappear. Yet we have seen just how important they are if one wishes to retain the crucial idea that the state is a 'special machine' possessing a special body and destined to be the 'instrument' of the dominant class in order to serve, guarantee and perpetuate its class domination. The specific reality of the state clearly does disappear in a formula in which Hegemony = Force + consensus, or political society + civil society,[166] and so on. When the realities of class struggle are treated *in the guise of Hegemony-effects alone*, it is obviously no longer necessary to scrutinize *either* the nature *or* the function of the state as a 'special machine'. In particular, one brackets out (and here it is difficult to imagine that the function of these apparatuses is stable!) the state apparatuses of Force (the army, the police, the other forces responsible for maintaining pubic order, the apparatuses of the courts, and so on). This is hardly serious – unless we assume that all these realities can be *regarded as nonexistent because they have been cancelled out of the equation, politically and historically.* Here we again meet the presupposition mentioned a moment ago. I just said that, in Gramsci, it is quite as if the infrastructure and its effects were treated as nonexistent or constant, and therefore cancelled out, since, at the level of the state, and contrary to the famous phrase of Marx's in Volume Three of *Capital*, we no longer have to take into account the determination of the state on the basis of the productive relation. Similarly, in the present instance, it is quite as if Gramsci's argument, about the state this time, were predicated on the absolute hypothesis that the state apparatus exercises a constant effect, that is, has effectively been cancelled out.

Yet it is rather facile to suppose that the state is cancelled out [*neutralisé*] (a formula which, it will be granted, can easily be transformed into the bourgeois idea that the state is neutral ...). And the paradox is that this consequence can be deduced from texts by a man who had to jot them down in a school notebook after being condemned to the harshest of prisons by a fascist state.... It is so facile that it is not very serious. In building up his arguments in *Capital*, Marx assumes that one and then another variable is constant, but he does so for the sake of the argument; after finishing the demonstration that he has set out to make, he corrects the assumption that such-and-such a variable could be cancelled out, precisely because the variable in question *is not neutral.* Strikingly, Gramsci never rectifies the presupposition that the state or the infrastructure can be treated as neutral. This is no doubt proof – as the diversity of the historical examples he cites makes superabundantly clear – that he had in mind a model of the elements of the state, and of their unity amid the difference of these elements, balanced or not, which he treated as the essence of any possible state. Yet, paradoxically, he had his sights trained on very disparate modern states.

It does not much matter which arguments are brought to bear here. They all boil down to the fact that, since Gramsci talks about a 'crisis of Hegemony', and thus about Hegemony itself as if it were the last word on the state, the effect of his little formulas is to hide the question of the material nature of the state-machine behind a hyper-allusive invocation of Hegemony. This breeds all manner of misunderstanding. It can also give rise to every imaginable sort of reformist lucubration about the nature of the state and the 'development of the party into the state'.

These views naturally culminate in the reduction of ideology to culture, or, more exactly, in a theory of the nonexistence of ideology (except as a 'cement' for groups of men, with no mention of classes) and the exaltation of the theoretical value of a notion that is altogether vacuous, the notion of 'culture'. Moreover, Gramsci does not identify, at least not directly, the specific element designated by the notion of culture that cannot be located within the notion of ideology. Anyone can imagine the consequences, political consequences included, which can flow from *replacing the notion of ideology with that of culture*: the intellectuals of the Italian Party are living proof of them. For if ideology rather quickly comes to mean ideological struggle, hence an inevitable, necessary form of class struggle, the notion of culture leads straight to the ecumenism of the notion that an elite (in the Party as well as in bourgeois society) is the guardian of culture's own values of 'production' ('creators') and consumption ('connoisseurs', 'art-lovers', and so on). I shall not labour the point; it would be too easy.

We can draw another consequence, perhaps still more serious, from Gramsci's nebulous treatment of both the state and private 'civil society', as well as of the sublimation of the state into Hegemony. It is what has traditionally been called, and for a long time now, '*the autonomy of politics*' or 'of the political'. I did nothing more than give its philosophical name to this thesis, inevitable in Gramsci's system of thought, when I said that, in the final analysis, Hegemony (in sense no. 2) as the sublimation of the unity of 'political society' (the state) and 'civil society', had necessarily to present itself as '*causa sui*', as that reality which, encompasssing everything, has no outside. But this 'practical autonomy of hegemony' is reproduced in the practical autonomy of its 'essence': since everything is political, Hegemony is for Gramsci the high point, the summa and the summit of politics. Gramsci is political through and through, and he says so. As we have seen, he is political to the point of thinking the political question of the strategy of the future workers' movement (at least in our societies, which have struck 'the proper balance between Force and Hegemony' [in sense no. 1]) in terms of the manipulation and modification of concepts taken over from bourgeois political science and haunted, in their fashion, by class struggle. In his views on the state, its two moments, and, especially, in his views on Hegemony as encompassing the two moments of the state – in, therefore, Hegemony – Gramsci remains just as political, just as universally political ('everything is political'). The difference is that, in his final theory of Hegemony, he actually declares that, for him, politics (and the politician, its agent) are *causa sui*, autonomous – and *by rights*, or, rather, by destiny. That 'everything is political' by no means contradicts 'the autonomy of politics', since, as is shown by the sublimation of the whole reality of the state (and, as a result of Gramsci's silences, of the superstructure and even the infrastructure) into Hegemony, it is the autonomy of this Hegemony which embraces everything: 'everything is political'. It thus coincides with the autonomy of all politics, and thus proclaims, beyond the shadow of a doubt, 'the autonomy of politics'.

There is a great deal to be said about this thesis of the autonomy of the political or of politics, particularly about the fact that it can be understood neither as the autonomy of the party from the masses in the class struggle, nor as that of political leaders in the life of the Party, and so on. Yet the fact is that this aberrant thesis brings us to the threshold of another 'absolute limit' of Marxist thought: namely, its inability to think 'politics'. It will be objected that this is to court paradox: the work of Marx and Lenin is full of 'politics'. It is indeed full of politics, full of political analyses. But our authors have never given us, except in the form of lists or descriptions, even the rudiments of an analysis responding to the question: *just what might politics be?* Where is politics to be found? In what forms? What distinguishes it from non-political forms, and how then should we designate these other forms? Unless we broach these questions, we risk remaining, for a long time yet, 'in the night in which all cows are grey'. And, colour for colour, our hands will most assuredly not be white.

For to ask what politics might be implies that one state one's views on the Party. But what does one do in the Party, if not politics?[167]

Notes

1 'Ce qui ne peut plus durer dans le Parti communiste français', *Le Monde*, 24–27 April 1978; 'What Must Change in the Party', trans. Patrick Camiller, *New Left Review*, no. 109, May–June 1978, pp. 19–45. Althusser published a slightly revised version of his text in book form in May 1978. [*Trans.*]

2 Gérard Duménil's *Le Concept de loi économique dans Le Capital*, Paris, 1978; 'CM'; 'MT'. [*Trans.*]

3 This is a literal translation of the French title of a paper (translated into English as 'CM') that Althusser delivered in Italian at a November 1977 conference in Venice.

4 Lenin, 'Opportunism and the Collapse of the Second International', *LCW* 21: 438–53.

5 The first draft reads 'the most serious conflicts'.

6 At the Twentieth Congress of the CPSU, Nikita Khrushchev delivered his 'secret speech' on 'Stalin's crimes'.

7 These were the main counts in Khrushchev's indictment of the practices of the Stalinist period. In addition to 'Marxism and Humanism' (*FM* 219–47) and 'Note on "The Critique of the Personality Cult"' (appended to 'RTJL' 115–32), Althusser wrote two texts on alienation and the 'personality cult' in 1964, both of them more overtly political than the published texts. He worked for a long time on these two manuscripts, but finished neither.

8 The Chinese Communist Party's official break with the Soviet Party sealed the 1963 'split in the international Communist movement'.

9 Althusser published an anonymous essay on the Chinese Cultural Revolution, 'Sur la révolution culturelle', in *Cahiers marxistes-léninistes*, no. 14, November–December 1966, pp. 5–16.

10 The first draft reads 'crisis of Marxism'.

11 In the 1980 'Livre sur le communisme' (A28–03.05, p. 1), Althusser attributes this phrase to Jacques Derrida. The allusion is to the 'New Philosophers' and especially to André Glucksmann's *The Master Thinkers*, trans. Brian Pearce, Brighton, 1980 (1977), pp. 120–2. A number of Althusser's letters indicate that while he considered Glucksmann's book a very poor one, he was hurt by the tone of the attacks on him contained in it; he felt that Glucksmann had caricatured him, presenting him as what he had always feared he might become – an intellectual tyrant.

12 A slogan of George Marchais's, Secretary General of the PCF at the time Althusser was writing 'Marx in his Limits'.

13 'Count on your own strength', a slogan of Mao Zedong's famous in its day.

14 See 'What Must Change in the Party', pp. 41–2.

15 'The main tendency is towards revolution', a slogan of Mao Zedong's famous in its day.

16 In a 2–3 November 1882 letter to Edouard Bernstein (trans. Peter and Betty Ross, *MECW* 46: 356), Engels reports that Marx once said this, in French, to Lafargue. See also Engels, Letter of 5 August 1890 to Conrad Schmidt, in Marx and Engels, *Selected Correspondence*, 3rd edn, ed. S. W. Ryazanskaya, trans. I. Lasker, Moscow, 1975, p. 393; and Karl Kautsky, 'Mein zweiter Aufenthalt in London', in Benedikt Kautsky, ed., *Friedrich Engels' Briefwechsel mit Karl Kautsky*, Vienna, 1955, p. 90.

17 *C1* 90, 93.

18 Marx, *Grundrisse*, trans. Martin Nicolaus, Harmondsworth, 1973, pp. 471–514. Althusser's extended correspondence with the management of the PCF publishing house Éditions sociales – especially in 1966–67 with its director, Guy Besse – testifies to his intention to publish this section of the *Grundrisse* (often abbreviated '*Formen*') in the collection 'Théorie' at a time when the text had not yet appeared in French. After having it translated, he gave up the idea of publishing it himself at the request of Éditions sociales, to which he had sent the translation on 13 August 1966. Éditions sociales ultimately published a different translation in the collection *Sur les sociétés précapitalistes* (Paris, 1970). As Althusser's letters show, this experience left him with the impression that he had been taken for a ride.

19 Marx, Letter of 17 April 1867 to Johann Philipp Becker, *MECW* 42:358. [*Trans.*]

20 Althusser would appear to be thinking of a passage from a review of *Capital* that Marx approvingly cites in the Postface to the second German edition (*C1* 101–2); the reviewer, I. I. Kaufman, says that criticism consists, for Marx, in 'confronting and comparing a fact with another fact'. [*Trans.*]

21 'Communism is for us not a *state of affairs* which is to be established, an *ideal* to which reality [will] have to adjust itself. We call communism the *real* movement which abolishes the present state of things. The conditions of this movement result from the now existing premise'. Marx and Engels, *The German Ideology*, trans. Clemens Dutt *et al.*, *MECW* 5: 49.

22 *C1* 98. [*Trans.*]

23 In what he would later call his 'theoreticist' period, Althusser took a position that was at the opposite extreme from the one he defends in this chapter. See 'Theory, Theoretical Practice, and Theoretical Formation', trans. James H. Kavanagh, *PSPS* 16 (an essay that remains unpublished in French): 'Marxist-Leninist science, which serves the objective interests of the working class, could not be the spontaneous product of proletarian practice; it was produced by the theoretical practice of intellectuals possessing a very high degree of culture (Marx, Engels, Lenin), and "introduced from without" into proletarian practice.' See also *SH* 246.

24 *Kritisch-revolutionär*: *C1* 103. The line of the *Internationale* to which Althusser is alluding runs: 'le monde va changer de base': literally, 'the world

will change its base'. The equivalent line in the most common English version of the *Internationale* is 'the earth shall rise on new foundations'.

25 Best known for his *History and Constitution of the Icarian Community* (trans. Thomas Teakle, New York, 1975), Étienne Cabet (1788–1856) came under the influence of Robert Owen after emigrating to England during the July monarchy. He subsequently attempted to found communal settlements in Illinois and Missouri.

26 Wilhelm Weitling (1807–71), a tailor, is one of the major figures of German 'utopian communism'. Among his works are *Garantien der Harmonie und der Freiheit* (1842), a book Marx held in high esteem, and *The Poor Sinner's Gospel.* Marx broke with Weitling in 1846.

27 The first draft reads 'from a proletarian point of view'.

28 Marx, Letter of 5 March 1852 to Joseph Weydemeyer, trans. Peter and Betty Ross, *MECW* 39: 62, 65.

29 'P' 264.

30 This and the following interpolation are Althusser's.

31 Karl Kautsky, 'On the New Draft Programme of the Austrian Social-Democratic Party', *Die Neue Zeit*, 20, 1901–02, I, no. 3, p. 79, cited in Lenin, *What Is To Be Done?*, trans. Joe Fineberg and George Hanna, *LCW* 5: 383–4. Althusser quotes the text from the French translation of Lenin's *What Is To be Done?* published in Moscow.

32 The organ of the Russian Social-Democratic Workers' Party and, subsequently, the Bolshevik Party.

33 1904–05.

34 Lenin, 'Preface to the Collection *Twelve Years*', trans. Bernard Isaacs, *LCW* 13: 101–2, 107–8. The translation has been modified to bring it into line with Althusser's. The interpolations are Althusser's. [*Trans.*]

35 The manuscript reads 'Trotsky'.

36 This paragraph is an addendum inserted into the manuscript by Althusser.

37 See *FM* 63–4: 'If the problem of Marx's Early Works is really to be posed, the first condition to fulfil is to admit that *even philosophers* are young men for a time. They must be born somewhere, sometime, and begin to think and write.'

38 Auguste Cornu, *Karl Marx et Friedrich Engels*, vol. 3, Paris, 1962. Althusser took most of his biographical information about Marx and Engels from this work. He dedicated 'On the Young Marx', included in *FM*, to Cornu.

39 'P' 264. [*Trans.*]

40 Engels, 'Outlines of a Critique of Political Economy', *MECW* 1.

41 *FM* 28.

42 'Hegelianized' is a handwritten addendum to the manuscript.

43 'Not only does Proudhon write in the interest of the proletarians, he is himself a proletarian, an *ouvrier*. His work is a scientific manifesto of the French proletariat.' Marx, *The Holy Family*, trans. Richard Dixon and Clemens Dutt, *MECW* 4: 41.

44 'P' 265.

45 Marx, 'Introduction to *Outlines of the Critique of Political Economy*', trans. Ernst Wangermann, *MECW* 28: 17–48.

46 The translation in *C1* 95 is more accurate: 'the appreciation which *Das Kapital* rapidly gained in wide circles of the German working class is the best reward of my labours'.

47 *C1* 112.

48 Marx's 1875 'Critique of the Gotha Programme' was first published, by Engels, in *Die Neue Zeit* of 31 January 1891.

49 Karl Kautsky, *Les Trois Sources de la pensée de Karl Marx* (1907), Paris, 2000; Lenin, 'The Three Sources and the Three Component Parts of Marxism', trans. George Hanna, *LCW* 19: 23–8.

50 Compare Hegel's *Phenomenology of Mind*, trans. A. V. Miller, Oxford, 1977, p. 56; *Hegel's Logic*, trans. William Wallace, Oxford, 1975, §25. Althusser was fond of the Hegelian phrase 'behind its back', citing it from memory in his 1947 Master's Thesis, 'On Content in the Thought of G. W. F. Hegel' (*SH* 111) and giving it a prominent place in the 1976 'La Transformation de la philosophie' (*Sur la philosophie*, Paris, 1994, p. 153). [The passage referred to here was included in the Spanish version of 'La Transformation de la philosophie', on which the English translation was based, but was edited out of the published English translation (see 'TP' 249). It has been incorporated into 'Philosophy and Marxism'; see p. 275 below.]

51 In *Dialectical and Historical Materialism* (Moscow, 1941, p. 3), Stalin says that historical materialism is an 'extension' and 'application of the principles' of dialectical materialism. [*Trans.*]

52 See esp. Engels, *Herr Eugen Dühring's Revolution in Science* [*Anti-Dühring*], trans. Emile Burns, *MECW* 25: 125–9.

53 *C3* 959 ff, 1016 ('the full development of individuality'); Paul Lafargue, *Le Droit à la paresse* (1881).

54 Marx, 'Marginal Notes on Adolph Wagner's *Lehrbuch der politischen Oekonomie*', trans. Barrie Selman, *MECW* 24: 531–59.

55 Engels, 'Foreword to *Ludwig Feuerbach and the End of Classical German Philosophy*', trans. anon., in Marx and Engels, *Selected Works*, Moscow, 1970, vol. 3, p. 336.

56 'P' 263.

57 *C1* 89.

58 Marx, 'Introduction to *Outlines of the Critique of Political Economy*',

MECW 28: 37–45. Let us note that the theory of 'theoretical practice' that Althusser put forward in his 1963 essay 'On the Materialist Dialectic' included in *FM* is based mainly on this text.

59 Althusser owned a copy of Galvano Della Volpe's *La Libertà communista*, Milan, 1963, containing a handwritten dedication by the author. He read one of the essays in it very closely; entitled 'Sulla dialectica', it focuses on Marx's 1859 Introduction.

60 'I have completely demolished the theory of profit as hitherto propounded. What was of great use to me as regards *method* of treatment was Hegel's Logic, at which I had taken another look by accident; Freiligrath having found and made me a present of several volumes of Hegel, originally the property of Bakunin. If ever the time comes when such work is again possible, I should very much like to write two or three sheets making accessible to the common reader the *rational* aspect of the method which Hegel not only discovered but also mystified.' Marx, Letter of 16 January 1858 to Engels, *MECW* 40: 249. [*Trans.*]

61 *C1* 321 ff.

62 'P' 261.

63 'The dialectic became the fashion in Germany, because it seemed to transfigure and glorify what exists.' (*C1* 103)

64 'The Marxist doctrine is omnipotent because it is true.' (Lenin, 'The Three Sources and the Three Component Parts of Marxism', *LCW* 19: 23).

65 'P' 263.

66 'It is this circumstance alone which has made it possible for Marx and myself not to disassociate ourselves publicly from a programme such as this.' Engels, Letter of 12 October 1875 to August Bebel, trans. Peter and Betty Ross, *MECW* 45: 98.

67 Engels, Letter of 18–28 March 1875 to August Bebel, trans. Peter and Betty Ross, *MECW* 45: 65, translation modified.

68 'I have spoken and saved my soul.' It is with this phrase that Althusser begins a text written in 1982 and incorporated into a manuscript partially published in the present volume under the title 'The Underground Current of the Materialism of the Encounter.' The 1982 text was posthumously published as 'Sur la pensée marxiste', *Futur antérieur*, special issue: *Passages, Paris*, 1993, 11–29. Too much of it has been drawn from 'Marx in his Limits' to warrant republication here.

69 'And could therefore also hold his tongue' is an addendum to the manuscript.

70 'Buried in the files' is an addendum to the manuscript.

71 Althusser mistakenly interpolates the word *Erfahrung*, and translates 'experience'; Marx wrote *Erforschung* ('study' or 'research into'). [*Trans.*]

72 'P' 261–3.

73 Althusser's translation, which differs somewhat from his 1969 translation of part of the same passage (see *SR* 244–5), is in fact rather similar to the one in Gilbert Badia and Maurice Husson, *Contribution à la Critique de l'Économie politique*, a text published by the PCF's publishing house, Éditions sociales, in 1957 to replace a translation by Jacques Molitor, which itself replaced one by Marx's daughter Laura Lafargue. Among the changes Althusser made in Badia and Husson's translation (which corresponds quite closely to the translation in *MECW* reproduced here), the following are noteworthy: 'the general conclusion at which I arrived' becomes 'the conclusion that offered itself up to me' [*qui s'offrit à moi*]; in the famous phrase, 'it is not the consciousness of men that determines their existence, but their social existence that determines their consciousness', Althusser twice substitutes 'conditions' for 'determines'; 'at a certain stage of development' becomes 'at a certain degree of their development'; 'determined with the precision of natural science' becomes 'that one can observe in a manner faithful to that of the natural sciences' [*qu'on peut constater fidèlement à la manière des sciences de la nature*]; 'no social order is ever destroyed before' becomes 'no social formation can ever die before' (furthermore, as in Badia and Husson's translation, the rest of the sentence, 'before all the productive forces for which it is sufficient [*für die sie weit genug ist*] have been developed' is rendered literally: 'before all the productive forces that it is large enough to contain'). It should also be noted that where the English translation used here has 'social order', Althusser's as well as Badia and Husson's translations have *formation sociale* (the German is *Gesellschaftsformation*).

The interpolations from the original German text are all Althusser's. [*Trans.*]

74 *Séparé*, which is both the past participle of *séparer*, to separate, and an adjective meaning 'separated'. [*Trans.*]

75 The first draft reads 'had been sly enough'.

76 The parenthetical phrase is in English in the original text.

77 The subtitle initially chosen by Feuerbach was *Contribution to the Critique of Pure Unreason*.

78 In 1836, Feuerbach married Bertha Löw, heir, along with other members of her family, to Brucherg Castle and the porcelain manufactory housed in it.

79 *Le genre humain*, which also means 'the human race', is often translated the 'human species' (whence 'species-being'). [*Trans.*]

80 The *sic* is Althusser's interpolation.

81 See Marx, Sixth Thesis on Feuerbach, *MECW* 5: 4: 'Feuerbach … is obliged … to abstract from the historical process'; or, again, Marx and Engels, *The German Ideology*, *MECW* 5: 41: 'As far as Feuerbach is a materialist he does not deal with history, and as far as he considers history, he is not a materialist.'

82 According to the Fifth Thesis on Feuerbach, 'Feuerbach, not satisfied with *abstract* thinking, wants [*sensuous*] *contemplation*, but he does not conceive sensuousness as *practical*, human-sensuous activity.' Cf. the First Thesis on Feuerbach, which runs: '[Feuerbach] regards the theoretical attitude as the only genuinely human attitude, while practice is conceived and defined only in its dirty-Jewish form of appearance.' *MECW* 5: 3.

83 Most of Marx's 'Contribution to the Critique of Hegel's Philosophy of Law' was first published in 1927.

84 The first draft reads 'rudiments'.

85 See especially 'The Historic Significance of the 22nd Congress', trans. Ben Brewster, *New Left Review*, no. 104, July–August 1977, pp. 3–22.

86 Timbaud and Michels were executed on 22 October 1941, along with other Communist internees selected for execution by the Interior Minister of the Vichy regime. [*Trans.*]

87 Francs-Tireurs et Partisans. See Charles Tillon, *Les FTP*, 2nd edn, Paris, 1967.

88 De Gaulle addressed this appeal to the French people from London on 18 June 1941. [*Trans.*]

89 Maurice Thorez was the General Secretary of the French Communist Party. Conscripted in 1939, he deserted and left for the USSR, where he remained until 1944. [*Trans.*]

90 The *Compagnie républicaine de sécurité*, the National Security police.

91 *C1* 340–416.

92 The manuscript contains the following paragraph, which Althusser ultimately dropped:

> Not once, not for a moment, was he willing to be party to any practice other than that of an appeal to the duties of the citizens *vis-à-vis* the state of the oppressed and humiliated French nation. In other words, he invoked – in other words, exploited – the values of the state: obey the legitimate state, the legitimate leader of the legitimate state, that of Free France, and refrain from engaging in politics, because if you, as soldiers, whether in uniform or not, engage in politics, the state will be torn asunder and perish. To be sure, this meant that he had to walk down a tightrope [*corde raide*], but De Gaulle had the stiffness of character [*raideur*] required, and it was from this stiffness of character that he drew his strength, as Churchill eventually learnt. Yet the fact is that this was the right card to play, because, playing it for all it was worth, De Gaulle finally came out on top, defeating even the organizations and fighters of the domestic resistance, who, for their part, did not all have quite the same 'appreciation of the state', since they, for their part, thought they had a right to 'engage in politics'. But their status was ambiguous, after all; they were not real soldiers, as De Gaulle brought home to them in no uncertain fashion when, amid the

confusion of ranks characteristic of the Résistance, he compelled them to accept demotions and fall back into line.

93 A big scandal involving international corruption which, among other things, led Prince Bernhard of the Netherlands to resign from all his public offices.

94 Maurice Grimaud, *En mai, fais ce qu'il te plaît*, Paris, 1977. Grimaud was chief of police in Paris at the time of the May 'events', in which he played a key role.

95 The first draft reads 'an inanity'.

96 The first draft reads 'albeit by different means'.

97 Lenin, 'The State: A Lecture Delivered at the Sverdlov University, July 11, 1919', trans. anon., *LCW* 29: 470–88. A French translation of this text may be found in an appendix to Étienne Balibar, *Sur la dictature du prolétariat*, Paris, 1976. Althusser's library included the volume of the French edition of Lenin's collected works containing the lecture on the state as well as Balibar's book; he extensively annotated the text in both.

98 The first draft reads 'like the Paris Municipal Museum of Modern Art'. The *Conseil d'État* or Council of State is the highest administrative tribunal in France.

99 Marx was in fact born in 1818. [*Trans.*]

100 Charles Babbage (1792–1871) was an English mathematician and mechanical engineer; he was the author of *On the Economy of Machinery and Manufacture* (2nd edn London, 1882), among other works. This sentence is quoted in *C1* 497n.

101 *C1*, p. 494 (Althusser's emphasis).

102 The question of the dictatorship of the proletariat was one of Althusser's central concerns in the 1975–78 period. He discusses it in 'The Historic Significance of the 22nd Congress', and in a number of lectures that he gave on the subject in France and Spain. He also devoted a typed, repeatedly revised 215-page manuscript to it: *Les Vaches noires: Interview imaginaire.*

103 The first draft reads 'but something necessitated by class relations'.

104 *C3* 926.

105 Ibid. (Althusser's emphasis.)

106 Ibid., 927–8 (Althusser's emphasis throughout the passage).

107 The first draft reads 'we know a little something about'.

108 The blanks are to be found in Althusser's manuscript. Compare 'the hand-mill gives you society with the feudal lord; the steam-mill, society with the industrial capitalist' (Marx, *The Poverty of Philosophy: Answer to the Philosophy of Poverty by M. Proudhon*, trans. Frida Knight., *MECW* 6: 166).

109 *EI* 1–60.

110 See note 97 on this page.

111 French civil servants are organized into corps. Throughout 'Marx in his Limits', Althusser plays on the fact that *corps* also means 'body'. Thus the literal meaning of *l'esprit de corps* is 'the spirit of the body', while the French equivalent of 'the body of the state', *le corps de l'État*, silently evokes the *corps* of civil servants. [*Trans.*]
112 Althusser originally wrote *violence publique*, which he deleted and replaced by *force publique*. [*Trans.*]
113 The *grands corps* are the highest state agencies and administrations: the Council of State, the diplomatic corps, the tax inspectorate, and so on. [*Trans.*]
114 In France, public school teachers, from primary school to university, are civil servants. [*Trans.*]
115 Louis Hubert Gonzalves Lyautey, a French Marshall and Minister of War who served mainly in the colonies. [*Trans.*]
116 See note 94.
117 I have changed Althusser's examples (*machine à percussion* and *machine à impression*) for the sake of readability. [*Trans.*]
118 In the manuscript, *par* (by) has been deleted and replaced by *sur* (on); the original reading has been retained here. [*Trans.*]
119 See p. 84 above.
120 The first draft reads 'contradictory'. Althusser uses the phrase *différence conflictuelle* in a similar sense in 'ISMBP?', 205 ('*une philosophie … n'existe donc que par sa différence conflictuelle*', *SM* 201); the English translation reads: 'a philosophy … exists only in so far as … conflict has made it something distinct'. [*Trans.*]
121 Althusser is alluding to the 1908 song *Gloire au 17ème*, by Gaston Montheus (Mardochée Brunswick). The song pays homage to the soldiers of the 17th regiment who rebelled against their officers at Agde in June 1907 rather than fire on striking winegrowers. Montheus also composed *La Jeune garde*, a song much in vogue on the French Left in the 1960s.
122 Enrico Berlinguer, General Secretary of the Italian Communist Party from 1972 to 1983, wrote a series of 1973 articles in *Rinascita* on the defeat of the Popular Unity government in Chile that justified the new PCI strategy of 'historic compromise' with Italy's Christian Democrats. See Berlinguer, *La questione comunista*, Rome, 1975, vol. 2, 632–3.
123 The salaries, pensions, employment conditions, possibilities for career advancement, etc., of French civil servants are governed by conventions [*régimes*] that vary with the category of public service. Among the advantages all these conventions confer, besides guaranteed employment, are regular bonuses and pensions determined in accordance with rules rather more generous than those applied to private sector employees. Among the perquisites reserved for the elite *grands corps* are sizeable bonuses. [*Trans.*]

124 The manuscript contains the following deleted passage: 'For, on all these questions, even after the experience of the Commune which suggested certain measures, although their exact significance and the conditions under which they were to be applied was never clearly understood, Marxist theoreticians and leaders had made very little progress. One does not get very far by saying that the state is a bludgeon, or by confounding the political dictatorship of the Supreme Soviet with the hegemony of the working class.'

125 The signs in question have since been replaced by others bearing precisely the same warning. *Au-delà de cette limite votre ticket n'est plus valable* is the title of a celebrated novel that Romain Gary published in 1975. [*Trans.*]

126 The particular target of this section of 'Marx in his Limits' is a book by three 'Eurocommunist' theoreticians, Lucien Sève, Jean Fabre, and François Hincker (*Les communistes et l'Etat*, Paris, 1977, esp. pp. 180–2), who, in the course of a defense of the PCF's decision to 'abandon' the dictatorship of the proletariat, lay out a plan for transforming the State adminstration into a 'public service' and 'democratizing' the state apparatus after the expected electoral victory of the Union of the Left. [*Trans.*]

127 Karl Wittfogel, *Oriental Despotism: A Comparative Study of Total Power*, New Haven, 1957.

128 The first draft reads, 'does not take place in the clouds'.

129 Paul Boccara was, at the time, one of the key members of the PCF Central Committee's section for economics, and a leading editor of the review *Économie et politique*. He took an active hand in the writing of *Traité marxiste d'économie politique: Le Capitalisme monopoliste d'État*, Paris, 1971, and published, among other works, *Études sur le capitalisme monopoliste d'État, sa crise et son issu*, Paris, 1973. In 1972–73, Althusser envisaged writing a book on imperialism; one of its objectives was to refute the theory of 'state monopoly capitalism' then underpinning the PCF's strategy for the Union of the Left. He wrote the preface for the book and several preliminary sketches, one of which is entitled 'The Mistake of the State Monopoly Capitalism Boys'.

130 Lenin, 'The Impending Debacle' (October 1917), trans. anon., *LCW* 24: 395–7.

131 Ludwig Feuerbach, *Sämtliche Werke*, eds Wilhelm Bolin and Friedrich Jodl, Stuttgart, 1903–10, vol. 7, p. 248. [*Trans.*]

132 The first draft reads 'in his clumsily constructed book'. Engels, *The Origins of the Family, Private Property and the State*, trans. anon., *MECW* 26.

133 *LCW* 29: 472. [*Trans.*]

134 The phrase evokes Lacan's *ça parle or ça pense*, 'it speaks' / 'it thinks'. *Ça* is the French translation of the Freudian 'id'. [*Trans.*]

135 *C1* 165. [*Trans.*]
136 Ibid., 165–6. [*Trans.*]
137 The first draft reads 'terribly well'.
138 Althusser's emphasis. The translation given here reflects the French translation given by Althusser. Compare *C1* 176: 'the degree to which some economists are misled by the fetishism attached to the world of commodities, or by the objective appearance of the social attributes of labour'. The German reads, 'Wie sehr ein Teil der Ökonomen von dem der Warenwelt anklebenden Fetischismus oder dem gegenständlichen Schein der gesellschaftlichen Arbeitsbestimmungen getäuscht wird.' [*Trans.*]
139 'Labour is *not the source* of all wealth. *Nature* is just as much the source of use-values (and it is surely these which make up material wealth!).' Marx, 'Critique of the Gotha Programme', in Marx, *The First International and After: Political Writings*, vol. 3, trans. David Fernbach, London, 1974, p. 341. [*Trans.*]
140 The first draft reads 'this theory, a handy little theory'.
141 The kind of analysis that Althusser has in mind here is exemplified by a passage from Jean-Marie Vincent, 'Le théoricisme et sa rectification', in *Contre Althusser*, ed. Denise Avenas et al., Paris, 1974, p. 227: 'The different modulations of the value-form are reproduced, at all levels, as if they were the result of a natural movement. Juridical, political, or libidinal relations are fetishized, becoming "natural" properties … which people utilize, but to which they also submit because they are natural.' [*Trans.*]
142 Engels, *Ludwig Feuerbach and the End of Classical German Philosophy*, trans. Nicholas Jacobs *et al.*, *MECW* 26: 392. Althusser's translation makes the state 'the greatest ideological power on earth'.
143 Marx, *The Poverty of Philosophy*, *MECW* 6: 211.
144 Georgy Plekhanov, *Fundamental Problems of Marxism*, eds James S. Allen and V. A. Fomina, trans. Julius Katzer, London, 1969. A heavily annotated version of the French translation of Plekhanov's book was found in Althusser's library.
145 'IISA'.
146 Foreword to *Lenin and Philosophy and Other Essays*, trans. Ben Brewster, London, 1971, pp. 7–9; Postscript to 'IISA', *EI* 57–60. [*Trans.*]
147 *SPN* 261. Althusser underlined the following passage in Christine Buci-Glucksmann, *Gramsci and the State*, trans. David Fernbach, London, 1980, p. 70: 'But what does that signify if not that by "State" should be understood not only the apparatus of government, but also the "private" apparatus of "hegemony" or civil society?' (*SPN* 263).
148 The manuscript contains the words 'Sorel, or even Bergson', which have been deleted. Gaetano Mosca (1858–1941) was an Italian legal scholar and politician who is sometimes regarded as a 'Machiavellian'. His works includes *The Ruling Class*, ed. Arthur Livingston, trans. Hannah D. Kahn, London, 1939.

149 Palmiro Togliatti, General Secretary of the PCI until his death in 1964.
150 The first draft reads 'a problematic of stupefying simplicity'. [*Trans.*]
151 In an unpublished 95-page manuscript entitled 'What is To Be Done?', Althusser offers a long analysis of Gramsci's reading of Machiavelli, which is also evoked in *MU*.
152 The manuscript reads 'him'.
153 See p. 104, footnote m.
154 The first draft reads 'this enormity'.
155 Valentino Gerratana, the general editor of the definitive Italian edition of Gramsci.
156 The first draft reads, 'but not even this is certain'.
157 See, for example, *Note sul Machiavelli, sula politica e sullo stato moderno*, Turin, 1949, pp. 68 ff.
158 *SPN* 238 ('In Russia the state was everything').
159 Ibid., p. 263.
160 The following words have been deleted from the manuscript: 'which would have horrified Mao'.
161 'Hegemony is born in the factory and does not need so many political and ideological intermediaries.' Antonio Gramsci, *Prison Notebooks*, vol. 1, ed. Joseph Buttigieg, trans. Buttigieg and Antonio Callari, New York, 1992, p. 169.
162 The first draft reads 'unbelievable'.
163 Jean-Jacques Rousseau, *The Social Contract*, in *The Social Contract and Discourses*, ed. P. D. Jimack, trans. G. D. H. Cole, London, 1993, p. 185.
164 Compare 'Every relationship of "hegemony" is necessarily an educational relationship' (Gramsci, *Further Selections from the Prison Notebooks*, ed. and trans. Derek Boothman, London, 1995, p. 157).
165 *SPN* 267.
166 'State = political society + civil society, that is, hegemony protected by the armour of coercion.' (*SPN* 263) 'In politics the error occurs as a result of an inaccurate understanding of what the State (in its integral meaning: dictatorship and hegemony) really is.' (*SPN* 510) See also 'CM' 219: 'Something pathetic strikes you when you re-read in the same light Gramsci's little equations written in prison (the State = coercion + hegemony, dictatorship + hegemony, force + consensus, etc.) which are the expression less of a theory than of a search, in terms borrowed from "political science" as much as from Lenin, for a political line aiming at the conquest of state power by the working class.'
167 These are the last words of the manuscript, which Althusser probably considered unfinished.

The Underground Current of the Materialism of the Encounter[1]

In July 1982, first in a clinic at Soisy-sur-Seine and then in his Paris apartment, Althusser began writing again. In a few months, he had completed a dozen texts on both the political conjuncture and what he would henceforth call 'the materialism of the encounter'. That autumn, he decided to recast these texts as a book. He photocopied some of them and wrote several new transitional passages and chapters, eventually producing a manuscript comprising sixteen chapters and 142 typed pages. The two, three, or even four page numbers on certain pages of the projected book show that he tried piecing the parts of it together in several different ways; one would be hard put to reconstruct these various 'montages' today. Since the document that survives in Althusser's archives is not the original manuscript, but a set of photocopies, re-creating the history of these texts would be a formidable task: although it seems that the countless handwritten emendations photocopied along with the rest originated in different periods, the fact that we have them in this form alone makes any attempt to date them an altogether aleatory affair.

It quickly became apparent that we could not publish the whole of Althusser's manuscript as it stands, since some passages in it occur twice.[2] *But since the repeated passages crop up in the middle of others that they suddenly turn in a new direction, it proved impossible to solve the problem by simply excising them, since that would have meant breaking the thread of Althusser's argument. This is not the only problem with his montage: one or more pages are often intercalated in the midst of sentences that they unceremoniously interrupt, leaving many passges of the manuscript altogether incomprehensible. Thus it was obvious that, whatever editorial policy was adopted, the published version of the text would have to be an a posteriori construction. Rather than try to maintain the greatest possible fidelity to Althusser's intentions – an editorial policy which, no matter how it was applied, would have yielded an unsatisfactory result – it seemed to us preferable to adopt a procedure exactly opposite to the one used in editing all the other texts in the present volume. Some sections of the manuscript, especially chapters 2 and 3, both entitled 'What Is To Be Done?', merit the kind of severe criticism that Althusser expressed in the November 1987 letter to Fernanda Navarro in which he asked her to suppress several chapters of her Interview with him. 'These are merely exchanges of opinion, of dubious value because they are not justified, not defended, not supported by textual citations or convincing examples – in short, they're feeble, at the level of mere journalism, and it's a pity, a real pity! So forget the "politico-strategic" ambition (with which I imprudently infected you), and stick to philosophy.'*[3]

Other passages, written weeks after those they were supposed to develop, are plainly restatements of them. Since we had, at all events, to make a choice, we decided to reduce Althusser's manuscript to the core section on the 'underground current of the materialism of the encounter'. In so doing, we inevitably altered the overall economy of the projected book.

Althusser decided to produce this book for the same reason he wrote The Future Lasts a Long Time *in 1985: he wanted to speak out in public again. At the beginning of the volume, he placed the following dedication: 'For Hélène / without whom / this book / in mourning', the last four words of which he later deleted. The text proper opens with a semi-autobiographical chapter:*

> I am writing this book in October 1982, at the end of a terrible, three-year-long ordeal. If an account of my ordeal can shed light on others like it, I may – who knows – provide one some day, relating both the circumstances surrounding this experience and also what I went through (psychiatry, etc.). For, in November 1980, in the course of a severe, unforeseeable crisis that had left me in a state of mental confusion, I strangled my wife, the woman who was everything in the world to me and who loved me so much that, since living had become impossible, she wanted only to die. In my confusion, not knowing what I was doing, I no doubt rendered her this 'service': she did not defend herself against it, but died of it.
>
> Subsequently, after it had been determined that there were no grounds for prosecution on the basis of three opinions delivered by

experts whose competence and independence I very much appreciated, I found myself in psychiatric clinics, living through that nameless time that does not pass, unaware of what was going on around me. Only later did I learn that the world had moved on. It saw the overwhelming[4] victory of the Left in the [presidential] elections of 10 May 1981 and the creation of a socialist government headed by [Prime Minister Pierre] Mauroy, under the 'serene' Presidency of François Mitterrand. It saw the first 'social' measures (should they be called 'socialist'?) unsettle the employers, and even make them tremble. (They are, of course, used to trembling – or do they just pretend to be? Still, they witnessed quite a few changes, from the court system to the minimum legal wage, to mention only those two extremes, the one involving the law, the other wages, the two pillars of our world.) The period also saw the Right attempting to pull itself back together; saw it win a few elections here and there, and play them up in order to convince itself that it still existed; and saw Mitterrand travelling around the world in quest of allies for peace and contracts for production. Quite a few other progressive reforms have been announced, reforms that will count as milestones, although, as everyone knows, one has 'to wait until the sugar dissolves': everything takes time to mature, and nothing is worse than the kind of premature development that opens the door to all sorts of misadventures. The France of 1792 or 1871 is well aware of this, in its wisdom and the popular memory which knows, precisely, how to bide its time until the moment is ripe, how to wait until things come to term. It waits, certain that the game is worth the candle, that everything can go awry, but that it must at least attempt this unhoped-for experiment, meditated and prepared long in advance; it is an experiment that can, the effort once made, open the way to a world of prosperity, security, equality and peace established on surer foundations.

Now, in better health, and freed from my terrible delusions, I am leaving the hospital (Soisy-sur-Seine) in which I was marvellously cared for – if one can ever talk about marvels in such matters – and am returning to this world that is entirely new to me, and, since I had never encountered it before, full of surprises. I am now living in a working-class neighbourhood, and can see with my own eyes what artisans are –

whether they are in disarray or not – and what a 'mode of production' and 'subcontracting' are (living in the École normale supérieure in the Fifth Arrondissement, I knew them only by hearsay or 'hear-read'). It seems to me that I understand better what Marx was trying, and, at least partially, failed, to say. Of course, these observations are joined with long reflections due to my vocation (one is not a 'philosopher' from the age of twenty-eight for nothing), and the result is this book – which will seem strange to anyone inclined only to leaf through it, and serious to anyone ready to read, if not study, it. I have condensed in it what I believe it is in my power to say in this autumn in which, the other day, the yellowed leaves were falling slowly on to the tombs of Père-Lachaise, near the Wall and elsewhere.[5] As always, I have said everything in a single breath, trusting, in some sort, to the movement of a form of writing that is, as it were, 'spoken' rather than 'written'; and trusting also that readers of goodwill will meet it with something like a movement of the same kind. I have swept past the difficulties flagged along the way, repeated established truths when necessary, and hastened towards the end in expectation of the sequel: a second volume on Marx, and, perhaps, a third on the countries of 'actually existing socialism'.[6]

The reader will, of course, consider me imprudent for thus 'showing my hand' from the start, particularly after the ordeal that I do not emerge from without trembling; but, after all, it is better that he know where he is going if he is to follow me, and it is therefore better that he know where I am going – where I would like to go, and, perhaps, am going; and it is better that he know that the 'philosophy of the encounter' whose existence, cause and fecundity I will be pleading has nothing at all speculative about it. It is, rather, the key to what we have read of Marx and, as it were, understood of what is thrust upon us: this world, torn between powers in collusion and the 'crisis' which unites them in its circle, diabolical because it is almost entirely unknown.

It only remains for me to wish my reader the courage to read as well as the fortitude to grant me a certain credit in advance, and also – but this is not indispensable – to ask him to begin this book by reading the provisional chapter pretentiously entitled, after Chernechevsky (from whom Lenin, in a time of disarray, borrowed his own title): *What Is To Be Done?*[7]

Hospitalized again at Soisy from 24 June to 28 July 1986, Althusser wrote out in longhand, and signed, what was no doubt the last series of philosophical texts he was to produce: 'On Analysis' (12 pages, undated); 'On History' (2 pages, 6 July); 'On Aleatory Materialism' (19 pages, 11 July); 'Portrait of the Materialist Philosopher' (2 pages, 19 July); 'Machiavelli as Philosopher' (13 pages, undated). Since it was hardly possible to publish the whole of this unfinished variation on the theme of aleatory materialism, we have culled the curious 'Portrait of the Materialist Philosopher' from it. It will readily be agreed that this is a particularly overdetermined text.

It is raining.

Let this book therefore be, before all else, a book about ordinary rain.

Malebranche wondered 'why it rains upon sands, upon highways and seas',[8] since this water from the sky which, elsewhere, waters crops (and that is very good), adds nothing to the water of the sea, or goes to waste on the roads and beaches.

Our concern will not be with that kind of rain, providential or anti-providential.[9]

Quite the contrary: this book is about another kind of rain, about a profound theme which runs through the whole history of philosophy, and was contested and repressed there as soon as it was stated: the 'rain' (Lucretius) of Epicurus' atoms that fall parallel to each other in the void; the 'rain' of the parallelism of the infinite attributes in Spinoza and many others: Machiavelli, Hobbes, Rousseau, Marx, Heidegger too, and Derrida.

That is the first point which – revealing my main thesis from the start – I would like to bring out: *the existence of an almost completely unknown materialist tradition in the history of philosophy: the 'materialism'* (we shall have to have some word to distinguish it as a tendency) *of the rain, the swerve, the encounter, the take* [*prise*]. I shall develop all these concepts. To simplify matters, let us say, for now, a *materialism of the encounter*, and therefore of the aleatory and of contingency. This materialism is opposed, as a wholly different mode of thought, to the various materialisms on record, including that widely ascribed to Marx, Engels and Lenin, which, like every other materialism in the rationalist tradition, is a materialism of necessity and teleology, that is to say, a transformed, disguised form of idealism.

The fact that this materialism of the encounter has been repressed by the philosophical tradition does not mean that it has been neglected by it: it was too dangerous for that. Thus it was very early on interpreted, repressed and perverted into an *idealism of freedom*. If Epicurus' atoms, raining down parallel to each other in the void, *encounter* one another, it is in order to bring out, in the guise of the swerve caused by the clinamen, the existence of human freedom even in the world of necessity. Obviously, producing this misreading, which is not innocent, suffices to preclude any other reading of the repressed tradition that I am calling the materialism of the encounter. Whenever one sets out from this misreading, idealist interpretations carry the day, whether what is in question is just the clinamen or all of Lucretius, as well as Machiavelli, Spinoza and Hobbes, the Rousseau of the second *Discourse*, Marx and even Heidegger (to the extent that Heidegger touched on this theme). What triumphs in these interpretations is a certain conception of philosophy and the history of philosophy that we can, with Heidegger, call Western, because it has presided over our destiny since the Greeks; and also logocentric, because it identifies philosophy with a function of the Logos charged with thinking the priority of Meaning over all reality.

To free the materialism of the encounter from this repression; to discover, if possible, its implications for both philosophy and materialism; and to ascertain its hidden effects wherever they are silently at work – such is the task that I have set myself here.

We can start with a surprising comparison: between Epicurus and Heidegger.

Epicurus tells us that, before the formation of the world, an infinity of atoms were falling parallel to each other in the void. They still are. This implies both that, before the formation of the world, there was nothing, and also that all the elements of the world existed from all eternity, before any world ever was. It also implies that, before the formation of the world, there was no Meaning, neither Cause nor End nor Reason nor Unreason. The non-anteriority of Meaning is one of Epicurus' basic theses, by virtue of which he stands opposed to both Plato and Aristotle. Then the clinamen supervenes. I shall leave it to the specialists to decide who introduced the concept of the clinamen, present in Lucretius but absent from the fragments of Epicurus. The fact that this concept was 'introduced' suggests that it proved indispensable, if only on reflection, to the 'logic' of Epicurus' theses. The clinamen is an infinitesimal *swerve,* 'as small as possible'; 'no one knows where, or when, or how' it occurs,[10] or what causes an atom to 'swerve' from its vertical fall in the void, and, breaking the parallelism in an almost negligible way at one point, induce *an encounter* with the atom next to it, and, from encounter to encounter, a pile-up and the birth of a world – that is to say, of the agglomeration of atoms induced, in a chain reaction, by the initial swerve and encounter.

The idea that the origin of every world, and therefore of all reality and all meaning, is due to a swerve, and that Swerve, not Reason or Cause, is the origin of the world, gives some sense of the audacity of Epicurus' thesis. What other philosophy has, in the history of philosophy, defended the thesis that *Swerve was originary*, not derived? We must go further still. In order for swerve to give rise to an encounter from which a world is born, that encounter must last; it must be, not a 'brief encounter', but a lasting encounter, which then becomes the basis for all reality, all necessity, all Meaning and all reason. But the encounter can also not last; then there is no world. What is more, it is clear that the encounter creates nothing of the reality of the world, which is nothing but agglomerated atoms, but *that it confers their reality upon the atoms themselves*, which, without swerve and encounter, would be nothing but *abstract* elements, lacking all consistency and existence. So much so that we can say that the *atoms' very existence is due to nothing but the swerve and the encounter* prior to which they led only a phantom existence.

All this may be stated differently. The world may be called *the accomplished fact* [*fait accompli*] in which, once the fact has been accomplished, is established the reign of Reason, Meaning, Necessity and End [*Fin*]. But *the accomplishment of the fact* is just a pure effect of contingency, since it depends on the aleatory encounter of the atoms due to the swerve of the clinamen. Before the accomplishment of the fact, before the world, there is only *the non-accomplishment of the fact*, the non-world that is merely the *unreal* existence of the atoms.

What becomes of philosophy under these circumstances? It is no longer a statement of the Reason and Origin of things, but a theory of their contingency and a recognition of *fact*, of the fact of contingency, the fact of the subordination of necessity to contingency, and the fact of the forms which 'gives form' to the effect of the encounter. It is now no more than *observation* [*constat*]: *there has been* an encounter, and a '*crystallization*' [*prise*] of the elements with one another (in the sense in which ice 'crystallizes'). All question of Origin is rejected, as are all the great philosophical questions: 'Why is there something rather than nothing? What is the origin of the world? What is the world's *raison d'être*? What is man's place in the ends of the world?' and so on.[11] I repeat: what other philosophy has, historically, had the audacity to entertain such theses?

I mentioned Heidegger a moment ago. One finds, precisely, a similar tendency in the thought of Heidegger, who is obviously neither an Epicurean nor an atomist. It is well known that he rejects all question of the Origin, or of the Cause and End of the world. But we find in Heidegger a long series of developments centred on the expression *es gibt* – 'there is', 'this is what is given' – that converge with Epicurus' inspiration. '*There is* world and matter, *there are* people … .' A philosophy of the *es gibt*, of the 'this is what is given', makes short shrift of all the classic questions about the Origin, and so on. And it 'opens up' a prospect that restores a kind of transcendental contingency of the world, into which we are 'thrown', and of the meaning of the world, which in turn points to the opening up of Being, the original urge of Being, its 'destining', beyond which there is nothing to seek or to think. Thus the world is a 'gift' that we have been given, the 'fact of the fact [*fait de fait*]' that we have not chosen, and it 'opens up' before us in the facticity of its contingency, and even beyond this facticity, in what is not merely an observation, but a 'being-in-the-world' that commands all possible Meaning. '*Dasein* is the shepherd of being.'[12] Everything depends on the *da*. What remains of philosophy? Once again – but in the transcendental mode – *the observation of the 'es gibt'* and its presuppositions, or, rather, its effects in their insurmountable 'givenness'.

Is this still materialism? The question is not very meaningful for Heidegger, who deliberately takes up a position outside the great divisions and the terminology of Western philosophy. But then are Epicurus' theses still materialist? Yes, perhaps, doubtless, but on condition that we have done with a conception of materialism which, setting out from the questions and concepts it shares with idealism, makes materialism the response to idealism. We continue to talk about a materialism of the encounter only for the sake of convenience: it should be borne in mind that this materialism of the encounter includes Heidegger and eludes the classical criteria of every materialism, and that we need, after all, some word to designate the thing.

Machiavelli will be our second witness in the history of this underground current of the materialism of the encounter. His project is well known: to think, in the impossible conditions of fifteenth-century Italy, the conditions for establishing an Italian national state. All the circumstances favourable to imitating France or Spain exist, but *without connections* between them: a divided and fervent people, the fragmentation of Italy into small obsolete states that have been condemned by history, a generalized but disorderly revolt of an entire world against foreign occupation and pillage, and a profound, latent aspiration of the people to unity, an aspiration to which all the great works of the period bear witness, including that of Dante, who understood nothing of all this, but was waiting for the arrival of the 'great hound'. In sum, an atomized country, every atom of which was descending in free fall without encountering its neighbour. It was necessary *to create the conditions for a swerve,* and thus an encounter, if Italian unity was to 'take hold'. How was this to be done? Machiavelli did not believe that any of the existing states – and, in particular, any of the papal states, the worst of all – could play the role of unifier. In *The Prince,* he lists them one after the next, but only to reject them as so many decaying components of the prior, feudal mode of production, including the republics that are its alibis and captives. And he poses the problem in all its rigour and stark simplicity.

Once all the states and their princes – that is, all the *places* and *people* – have been rejected, Machiavelli, using the example of Cesare Borgia, moves on to the idea that unification will be achieved if there emerges some nameless man who has enough luck and *virtù* to establish himself somewhere, in some *nameless* corner of Italy, and, starting out from this atomic point, gradually aggregate the Italians around him in the grand project of founding a national state. This is a completely aleatory line of reasoning, which leaves politically *blank* both the name of the Federator and that of the region which will serve as starting point for the constitution of this federation. Thus the dice are tossed on the gaming table, which is itself empty (but filled with men of valour).[13]

In order for this encounter between a man and a region to 'take hold', it has *to take place*. Politically conscious of the powerlessness of the existing states and princes, Machiavelli says nothing about this prince and this place. But let us not be fooled. This silence is a *political* condition for the encounter. Machiavelli's wish is simply that, in an atomized Italy, the encounter should take place, and he is plainly obsessed with this Cesare, who, starting out with nothing, made the Romagna a Kingdom, and, after taking Florence, would have unified all Northern Italy if he had not been stricken with fever in the marshes of Ravenna at the critical moment, when he was heading, despite Julius II, for Rome itself, to strip him of his office. *A man of nothing who has started out from nothing starting out from an unassignable place*: these are, for Machiavelli, the conditions for regeneration.

In order for this encounter to take place, however, another encounter must come about: that of fortune and *virtù* in the Prince. Encountering *Fortuna*, the Prince must have the *virtù* to treat her as he would treat a woman, to welcome her in order to seduce or do violence to her; in short, to use her to realize his destiny. Thanks to this consideration, we owe Machiavelli a whole philosophical theory of the encounter between fortune and *virtù*. The encounter may not take place *or* may take place. The meeting can be missed. The encounter can be brief or lasting: he needs an encounter that lasts. To make it last, the Prince has to learn to govern fortune by governing men. He has to structure his state by training up its men, commingling them in the army (see Gramsci), and, above all, by endowing this state with constant *laws*. He has to win them over by accommodating them, while knowing how to keep his distance. This dual procedure gives rise to the theory of seduction and the theory of fear, as well as the theory of the ruse. I leave aside the rejection of the demagoguery of love,[14] the idea that fear is preferable to love,[15] and the violent methods designed to inspire fear, in order to go straight to the theory of the ruse.

Should the Prince be good or wicked? He has to learn to be wicked, but in all circumstances he has to know how to *appear to be* good, to possess the moral virtues that will win the people over to his side, even if they earn him the hatred of the mighty, whom he despises, for, from them, nothing else is to be expected. Machiavelli's theory is well known: the Prince should be 'like the centaur of the Ancients, both man and beast'. But it has not been sufficiently remarked that *the beast divides* into two in Machiavelli, becoming both lion and fox, and that, ultimately, it is the fox who governs everything.[16] For it is the fox who obliges the Prince either to appear to be evil or to appear to be good – in a word, to fabricate a popular (ideological) image of himself that either does or does not answer to his interests and those of the 'little man'.[17] Consequently, the Prince is governed, internally, by the variations of this other aleatory encounter, that of the fox on the one hand and the lion and man on the other. This encounter *may not take place*, but it may also take place. It has to last long enough for the figure of the Prince to 'take hold' among the people – to 'take hold', that is, *to take form*, so that, institutionally, he instils the fear of himself as good; and, if possible, so that he ultimately *is* good, but on the absolute condition that he never forget how to be evil if need be.

The reader may object that this is merely *political* philosophy, overlooking the fact that a philosophy is simultaneously at work here too. A curious *philosophy which is a 'materialism of the encounter' thought by way of politics*, and which, as such, does not take anything for granted. It is in the political *void* that the encounter must come about, and that national unity must 'take hold'. But *this political void is first a philosophical void.* No Cause that precedes its effects is to be found in it, no Principle of morality or theology (as in the whole Aristotelian political tradition: the good and bad forms of government, the degeneration of the good into the bad). One reasons here not in terms of the Necessity of the accomplished fact, but in terms of the contingency of the fact to be accomplished. As in the Epicurean world, all the elements are both here and beyond, to come raining down later [*là et au-delà, à pleuvoir*] (see above, the Italian situation), but they do not exist, are only abstract, as long as the unity of a world has not united them in the Encounter that will endow them with existence.

It will have been noticed that, in this philosophy, there reigns an alternative: the encounter may not take place, just as it may take place. Nothing determines, no principle of decision determines this alternative in advance; it is of the order of a game of dice. 'A throw of the dice will never abolish chance.' Indeed! A successful encounter, one that is not brief, but lasts, never guarantees that it will continue to last tomorrow rather than come undone. Just as it might not have taken place, it may *no longer* take place: 'fortune comes and changes', affirms Borgia, who succeeded at everything until the famous day he was stricken with fever. In other words, nothing guarantees that *the reality of the accomplished fact* is *the guarantee of its durability*. Quite the opposite is true: every accomplished fact, even an election, like all the necessity and reason we can derive from it, is only a provisional encounter, and since every encounter is provisional even when it lasts, *there is no eternity in the 'laws' of any world or any state.* History here is nothing but the permanent revocation of the accomplished fact by another undecipherable fact to be accomplished, without our knowing in advance whether, or when, or how the event that revokes it will come about. Simply, one day new hands will have to be dealt out, and the dice thrown again on to the empty table.

Thus it will have been noticed that this philosophy is, in sum, a philosophy of the *void*: not only the philosophy which *says* that the void pre-exists the atoms that fall in it, but a philosophy which *creates the philosophical void* [*fait le vide philosophique*] in order to endow itself with existence: a philosophy which, rather than setting out from the famous 'philosophical problems' (why is there something rather than nothing?),[18] *begins by evacuating all philosophical problems,* hence by refusing to assign itself any 'object' whatever ('philosophy has no object')[19] in order to set out from *nothing*, and from the infinitesimal, aleatory variation of nothing constituted by the swerve of the fall. Is there a more radical critique of all philosophy, with its pretension to utter the truth about things? Is there a more striking way of saying that philosophy's 'object' *par excellence* is nothingness, nothing, or the void? In the seventeenth century, Pascal repeatedly approached this idea, and the possibility of introducing the void as a philosophical object. He did so, however, in the deplorable context of an apologetics. Here, too, it was only with Heidegger, after the false words of a Hegel ('the labour of the negative') or a Stirner ('all things are nothing to me'),[20] that the void was given all its decisive philosophical significance again. Yet we already find all this in Epicurus and Machiavelli: in Machiavelli, who evacuated [*fit le vide de*] all Plato's and Aristotle's philosophical concepts in order to think the possibility of making Italy a national state. One measures the impact of philosophy here – reactionary or revolutionary – despite the often baffling outward appearances, which have to be patiently and carefully deciphered.

If Machiavelli is read along these lines (the foregoing are just brief notes which have to be developed, and which I hope to develop some day[21]), how is it possible to imagine that his work is, under its political cloak, anything other than an authentically philosophical body of thought? And how is it possible to imagine that the fascination exercised by Machiavelli has been merely political, or centred on the absurd question of whether he was a monarchist or a republican (the very best philosophy of the Enlightenment was enamoured of this foolishness),[22] when the philosophical resonances of his work have been, unbeknown to Machiavelli himself, among the most profound to have reached us from this painful past? I would like to *displace* the problem, in order to challenge not simply the meaningless monarchist/republican alternative, but also the widespread thesis that Machiavelli merely founded political science. I would like to suggest that it is less to politics than to his 'materialism of the encounter' that Machiavelli basically owes the influence he has had on people who do not give a damn about politics, and rightly so – *no one is obliged to 'engage in politics'*; they have been partly misled about him, vainly striving to pin down, as Croce still was, the elusive source of this *eternally* incomprehensible fascination.

Someone understood this fascination less than a century after Machiavelli's death. His name was Spinoza. In the *Tractatus politicus*, we find high praise for Machiavelli, mentioned by name in a treatise whose subject, once again, would appear to be politics, whereas it is in reality philosophy as well.[23] In order to grasp this philosophy, however, we have to take a step back, since Spinoza's philosophical strategy is radical and extremely complex. This is because he was struggling in a full world and was stalked by adversaries ready to pounce on his every word, adversaries who occupied all the terrain, or thought they did. Moreover, he had to develop a disconcerting problematic – from the high ground, which dominates all the consequences.

Here, I shall defend the thesis that, for Spinoza, the object of philosophy is the void.[24] This is a paradoxical thesis, in view of the great many concepts that are worked out in the *Ethics*.[25] Yet we only need notice *how Spinoza begins*. He confesses in a letter that 'some begin with the world and others with the mind of man; I begin with God'.[26] The others: first, the Schoolmen, who begin with the world, and, from the created world, trace things back to God. The others are also Descartes, who starts with the thinking subject and, by way of the cogito, traces things back to the dubito and God as well. All of them take a path that leads through God. Spinoza shuns these detours and deliberately takes up his position *in God*. Hence one can say that he occupies, *in advance*, the common fortress, the ultimate guarantee and last recourse of all his adversaries, by starting with this *beyond-which-there-is-nothing*, which, because it thus exists in the absolute, in the absence of all relation, *is itself nothing*. Saying that one 'begins with God', or the Whole, or the unique substance, and making it understood that one 'begins with nothing', is, basically, the same thing: what difference is there between the Whole and nothing? – since nothing exists outside the whole.... What, for that matter, does Spinoza have to say about God? This is where the strangeness begins.

Deus sive natura, God *is only* nature. This comes down to saying that He is *nothing* else: He is only *nature*. Epicurus, too, set out from nature as that outside which nothing exists. What, then, is this Spinozist God? An absolute, unique, infinite substance, endowed with an infinite number of infinite attributes. This is obviously a way of saying that anything which can exist never exists anywhere other than in God, whether this 'whatever' is known or unknown. For we know only two attributes, extension and thought, and even then, we do not know all the powers of the body,[27] just as, when it comes to thought, we do not know the unthought power of desire. The other attributes – of which there are an infinite number, and which are themselves infinite – are there to cover the whole range of the possible and impossible. The fact that there is an *infinite* number of them, and that they are unknown to us, leaves the door to their existence and their aleatory figures wide open. The fact that they are *parallel*, that here everything is an effect of parallelism, recalls Epicurus' rain. The attributes fall in the empty space of their determination like raindrops that can undergo encounters [*sont recontrables*] only in this exceptional parallelism, this parallelism *without encounter or union* (of body and soul ...) known as man, in this assignable but minute parallelism of thought and the body,[28] which is still only parallelism, since, here as in all things, 'the order and connection of ideas is the same as the order and connection of things'.[29] In sum, a *parallelism without encounter*, yet a parallelism that is already, in itself, *encounter* thanks to the very structure of the relationship between the different elements of each attribute.

One cannot assess this unless one perceives the philosophical effects of this strategy and this parallelism. The result of the fact that God is *nothing* but nature, and that this nature is the infinite sum of an infinite number of parallel attributes, is not only that *there is nothing left to say about God*, but that there is also nothing left to say about the great problem that invaded all of Western philosophy with Aristotle and, especially, Descartes: *the problem of knowledge*, and of its dual correlative, the knowing subject and the known object. These great causes, which are the cause of so much discussion, are reduced to nothing. *Homo cogitat*, 'man thinks',[30] that is just how it is; this is the observation of a facticity, that of the 'this is how it is', that of an *es gibt* which already anticipates Heidegger and recalls the facticity of the falling atoms in Epicurus. Thought is simply the succession of the modes of the attribute 'thought', and refers us, not to a Subject, but, as good parallelism requires, to the succession of the modes of the attribute 'extension'.

Also interesting is the way in which thought is constituted in man. That he starts to think by thinking confused thoughts, and by hearsay, until these elements at last 'take' form, so that he can think in 'common notions' (from the first kind to the second, and then the third: by thinking singular essences)[31] is important, for man could well remain at the level of hearsay, and the thoughts of the first kind might not 'take hold' with those of the second. Such is the lot of most peoples, who remain at the level of the first kind and the imaginary – that is, at the level of the illusion that they are thinking, when they are not. That is just how it is. One can remain at the level of the first kind or not. There is not, as there is in Descartes, an immanent necessity that brings about the transition from confused thinking to clear and distinct thinking. There is no subject, no cogito, no necessary moment of reflection guaranteeing this transition. It may take place or it may not. And experience shows that, as a general rule, it does not, except in a philosophy which is aware that it is nothing.

What remains of philosophy once both God and the theory of knowledge, destined to establish supreme 'values' that provide the measure of all things, have been reduced to naught? No more morality, or, above all, religion. Better: a theory of morality and religion which, long before Nietzsche, destroys them right down to their imaginary foundations of 'reversal' – the 'inverted *fabrica*' (see the appendix to Book I of the *Ethics*).[32] No more finality (whether psychological or historical). In short, *the void that is philosophy itself.* And inasmuch as this result is a result, it is attained only after an immense amount of labour, which makes for all the interest of the *Ethics*, has been performed on concepts: 'critical labour', as it is usually called; a labour of 'deconstruction', as Derrida would say, following Heidegger. For what is destroyed is simultaneously reconstructed, but on other foundations and in accordance with an altogether different plan – witness the inexhaustible theory of the imagination or the imaginary, which both destroys and reconstructs the theory of knowledge, the theory of religion, the theory of history, and so on – but in their actual, political functions.

A strange theory, which people tend to present as a theory of knowledge (the first of the three kinds), whereas *the imagination is not by any means a faculty, but, fundamentally, only the only*[33] *world itself in its 'givenness'.* With this slide [*glissement*], Spinoza not only turns his back on all theories of knowledge, but also clears a path for the recognition of the 'world' as that-beyond-which-there-is-nothing, not even a theory of nature – for the recognition of the 'world' as a unique totality that is *not totalized, but experienced in its dispersion*, and experienced as the 'given' into which we are 'thrown' and on the basis of which we forge all our illusions [*fabricae*]. Basically, the theory of the first kind as a 'world' corresponds distantly, yet very precisely, to the thesis that God is 'nature', since nature is nothing but the world thought in accordance with ordinary notions, but given before them, as that prior to which there is nothing. For Spinoza, politics is then grafted on to the world's imaginary and its necessary myths. Thus Spinoza converges with Machiavelli in his profoundest conclusions and his rejection of all the presuppositions of traditional philosophy, the autonomy of the political being nothing other than the form taken by the rejection of all finality, all religion and all transcendence. But the theory of the imaginary as a world allows Spinoza to think the 'singular essence' of the third kind which finds its representation *par excellence* in the history of an individual or a people, such as Moses or the Jewish people. The fact that it is necessary means simply that it has been accomplished, but everything in it could have swung the other way, depending on the encounter or non-encounter of Moses and God, or the encounter of the comprehension or non-comprehension of the prophets. The proof is that it was necessary to explain to the prophets the meaning of what they reported of their conversations with God! – with the following limit-situation, of nothingness itself, which was Daniel's: you could explain everything to him for as long as you liked, he never understood a thing.[34] A proof by nothingness of nothingness itself, as a limit-situation.

Hobbes, that 'devil' or 'demon', will serve, in his fashion, as our transition from Spinoza to Rousseau. Chronology hardly matters in this business, because each of these bodies of thought is developed for itself, despite the intermediary role played by Mersenne, and because what is in question is, above all, the resonances of a tradition buried and then revived, resonances which must be registered.

All society is based on fear, Hobbes says, the factual proof being that you have *keys*. What do you have keys for? To lock your doors against attack from you don't know whom: it might be your neighbour or your best friend, transformed into a 'wolf for man' by your absence, and the occasion and desire to enrich himself.[35] From this simple remark, which is worth as much as our best 'analyses of essence', Hobbes draws a whole philosophy: namely, that there reigns among men a 'war of all against all', an 'endless race' which everyone wants to win, but which almost everyone loses, judging from the position of the competitors (whence the 'passions' about which he wrote a treatise [*sic*], as was then the fashion, in order to disguise politics in them), who are ahead, behind, or neck-and-neck in the race.[36] Whence the state of general war: not that it breaks out, here, between states (as Rousseau would logically claim), but, rather, in the sense in which we talk about 'the threat of an outbreak of foul weather' (it can start to rain at any time of the day or night, without warning); in short, as a permanent threat against one's life and possessions, and the threat of death which hangs, always, at every moment, over every man simply by virtue of the fact that he lives in society. I am well aware that Hobbes is thinking of something very different from competition, simple economic competition (as was once thought) – namely, the great revolts of which he was a witness (one is not a contemporary of Cromwell and the execution of Charles I with impunity), in which he saw the equilibrium of the minor fear of the 'keys' suddenly overturned in the face of the great fear of popular revolts and political murders. Beyond the shadow of a doubt, it is this great fear in particular that he means when he evokes the times of misfortune in which part of society could massacre the other in order to take power.

As a good theoretician of Natural Law, our Hobbes obviously does not restrict himself to these outward appearances, even if they are appalling; he wants to come to terms with the effects by tracing them back to their causes, and therefore proceeds to give us a theory of the state of Nature as well. To reduce the state of Nature to its elements, one has to pursue the analysis down to the level of the '*atoms of society*' constituted by *individuals endowed with conatus*, that is, with the power and will 'to persevere in their being' and create a void in front of themselves [*faire le vide devant eux*] in order to mark out the space of their freedom there. Atomized individuals, with the void as the condition for their movement: this reminds us of something, does it not? Hobbes does indeed contend that freedom, which makes the whole individual and the force of his being, resides in the 'void of impediments', the 'absence of impediments'[37] in the path of his conquering power. An individual joins the war of all against all only out of a desire to avoid every obstacle that would prevent him from forging straight ahead (one thinks here of the atoms descending in free fall parallel to each other); basically, he would be happy to encounter no one at all in a world that would in that case be empty.

It is an unfortunate fact, however, that *this world is full* – full of people pursuing the same goal, who therefore confront each other in order to clear the way before their own *conatus*, but find no other means of attaining their end than 'to bestow death upon' anyone who blocks their path. Whence the essential role of *death* in Hobbes's thought, which is a thought of infinite life; the role not of accidental death, but of necessary death, bestowed and received by man; the role of economic and political murder, which alone is capable of [*propre à*] maintaining this society of the state of war in an unstable but necessary equilibrium.

Yet these appalling men are also men; they think, that is to say, they '*calculate*', weighing up the respective advantages of remaining in the state of war or entering into a contractual state[38] which, however, is based on the inalienable foundation of any human society: *fear* or *terror*. They reason, then, and eventually conclude that it would be to their advantage to make a mutual pact, a curious, asymmetrical [*déséquilibré*] pact, in which they pledge (as atomistic individuals) not to resist the omnipotent power of the one to whom they then delegate, unilaterally and without receiving anything in exchange, all their *rights* (their natural rights): Leviathan – whether the individual of absolute monarchy or the omnipotent assembly of the people or its representatives. In making this pact, they make a mutual commitment to respect this delegation of power without ever violating it. If they did, they would incur the terrifying punishment of Leviathan, who, let us note, is not himself bound to the people by any contract; rather, he maintains the unity of the people through the exercise of an omnipotence to which all have consented, by making fear and terror reign at the limits of the law, thanks to his sense (what a miracle that he should possess it!) that it is his 'duty' to maintain the people thus subjugated in subjugation, so as to spare it the horrors of the state of war, infinitely worse than its fear of him.[39] A Prince bound to his people by nothing other than the duty to protect it from the state of war, a people bound to its Prince by nothing other than the promise – respected, or watch out! – to obey him in everything, *even in the realm of ideological conformity* (Hobbes is the first to think, if that is possible, ideological domination and its effects). It is here that we find all the originality and horror of this subversive thinker (his conclusions were correct, but he was a poor thinker, as Descartes would later say: his reasoning was faulty) and extraordinary theoretician, whom no one understood, but who terrified everyone. He thought (this privilege of thinking, which consists in not giving a toss about what people will say, or about the world, gossip, even one's reputation; in reasoning in absolute solitude – or the illusion of absolute solitude). What, then, did the accusations levelled at him (as they were also levelled at Spinoza) matter, accusations to the effect that he was an emissary of Hell and the Devil among men, and so on? Hobbes thought that every war was a preventive war, that no one had any other recourse against the Other he might some day face than to 'get the jump on him'. Hobbes thought (and with what audacity!) that all power is absolute, that to be absolute is the essence of power, and that everything which exceeds this rule by however little, whether from the Right or the Left, should be opposed with the greatest possible rigour. He did not think all this with a view to justifying what people would today call – using a word that blurs all distinctions, and therefore all meaning and all thought – 'totalitarianism' or 'etatism'; he thought all this in the interests of free economic competition, and the free development of trade and the culture of the peoples!

For, on closer inspection, it turns out that his notorious totalitarian state is almost already comparable to Marx's, which must *wither away*. Since all war, and therefore all terror, are preventive, it was sufficient for this terrible state to exist in order, as it were, to be so thoroughly absorbed by its own existence as not to have to exist. People have talked about the fear of the gendarme and the need to 'make a show of one's force so as not to have to make use of it' (Lyautey);[40] today we talk about *not* making a show of one's (atomic) force so as not to have to make use of it. This is to say that Force is a myth which, as such, acts on the imagination of men and peoples preventively, in the absence of any reason to employ it. I know that I am here extending an argument that never went this far, but I remain within the logic of Hobbes's thought, and am accounting for his paradoxes in terms of a Logic that remains his.

Be that as it may, it is painfully clear that Hobbes was not the monster that he has been made out to be, and that his sole ambition was to contribute to securing the conditions of viability and development of a world which was what it was, his own world, that of the Renaissance, then opening itself up to the monumental discovery of another, the New World. To be sure, the 'hold' of the atomized individuals was not of the same nature or as powerful as in Epicurus and Machiavelli; and Hobbes, unfortunately for us, was no historian, although he lived through so much history (these are not vocations that one can acquire by simple decree). Yet, in his way, he had arrived at the same result as his teachers in the materialist tradition of the encounter: *the aleatory constitution of a world*; and if this thinker influenced Rousseau (I shall discuss this some day) and even Marx as profoundly as he did, it is clearly owing to the fact that he revived this secret tradition, even if (this is not impossible) he was not aware of the fact. After all, we know that, in these matters, consciousness is only the Fly in the Coach;[41] what matters is that the horses pull the train of the world at the full gallop of the plains or the long slow plod of the uphill climbs.

Although there are no references to Epicurus or Machiavelli in Rousseau's second *Discourse* or the '[Discourse on] the Origin of

Languages', it is to the author of these works that we owe another revival of the 'materialism of the encounter'.

Not enough attention has been paid to the fact that the second *Discourse* begins with a description of the state of nature which differs from other such descriptions in that it is cut in two: we have a '*state of pure nature*' that is the radical Origin of everything, and the '*state of nature*' that follows certain modifications imposed on the *pure state.* In all the examples of the state of nature that the authors of the Natural Law tradition provide, it is clear that this state of nature is a state of society – either of the war of all against all, as in Hobbes, or of trade and peace as in Locke. These authors do indeed do what Rousseau criticizes them for: they project the state of society on to the state of pure nature. Rousseau alone thinks the state of '*pure*' *nature*, and, when he does, thinks it as a state lacking all social relations, whether positive or negative.[42] He uses the fantastic image of the primeval forest to represent it, recalling another Rousseau, Le Douanier, whose paintings show us isolated individuals who have no relations to each other wandering about: *individuals without encounters.* Of course, a man and a woman can meet, 'feel one another out', and even pair off, but only in a brief encounter without identity or recognition: hardly have they become acquainted (indeed, they do not even become acquainted: and there is absolutely no question of children, as if the human world, before *Émile*, were oblivious to their existence or could manage without them – neither children nor, therefore, father or mother: no *family*, in sum)[43] than they part, each of them wending his way through the infinite void of the forest. As a rule, when two people do encounter one another, they merely cross paths at a greater or lesser distance without noticing each other, and the encounter does not even take place. The forest is the equivalent of the Epicurean void in which the parallel rain of the atoms falls: it is a pseudo-Brownian void in which individuals cross each other's paths, that is to say, do not meet, except in brief con-junctions that do not last. In this way, Rousseau seeks to represent, at a very high price (the absence of children), a *radical absence* [*néant*] *of society* prior to all society; and – condition of possibility for all society – the radical absence of society that constitutes the essence of any possible society. That the radical absence of society constitutes the essence of all society is an audacious thesis, the radical nature of which escaped not only Rousseau's contemporaries, but many of his later critics as well.

For a society to be, what is required? The *state of encounter has to be imposed* on people; the infinity of the forest, as a condition of possibility for the non-encounter, has to be reduced to the finite by external causes; natural catastrophes have to divide it up into confined spaces, for example islands, where men are *forced* to have encounters, and forced to have encounters that last: forced by a force superior to them. I leave to one side the ingenuity of those natural catastrophes that affect the surface of the earth – the simplest of which is the very slight, the infinitesimal, tilt of the equator from the ecliptic, an accident without cause akin to the clinamen – in order to discuss their effects.[44] Once men are forced to make encounters and found associations which, *in fact*, last, *constrained relationships* spring up among them, social relationships that are rudimentary at first, and are then reinforced by the effects that these encounters have on their human nature.

A long, slow dialectic comes into play at this point; in it, with the accumulation of time, forced contacts produce language, the passions, and amorous exchanges or struggle between men: such struggle eventually leads to the state of war. Society is born, the state of nature is born, and war as well. Along with them, there develops a process of accumulation and change that literally *creates socialized human nature.* It should be noted that it would be possible for this encounter not to last if the constancy of external constraints did not maintain it in a constant state in the face of the temptation of dispersion, did not literally impose its law of proximity without asking men for their opinion; their society thus emerges behind their backs, so to speak, and their history emerges as the dorsal, unconscious constitution of this society.

No doubt man in the state of pure nature, although he has a body and, as it were, no soul, carries within himself a transcendent capacity for all that he is and all that will happen to him – *perfectibility* – which is, so to speak, the abstraction and transcendental condition of possibility for all anticipation of all development; and also a faculty that is perhaps more important: *pity*, which, as the negative faculty of

[not] being able to bear the suffering of one's fellow man, is society by virtue of its absence [*société par manque*], hence latent society, a negative society latent in the isolated man, athirst for the Other in his very solitude.[45] But all this, which is posed from the beginning of the state of 'pure' nature, is not active there, has no existence or effect, but is merely expectation of the future that awaits man. Just as society and the history in which it is constituted come about behind man's back, without his conscious, active involvement, so both perfectibility and pity are merely the negative [*nul*] anticipation of this future, in which *man has no hand.*

There have been studies of the genealogy of these concepts (Goldschmidt's book is definitive),[46] but there has not been enough study of the effects of this system as a whole, which is rounded off in the second *Discourse* by the theory of the *illegitimate contract*, a contract of force concluded with the obedience of the weak by the arrogance of the powerful, who are also the 'most cunning'. This determines the true meaning of the Social Contract, which is concluded and persists only under the constant threat of the *abyss* (Rousseau himself uses this word [*abîme*] in the *Confessions*) represented by a *re-lapse* [*re-chute*] into the state of nature, an organism haunted by the inner death that it must exorcize: in sum, *an encounter that has taken form* and become necessary, but against the background of the aleatory of the non-encounter and its forms, into which the contract can *fall back* at any moment. If this remark, which would have to be developed, is not wrong, it would resolve the classical aporia that constantly counterposes the *Contract* to the second *Discourse*, an academic difficulty whose only equivalent in the history of Western culture is the absurd question as to whether Machiavelli was a monarchist or a republican. … By the same token, it would clarify the status of the texts in which Rousseau ventures to legislate for the peoples (the Corsican people, the Poles, and so on) by reviving, in all its force, the concept that dominates in Machiavelli – he does not utter the word, but this hardly matters, since the thing is present: the concept of the *conjuncture.* To give men laws, one must take full account of the way the *conditions* present themselves, of the surrounding circumstances, of the '*there is*' this and not that, as, allegorically, one must take account of the climate and many other conditions in Montesquieu, of these conditions and their history, that is to say, of their 'having come about' – in short, of the encounters which might not have taken place (compare the state of nature: 'that state that might never have arisen')[47] and which have taken place, shaping the 'given' of the problem and its state. What does this signify, if not an attempt to think not only the contingency of necessity, but also the necessity of the contingency at its root? The social contract then no longer appears as a utopia, but as the inner law of any society, in its legitimate or illegitimate form, and the real problem becomes: *how does it happen that one never rectifies an illegitimate (the prevailing) form, transforming it into a legitimate form*? At the limit, the legitimate form does not exist, but *one has to postulate it* in order to think the existing concrete forms: those Spinozist 'singular essences', whether individuals, conjunctures, real states or their peoples – one has to postulate it as the transcendental condition for any condition, that is, any *history*.

The most profound thing in Rousseau is doubtless disclosed and covered back up [*découvert et recouvert*] here, in this vision of any possible theory of history, which thinks the contingency of necessity as an effect of the necessity of contingency, an unsettling pair of concepts that must nevertheless be taken into account. They make themselves felt in Montesquieu and are explicitly postulated in Rousseau, as an intuition of the eighteenth century that refutes in advance all the teleologies of history which tempted it, and for which it cleared a broad path under the irresistible impulsion of the French Revolution. To put it in polemical terms: when one raises the question of the 'end of history', Epicurus and Spinoza, Montesquieu and Rousseau range themselves in the same camp, on the basis, explicit or implicit, of the same materialism of the encounter or, in the full sense of the term, the same idea of the *conjuncture*. Marx too, of course – but Marx was constrained to think within a horizon torn between the aleatory of the Encounter and the necessity of the Revolution.

Let us hazard one last remark, which tends to bring out the fact that it is perhaps no accident that this curious pair of concepts interested, above all, men who sought, in the concepts of encounter and conjuncture, a means with which to think not only the *reality* of history, but, above all, the reality of *politics*; not only the essence of reality but, above all, the essence of *practice*, and the link between these two realities in their *encounter*: *in struggle* (I say struggle) and, at the limit, war (Hobbes, Rousseau). This struggle was the struggle for recognition (Hegel), but also, and well before Hegel, the struggle of all against all that is known as competition or, when it takes this form, class struggle (and its 'contradiction').[48] Is there any need to recall why and on whose behalf Spinoza speaks when he invokes Machiavelli? He wants only to think Machiavelli's thought, and, since it is a thought of practice, to think practice via that thought.[49]

All these historical remarks are just a prelude to what I wanted to call attention to in Marx. They are not, to be sure, accidental, but, rather, attest that, from Epicurus to Marx,[50] there had always subsisted – even if it was covered over (by its very discovery, by forgetfulness, and, especially, by denial and repression, when it was not by condemnations that cost some their lives) – the 'discovery' of a profound tradition that sought its materialist anchorage *in a philosophy of the encounter* (and therefore in a more or less atomistic philosophy, the atom, in its 'fall', being the simplest figure of individuality). Whence this tradition's radical rejection of all philosophies of essence (*Ousia*, *Essentia*, *Wesen*), that is, of Reason (*Logos*, *Ratio*, *Vernunft*), and therefore of Origin and End – the Origin being nothing more, here, than the anticipation of the End in Reason or primordial order (that is, the anticipation of Order, whether it be rational, moral, religious or aesthetic) – in the interests of a philosophy which, rejecting the Whole and every Order, rejects the Whole and order *in favour of* dispersion (Derrida would say, in his terminology, 'dissemination') and *disorder*.

To say that in the beginning was nothingness or disorder is to take up a position prior to any assembling and ordering, and to give up thinking the origin as Reason or End in order to think it as nothingness. To the old question 'What is the origin of the world?', this materialist philosophy answers: 'Nothingness!', 'Nothing', 'I start out from nothing', 'There is no beginning, because nothing ever existed before anything at all'; therefore 'There is no obligatory beginning of philosophy', 'philosophy does not start out from a beginning that is its origin'; on the contrary, it 'catches a moving train', and, by sheer strength of arm, 'hoists itself aboard the train' that has been running for all eternity in front of it, like Heraclitus' river. Hence there is no end, either of the world, or of history, or of philosophy, or of morality, or of art or politics, and so on. These themes, which, from Nietzsche to Deleuze and Derrida, from English empiricism (Deleuze) to (with Derrida's help) Heidegger, have become familiar to us by now, are fertile for any understanding not only of philosophy, but also all its supposed 'objects' (whether science, culture, art, literature, or any other expression of existence). They are crucial to this materialism of the encounter, however well disguised they may be in the form of other concepts. Today we are capable of translating them into plainer language.

We shall say that the materialism of the encounter has been christened 'materialism' only provisionally,[a] in order to bring out its radical opposition to any idealism of consciousness or reason, whatever its destination. We shall further say that the materialism of the encounter turns on a certain interpretation of the single proposition *there is* (*es gibt*, Heidegger) and its developments or implications, namely: 'there is' = 'there is nothing'; 'there is' = '*there has always-already been nothing*', that is to say, 'something', the 'always-already', of which I have made abundant use in my essays until now, although this has not always been noticed – since the always-already is the grip[51] (*Greifen*: grasp [*prise*] in German; *Begriff*: grasp or *concept*) of this antecedence of each thing over itself, hence over every kind of origin. We shall say, then, that the materialism of the encounter is contained in the thesis of the primacy of positivity over negativity (Deleuze), the thesis of the primacy of the swerve over the rectilinearity of the straight trajectory (the Origin is a swerve from it, not the reason for it), the thesis of the primacy of disorder over order (one thinks here of the theory of 'noise'), the thesis of the primacy of 'dissemination' over the postulate that every signifier has a meaning (Derrida), and in the welling up of

a This is why Dominique Lecourt is right to advance the term 'sur-materialism' in connection with Marx, in a remarkable work that has naturally been ignored by a University accustomed to responding with contempt whenever it feels that 'a point has been scored against it' (see *L'Ordre et les jeux*, Paris, 1981, last part).

order from the very heart of disorder to produce a world. We shall say that the materialism of the encounter is also contained in its entirety in the negation of the End, of all teleology, be it rational, secular, moral, political or aesthetic. Finally, we shall say that the materialism of the encounter is the materialism, not of a subject (be it God or the proletariat), but of a process, a process that has no subject, yet imposes on the subjects (individuals or others) which it dominates the order of its development, with no assignable end.

If we were to push these theses further, we would be led to formulate a number of concepts that would, of course, be *concepts without objects*, since they would be the concepts of *nothing*, and, inasmuch as philosophy has no object, would make this nothing into being or beings, to the point of rendering it unrecognizable and recognizable in them (which is why it was, in the last analysis, both misrecognized and anticipated). To illustrate these theses, we would refer to the first form, the simplest and purest, which they took in the history of philosophy, in Democritus and, especially, Epicurus. Democritus' and Epicurus' work, we would note in passing, did not fall victim to the flames by accident, these incendiaries of every philosophical tradition having paid for their sins in kind – the flames, produced by friction, which one sees bursting from the tips of the tallest trees, because they are tall (Lucretius),[52] or from philosophies (the great philosophies). We would then have, in this illustration (which must be renewed at every stage of the history of philosophy), the following first forms:

'*Die Welt ist alles, was der Fall ist*' (Wittgenstein):[53] the world is everything that 'falls', everything that 'comes about [*advient*]', 'everything that is the case' – by *case*, let us understand *casus*: *at once occurrence and chance*, that which comes about in the mode of the unforeseeable, and yet of being.

Thus, as far back as we can go, 'there is' = 'there has always been', there 'has-always-already-been', the 'already' being absolutely necessary in order to mark this priority of the occurrence, of the *Fall*, over all its forms, that is to say, all the *forms* of beings. This is[54] Heidegger's *es gibt*, the inaugural deal [*la donne*] (rather than what has been dealt out [*le donné*], depending on whether one wishes to highlight the active or passive aspect); it is always prior to its *presence*. In other words, it is the primacy of absence over presence (Derrida), not as a *going-back-towards,* but as a horizon receding endlessly ahead of the walker who, seeking his path on the plain, never finds anything but another plain stretching out before him (very different from the Cartesian walker who has only to walk straight ahead in a forest in order to get out of it,[55] because the world is made up, alternatively, of virgin forests and forests that have been cleared to create open fields: without *Holzwege*).[56]

In this 'world' without being or history (like Rousseau's forest), what happens? For *there are occurrences there*, taking this phrase in the impersonal, active/passive sense [*car il y advient: 'il', actif/passif impersonnel*]. *Encounters.* What happens there is what happens in Epicurus' universal rain, prior to any world, any being and any reason as well as any cause. What happens is that 'there are encounters' [*ça se rencontre*]; in Heidegger, that 'things are thrown' in an inaugural 'destining'. Whether or not it is by the miracle of the clinamen, it is enough to know that it comes about 'we know not where, we know not when', and that it is 'the smallest deviation possible', that is, the assignable nothingness of all swerve. Lucretius' text is clear enough to designate *that which nothing in the world can designate*, although it is the origin of every world. In the 'nothing' of the swerve, there occurs an encounter between one atom and another, and this event [*événement*] becomes *advent* [*avènement*] on condition of the parallelism of the atoms, for it is this parallelism which, violated on just one occasion, induces the gigantic pile-up and collision–interlocking [*accrochage*] of an infinite number of atoms, from which a world is born (one world or another: hence the plurality of possible worlds, and the fact that the concept of possibility can be rooted in the concept of original disorder).

Whence *the form of order* and the *form of beings* whose birth is induced by this pile-up, determined as they are by the *structure* of the encounter; whence, once the encounter has been effected (but not before), the primacy of the structure over its elements; whence, finally, what one must call an *affinity* and a complementarity [*complétude*] of the elements that come into play in the encounter, their 'readiness to collide–interlock' [*accrochabilité*], in order that this encounter 'take hold', that is to say, 'take *form*', *at last give birth to Forms, and new Forms* –

just as water 'takes hold' when ice is there waiting for it, or milk does when it curdles, or mayonnaise when it emulsifies. Hence the primacy of 'nothing' over all 'form', and *of aleatory materialism over all formalism.*[57] In other words, not just anything can produce just anything, but only elements destined [*voués*] to encounter each other and, by virtue of their affinity, to 'take hold' one upon the other – which is why, in Democritus, and perhaps even in Epicurus, the atoms are, or are described as, 'hooked', that is, susceptible of interlocking one after the other, from all eternity, irrevocably, for ever.

Once they have thus 'taken hold' or 'collided–interlocked', the atoms enter the realm of Being that they inaugurate: they constitute *beings*, assignable, distinct, localizable beings endowed with such-and-such a property (depending on the time and place); in short, there emerges in them a structure of Being or of the world that assigns each of its elements its place, meaning and role, or, better, establishes them as 'elements of …' (the atoms as elements of bodies, of beings, of the world) in such a way that the atoms, far from being the origin of the world, are merely the secondary consequence of its assignment and advent [*assignement et avènement*]. If we are to talk about the world and its atoms in this way, it is necessary that the world exist, and, *prior to that*, that the atoms exist, a situation which puts discourse on the world *for ever in second place*, and also puts in *second place* (not first, as Aristotle claimed) the philosophy of Being – thus making for ever intelligible, as impossible (and therefore explicable: see the appendix to Book I of the *Ethics*, which repeats nearly verbatim the critique of all religion found in Epicurus and Lucretius) any discourse of *first philosophy*, even if it is materialist (which explains why Epicurus, who knew this, never subscribed to the 'mechanical' materialism of Democritus, this materialism being only a resurgence, within a possible philosophy of the encounter, of the dominant idealism of Order as immanent in Disorder).

Once these principles have been set out, the rest follows naturally, if I may be forgiven the expression.[58]

1. For *a being* (a body, an animal, a man, state, or Prince) *to be*, an encounter has *to have taken* place (past infinitive). To limit ourselves to Machiavelli, an encounter has to have taken place between beings

with affinities [*des affinissables*]; between such-and-such an individual and such-and-such a conjuncture, or Fortune, for example – the conjuncture itself being junction, con-junction, congealed (albeit shifting) encounter, since it has already taken place, and refers in its turn to the infinite number of its prior causes, just as (let us add) a determinate [*défini*] individual (for instance, Borgia) refers to the infinite sequence [*suite*] of prior causes of which it is the result.

2. There are encounters only between series [*séries*] of beings that are the results of several series of causes – at least two, but this two soon proliferates, by virtue of the effect of parallelism or general contagion (as Breton put it, profoundly, 'elephants are contagious').[b] One also thinks here of Cournot, a great but neglected thinker.

3. Every encounter is aleatory, not only in its origins (nothing ever guarantees an encounter), but also in its effects. In other words, every encounter might not have taken place, although it did take place; but its possible nonexistence sheds light on the meaning of its aleatory being. And every encounter is aleatory in its effects, in that nothing in the elements of the encounter prefigures, before the actual encounter, the contours and determinations of the being that will emerge from it. Julius II did not know that he was harbouring his mortal enemy in his Romagnol breast, nor did he know that this mortal enemy would be lying at death's door, and so find himself outside history [*hors histoire*] at the critical hour of Fortune, only to go off and die in an obscure Spain before the walls of an unknown castle.[59] This means that no determination of the being which issues from the 'taking-hold' of the encounter is prefigured, even in outline, in the being of the elements that converge in the encounter. Quite the contrary: no determination of these elements can be assigned except by *working backwards* from the result to its becoming, in its retroaction. If we must therefore say that there can be no result without its becoming (Hegel), we must also affirm that there is nothing which has become except as determined by the result of this becoming – this retroaction itself (Canguilhem). That is, instead of thinking contingency as a modality of necessity, or

b Compare Feuerbach citing Pliny the Elder: 'elephants [...] have no religion'. Ludwig Feuerbach, *The Essence of Christianity*, trans. George Eliot, Amherst, New York, 1989, p. 1.

an exception to it, we must think necessity as the becoming-necessary of the encounter of contingencies.

Thus we see that not only the world of life (the biologists, who should have known their Darwin, have recently become aware of this[c]), but the world of history, too, *gels* at certain felicitous moments, with the taking-hold of elements combined in an encounter that is apt to trace such-and-such a figure: such-and-such a species, individual, or people. Thus it happens that there are aleatory men or 'lives', subject to the accident of a death bestowed or received, as well as their 'works', and the great figures of the world to which the original 'throw of the dice' of the aleatory has given their form: the great figures in which the world of history has 'taken form' (Antiquity, the Middle Ages, the Renaissance, the Enlightenment, etc.). This makes it all too clear that anyone who took it into his head to consider these figures, individuals, conjunctures or States of the world as either the necessary result of given premisses or the provisional anticipation of an End would be mistaken, because he would be neglecting the fact (the '*Faktum*') that these provisional results are doubly provisional – not only in that they will be superseded, but also in that they might never have come about, or might have come about only as the effect of a 'brief encounter', if they had not arisen on the happy basis of a stroke of good Fortune which gave their '*chance*' to 'last' to the elements over whose conjunction it so happens (by chance) that this form had to preside. This shows that we are not – that we do not live – in Nothingness [*le Néant*], but that, although there is no Meaning to history (an End which transcends it, from its origins to its term), there can be meaning *in* history, since this meaning emerges from an encounter that was real, and really felicitous – or catastrophic, which is also a meaning.

From this there follow very important consequences as to the meaning of the word 'law'. It will be granted that no law presides over the encounter in which things take hold. But, it will be objected, once the encounter *has* 'taken hold' – that is, once the stable figure of the

c See the fine and very successful conference on Darwin recently organized in Chantilly by Dominique Lecourt and Yvette Conry [Conry, ed., *De Darwin au Darwinisme: Science et idéologie*, Paris, 1983].

world, of the *only* existing world (for the advent of a given world obviously excludes all the other possible combinations), has been constituted – we have to do with a stable world in which events, in their succession [*suite*], obey 'laws'. Hence it does not much matter whether the world, our world (we know no other; of the infinity of possible attributes, we know only two, the understanding and space: '*Faktum*', Spinoza might have said), emerged from the encounter of atoms falling in the Epicurean rain of the void, or from the 'Big Bang' hypothesized by the astrophysicists. The fact is that we have to do with *this* world and not another. The fact is that this world '*plays by the rules*' [*est régulier*] (in the sense in which one says that an honest player does: for this world plays, and – no mistake about it – plays with us), that it is subject to rules and obeys laws. Hence the very great temptation, even for those who are willing to grant the premisses of this materialism of the encounter, of resorting, once the encounter has 'taken hold', to the study of the laws which derive from this taking-hold of forms, and repeat these forms, to all intents and purposes, indefinitely. For it is also a fact, a *Faktum*, that there is order in this world, and that knowledge of this world comes by way of knowledge of its 'laws' (Newton) and the conditions of possibility, not of the existence of these laws, but only of knowledge of them. This is, to be sure, a way of indefinitely deferring the old question of the origin of the world (this is how Kant proceeds), but only in order to obscure all the more effectively the origin of the second encounter that makes possible knowledge of the first in *this* world (the encounter between concepts and things).

Well, we are going to resist this temptation by defending a thesis dear to Rousseau, who maintained that the contract is based on an 'abyss' – by defending the idea, therefore, that the necessity of the laws that issue from the taking-hold induced by the encounter is, even at its most stable, haunted by a *radical instability*, which explains something we find it very hard to grasp (for it does violence to our sense of 'what is seemly'): that laws can change – not that they can be valid for a time but not eternally (in his critique of classical political economy, Marx went that far, as his 'Russian critic' had well understood,[60] arguing that every historical period has its laws, although he went no further, as we shall see), but that they can change at the drop of a hat, revealing the aleatory basis that sustains them, and can change without reason, that is, without an intelligible end. This is where their *surprise* lies (*there can be no taking-hold without surprise*) [*il n'est de prise que sous la surprise*].[61] This is what strikes everyone so forcefully during the great commencements, turns or suspensions of history, whether of individuals (for example, madness) or of the world, when the dice are, as it were, thrown back on to the table unexpectedly, or the cards are dealt out again without warning, or the 'elements' are unloosed in the fit of madness that frees them up for new, surprising ways of taking-hold [*de nouvelles prises surprenantes*] (Nietzsche, Artaud). No one will balk at the idea that this is one of the basic features of the history of individuals or the world, of the revelation that makes an unknown individual an author or a madman, or both at once: when Hölderlins, Goethes and Hegels come into the world conjointly; when the French Revolution breaks out and triumphs down to the march of Napoleon, the *Zeitgeist*, beneath Hegel's windows at Jena; when the Commune bursts forth from treason; when 1917 explodes in Russia, or, *a fortiori*, when the 'Cultural Revolution' does, a revolution in which, truly, almost all the 'elements' were unloosed over vast spaces, although the lasting encounter did not occur – like the 13th of May,[62] when the workers and students, who ought to have 'joined up' (what a result would have resulted from that!), saw their long parallel demonstrations cross, but *without joining up*, avoiding, at all costs, joining up, conjoining, uniting in a unity that is, no doubt, still for ever unprecedented (the rain in its *avoided* effects).

To[63] give some sense of the underground current of the materialism of the encounter, which is very important in Marx, and of its repression by a (philosophical) materialism of essence, we have to discuss the mode of production. No one can deny the importance of this concept, which serves not only to think every 'social formation', but also to periodize the history of social formations, and thus to found a theory of history.[d]

d See [Althusser *et al.*,] *Lire le Capital*, I [ed. Étienne Balibar, Paris, 1996, pp. 1–244].

In fact, we find *two* absolutely unrelated conceptions of the mode of production in Marx.

The first goes back to Engels's *Condition of the Working-Class in England*; its real inventor was Engels. It recurs in the famous chapter on primitive accumulation, the working day, and so on, and in a host of minor allusions, to which I shall return, if possible. It may also be found in the theory of the Asiatic mode of production. *The second* is found in the great passages of *Capital* on the essence of capitalism, as well as the essence of the feudal and socialist modes of production, and on the revolution; and, more generally, in the 'theory' of the transition, or form of passage, from one mode of production to another. The things that have been written on the 'transition' from capitalism to communism over the past twenty years beggar the imagination and are past all counting!

In untold passages, Marx – this is certainly no accident – explains that the capitalist mode of production arose from the '*encounter*' between 'the owners of money'[64] and the proletarian stripped of everything but his labour-power. 'It so happens' that this encounter took place, and 'took hold', which means that it did not come undone as soon as it came about, but *lasted*, and became an accomplished fact, the accomplished fact of this encounter, inducing stable relationships and a necessity the study of which yields 'laws' – tendential laws, of course: the laws of the development of the capitalist mode of production (the law of value, the law of exchange, the law of cyclical crises, the law of the crisis and decay of the capitalist mode of production, the law of the passage – transition – to the socialist mode of production under the laws of the class struggle, and so on). What matters about this conception is less the elaboration of laws, hence of an essence, than *the aleatory character of the 'taking-hold' of this encounter, which gives rise to an accomplished fact* whose laws it is possible to state.

This can be put differently: the whole that results from the 'taking-hold' of the 'encounter' does not precede the 'taking-hold' of its elements, but follows it; for this reason, it might not have 'taken hold', and, *a fortiori*, 'the encounter might not have taken place'.[65] All this is said – in veiled terms, to be sure, but it is said – in the formula that Marx uses in his frequent discussions of the 'encounter' [*das*

Vorgefundene] between raw labour-power and the owners of money. We can go even further, and suppose *that this encounter occurred several times in history before taking hold in the West*, but, for lack of an element or a suitable arrangement of the elements, failed to 'take'. Witness the thirteenth-century and fourteenth-century Italian states of the Po valley, where there were certainly men who owned money, technology and energy (machines driven by the hydraulic power of the river) as well as manpower (unemployed artisans), but where the phenomenon nevertheless failed to 'take hold'. What was lacking here was doubtless (perhaps – this is a hypothesis) that which Machiavelli was desperately seeking in the form of his appeal for a national state: *a domestic market* capable of absorbing what might have been produced.

The slightest reflection on the presuppositions of this conception suffices to show that it is predicated on a very special type of relationship between the structure and the elements which this structure is supposed to unify. For what is a mode of production? We provided an answer to this question, following Marx: *it is a particular 'combination' of elements*. These elements are an accumulation of money (by the 'owners of money'), an accumulation of the technical means of production (tools, machines, an experience of production on the part of the workers), an accumulation of the raw materials of production (nature) and an accumulation of producers (proletarians divested of all means of production). The elements do not exist in history *so that* a mode of production may exist, they exist in history *in a 'floating' state* prior to their 'accumulation' and 'combination', each being the product of its own history, and none being the teleological product of the others or their history. When Marx and Engels say that the proletariat is 'the product of big industry', they utter a very great piece of nonsense, positioning themselves within the *logic of the accomplished fact of the reproduction of the proletariat on an extended scale*, not the aleatory logic of the 'encounter' which produces (rather than reproduces), as the proletariat, this mass of impoverished, expropriated human beings as one of the elements making up the mode of production. In the process, Marx and Engels shift from the first conception of the mode of production, an historico-aleatory conception, to a second, which is essentialistic and philosophical.

I am repeating myself, but I must: what is remarkable about the first conception, apart from the explicit theory of the encounter, is the idea that every mode of production comprises *elements that are independent of each other*, each resulting from its own specific history, in the absence of any organic, teleological relation between these diverse histories. This conception culminates in the theory of *primitive accumulation*, from which Marx, taking his inspiration from Engels, drew a magnificent chapter of *Capital*, the true heart of the book. Here we witness the emergence of a historical phenomenon whose result we know – the expropriation of the means of production from an entire rural population in Great Britain – but whose causes bear no relation to the result and its effects. Was the aim to create extensive domains for the hunt? Or endless fields for sheep-raising? We do not know *just what* the main reason for this process of violent dispossession was (it was most likely the sheep), and, especially, the main reason for the violence of it; moreover, it doesn't much matter. The fact is that this process took place, culminating in a *result* that was promptly *diverted* from its possible, presumed end by 'owners of money' looking for impoverished manpower. *This diversion is the mark of the non-teleology of the process* and of the incorporation of its result into a process that both made it possible and was wholly foreign to it.

It would, moreover, be a mistake to think that this process of the aleatory encounter was confined to the English fourteenth century. It has always gone on, and *is going on even today* – not only in the countries of the Third World, which provide the most striking example of it, but also in France, by way of the dispossession of agricultural producers and their transformation into semi-skilled workers (consider Sandouville: Bretons running machines[66]) – as a permanent process that puts the aleatory at the heart of the survival and reinforcement of the capitalist 'mode of production', and also, let us add, at the heart of the so-called socialist 'mode of production' itself.[e] Here Marxist scholars untiringly rehearse Marx's fantasy, thinking the *reproduction* of the proletariat in the mistaken belief that they are thinking its production;

e See Charles Bettelheim's remarkable *Class Struggles in the USSR*, trans. Brian Pearce, vol. 2: *Second Period*, New York, 1978 (1965).

thinking in the accomplished fact when they think they are thinking in its becoming-accomplished.

There are indeed things in Marx that can lead us to make this error, whenever he cedes to the other conception of the mode of production: a conception that is totalitarian, teleological and philosophical.

In this case, we are clearly dealing with all the elements mentioned above, but so thought and ordered as to suggest that they were from all eternity destined to enter into combination, harmonize with one another, and reciprocally produce each other as their own ends, conditions and/or complements. On this hypothesis, Marx deliberately leaves the aleatory nature of the 'encounter' and its 'taking-hold' to one side *in order to think solely in terms of the accomplished fact of the 'take' and, consequently, its predestination.* On this hypothesis, each element has, not an independent history, but a history that pursues an end – that of adapting to the other histories, history constituting a whole which endlessly *reproduces* its own [*propre*] elements, so made as to [*propre à*] mesh. This explains why Marx and Engels conceive of the proletariat as a 'product of big industry', 'a product of capitalist exploitation', *confusing the production of the proletariat with its capitalist reproduction on an extended scale*, as if the capitalist mode of production pre-existed one of its essential elements, an expropriated labour-force.[f] Here *the specific histories no longer float in history*, like so many atoms in the void, at the mercy of an 'encounter' that might not take place. Everything is accomplished in advance; *the structure precedes its elements and reproduces them in order to reproduce the structure.* What holds for primitive accumulation also holds for the owners of money. Where do they come from in Marx? We cannot tell, exactly. From mercantile capitalism, as he says? (This is a very mysterious expression that has spawned many an absurdity about 'the mercantile mode of production.') From usury? From primitive accumulation? From colonial pillage? Ultimately, this is of small importance for our purposes, even if it is of special importance to Marx. *What is essential is the result: the fact that they exist.* Marx, however, abandons this thesis for *the thesis of a mythical 'decay' of the*

f On this point, Engels's 'The Principles of Communism' [*MECW* 6: 346] leaves no room for doubt: the proletariat is the product of the 'industrial revolution' (*sic* – Louis Althusser).

feudal mode of production and the birth of the bourgeoisie from the heart of this decay, which introduces new mysteries. What proves that the feudal mode of production declines and decays, then eventually disappears? It was not until 1850–70 that capitalism established itself firmly in France. Above all, given that the bourgeoisie is said to be the product of the feudal mode of production, what proves that it was not a class of the feudal mode of production, and a sign of the reinforcement rather than the decay of this mode? These mysteries in *Capital* both revolve around the same object: money and mercantile capitalism on the one hand, and, on the other, the nature of the bourgeois class, said to be its support and beneficiary.

If, to define capital, one contents oneself with talking, as Marx does, about *an accumulation of money* that produces a surplus – a money profit (M" = M + M') – then it is possible to speak of money and mercantile capitalism. But these are *capitalisms without capitalists*, capitalisms *without exploitation of a labour force*, capitalisms in which exchange[67] more or less takes the form of a levy governed not by the law of value, but by practices of pillage, either direct or indirect. Consequently, it is here that we encounter the great question of the *bourgeoisie.*

Marx's solution is simple and disarming. The bourgeoisie is produced as an antagonistic class by the decay of the dominant feudal class. Here we find the schema of dialectical production again, a contrary producing its contrary. We also find the dialectical thesis of negation, a contrary naturally being required, by virtue of a conceptual necessity, to replace its contrary and become dominant in its turn. But what if this was not how things happened? What if the bourgeoisie, far from being the contrary product of the feudal class, was its culmination and, as it were, acme, its highest form and, so to speak, crowning perfection? This would enable us to resolve many problems which are so many dead-ends, especially the problems of the bourgeois revolutions, such as the French Revolution, which are supposed, come hell or high water, to be capitalist,[g] yet are not; and a number of other problems that are so many mysteries: what is this strange

g [Albert] Soboul [1914–82] stubbornly devoted the whole of his short life to trying to prove this.

class – capitalist by virtue of its future, but formed well before any kind of capitalism, under feudalism – known as the bourgeoisie?

Just as there is not, in Marx, a satisfactory theory of the so-called mercantile mode of production, nor, *a fortiori*, of merchant (and money) capital, *so there is no satisfactory theory of the bourgeoisie in Marx* – excepting, of course, for the purpose of eliminating problems, a superabundant utilization of the adjective 'bourgeois', as if an adjective could stand in for the concept of pure negativity. And it is no accident that the theory of the bourgeoisie as a form of antagonistic disintegration of the feudal mode of production is consistent with the philosophically inspired conception of the mode of production. In this conception, the bourgeoisie is indeed nothing other than the *element predestined* to unify all the other elements of the mode of production, the one that will transform it into another combination, that of the capitalist mode of production. It is the dimension of the whole and of the teleology that assigns each element its role and position in the whole, reproducing it in its existence and role.

We are at the opposite pole from the conception of the '*encounter between the bourgeoisie*', an element that 'floats' as much as all the others, and *other* floating *elements*, an encounter that brings an original mode of production into existence, the capitalist mode of production. Here there is no encounter, for the unity precedes the elements, *for the void essential to any aleatory encounter is lacking.* Whereas it is in fact still a question of thinking *the fact to be accomplished*, Marx deliberately positions himself within *the accomplished fact*, and invites us to follow him in the laws of its necessity.

Following Marx, we[68] defined a mode of production as a double combination (Balibar), that of the means of production and that of the relations of production (??). To pursue this analysis, we need to distinguish certain elements in it, 'productive forces, means of production, those who possess the means of production, producers with or without means, nature, men, etc.'. What then comprises the mode of production is a combination which subjects the productive forces (the means of production, the producers) to the domination of a totality, in which it is the owners of the means of production who are dominant. This combination is essential [*est d'essence*], is established once and for all, and corresponds to a centre of references; it can, to be sure, disintegrate, but it still conserves the same structure in its disintegration. A mode of production is a combination because it is a *structure* that imposes its unity on a series of elements. What counts in a mode of production, what makes it such-and-such, is the *mode of domination* of the structure over its elements. Thus, in the feudal mode of production, it is the *structure of dependence* which imposes their signification on the elements: possession of the manor, including the serfs who work on it, possession of the collective instruments (the mill, the farmland, etc.) by the lord, the subordinate role of money, except when, later, pecuniary relations are imposed on everyone. Thus, in the capitalist mode of production, it is the structure of exploitation that is imposed on all the elements, the subordination of the means of production and the productive forces to the process of exploitation, the exploitation of workers stripped of the means of production, the monopoly of the means of production in the hands of the capitalist class, and so forth.

Notes

1 Althusser left his manuscript untitled; the present text takes its title from a phrase that occurs on p. 196 above. Published here are chapters 4–9 and 12 of the projected book described on p. 163 above.

2 Thus pp. 109–16 of the photocopy are identical with pp. 56–63, and pp. 119–25 with pp. 69–75.

3 Althusser, Letter of 3 November 1987 to Fernanda Navarro, p. 245 below. [*Trans.*]

4 The Left's victory in the presidential elections was in fact a narrow one, although it carried the ensuing legislative elections with a solid majority. [*Trans.*]

5 Père-Lachaise is a cemetery in Paris's Twentieth Arrondissement. In May 1871, it saw a fierce battle that sealed the defeat of the Paris Commune at the hands of the liberal regime headed by Louis Adolphe Thiers. After the fighting, the Communards who had survived it were shot down in cold blood; the *Mur des Fédérés*, in the south-eastern corner of the cemetery, memorializes the massacre. The apartment in which Althusser lived in the 1980s stands not far from this wall. [*Trans.*]

6 Neither of these two volumes was ever written.

7 Althusser later deleted this paragraph, which originally formed the conclusion to the first version of his preface.

8 Nicolas Malebranche, *Dialogues on Metaphysics and on Religion*, trans. Morris Ginsburg, London, 1923, p. 245.

9 See Nicolas Malebranche, *A Treatise of Nature and Grace*, trans. anon., London, 1695, p. 22, translation modified: 'I use the examples of the irregularity of ordinary rain to ready the soul for another rain, which is not given to the merits of men, no more than the common rain which falls equally upon lands that are sown, as well as those that lie fallow.'

10 Althusser intended to insert a note here. It would probably have been a reference to Lucretius, *De rerum natura*, Book 2, ll. 217–20. [*Trans.*]

11 Leibniz, 'Principles of Nature and of Grace, Based on Reason', §7, in *idem*, *Philosophical Writings*, ed. G. H. R. Parkinson, trans. Parkinson and Mary Morris, London, 1973, p. 199. I thank V. Morfino for help with this and other notes. [*Trans.*]

12 Martin Heidegger, 'Letter on Humanism', trans. Frank A. Capuzzi and J. Glenn Gray, in *Heidegger, Basic Writings*, ed. David Farrell Krell, London, 1993, p. 245; translation modified. [*Trans.*]

13 The first draft reads 'itself empty (yet full)'.

14 *P* 62–3 ('How to Avoid Hatred'). [*Trans.*]

15 Ibid., p. 38 ('Cruelty Prudently Used'). [*Trans.*]

16 Ibid., pp. 64–5 ('The Prince Must Fight as Both Animal and Man'). [*Trans.*]

17 Ibid., p. 66 ('The Prince Ready, in Necessity, to Abandon Conventional Ethics'). [*Trans.*]

18 See n. 11 above. [*Trans.*]

19 'LP' 193. [*Trans.*]

20 This is the first line of Goethe's 'Vanitas! Vanitatum vanitas', from which Max Stirner took the epigraph to *The Ego and His Own*. [*Trans.*]

21 Here, Althusser is thinking of *MU*, a text based on the many courses on Machiavelli that he gave over the years. He seriously considered publishing it on a number of occasions.

22 Althusser intended to insert a note here. It would probably have been a reference to 'RSC' 118 (Book 3, ch. 6): 'Under the pretence of teaching kings, it has taught important lessons to the people. Machiavelli's *Prince* is a handbook for Republicans.'

23 Althusser intended to insert a note here. It would probably have been a reference to *TP*, V, 7. [*Trans.*]

24 As Althusser was writing these lines, Pierre Macherey was defending much the same paradoxical thesis at an October 1982 conference held in Urbino to commemorate the 350th anniversary of Spinoza's birth. His paper, 'Entre Pascal et Spinoza: Le vide' (1982), was later published in Macherey, *Avec Spinoza*, Paris, 1992. See especially pp. 165 ff:

If we look beyond Pascal's literal formulation to the meaning that he is trying to communicate, does he say anything different [from Spinoza]? In relating his 'feeling' about the void, he plainly means to postulate the infinity, that is, indivisibility of extension, which, as such, is irreducible to any physical component of nature whatsoever, so that we must be able to think it in and of itself, independently of the presence of any finite material reality. Whether one calls this infinity full or empty is, after all, merely a question of the name one chooses to give it, and has no bearing on the content of the reasoning that name designates.

25 Compare *E* II, P 15, S. [*Trans.*]

26 The remark that Althusser attributes to Spinoza was in fact jotted down by Leibniz after a discussion of Spinoza with Tschirnhaus.

27 *E* III, P 2, S. [*Trans.*]

28 This section of the text is so thickly covered with handwritten emendations that it is difficult to decipher. The original versions reads: 'The attributes fall in the empty space of their indetermination like the drops of rain that have encountered each other only in man, in the assignable, but minute parallelism of thought and the body.'

29 *E* II, P 7. [*Trans.*]

30 *E* II, A 2. [*Trans.*]

31 *E* II, P 40, S 2. [*Trans.*]

32 *E* I, Appendix, p. 74: 'This doctrine concerning the end turns Nature completely upside down. For what is really a cause, it considers as an effect, and conversely.' Elsewhere, Althusser translates Spinoza's phrase *tota illa fabrica*, which occurs in the Appendix to Book I of the *Ethics* shortly before the sentence just quoted, as 'an entire "apparatus"', likening it to his own concept of the 'Ideological State Apparatus'. [*Trans.*]

33 It would appear that two handwritten emendations are juxtaposed here; the first does not appear to have been deleted.

34 *TTP* 78. [*Trans.*]

35 *L* 186.

36 Thomas Hobbes, *The Elements of Law, Natural and Politic*, ed. Ferdinand Tönnies, 2nd edn, London, 1969, p. 47 (Part 1, ch. 9, §21). [*Trans.*]

37 *L* 261. [*Trans.*]

38 *À rester dans un état de guerre ou à entrer dans un État de contrat: état* means 'state' in the sense of 'political state', 'nation-state,' when it begins with a capital letter, and 'state' in the sense of 'condition' when it begins with a small letter. [*Trans.*]

39 *L* 170. [*Trans.*]

40 See p. 103 and note 115 on p. 159 above. [*Trans.*]

41 The common French expression *la mouche du coche* comes from Lafontaine's fable 'Le coche et la mouche' (*Fables*, Book VII, fable 8). A coach gets stuck; the horses finally succeed in pulling it up the hill; the fly, whose

contribution consists in buzzing around and biting them, concludes that she is the one who 'makes the machine go', taking all the glory for the exploit and complaining that she had to do all the work herself. [*Trans.*]

42 'RSD' 132, 215–16 (Exordium §5; Note XII, §7). [*Trans.*]

43 Ibid., p. 145 (Part 1, §25). [*Trans.*]

44 'ROL' 273; Rousseau, 'L'influence des climats sur la civilisation', in Rousseau, *Œuvres complètes*, vol. 3, Paris, 1964, p. 531. [*Trans.*]

45 'RSD' 151–4 (Part 1, §§35–8). [*Trans.*]

46 Victor Goldschmidt, *Anthropologie et politique: Les principes du système de Rousseau*, Paris, 1974.

47 'RSD' 159 (Part 1, §51). In the passage that Althusser cites here, Rousseau in fact says that the conditions whose convergence precipitated the transition to the state of *society* might never have arisen. [*Trans.*]

48 This sentence is so thickly covered with handwritten emendations that it is difficult to decipher.

49 Althusser intended to cite an unspecified passage from *TP*, V, 7 here. See note 23 above.

50 In a handwritten addendum to an earlier version of the present text, Althusser here inserts: 'who, let us note, devoted his doctoral thesis to him, basing it on a splendid piece of nonsense, which the thought of his "youth" made inevitable: an interpretation of the "clinamen" as "freedom"'. [*Trans.*]

51 The French word here translated 'grip' [*griffe*] also designates a wide variety of tools used for clutching or clamping; a stamped signature; and the tag that identifies the designer or manufacturer of a garment. [*Trans.*]

52 See Lucretius, *De rerum natura*, Book V, ll. 1094–1100. [*Trans.*]

53 'The world is everything that is the case.' This is the opening sentence in Wittgenstein's *Tractatus Logico-Philosophicus*, which Althusser quotes in very approximate German.

54 In a handwritten addendum to another version of the text, Althusser specifies: 'but interpreted in the sense, not of thrownness (*Geworfenheit*), but of the aleatory'. [*Trans.*]

55 René Descartes, *Discourse on Method*, trans. Robert Stoothoff, in Descartes, *Philosophical Writings*, vol. 1, trans. John Cottingham *et al.*, London, 1985, p. 123. [*Trans.*]

56 Althusser's library contained a copy of the 1952 German edition of Heidegger's *Holzwege*.

57 This phrase is a handwritten addendum, and the sole occurrence of the phrase 'aleatory materialism' in the present text. Althusser entitled one of his last texts, written in 1986, 'On Aleatory Materialism' [*Sur le matérialisme aléatoire*, ed. François Matheron, *Multitudes* 21, 2005, pp. 179–94].

58 *Coule de source*, a rather unaleatory idiom that means, literally, 'flows from the source/spring'. [*Trans.*]

59 Cesare Borgia died fighting before the Castle of Viana, in Navarre, on 12 March 1507. [*Trans.*]

60 *C1* 100n., 101–2. See p. 17 and note 20 on p. 152 above.

61 Here, as well as a few lines later, Althusser plays on the links between *prise* (here translated as 'taking-hold') and *surprise*, which, besides meaning what it also means in English, silently evokes a neologism, *sur-prise*, roughly analogous to 'surrealism'. *Surprendre*, to surprise, thus comes to carry the same connotations as *sur-prise.* The French word for 'overdetermination', it should be noted, is 'surdétermination'. Compare footnote a above, p. 189. [*Trans.*]

62 An allusion to the biggest of the demonstrations that took place in France in May 1968. The words 'or, a fortiori, when "the Cultural Revolution"' are a handwritten addendum to the text; the reference is to May 1968 alone in the original version, in which the 'workers' and 'students' who failed to 'join up' are faulted for lacking the will to move beyond 'derisory refusal'.

63 The pages that follow originally constituted chapter 12 of the projected book described in the editors' introduction to the present text, pp. 164–5 above. They represent a lightly revised version of a text initially entitled 'On the Mode of Production'.

64 *C1* 874. [*Trans.*]

65 See Gilles Deleuze and Félix Guattari, *Anti-Oedipus: Capitalism and Schizophrenia*, trans. Robert Hurley, Mark Seem and Helen R. Lane, Minneapolis, 1983, p. 225. [*Trans.*]

66 The allusion is to the Renault plant at Sandouville, in Normandy.

67 Presumably a slip for 'exploitation'. [*Trans.*]

68 We have reproduced the original version of the following passage here, because the changes Althusser made in it so as to incorporate it into his projected book (see note 63 above) yielded a patently unsatisfactory result. 'We' in Althusser's text doubtless means the authors of *Reading Capital.*

Correspondence about 'Philosophy and Marxism'

Editorial Note

All of Louis Althusser's letters to Fernanda Navarro published below have been taken from their 1984–87 correspondence, which includes more than thirty typed or handwritten letters by Althusser pertaining to the preparation and publication of his Interview with her. We have selected those letters that bear mainly on the subjects discussed in the Interview. Certain passages in the letters mentioning third parties have not been reproduced here (these passages are marked [***]).

The dating of the letters has been standardized. When Althusser dated a letter, the date given is his; the other dates have been deduced, as a rule, from Navarro's letters. Dates that have been so reconstructed have been put in square brackets, like all other editorial interpolations (corrections of punctuation or minor slips of the pen aside), whether they involve clarification of the context or the elimination of syntactical and grammatical errors.

Althusser's correspondence with Navarro is preceded by a letter he wrote to his friend Mauricio Malamud, who introduced him to her.

This edition of Althusser's letters was of course prepared with the consent of François Boddaert, Louis Althusser's sole legatee.

Olivier Corpet
Director, Institut Mémoires de l'édition contemporaine

Letter to Mauricio Malamud[1]

Typed letter [Paris,] 8 March 1984

My dear Malamud,

I haven't stopped thinking of you since you came to visit with Fernanda. I treated you abominably, and am still ashamed of the way I behaved. But Fernanda tells me you're generous and won't hold it against me….

In any case, it's a blessing for me that Fernanda is in Paris. She helps me to live; for, as you can imagine, now that my wife is dead, the hardest thing to bear is the loneliness. For almost four years now, various friends of mine have been making all sorts of sacrifices to keep me company, some coming for an hour or two, others for a day; when I was in a very bad way, a few even stayed with me in shifts, so that there would be someone here at night (I would get up without knowing where I was, open the door, and stumble into the hall or the stairwells). Fernanda tells me about her life in Mexico, about what she's done for Chile, and about you. For my part, I show her a few texts from the period before the tragedy I went through; but, thanks to all my friends, and to her, since she's come at just the right time to take over from the others for a while, I'm beginning to get down to putting my books and files in order, reading certain texts (F[ernanda] will bring you some of them), and even trying to revise one or two that might be publishable. In other words, I'm doing better, thanks to a very new antidepressant, called Upstene,[2] that works miracles in the chemical line. I call it to your attention – who knows? – You might have a depressed friend who will need it some day.

In short, I'm doing considerably better; a month ago, I would have been incapable of writing you this letter.

I've been thinking about all that we (my little group and I) have done since 1965, or, let's say, did from 1965 to 1975, and I think that I now have a pretty good sense of our enterprise. I haven't yet shared this retrospective judgement with anyone; for a long time, you will be the only one to know about it.

We tried to make the works of Marxism, Marxism itself, and, in the final analysis, the work of Marx himself, *readable and thinkable.*

Which means that, previously, it scarcely was … it contained contradictions, theoretical dead-ends, misunderstandings, and huge gaps. We held that there was a scientific kernel in Marx, a kernel of indisputable theoretical knowledge – everything that the tradition recognizes under the name of historical materialism, the most highly developed contribution to which, bequeathed us by Marx, is known as *Das Kapital.* The biggest gap in Marxism, the work of Marx and even Lenin included, was philosophy. You know how the matter stands. Marx jotted down in pencil, on a sheet of paper, a few sentences that Engels published after his death under the title 'Theses on Feuerbach': they are incoherent, except that [one] *feels* a revolutionary appeal in them. But to feel is not to think. In *The German Ideology*, what dominates is a form of geneticist positivism and the affirmation of the end of all philosophy. This isn't a philosophy, then.... Afterwards, we have occasional acrobatics about the inversion of Hegelian method, as well as Marx's declaration to the effect that if he had a week, he would write twenty pages on the dialectic. If he didn't write them, it's not because he couldn't find a week's time to do it, but because he didn't know, in the state his work was in, just what he could find to say on the subject. And we latched on to Lenin: 'Marx's logic is to be found in *Capital*', but in a latent state; we tried to bring it out of this latent state.

We did so not on a whim, but out of a profound necessity: to make it possible to read and to think Marx's thought, we had to bring out the philosophy implicit in it, the only philosophy capable of clarifying the difficulties in his great work, *Capital* – capable, in a word, of rendering it thinkable, that is, *rational and coherent.* Turning every possible clue to advantage, then, we set out to acquire – to discover and elaborate – what was massively absent from it [*cette grande absente*]: Marx's philosophy. And we fabricated for Marx, really and truly *fabricated*, the philosophy that he lacked: this rational, coherent philosophy.

It so happens that this rational, coherent philosophy 'flirted' with the structuralist ideology at work in linguistics, ethnology, the history of philosophy (Saussure, etc.; Lévi-Strauss; Guéroult, etc.). But if we 'flirted' with structuralism, it was not only because it was in vogue; it was also because one finds formulas in *Capital*, well-developed formulas, that come close to authorizing the use of structuralism or, at least, 'flirting' with it (*kokettieren*, says Marx, in a discussion of his flirt with Hegel). In discussing his flirt with Hegel, Marx really did substantiate our position: to think his work, *it was necessary to have Marx's philosophy*, which was missing. If Marx flirted with Hegel's philosophy, this was because, to make his work thinkable and coherent – rationally coherent, and therefore thinkable – he needed a philosophy; in the event, the one closest to his own. But it was easy to see, in the texts themselves, that Hegel's philosophy, even 'inverted', wouldn't 'do the trick', that it didn't work: the fact is that *Capital* doesn't 'run on Hegelian philosophy', even if it is 'inverted' (this was the point of the first essays in *For Marx*). On the contrary, the 'inversion' simply succeeds in reproducing the structure of Hegelian philosophy, as we can see in countless projects, for example – in the theory of fetishism, and, especially, the theory of history developed by Marx (who, every other year, expected to see the worldwide revolution break out).

So we fabricated a rational, coherent philosophy that enabled us to read and, consequently, think the thought of Marx. Raymond Aron was right – I admit, now, that he was right; we fabricated, *at least in philosophy, an 'imaginary Marxism'*,[3] a solid little philosophy, which can be used to help think both Marx's thought and the real, but had the one little disadvantage that it, too, was missing from Marx. Naturally, this philosophy had its theoretical repercussions – on our way of reading, that is, interpreting, *Capital* and all the other works of Marxism, correcting them when the need arose, or roundly criticizing them when that was in order (for example, the philosophy elaborated in Engels's *Anti-Dühring* or *Ludwig Feuerbach*).

This operation had, then, a twofold result at the level of the theoretical works: (1) the fabrication of a thinkable, coherent philosophy; and (2) the rectification, made possible by this philosophy, of various passages in *Capital*, or the critique of certain of Marx's theses (above all, his philosophy of history). In Marx, and, *a fortiori*, in his disciples.

But reality, in this matter, is rather different, after all! For a long time, we celebrated the '*fusion*' of the workers' movement and Marxist theory as a historic event, repeating Engels's and Lenin's formulas after Marx's, without considering the fact that this 'fusion' had either not been realized at all, or had just barely been realized, and that, where it seemed to have, it had been realized rather badly. This negative experience (the USSR offered the worst imaginable examples of its excesses: the camps, economism, etc.) forced us to admit that the matter was rather more complicated than we had thought.

Today I would say that there exists an autonomous reality, a reality that is relatively autonomous *at the base: the workers' movement*, with its specificity, national diversity, obstinacy, traditions, and so on – an unpredictable movement. There are also its organizations: those that are now the closest to it, such as the trade unions and, sometimes, the Communist Parties. The workers' movement takes its own course, anchored in its own spontaneity and its fighting traditions, which the activity of organizations inspired *by Marxist theory can modify to one degree or another*, depending on (1) the period, (2) the country, (3) the conjuncture, (4) the traditions existing in the working class, and so on. As for Marxist theory, it is not primarily, or first and foremost, *at the base*: it was produced 'in the heads of bourgeois intellectuals' (Marx) who had rallied to the cause of the workers' movement and social revolution. Thus it was produced at a distance from the workers' movement, initially, and for a long time floated above it, for more than half a century before Marx's first theses began, by way of organizations of Marxist inspiration, with programmes inspired by Marx – and, even then, in what were called social-democratic parties (see the 'Critique of the Gotha Programme') – to penetrate parts of the workers' movement. The possibility that Marxist theory can virtually disappear, even after the supposed 'fusion', leaving the workers' movement to nothing but its instincts and traditions – the possibility that the workers' struggle can be pursued in virtual independence of Marxist theory – is today a reality in Western Europe, where only scraps of Marxist theory can still be found in the workers' movement. But the workers' movement still exists; it is forging ahead on its own path, despite its defeats.

Above all, the apparatuses of the Communist Parties are still in place; they are untouchable, with their permanent staffs paid by the leadership of the CPs, and their own sources of funding (in France, the municipal governments and other resources they are less inclined to talk about): they may well take their knocks, but they remain in place, and continue to try to win the allegiance of the working masses disorientated by their 'turns'. They may have to wait a long time, for they themselves no longer know where they are headed.

What has had an effect in history is not 'the logic of *Capital*', understood as Marx's true philosophy, the proper version of which we tried to provide. Rather, it is a few formulas taken from Marx and Engels, which the political apparatuses of the Socialist and then Communist parties seized on, without first putting them to the test. Hence it is in part the bad philosophy of Marx and Engels, the inverted Hegelianism that continues to sustain an impossible, unthinkable philosophy of history: 'Let us unite, and *tomorrow* … the International *will be* the human race.'[4] But this bad philosophy finds a spontaneous echo in the vulgar ideology of working-class spontaneism (the inevitable revolution as the End of Time, the full development of the human essence, and so on). Behind this ideology lie two realities: the party apparatuses, and the workers' movement with its spontaneity, embryonic perspectives, traditions of action and organization, and so on.

If all this is borne in mind, it can be said that, in principle, our work was salutary: it made it possible to 'read' *Capital* somewhat better, and to arrive at a clearer understanding of its various 'deviations'. A few political groups seized on this work, but foundered on the rock of May 1968,[5] which they understood no better, or hardly better, than the leaderships of the CPs. That our research has had theoretical repercussions is certain, and they have not ceased to produce their effects; but it has had little effect in the CPs, which are attached to, first, the principles of their survival, and, second, what they perceive of/collect from [*percevoir*] the workers' movement. We waited a long time before attacking the structure of the CPs, or, at any rate, that of our own. As for the workers' movement, we didn't really pay any attention to it (can you imagine … ?), confident as we were that the 'fusion' had been realized, and that we really could consider the CPs to be the *authentic* representatives of the revolutionary revolt of the workers, and the *authentic* representatives of Marxist theory.

If we take the measure of this situation, of the reality of what we did and neglected to do, I think that we can continue to advance, and with a bit more success this time: because, for the purpose of coming to grips with the reality of the workers' movement, as well as that of the CPs, the capitalist mode of production, imperialism, and so on, we have a rather good philosophy, the one that we have constructed: it must, of course, be developed, but it is a solid base to build on.

Forgive me for going on at such length, Malamud, and rest assured of my affectionate friendship.

Louis Althusser

Letters to Fernanda Navarro

1

Typed letter [Paris,] 11 June [1984]

Already 11 June, my very dear F'tana, and, since I haven't heard from you, I'm writing you this note amid a spring sprung without warning from days and days of rain, real downpours in Paris. Amid problems with my oesophagus, too, that are giving me a great deal of grief, since it was only a few months ago that they were slipping 'olives' down the alimentary canal in question. Insh'Allah. In any case, the situation is no longer desperate – just one more little setback, but it means that I have to get along on a diet of nothing but milk and soup. I'm back in touch with the specialists.

I'd be happy to hear how you are, and how Mauricio is, and whether there's any chance that my letter to an unknown psychiatrist will bring him a little relief, and whether it's possible to obtain the drug locally or through middlemen, in the USA, or ordered in France through a pharmacy.

You can also ask me theoretical questions by letter, and I'll answer you. I have a sort of perverse talent for turning out administrative letters and writing theoretical or political letters....

I've reread an Ms. on philosophy[6] which, though it's not finished, seems pretty good to me; at any rate, I read it through to the end. One of the subjects discussed in it is the absolute beginning of philosophy, and Descartes's feint in his 'order of reasons'. Did you read it [while in Paris]? I don't disavow it. But other Mss, although they begin acceptably enough, rapidly metamorphose into theoretical raving. I must have been in a terribly manic phase.

Something quite surprising happened to me recently: the handwritten account of the dream that you found, dated 1964, had an astonishingly premonitory cast, because it involved the murder of my mother, strangled by me.[7] It allowed me and D[iatkine][8] to work well on the unconscious impulse that culminated in the tragedy. I think I've re-established a positive, productive relationship with him. I owe that to you....

Then there were the matches at Roland Garros, which distracted me from all (difficult) reading: the fascination of the little round ball, interminable. The players from Latin America did very well, not all the way to the end, but still – also a Spaniard who almost managed to make MacEnroe 'bite the dust'.

Derrida has just brought out a short book called *Otobiographies*; it has to do with the ear (oto). I'm to receive a copy. Some say it's very good, others that it's no good at all. And Le Seuil has just published Lacan's old article from the *Encyclopédie Wallon* on 'the family'. I read it a long time ago in the *Encyclopédie*, but don't remember it at all. Worth taking a look at.

What shall I tell you? I'm struggling hard to cut down on the drugs, gradually, keeping an eye on myself, but I still take a good dose of them. The night before last, I forgot to take my Temesta: I had a very hard day that brought back bad memories. I didn't forget them last night, and this morning, as I write, I'm fine.

You're in my thoughts, dearest F'tana, and I embrace you with all my heart – yes indeed!

Louis

2

Typed letter [Wassy,][9] 10 July [1984]

Dear Fontana, let me begin by giving you, if I haven't already, the address I'll be at from 14 July to 30 August: c/o M[ichelle] Loi [***]. Don't forget to send me news of Mauricio, whose condition worries me, to judge by what you say of it. Give him my fraternal greetings.

Yes, I'm willing to answer, or try to answer, your theoretical questions.

You raise, with materialism, the hardest question of all. Here's what I think I can say about it.

The term 'materialism' belongs to the history of our philosophy, which, as you know, was born in Greece, under Plato's patronage and within his general problematic. It is in Plato that we find the primary, fundamental distinction between the 'friends of the Forms' and the 'friends of the Earth'.[10] Both terms in this pair are posited as being essential to constituting the pair, in which each term commands the *other*. Thus there exist friends of the Earth only because there exist friends of the Forms; this distinction or opposition, is the work of a philosopher, the inaugurator of our philosophical history, who considers himself a 'friend of the Forms' opposed to the 'friends of the Earth', among whom he ranges the empiricists, sceptics, sensualists and historicists. (See Protagoras' myth, which explains the origin of humankind and human societies; it is a lovely materialist myth – unlike animals, people are 'born naked', so that they have to work and invent arts and techniques to survive.)[11]

The intrinsic tie that we find in the pair of opposites idealism/materialism is therefore *primary* with respect to both idealism and materialism, with the important distinction that because idealism has been the *dominant* tendency or current in all of Western philosophy, the idealism/materialism pair itself is clearly based on the dominant tendency, idealism.

I don't know if Heidegger has explained his views on this point, but, when we set out from what he says about the domination of logocentrism over all of Western philosophy, it is easy to imagine his position: every time it is a question of *pronounced materialism* in the history of our philosophy, the term 'materialism' reproduces as, so to speak, its negation and mirror opposite, the term 'idealism'. Heidegger would say that idealism, just like materialism, obeys the 'principle of reason', that is, the principle according to which everything that exists, whether ideal [*idéel*] or material, is subject to the question of the *reason for its existence* (ultimately: 'why is there something rather than nothing?', the question of the 'origin of the world', a question which makes it easy to see that philosophy comes into the world as religion's heir), and the existence of this question opens up a hinterworld (Nietzsche), a 'behind' the thing, a reason hidden beneath the appearance of the immediate, the empirical, the thing given here and now. If this is how we conceive the reign, generalized to philosophy, of the 'principle of reason' (expressed with the greatest possible clarity by Leibniz, who demands that one show, for each thing and each relation, the *ratio rationis*), we can readily see that philosophies which are called 'materialist' (such as those of the eighteenth century, or many passages in Engels) meet this idealist criterion.[12] Matter stands in for the ultimate reason, the ratio for each thing; the only difference, according to Engels, is that instead of being conceived mechanically, this ratio is conceived dialectically (dialectic = movement), and movement is defined as an attribute of matter (just as, in idealism, there exist attributes of God, the *ratio rationis*).

I would therefore say that, in the philosophical tradition, the evocation of materialism is *the index of an exigency*, a sign that idealism has to be rejected – yet without breaking free, without being able to break free, of the speculary pair idealism/materialism; hence it is a sign, but, *at the same time, a trap*, because one does not break free of idealism by simply negating it, stating the opposite position or – I've gone on about this often enough – 'standing it on its head'. We must therefore treat the term 'materialism' with suspicion: the word does not give us the thing, and, on closer inspection, most materialisms turn out to be inverted idealisms – that is to say, are still idealisms.

Let us go a little further: how can we characterize idealism? Obviously not simply by the existence of an external world independent of consciousness or the mind, for what do these three terms signify beyond the reference to a whole philosophical problematic?

We can recognize idealism, I think, by the fact that it is haunted by a single question which divides into two, since the principle of reason bears not only on *the origin*, but also on *the end*: indeed, the Origin always, and very naturally, refers to the End. We can go further still: in idealism, the question of the Origin is a question that arises on the basis of the question of the End. Anticipating itself, the End (the meaning of the world, the meaning of its history, the ultimate purpose of the world and history) projects itself back on to and into the question of the origin. The question of the origin of anything whatsoever is always posed as a function of the idea one has of its end. The question of the 'radical origin of things' – Leibniz – is always posed as a function of the idea one has of their Final Destination, their End, whether it is a question of the Ends of Providence or of Utopia.

That is why I would say that *if certain* philosophies escape this materialism/idealism pair, which is dominated by idealism right down to its very 'opposite', they can be recognized by the fact that they escape, or attempt to escape, questions of origin and end, that is, in the final analysis, the question of the End or Ends of the world and human history. These philosophies are 'interesting', for, in escaping the trap, they express the exigency to abandon idealism and move towards what may be called (if you like) materialism.

There are not many of them, of these non-apologetic, truly non-religious philosophies in the history of philosophy: among the great philosophers, I can see only Epicurus, Spinoza (who is admirable), Marx, when he is properly understood, and Nietzsche.

(I have to interrupt this raving, because I need to get ready to leave for Wassy. But I'll come back to this letter; or, rather, I'll rewrite it, since I'm not very happy with it. Matters are both simpler and more complicated.)

I wish you the very best and embrace you warmly,

Louis

Remind me that I have to tell you about the mutual encroachment [*empiétement*] of idealism and materialism. I had another idea, but I've forgotten it – ah, yes, 'the PHILOSOPHY-EFFECT', which is very important.

3

Typed letter [Wassy,] 18 July [1984]

Dearest Fernanda, it's summer, the weather is rainy or else foggy, which I don't mind at all; it's as if I were in a nice warm bed, protected from the cold out-of-doors. There are plenty of things to do in the garden: I join in, picking gooseberries and raspberries (you must have tried the jam Michelle [Loi] makes from them on one of your visits to my flat). We also go and pick the wild strawberries that dot the gravel paths; there were just as many in Régis [Debray]'s garden when, years ago, I went to see him. I'm reading a great deal – I haven't read as much in years, though I don't always understand what I read: the Sartre of the *War Diaries: Notebooks from a Phoney War* is very moving when he talks about himself and his buddies in the camp, and very boring when he launches out on long philosophical discourses, except when he discusses Heidegger, Husserl, and a few abstract–concrete subjects like love. I've also read *Les Mots*, which I thought I'd read before, but I'll be hanged if I recalled any of it. These stories of his childhood are quite sinister. I was hoping he'd talk about his youth and his life, but no, nothing but his childhood: how, for the solitary, arrogant little boy that he was, praised to the skies by his family, but practically friendless, the world became a 'catch' [*prise*] – he caught it in words the way you catch birds in a net. To change these gloomy perspectives a little, which match my mood rather too well, I'm going to change authors and read some Nietzsche and Heidegger and … novels. I've already read a very beautiful book by an Italian, Ferdinando Camon, called *La maladie humaine*. It's his account of his psychoanalyses, and contains astonishing formulas about psychoanalysis; it's very moving. I recommend it to you if you can find it in Spanish; if not, I'll put it aside for you here. When the church bell of the very beautiful twelfth-century church starts pealing madly at midday, that means there's to be a christening. This is a big village where you can find just about everything: doctors, a physiotherapist, a hospital with X-ray equipment, and all within 100 metres of the house. It's ultra-convenient. I'm taking advantage of the situation to have my kidneys X-rayed (I have a splendid ailment of the arteries; the technical term escapes me whenever I need it). In Paris they diagnosed the same thing in my neck, in which the vertebrae are stuck together; the bones have been pushed towards the arteries, and I was told that that reduced the size of the 'hole' which the nerves and arteries[13] that go up to the brain run through. The result is that when I turn my head, the hole gets smaller, which reduces the blood supply to my brain. Whence my dizzy spells. So, the cause has been discovered at last, and the prescription is massage. I'm getting massages here, although they only seem to make the dizzy spells worse … but let's wait and see.

Forgive me for talking about myself first; I'll come to you in a minute. I'm plainly much better than I was when I was here last year, as far as depression is concerned; I'm more active, I don't necessarily stay in bed, etc. But I'm overwhelmed by my infirmities. I'm attacking them head-on, as you can see, but it's pretty rough going. My oesophagus has started acting up again, with an obstinacy that brings back bad memories, although I received extensive treatment for it in Paris, before leaving. Try and make sense of that…. I vomit almost constantly, up to three times in succession, even when I try to eat things that are almost liquid. I stop eating, wait a few hours, and, timidly, try crackers dunked in hot milk … which I manage to get down.

I'm tired of all these afflictions. Meanwhile, my dreams are slowly evolving. It's still the story about changing professions – another exam to take, I try to get out of it, don't have the time, have forgotten to study for it – but for the past few nights I've been sitting the exam, under good conditions, and I've been having all sorts of erotic encounters (exclusively visual ones, I have to admit); it's curious, after all, this long series of dreams that are all on the same theme, yet slowly evolve.

I've received your letters, including the one with the transcription.[14] What drudgery! I wonder if it's really necessary to impose this chore on you: or, if you do do it, you can bring the texts with you when you come to Paris. I have the feeling that the more time goes by, the more remote my projects to write something are becoming. You can make use of anything that I've said to you or that I manage to write to you, but provisionally; I'm not particularly eager to publish anything at all, either in France or in Mexico. I'm not in the mood. I feel that I'm still a long way from where I need to be. For the moment, I'm just thinking of 'educating' myself a little (Sartre, Nietzsche, Heidegger and others, and novels, and … detective novels, of which there is a good supply here, and Char, a little poetry), and the sessions with the physiotherapist and the exercises that he recommended (holding an nine-pound sandbag on my head for an hour a day to strengthen the muscles of the *neck* ...) and the hikes we plan to take, perhaps to look for mushrooms in the woods.

I wanted, despite all, to add something about philosophy and the idealism/materialism pair.

The first thing is that a good materialist shouldn't judge a work or a philosophy by its self-conception, but by what it in fact is. For example, Sartre says that he has at last abandoned the 'idealism' of his youth, giving his reader to understand that he has at last attained materialism. For example, Feuerbach declares that he is a materialist, whereas he is obviously only an idealist of Man; and so on.

By what criterion should we judge a philosophy if we refuse, as a point of method, to judge it by its declarations of intention? By its acts, its mode of action, which is not just any mode of action, but the specific mode by which a philosophy acts: by which it acts on ideologies, and, by way of those ideologies, on practices. You know that, limit-cases aside, a philosophy never acts directly on practices, but almost always acts by way of the ideologies. This is what might be called, in order to bring out its specificity, the 'philosophy-effect'. It follows that in order to be able to characterize a philosophy (leaving its self-conception to one side), we have to consider it *in its effects* on practices: does it exploit them or does it respect and help them, etc. This is what I tried to show, a bit, in *The Spontaneous Philosophy of the Scientists*. The closer a philosophy comes to the practices – the more it respects them, the more it assists them through the relay of the ideologies – the more it tends towards materialism, a materialism other than the one inscribed in the idealism/materialism pair, which is a speculary pair. (Dominique [Lecourt] has tried to break out of this pair by using the term sur-materialism, bearing in mind that Bachelard talks about the 'sur-rationalism' of modern physics, and doubtless thinking of Breton's 'sur-realism' as well.)[15]

So. I'm feeling a bit under par today, and won't talk to you this time about the encroachment of one philosophy on the philosophies that have preceded it, hence about the encroachment of an idealist philosophy on a materialist philosophy. This is tied in with the 'polemical' nature of all philosophy (Kant's *Kampfplatz*).

It's still as cold as it was. Embracing you will warm me up again, so, I embrace you very tenderly. Here's to you, dear Fontana.

Louis

4

Typed letter [Wassy,] 19 July 1984

Dear F'Tana,

Your beautiful grey envelope just arrived; but you're mistaken, I'm not going back to Paris at the end of July, but only on the 4th or 5th of September! However, if you've written to me in Paris in the meantime, it makes no difference; my mail is being forwarded.

It has occurred to me that there's a book which would be useful to you in philosophy, by an old student of mine, Pierre Raymond: *Le passage au matérialisme* (Maspero).[16] It's been translated into Spanish by Siglo XXI, hasn't it? The leading idea of this book is that, in every great philosophy, there are elements of idealism and materialism; that, in an idealist philosophy (Plato, for example), there is a point of 'reversal' [*rebroussement*], (of turning back) towards materialism, and vice versa. Raymond examines the great philosophies from this standpoint. This is a notable improvement over Engels's and Lenin's thesis that philosophies are either idealist or materialist, or stand 'shamelessly' between the two.[17] One can get down to work with this, dissecting the philosophies of history from this point of view, while noting that idealist or materialist elements are better conceived of as 'tendencies' ('tendency' rather than 'element'). But, that said, Raymond's book is very interesting, even if it operates on the terrain of the idealism/materialism pair. I believe that Macherey was the first to state the idea that there are materialist and idealist elements in all philosophy. But, in my humble opinion, we have to go much further.

One can go further, even while maintaining Raymond's perspective. I believe that we can think the relation between idealist elements (or the idealist tendency) and materialist elements (or the materialist tendency) in terms of the concept of encroachment (rather than 'reversal', the concept we find in Raymond). For the concept of 'reversal' is merely *descriptive.* Even if it introduces *movement* into the history of philosophy and the life of each philosophy, it does not say *why* we find this contradiction between elements or tendencies in every philosophy. We understand this better once we have grasped that every philosophy is *polemical*, that it exists only in a state of theoretical *war* against another philosophy or philosophical current. Thus every philosophy takes up a *position* against another philosophy, and, within the current in which it is situated, against the opposed current. We can derive this conception from what I have explained about the nature of philosophical *theses*. Thesis = position; but there is no position unless it is taken = the taking of a position within the space of philosophy, and taken against adversaries, or an adversary, occupying historical positions in their turn. Thus every thesis is an antithesis or counter-thesis. And every philosophy strives to besiege the positions occupied by its adversary or adversaries (this is confirmed all the time, or almost): this literally happens as it would in a *war of position*, with an entire conceptual strategy and tactics. Naturally, the *occasions* for philosophical interventions change; from Plato down to our day, they have changed significantly; but because, *grosso modo*, philosophy always functions in the same way, it is to be expected that new philosophies will forever continue to reflect on the history of philosophy, indefinitely, and that they will pursue their reflections within the history of philosophy, in order to take up a position *vis-à-vis* the whole previous history of philosophy, finding their arguments and philosophical categories in it [***]. It is in this war of position, which is usually a *preventive* war, that we find the reason for what R[aymond] calls 'reversals', whether materialist or idealist: these reversals are in fact encroachments, that is to say, positions gained on [*prise sur*] the adversary's. That is why any philosophy, idealist or materialist, contains its opposite, *its enemy*: it is by besieging the enemy, by encroaching on him – on his positions – that a philosophy can hope to prevail over its enemy. If it is true that the adversary's positions are occupied in this way, it is not surprising that a philosophy should contain – but *occupied in its fashion* – what we have referred to as the adversary's positions. It is not surprising that each philosophy *must* (this is an effect of the war between philosophies, between philosophical tendencies) strive to occupy the adversary's positions, the adversary's theses, inside itself. Partially or wholly.

When we begin to look at things from this standpoint – when we adopt this polemical conception of the nature of philosophy – we shift from the description (Raymond) of a fact that can indeed be observed in the history of philosophy to an understanding of its *necessity*.

We could leave matters at that, at this view which it is easy to develop further. It sheds a great deal of light both on what a given philosophy is, and on what a genuine *history* of philosophy might look like (what is the connection between the philosophies that follow one another as consequences of different concrete conjunctures?), although I would say that philosophy always functions in the same way, that it is eternal (just as the Freudian unconscious is eternal = repeats itself at the level of its functioning): unless, in the last hundred years, something has changed in philosophy ... which is something that should be looked into.

All this is well and good; but it still does not explain what the materialism whose presence and effects we observe in the history of philosophy might be, and what idealism might be.

To take another step, but one that is more difficult, we have to go back to the idealism/materialism pair and note, as I have already said, that it is speculary and circular, and was imposed in its initial form by Plato, when he contrasted the friends of the Forms with the friends of the Earth. Historically, then, materialism is defined by Platonic idealism as its opposite. Thus the history of philosophy has been, from its beginnings down to our day, dominated by idealism.

What, then, are we to understand by idealism? It is usually said that it means the primacy of thought over Being, or Mind over matter, and so on.

This was not the meaning of idealism in Plato. For him, the Ideas were not modes of Thought or of Mind, but realities in and of themselves, above Thought or Mind; as such, they were the ground for the properties of the concrete realities in which they 'participated' (this is the theory of participation). This is where the 'philosophy-effect' comes into play. For Plato situated these ideas in a heaven above all sensual reality – not only in order to ground the properties of concrete things, but also to make the *Idea of the Good* shine down upon things and the world, which were dominated by it. Hence Nietzsche could say, rightly, that Plato's idealism was the idealism of an *Ideal*, the idealism of a morality and a politics which the philosopher defended and thought he could demonstrate for his contemporaries. Over against the idea of the Good there stood, in the view of this aristocrat, the evil that reigned in the democracy of Pericles.

What I mean is that we can clearly see in Plato that the basis of his idealism is the struggle for an *ideal*, and war against those who didn't accept it: the atomists, the Sophists, and so on. We can clearly see that philosophy is a *practice*, a struggle for a moral, social and political ideal situated outside the world. That kernel, which is essential, was subsequently, and very soon (beginning with Aristotle), covered over by an idealism of *knowledge* (the primacy of mind over matter). But I think that I'm getting tangled up in my ideas. I think that my last remark is important (the determination of everything as a function of knowledge: this is profoundly idealist in the modern sense, from Descartes to Kant), but I'm not capable of developing it. Forgive me. Some other time.... I embrace you very affectionately,

Louis

5

Typed letter [Wassy,] 30 July 1984

Dear Fernanda, I'm writing to you from Wassy, as I must have indicated that I would be in my last letter. For three days, it has been scorching hot here. I stay indoors all the time, except when I 'venture out' to go and see the local physiotherapist – it's amazing, but in this village of 4,000 souls, there is a hospital with X-ray equipment (I've had my kidneys X-rayed there), and doctors, two pharmacies, a physiotherapist, and even a woman who does acupuncture! Getting medical treatment, and reading, plus meals, are my sole occupations; I also spend quite a few hours in bed (and have, most of the time, awful nightmares). I'm reading some Nietzsche, whom I didn't know well at all; that's all I do.

How are you doing, and how is Mauricio [Malamud]? Send me news of him; I'm very worried about his health.

The further along I get into the summer, the more remote the idea of my writing anything at all gets. I've very clearly understood what my best friends have told me: that I cannot write on any subject whatsoever in France, in short, reappear on the philosophical-political scene, without first saying something about myself – without first presenting myself and shedding some light on at least a part of my life. But that project, which once seemed sensible to me, now seems to me to be beyond my reach. To tell the truth, I don't feel like doing much of anything. Probably just a moment to get over, the underlying reasons for which escape me.

[***]

In short, I'm not in the best shape, and, as you can see, I feel the need to complain … (whereas Spinoza is against all tears and complaining!).

So, for the time being, I'm a long way from the idea of trying to write anything at all, or even pursuing the reflections on philosophy that I had begun sending you *for your own personal use.* But I'm still reading, with fierce determination, the texts by Nietzsche that I brought with me. I don't know N[ietzsche] well at all, but, believe it or not, this ignorance, like my shocking ignorance of so many other things (the result of which is that I 'have no culture', you'll recall what I said), undoubtedly *has helped me to write what I have written,* and even, quite simply, has helped me to write. Do you know the passages from Freud that I'll copy out for you below? I didn't; I just discovered them:

1. 'I have denied myself the very great pleasure of reading the works of Nietzsche, with the deliberate object of not being hampered in working out the impressions received in psycho-analysis by any sort of anticipatory ideas.'[18] Nietzsche, another philosopher whose guesses and intuitions often agree in the most astonishing way with the laborious findings of psycho-analysis, was for a long time avoided by me on that very account.'[19]

(and, above all) 2. (in connection with the theory of insanity in Schopenhauer, which) 'coincides with my conception of repression so completely that once again I owe the chance of making a discovery to my *not being well-read.* Yet others have read the passage and passed it by without making this discovery.'[20]

I can't tell you what a profound consolation these remarks of Freud's have been for me (here, a touch of your Spanish irony would be in order), but when I think about all that has happened to me, about how little I have read (perhaps a book a year, if that) – in other words, of my infinitesimal (!) culture – I have to acknowledge that, somewhat like Freud, I had the good fortune to call attention to certain points in philosophy precisely because I didn't really know much. Nietzsche, for example: if I had really known him, I believe I would have *overlooked* certain things that I more or less 'discovered'. I shall have to delve more deeply into this question, for it seems to me to be of the highest importance, at least as far as I am concerned.

With that I have, perhaps, found an angle of attack for talking about myself, if ever I feel the desire to. (Apparently Einstein once said something quite similar to what Freud says: he explained his discoveries by the fact that, because he had been a poor student at *lycée*, nothing of what they taught there made the slightest impression on him, which left him with an open mind for what came after....) I close this letter with those encouraging words, and embrace you very affectionately, my dear F'tana.

Louis

6

Typed letter [Paris, 10] Sept. [1984]

Dear Fernanda, this letter comes to you from Paris in response to yours, received today, the one in which you tell me that Mauricio is better. These sudden swings in his condition are astonishing. I've looked into the matter: the phenomenon is apparently rare, but it exists. As for the ways and means of preventing, and so fighting, a *lapse into the manic phase*, there are two ways of proceeding. The more classic is lithium, which you're familiar with: it has the merit of abrading (gradually wearing down) the state of excitation (it takes effect over the long term, so one should take it all the time, *preventively*). When lithium has no effect (as in my case), one uses *Tegretol* (I enclose a brochure about it). I take it, and it seems to work well for me. I say 'for me', because all these drugs can, for mysterious reasons, work or not, depending on the individual.

It's cold in Paris: there's fruit on all the stands, but it's a lot more expensive than in eastern France. I was well advised to undergo my fruit-cure of white peaches, a real treat, while I was still there …

[***]

It was quite hard for me to come back home, with all my infirmities (I had been battling them ferociously for months, but to no avail), and my fear of being alone. But you know all that.

I ended up reading a great deal at Wassy: Nietzsche, Heidegger. Educated myself a little bit. But I'm a long way from having come to terms with these authors. When I read an author, I always have, after laying him aside for a long time, to go back to him with the need to grasp him (*begreifen*), to hold him tight in my hand. I think this is possible with Nietzsche, who isn't all that complicated, but it's a different story with Heidegger.[21]

I've done a lot of chores so that I can have my peace. I've found a cleaning-lady who will come one afternoon per week. I'll need to procure other books so as not to be alone…. I'm also going to try to listen to music a little.

Thank you for the detailed information on how you plan to utilize my notes/interviews. If it's any help to any of you, you can – as goes without saying – use the 'substance' of them in your courses; but don't publish anything. I'm once again starting to think that I could perhaps write something that our Latin American friends would find useful. I read about the trial of Father Boff (a Brazilian, I believe) in *Le Monde*; he said that, for his 'liberation theology', he made use of the writings of 'Gramsci and Althusser'. Encouraging (although I'm not very keen on that kind of theology).

I embrace you, my dear Fernanda. Give my best regards to Malamud.

Louis

[***]

7

Typed letter [Wassy,] 18 September 1984

Dear Fernanda,
nothing but letters from you! I want to thank you from the bottom of my heart both for writing to me and for sending me so much news. I'm glad to hear that Malamud is better; give him my regards, and tell him that, as a veteran of the war against depression, I fully understand what he's up against. Tell him that I have also gone through manic phases and that they are the hardest for one's family and friends to bear – unfortunately, one always realizes that after the event, because one is so intoxicated with one's freedom, strength and intelligence in the critical period....

I'm reading Heidegger attentively after having read Nietzsche. I see now that all this was missing from my 'culture'. It always takes me quite a while to assimilate an author's thought, and to 'digest' and 'master' it. This reading has naturally thrown up certain 'questions' for me. I need to gain some perspective and let some time go by before I can tell how the internal equilibrium of what I have been able to think (and write out in manuscripts) will be modified by these readings. I always need a great deal of time to bring ideas to maturity, even if things go rather quickly once I sit down to write. Add to that the fact that these readings inevitably lead me on to others, to things that I either haven't read or have read in another context and, what is more, have completely forgotten (for instance, Derrida: in what respect, and how, has he criticized Heidegger even while basing himself on him, etc.), to say nothing of Hegel, who remains, after all, the fundamental reference for everyone, since he is himself such a 'continent' that it takes practically a whole lifetime to come to know him well....

I'm not at all averse to this new experience of putting things in 'suspension', this experience of the epoche of inner reflection (as opposed to developing a body of thought). This does not rule out the project of writing something for our Latin American friends, which I've tucked away somewhere in my mind – but I'm inclined to write something about the state rather than philosophy. What do you think? It's a remote project, like all my projects, but it's a project, after all (rather than that 'autobiography', about which I would first need to know if it can be an intellectual autobiography or not; I find the idea, which has been suggested by several of my friends, troubling and irritating. I toyed with it for a while this summer, but all that did was to make me back away from it). I'm also reading a few poets (Char, Baudelaire: what a grand old fellow Baudelaire was!).

My infirmities (my feet, dizzy spells, eyesight, etc.) continue to plague me. I don't know if I'll ever manage to rid myself of them (I've seen so many doctors already, and tried so many different types of treatment).

I often see Michelle, who is always a great help. I help her to orientate herself a bit in various areas, professional and otherwise. She's not doing too badly at the moment.

I'm sleeping better than before, and almost without drugs: a satisfactory result, but one I pay for with terrible nightmares every night, on themes that come back again and again by way of the variations on them....

It's a rather steady sort of life, against a backdrop of loneliness (visits by friends don't change this), in which nothing happens apart from the reading I've been telling you about, and the attention I pay to political and other news thanks to *Le Monde* and TV. Have you read about the brouhaha involving the Vatican and the Brazilian liberation theologians who say that they take their inspiration from Gramsci and Althusser?

Here's to you, my dear Fontana, from the bottom of my heart, and with thanks for your lovely letters.

Louis

8

Handwritten letter [Paris,] 11 October 1984

Dearest Fontana

[***]

Don't push me too hard to have 'ideas' about philosophy. I need a (long) quiet period of reflection in order to understand a little better what is going on with me after all these ordeals (personal and historical), while also reaping the benefit of the readings I'm currently engaged in. I haven't reached the end of my labours yet – far from it.

Yes, I thought that Marxism had something objective and 'relatively' universal to say about philosophy – as I said in 'Lenin and Philosophy' – and, in a certain sense, I still think so. But not just Marxism; psychoanalysis too, and perhaps other theories as well. This is something that should be looked into. I've become cautious, now that I'm educating myself a little.

My main idea can be summed up in a few words: philosophy is, as it were, the theoretical laboratory, solitary and isolated, despite all the links tying it to the world, in which categories are developed that are appropriate for [*propres à*] thinking, and, above all, unifying/diversifying – appropriate for thinking the various existing ideologies in unitary/unifying forms. Engels utters, somewhere, a great piece of foolishness: about the 'eternal need of the human spirit' to 'overcome contradiction', and therefore to think the real in the form of unity, or even a non-contradictory system. What is involved is, to be sure, *language*, well and good; but, behind language, there is a need for unification that has to do, indirectly, with the imperative to *unify* diverse (and contradictory) ideologies in order to draw them into the process (a process that is never completed, that is infinite; see Kant's regulative idea) of constituting what can be called the *dominant ideology* (today our adversaries are challenging this idea of a dominant ideology).

This idea, which you have perhaps come across in my manuscripts, remains Top Secret for the moment. Keep it to yourselves. I think that it is still valid, but *it is not the only one to come into play* (there is the unconscious as well, and also language games, the effects of the unconscious and the effects of language).

(One would have to see what there is about philosophy in Freud – that's something to look into – and about the role of language, on which Nietzsche insists heavily, as does Derrida.)

Give some thought to all this, but, for the moment, *keep it to yourselves.*

Affectionately,

Louis

[***]

9

Typed letter [Paris,] 27 October [1984,] noon

Dearest Fontana, I'm writing to you from my office, in the broad autumn sunlight that has returned after a two-day absence (earlier, we were 'swimming' in rain). Yes, I receive your letters (more frequent than mine) with the same pleasure. I'm happy to learn that, all in all, things seem to be looking up for you, your work, and Mauricio.

As for me, I go through good moments and bad. Sometimes I read, as I did this summer, either Nietzsche, or Heidegger, or essays about them; sometimes they bore me, and I stop reading, sink into a pernicious inactivity, and don't know what to do. When that happens, I latch on to the television … but the films are too idiotic, so I stop and go out for a while; but my feet hurt, so I come back home soon enough. I don't have too many visitors these days, apart from the ever-faithful Michelle. [***]

I've seen Father Breton again; we have rather comical philosophical exchanges that cheer me up. I admire his devotion, as well as his knowledge of philosophy and his general culture. He knows the whole world, because his order sends him to give lectures here and there; it's implanted in most countries, even Hong Kong! He's always telling me priceless stories, and, what's more, he knows – don't ask me how (doubtless thanks to his conferences) – an incredible number of people. He's an extremely valuable friend.

Needless to say, I have my problems with Heidegger (not with Nietzsche), however fascinating he is, but I find that he is (1) an extraordinary historian and interpreter of philosophy; and (2) a kind of unctuously refined country priest (he started out by studying Catholic theology, and read Meister Eckhart and others). I can easily see why Derrida has criticized him, even while declaring that, without him, he (Derrida) could not have done what he has tried to do. But I don't know Derrida well at all. One more gap in my 'culture' to fill in.

I recently read a number of short stories by Musil (instead of his great book, *The Man Without Qualities*[22]); they left a deep impression on me. Do you know him? Also read some admirable Baudelaire. Heidegger has 'his' poets, first and foremost Hölderlin – 'thinking poets', as he says, *'denkende Dichter'* – but Baudelaire isn't among them. He has built up a veritable cult around Hölderlin, his 'god'.

There you have my life: very reclusive and very restricted. I'm stubbornly trying to get the doctors to tell me about the nature of my maladies, which you know about, but each specialist passes the buck to the next.

Still, all things considered, and taking the 'variations' into account, I'm not doing too badly, after all.

I'm waiting for Michelle, who has gone to Roissy to wait for a Chinese aquaintance of hers. She's been waiting since 5 o'clock this morning, and just called to say that the aeroplane only just landed (at 11:50 a.m.), but no Chinese aquaintance. There's one hypothesis left: that he got lost while looking for his luggage.

I embrace you very affectionately,

Louis

10

Typed letter [Paris,] 20 November 1984

Dearest Fontana,

I haven't written for a while. But I've been receiving your good, lovely letters, with the thousands of little nocturnal candles on the shores of your little lake.

For three weeks now, I've been having a rough time. After reading philosophy (Nietzsche and Heidegger) this summer and in September/October, I suddenly lost interest in it, pretty abruptly, and I now find myself in a sort of vacuum of inactivity that is quite unpleasant.

I looked into the matter with Diatkine, and realized that it was no doubt a form of my 'work of mourning', which goes well beyond Hélène to all that I have lost: the Ecole [normale supérieure], my flat there, my work, my students, my political activities, and so on. But, throughout all this torture, I still had the feeling that I could perhaps take up one or two of the *ideas* that I was holding in reserve in my mind (they had to do with philosophy, as you know): it was in this perspective that I began reading Nietzsche and Heidegger, in order to fill in some enormous gaps and be better armed in case I took up this couple–three ideas again. This was *on a continuum* with the period before the torture began; these were, as I saw it, ideas that I hadn't lost, and was therefore not obliged to give up. But experience has shown that these ideas were well and truly a part of *before*, of all that I had to lose – and that I had to mourn their passing along with the rest: a need to mourn of which they cruelly reminded me by tearing the books of philosophy from my hands.

That said, there is nothing to prove that I won't come back to these ideas some day. For the time being, however, it is clear that I have to include them in the work of mourning and treat them as something that I must give up with the rest.

This fact, this necessity, have left me in a disagreeable state bordering on anguish ... let's hope that I won't sink any further into the logic of depression, but will return to more hospitable shores.

My visits to the doctors have also kept me extremely busy. In our medical system, the division of labour is such that you go and see a (so-called) general practitioner: he sends you to a first specialist, who examines you and sends you to a second, who examines you and sends you to a third, and so on and so forth.

This afternoon, I think, I just saw the last specialist in this round. But he's going to write to the first one I saw, who will want to see me to comment on the results the last one arrived at....

To combat this fragmentation and its ideology, I went to see a real general practitioner, a Frenchman – that is, a doctor with a French diploma – who has, however, been practising acupuncture for twenty years. The acupuncturists are virtually the only serious generalists in existence (in my opinion). And what they do interests me a great deal. There is a book waiting to be written (and, first, an investigation waiting to be carried out; I had been thinking of doing this, before my terrible years) on Western medical ideology. To show that it is based on the dissection of cadavers, on pinpointing organs, on the secondary character of functions with respect to organs, that it is analytic, and so on. Chinese medicine doubtless has its limits and its faults, but those aren't among them. It *sets out from functions* and 'parcels them out' among several organs; for Chinese medicine, the whole represented by the function has priority over the parts represented by the organs. I'm telling you very elementary things, but they're real.

Yesterday I heard about the terrible explosion in Mexico City. I pray heaven that no one, none of your loved ones, or Mauricio's, or those of your friends, was injured in it.

The political situation in France is becoming uglier and uglier (it's the Right's doing). Workers and foreigners have been shot at: four have died in the past few days. A sad turn of events.

I embrace you very affectionately, dear Fernanda. I'm hoping I'll manage to sort things out....

Louis

11

Typed letter [Paris,] 7 January 1985

Dearest F'tana, I don't write much, it's not my nature to write much, but I read your letters very attentively. [***]

On the substantive and substance: Nietzsche built his whole critique of philosophy on a critique of the language of substantification, of the transformation of the words of language, verbs, and so on, into substance. I find this critique a bit thin, for many other things come into play in the notion of substance, but it can at least help us to take our bearings. Whence, in Nietzsche, the quest for another form of language, a poetic and aphoristic form, almost without reasoned argument, as you know. But I think that the notion of substance, which was heavily criticized before Nietzsche (for example, in the eighteenth century, by Hume and others) depends on the form of the philosophy in which it is inserted. This philosophy looks above all for guarantees for what it advances, even while reflecting in a certain manner – which depends on the first – something of common practice, and also of scientific practice conceived in terms of the ideology *of* this common practice. Substance is opposed to phenomenon; the phenomenon is transitory, but, in everyday life, it is necessary to have the certitudes of permanence so that practice can recognize itself amid the diversity of transitory phenomena. This spontaneous ideology of the recognition of the stable, of the subject, of the stable and permanent which underlies transitory phenomena, has naturally entered into scientific practice and philosophy – or, rather, has passed from philosophy into scientific practice. Here we find Nietzsche again: the spontaneous notion that there exists a hinterworld beneath phenomena, and that it is the world of ideas, or substances.

Derrida has also, in the Nietzschean tradition, mercilessly criticized everything that bears even a remote resemblance to substance and substantification.

Of course there are, as you say, 'possibilities' within social determination, if only because there are several different orders of social determination and because this creates a *play* – of gaps, blank spaces, or margins in which the subject may find his path determined or not determined by social constraints; but this non-determination is an effect, a sub-effect, of determination, of determinations; what I called not only overdetermination, but underdetermination.... Do you see what I mean?

[***]

I embrace you with all my heart,

Louis

12

Typed letter [Paris,] 7 April 1985

Dearest Fernanda,

I was shaken by your last two letters. I didn't write back because I thought that you might still be able to come, or, if not, that you might send me a telegram. Now that I know you're going to be staying with your mother for a long time yet, I've decided to write.

[***]

I'd been waiting for you. Michelle left for China almost a month ago, but I made up my mind to make the best of the situation: I set out to organize my life in my semi-solitude, and did a rather good job of it. I can therefore give you much more positive news about myself. I'm doing much better, and am in a state in which, neither manic nor depressive, I've attained an equilibrium of the kind I hadn't enjoyed for a long time. And now, at last, it's spring in France! I've taken initiatives that I'd long renounced; in short, I believe that I've begun to live normally, with an important, non-philosophical project in mind that I'll tell you about once it has matured. This must mean that I've finished my 'work of mourning', thanks to the help of my analyst and also of a very remarkable acupuncturist whom I've been seeing for two months now. There's also the work on myself that I undertook alone, courageously, a year ago. I've put my affairs in order, then, my medical affairs included (by no means the easiest task was carefully to delimit the area assigned to each of my various doctors). I'm steadily reducing my intake of drugs, cautiously, but I don't really take much of anything any more, even to sleep. That's obviously extremely important as well.

I've adopted a strategy and tactics of 'little steps', not anticipating the future in any way and waiting for things to sort themselves out at their own pace, without, above all, trying to force things. It was about a month ago that I really started feeling better.

All this by way of telling you that I'm not making any plans for next summer; that's too far off to be foreseeable, and I prefer to let things develop on their own. In any event, I doubt (but you never know) that I can come and see you this year, beside the little lake: for one thing, it's a long way away for me, and, for another, I need – when it comes to travel, which I've always shied away from, more than ever for the last six years – transitions. I think I also need, if I can, to go and spend some time near an ocean that can reinvigorate me, such as the Atlantic, although I don't know if I'll be up to it. No, I wasn't 'bored' on my holiday last summer; I wasn't well yet, that's all. I was with Michelle and her husband in their house in Lorraine, where I rested and read a great deal of … Heidegger and Nietzsche (a little), the first time that I've reread a little philosophy in systematic fashion. Since then, I've finished with Nietzsche, having, I think, grasped the essentials, and also with Heidegger, who, in the end, annoyed me because of the streak of 'country priest' in him. I've turned the page. Since then, I've read hardly anything, except for one or two books that I found striking – for example, *Interpreting the French Revolution*,[23] by

F[rançois] Furet, a book of gripping intelligence which confirmed ideas that I've preserved and tended very carefully for a good thirty years, sharing them with only a very few intimates, including yourself (you must have read a text of mine on the philosophy of the 'encounter',[24] which I'm jealously sitting on – not the text, but the intuitions that are set down in it).

The situation in France is far from good. The left is going to lose the 1986 legislative elections, despite the divisions in the Right. The greatest danger is the rise of the racist, xenophobic National Front: it brings back sinister memories.[25] And the general state of the world (except for the re-emergence, at last, of democracies in South America) worries me terribly. Apart from its traditional core, which has itself shrunk considerably, the PC is in the midst of a full-blown crisis; for the first time, it has even had trouble coping, at the heart of its upper management levels (the CC) [Central Committee], with an opposition that is determined, but unfortunately has no line and no perspective. They (the members of the internal opposition) only attack the 'leadership', as if that were the key problem.

Might you or one of your friends have kept articles from the press at the time of Hélène's death (16 November 1980), or could you procure them? I'm trying to find out what kind of 'commentaries' were made on the event every place where people knew of me. It's important for me, the disgusting articles included, of course (to see their arguments). I'm now in a state to examine all that very objectively; it won't have the least effect on me.

I hope you'll carry the day against your philosophical opponent!

Do give my regards to Mauricio, dearest Fernanda, while keeping my very tender affection for yourself.

Louis

13

Typed letter [Paris,] 8 April 1986

Dearest Fernanda, I've received the text of your 'intervista'[26] and I think it is *excellent*. Let me make you the following proposition (concerning publication). We can turn your text into a short book (it would run to some 80 pages). To bring it out in published form (if you agree with the idea), you could address yourself, on my behalf, to Orfila [Reynal] (whom I know well), the head of the publishing house Siglo XXI in Mexico City. As far as the contract and so on goes, all he has to do is to write to me: this edition would be for Latin America *exclusively* (hence in Spanish and, if possible, Portuguese for Brazil). I personally reserve the right to bring out future editions, if any, in other languages (I'll think it over), and also retain the option to expand the text or present it differently. But, as it stands, it seems to me that it would serve a purpose in Latin America. *What do you think?*

That said, I'd like to make a few suggestions as to how, on certain points, you could improve the text of your 'interview' somewhat.

First, I'd like you to drop the passage about 'lines of demarcation' in the sciences, particularly the demarcation between the scientific and *the ideological*, as well as everything pertaining to the difference between ideology *and* the ideological. That section is not ready yet, and ought to be rewritten.

I'd like you to modify your use of the term 'dominant class' to take certain nuances into account. There is never *a single* dominant class, but, rather, a group of classes or fractions of classes 'in power', as Gramsci clearly saw when he talked about the '*bloc* (of classes) *in power*', an excellent expression (taken over from Sorel) which describes things more concretely.

Similarly, be careful with the term *dominant ideology*. Historical periods marked by a dominant ideology that is truly one and truly unified are rare: the dominant ideology is always more or less contradictory, tending toward a controlling [*dominateur*] unity, but attaining it only very rarely and with great difficulty. It would be preferable to speak, as you do elsewhere, in terms of the (contradictory) tendency of an ideology which seeks to constitute itself as a (non-contradictory) *unity* and aspires to domination over ideological elements inherited from the past, elements which it never succeeds in truly *unifying* as a unique, dominant ideology.

A few other comments.

– The principle informing Marx's thesis that 'so far, philosophies have only *interpreted* the world; now the point is to change it [*sic*]' is inaccurate. Marx's meaning seems to be (in this short, improvised sentence left in the form of a draft; it was Engels who later published the 'Theses on Feuerbach') that *to interpret* the world is to have a *speculative* attitude, hence an abstract and, above all, *passive* attitude, hence a conservative one. In reality, *every philosophy* is *active*, and always aims to *act upon the world* (by way of its work on the ideologies), by orientating it in a revolutionary direction (Marx), or in a *reactionary* direction (a turning back; for example, Plato, in his deepest political inspiration – although there are infinite riches in Plato, and even materialism, as you know), or, again, in a conservative direction (to maintain the world in the state in which it finds itself is to struggle against the ideologies or philosophies that seek to change it, and is therefore – here too, as always – to act, to be active). Heidegger himself recognized this; he's no one's fool.

– p. 33 of your text: emphasize the *practical* nature of all ideology, in order to move, as I've always tried to, towards the *materiality* of all ideology. This is a crucial point that I emphasized in my essay on the ISAs [Ideological State Apparatuses]; it is absolutely essential that it be reiterated, with renewed emphasis on this materiality, which Foucault clearly perceived. Otherwise, one remains hopelessly trapped in an idealist conception of the ideologies. This is very important, because, without it, the *essential* meaning of my theses about the ISAs goes by the board.

– p. 31, don't forget the 'class struggle'!

I'm surprised that you make no reference to the different definitions of philosophy that I've proposed. First (in *Reading Capital*), 'the theory of theoretical practice', a positivist formula (philosophy = the science of the sciences) which I soon abandoned in order to replace it with (1) the formula in 'Lenin and Philosophy' (philosophy represents politics with the sciences and scientificity with the practices – the wording should be checked);[27] and (2) the definitive formula: philosophy is class struggle in theory – an abrupt, provocative formula, but one whose validity can be demonstrated, precisely as a function of philosophy's, any philosophy's, role and partisan position in the ideological–theoretical struggle. This isn't very easy to explain in a few words (especially not in three words!), but it's possible, and the attempt has to be made. You can try yourself, or else I'll help you.

– p. 40 of your Ms.: don't forget Gramsci's phrase (which I didn't know at the time): 'hegemony is born in the factory':[28] any mode of organization of labour, the forms of its exercise and submission, comes about under an ideology – the ideology of submission to exploitation, of illusions about the nature of wages, and so forth.

– p. 40: '*El reconocimiento a toda forma de autoridad*.' A *very important* point. The interpellation of the individual as subject, which makes him an ideological subject, is realized not on the basis of a *single* ideology, but of *several ideologies* at once, under which the individual *lives* and *acts* [*agit*] his practice. These ideologies may be very 'local', such as a subject in his *family* and at *work*, in his immediate relations with his family and friends or his peers; or they may be broader, 'local' in the broad sense, either 'regional' or 'national'. Such ideologies are, for the most part, always initially inherited from the past, the tradition. What results is a *play and a space* of multiple interpellations in which the subject is caught up, but which (as contradictory play and as space) constitutes the 'freedom' of the individual subject, who is *simultaneously* interpellated by several ideologies that are neither of the same kind nor at the same level; this multiplicity explains the *'free' development of the positions adopted by the subject-individual.* Thus the individual has at his disposal a 'play of manoeuvre' [*jeu de manœuvre*] between several positions, between which he can 'develop', or even, if you insist, 'choose', determine his course [*se déterminer*], although this determination is itself determined, but in the play of the plurality of interpellations. This explains the persistence of tendencies in the working class and the other classes as well as the shifts, noted by Marx, of subject-individuals from one political-ideological position to another (for example – alas, this is the only example Marx cites – intellectuals who go over to the ideological positions of the working class, *although they are themselves originally bourgeois* – as were Marx and Engels themselves). But one would have to take this much further, examining, *in the working class itself*, these *shifts* from one position to another: reformist, anarchist, revolutionary, to say nothing of the workers who vote straight out for the bourgeois parties, or – a much more extreme case – those who, in Germany, for example, rallied to fascism *en masse*. The theory of the ISAs is therefore quite the contrary of a determinist theory in the superficial sense.

You say nothing about the dialectic; and, all things considered, I think you are right in this, because long explanations are needed to explain that the dialectic (not only in the form given it by Engels: the science of the laws of motion of matter) is *more than dubious; indeed, it is harmful*, that is, always more or less teleological. If I have the strength, I'll try to show this some day.

I'm not at all well – but I embrace you with all my heart.

Write to me to tell me what you think of this letter and the various projects.[29]

Louis

14

Handwritten letter [Paris,] 2 June 1986

Dear Fernanda,

I write this note to you after a long silence (for months, I was going through some very rough moments). It's been only two weeks that I've been feeling better, and able (cautiously) to read and write.

I'm in the process of *finishing* a long preface to your interview (around forty typed, double-spaced pages). I'll have to get the advice of my friends in order to revise it. It's a *very political text* in which I try to explain to Latin American readers the conditions of class struggle, war and resistance (and their consequences) in which the French Party was formed, and the 'strategy' I had to pursue to try to change something in the Party. As it's a theoretico–*political* text, I have to get as many guarantees as possible. I think I can send it to you by August *if all goes well.*

I hope that you've been able to revise your interview as I indicated. Let me add that the last section, in which you discuss the teaching of philosophy without any intervention on my part, doesn't seem to me to be ready yet. It should be reworked. In any case, I'm impatiently awaiting the revised text of your interview.

I embrace you with all my heart,

Louis

15

Handwritten letter [Paris,] 23 June 1986

I'm in the process of translating the interview into French, correcting it as I go and, above all, adding passages on ideology and politics that are of the highest importance.

I still have a week's work ahead of me. I'll send you the French text, which is to be released in the new 'Strategy' series, edited by Louis Althusser and published by Orfila.[30]

Work everything out with Orfila and make it very clear to him that he'll be receiving, once you've translated my text of the interview into Spanish – and then, by an excellent woman translator, into Portuguese – not just the text of the interview, but also *a long postface*, in which I explain to Latin American readers *why and how I had*, in 1950 and thereafter, to intervene *politically* in the French CP and the progressive international movement – to intervene by seizing *the only opening I could: philosophy*; and also *how and why* – while offering a revolutionary interpretation of Marx and *Capital*, and flirting with structuralism – *I was able*, despite the Party leaders' fierce hostility towards me, to 'trap them completely', and prevent them from expelling, condemning, or even criticizing me (*there were three lines of cautious critique* in *L'Huma*[*nité*][31] after my broadside *What Must Change in the Party*,[32] a grand total of three lines in forty-two years!).

Carefully translate this postface as well and send it to Orfila for publication immediately after the interview, in the same volume, under a title we'll need to discuss. Perhaps simply:

Interview with L. A. on philosophy by F. N.
(the ideological and political reasons for his philosophical battle
in the conjuncture of the PCF and the international conjuncture
between 1948 and 1986)

Thanks for everything. All my affection. You'll receive the French texts as soon as they're translated and typed up in two copies, as soon as possible. In any event, I'll post them to you airmail by around 10 July.

Affectionately,

Louis

16

Typed letter [Paris,] 3 November 1987

Dearest Fernanda,

have received your letters, the cassette, etc. Glad you're well and busy. As for me: like Malamud, but less serious – ups and downs, but I haven't had an up for three years now. I've sunk into a terrible pit of anguish, with all my infirmities on top of everything else. I don't think you can really know what it's like from a distance; moreover, when we met, I was in a manic phase. The result is that I make stupid mistakes and do foolish things and lead my friends, you in particular, to follow suit.

Your text[33] is very often excellent, but it is completely *unbalanced. I'm to blame.* I incorporated so many new arguments into my revised version of your interview, and I imprudently advanced so many ideas, so many *words* (*just words, not demonstrations*) that I lapsed into a sort of political-verbal vertigo (about interstices, margins, the primacy of movements over organizations, about 'thinking differently', etc., etc.) and *dragged you in after me,* with the following complication: *I* had reasons for talking the way I did, but I kept them to myself (for lack of time and explanations, and also because I hadn't looked up, in the ponderous text of *Capital*, the crucial lines I had in mind). *You* couldn't do anything other than what you did. (1) In fact, you found yourself confronted with *two texts*, the old and the new (*grosso modo*); (2) with an insoluble problem (my fault): finding a way to *unify* these two texts; (3) you thought you had found a solution with '*conversando con Alth.*'. In fact, this programme was nothing but a hollow declaration, an artificial, fictitious unity. That stands out big as a barn door ... when one reads the whole thing, which is totally unbalanced, hence is *weak, becomes weak.* Again, I'm to blame; you just followed my lead, without being able to put anything to rights.

There are three excellent passages in the section '*Conversando*':

1) Chapter 1, which I would like to call 'A Philosophy for Marxism: The "Line of Democritus"' (Lenin, *Materialism and Empirio-Criticism*).[34] This text is new, and it is excellent. You can count on it; I'll see – once I feel better, and once we've had a chance to talk to Father Breton

(who is also ill) – whether there aren't a few details that could be improved, but *very little is involved here.* Here you've understood me well, or I've explained myself well. But I think, above all, that you've understood me well, because you have a truly philosophical mind – whereas you're not as gifted when it comes to politics (or so it seems … sorry!).

2) What is excellent, then, is chapter 1 (except the very beginning) and *the two appendices* (except the end of the second, where you try to establish a continuity with Sartre. It would be better not to discuss Sartre at all, or, if it's important to you, to do so in a short note somewhere).

Together, these three texts will make an excellent little book – clear, dense, systematic and rigorous: the ideal combinatioin.

However, chapters 2, 3, 4 and 5 are not on the same level. These are merely exchanges of opinion, of dubious value because they are not justified, not argued, not supported by textual citations or convincing examples–in short, they're feeble, at the level of mere *journalism*, and it's a pity, a real pity! So forget the 'politico-strategic' ambition (with which I imprudently inoculated you) and *stick to philosophy*. You already have a bombshell!

I know I'm asking you to make a big sacrifice, but think of the sacrifices that I've imposed on myself in not publishing all the manuscripts you've seen…. And don't talk about, or have me talk about, the 'old closet'; say 'my files'. No need to exaggerate…. I'm asking you to make a big sacrifice and, at the same time, I'm offering you the key to the solution. In sum, a good trade-off.

Let me give you a piece of advice: *drop everything that is too autobiographical, both about me* (don't discuss my tragedy or my illness) *and about you* […], and *don't say*: (1) that I'm no longer in the Party – that's none of their business – or (2) anything about my reasons for '*breaking*' my silence. If I kept silent, it is because I'm ill, full stop; that's none of their business, either, in the form of a written affirmation. It's possible to *say* that; it's possible, incidentally, to say many things, about the interstices as well,[35] but *that isn't ready to be written out and published.* Do you see the difference? I don't mean to prevent you from thinking, or even talking with others, about the subject matter of your chapters 2,

3, 4 and 5, but do so *in your own name and your own manner*, qualifying what you say: 'I believe that A. even thinks that …'; 'if I'm not mistaken, I believe that he is even more optimistic than not', for such-and-such a reason. But *mezzo voce*, and tangentially with respect to our common fortress: the text on philosophy. And *never in written form.*

Taking these last scruples into account (I assure you that they count: a published text breeds others, and nothing it contains is neutral) will require *cutting my preface down to a few words* (I'll take care of that), without mentioning my age or my tragedy, and deleting the last paragraph, since I shall not be discussing political life in France in this text. You'll also have to *reorganize your prologue*, take out the phrase '*A. rumpe il silencio*' and everything that you derive from it, say nothing about my tragedy, and drop *the autobiographical section about yourself*, which is too long. Relate the circumstances of our encounter more simply, in three lines. Naturally, this also implies a solution: *that you not mention the new problem of the integration of the two texts* and the dubious *mélange* it would unfailingly produce.… Here too, then, I get you out of a difficult business that would be incomprehensible for your friends. *Finally, I would ask you to take out all of pages 6–7*, about the Party. One has to be in France to understand these things. In Mexico, all that is just going to sow confusion, I promise you, confusion and nothing else … (*I already say enough* about my strategy *vis-à-vis* the Party).

My text on the political situation in France (don't refer to it in your book, it's better that way; in this case, too, they wouldn't understand why I'm not publishing it) runs to 85 pages in large format … good things and bad. Once my health improves, I'll revise it and send it to you. But that can wait, whereas your text,

Philosophy and Marxism
Interview with L. Althusser
by Fernanda Navarro

beautiful cover, beautiful lettering, etc., *beautiful everything*!!
is virtually ready; there's very little work left to do.

Practically, I would propose the following procedure, to save time:

1. I keep your basic manuscript here: I mean *chapter 1 and the appendices*,[36] together with my short preface, which I'll rewrite.

2. You work on the points I've indicated above, using your best judgement, and you send me *only* the revised passages, telling me only: page such-and-such has been *dropped* or *modified as follows*, or *page such-and-such and following* (for example, pp. 19 f.): new page to be intercalated, etc.

3. You send me these modifications as soon as you can. I go over them with Breton, and we send the text back to you with the final modifications of a few small details, or no modifications at all, *passing it for press. You enter into no negotiations with anyone at all until I send you a statement that the text has been 'passed for press'*.

I have no objection to your plans for a joint publication with the University, but I don't know how Orfila will react. You can tell him, cautiously, that you have my agreement.

I've just made, over the past two hours, a tremendous effort to write you this text. Many more explanations would have been in order. I'm counting on you to trust me, but I'm at the end of my strength. I've capitalized on a sleepless night to write to you. It's 4 a.m., and I'm going to try to get a little sleep. Heaven help me so that the doctors won't send me to the hospital and I can get over this alone in my empty house, for I really have very few visitors. Solitude is terrible. 'Solitude is when nobody is waiting for you.'

I embrace you tenderly,

Louis

Notes

1 A professor of philosophy from Argentina and a Communist militant, Mauricio Malamud was persecuted by the Argentinian military junta and, in 1975, sent to prison for eighteen months. He was subsequently forced into exile in Mexico, where he taught in the Philosophy Department of the University of Michoacán de San Nicolás de Hidalgo. After a long depression, he returned to Argentina in 1987. He died in Mexico in September 1989. Malamud was a friend of Althusser's, and one of the earliest and most enthusiastic proponents of his work in Argentina. Apart from a handful of essays, he left no written work.

2 Upstene was sometimes prescribed in cases of severe depression and anxiety. It has been taken off the market, in part because the active ingredient, indalpine, tends to reinforce suicidal tendencies. [*Trans.*]

3 Raymond Aron, *Marxismes imaginaires: D'une sainte famille à l'autre*, Paris, 1970, pp. 175–323. [*Trans.*]

4 The last two lines of the chorus of the *Internationale*. The most common English version runs: 'So comrades, come rally / And the last fight let us face/ The International / Unites the human race.' [*Trans.*]

5 In an unpublished manuscript initially intended as a preface for 'Philosophy and Marxism' (see note 33 below), Althusser is more explicit:

> The very dynamic, very active [French Maoist] movement disappeared almost overnight in 1968 owing to a serious political mistake on the part of its leader, who, throwing his considerable personal prestige into the balance, convinced his comrades that the student revolt of May 1968 was nothing but a police manipulation designed by the French bourgeoisie to divide the immense working-class movement of May 1968.

(A30–02.03, p. 4) [*Trans.*]

6 *Être marxiste en philosophie*, a 140-page-long manuscript.

7 The complete text of this August 1964 dream may be found in *L'Avenir dure longtemps*, 2nd edn, Paris, 1994, pp. 429–31. At the manifest level, at any rate, Althusser murders his sister, not his mother.

8 René Diatkine, one of the psychoanalysts who treated Althusser. [*Trans.*]

9 In summer 1984, Althusser was on holiday in the country home of Michelle Loi in Wassy, in the Département of Haute-Marne in Eastern France.

10 *The Sophist*, pp. 246 ff. [*Trans.*]

11 *Protagoras*, pp. 321–2. [*Trans.*]

12 See p. 170 and note 11 on p. 204 above. [*Trans.*]

13 Althusser writes 'vertebrae'. [*Trans.*]

14 Althusser is referring to the first, eight-page transcription of a conversation that Fernanda Navarro held with him just before going back to Mexico in 1984.

15 See footnote a on p. 189 above. [*Trans.*]

16 Pierre Raymond, *Le passage au matérialisme: Idéalisme et matérialisme dans l'histoire de la philosophie*, Paris, 1973. The book was published in the series 'Théorie', whose general editor was Althusser.

17 *LCW* 14: 33. [*Trans.*]

18 Sigmund Freud, 'On the History of the Psycho-Analytic Movement', in James Strachey, ed., *The Standard Edition of the Complete Psychological Works of Sigmund Freud*, trans. Strachey *et al.* (hereafter *SE*), vol. 14, London, 1957, pp. 15–6. [*Trans.*]

19 Freud, 'An Autobiographical Study', *SE*, vol. 20, London, 1959, p. 60. [*Trans.*]

20 Freud, 'On the History of the Psycho-Analytic Movement', p. 16. [*Trans.*]

21 In a letter dated 6 August, not included in the present volume, Althusser writes: 'I'm tired of Nietzsche and I'm scared of Heidegger.'

22 Althusser writes '*The Man Without Utility*'.

23 François Furet, *Interpreting the French Revolution*, trans. Elborg Foster, Cambridge, 1981. In another letter, Althusser praises Furet because – unlike Albert Soboul, a French Communist historian of the French Revolution – he 'does not take the revolutionaries' consciousness for the reality of the Revolution'. See p. 201 footnote g above. [*Trans.*]

24 The reference is to the 1982–83 manuscript from which 'The Underground Current of the Materialism of the Encounter' was culled.

25 With the victory of the Right in the March 1986 elections to the French National Assembly, Jacques Chirac became Prime Minister. Almost 10 per cent of the ballots cast went to the National Front, which has gone on to greater electoral successes since. [*Trans.*]

26 Althusser is referring to a typed, 71-page Spanish text, dated April–May 1984, entitled *Acerca de la filosofía (Desde une posición materialista). Entrevista al filósofo francés Louis Althusser.* This is the text that he would subsequently translate into French (see his letter of 23 June 1986), apparently without realizing that it included Spanish translations of texts of his already published in French. He also made extensive modifications in the last part of the 'interview,' and introduced a number of passages on the political conjuncture in France.

27 The exact formulation is: 'philosophy represents politics in the domain of theory or, to be more precise: *with the sciences* – and, vice versa, philosophy represents scientificity in politics' ('LP' 199).

28 See p. 145 and note 161 on p. 162 above. [*Trans.*]

29 Among the projects Althusser was considering at this time, as he indicates in a June letter, was that of founding an 'international cultural-theoretical association' that would unite 'former Communists, Trotskyists, anarchists, ultra-leftists, members of alternative groups, veterans of the Résistance, believers, young people and old' in an 'International Liberation Movement'. [*Trans.*]

30 Here Althusser is referring to his intention to propose this project for a series of books to Orfila Reynal, the head of Siglo XXI, in a 28 May 1986 letter. In the end, the letter was not posted, although Althusser kept a copy in his files. The planned series was to contain 'short books' ('I'm for short books aimed at a broad public'), the first of which was to be the interview with Navarro. Among the other books he planned to release in it was his autobiography, *The Future Lasts a Long Time*. In the letter, he tells Orfila that he intended to rewrite the first version, which was 'too rushed'; yet he also writes: 'This book is, as I think I can say without any vanity whatsoever, unprecedented, and it should "*faire un tabac*", as the French phrase goes; that is, make a very big splash.' (For more detail, see the discussion in *L'Avenir dure longtemps*.)

It should be pointed out that on 1 March 1987, Althusser sent Orfila the following short handwritten note regarding publication of his interview with Navarro:

> Dear Orfila,
> The text that Fernanda has in her posssession is for Latin America ONLY – rights for all other countries are withheld.
> I accord Fernanda the right to revise the text and publish it directly with your firm, even if I am unable to revise it.
>
> Heartfelt thanks,
> Louis Althusser

31 The French Communist Party daily. [*Trans.*]

32 Published in four instalments from 25 to 28 April 1978 in the daily *Le Monde*, and, in expanded form, in a book released in May: *Ce qui ne peut plus durer dans le parti communiste*. The *Le Monde* articles have been translated into English by Patrick Camiller as 'What Must Change in the Party', *New Left Review*, no. 109, May–June 1978, pp. 19–45. [*Trans.*]

33 Althusser is referring to a new Spanish version of the interview comprising 104 typed pages. It includes several passages from an unpublished manuscript of his that Navarro had consulted while in Paris and later incorporated into the text of the interview, together with many of the arguments featuring in the 'Preface' of 82 typed pages, entitled 'To my Latin American Readers' and dated 20 May 1986 that he sent her in Mexico (see the letters of 2 and 23 June above).

34 *LCW* 14: 130. [*Trans.*]

35 Althusser is alluding to a topic discussed in the version of the interview that he criticizes here.

36 Appendix 1 of this 'basic manuscript', as established by Fernando Navarro in 1987, subsequently became Part 2 of the interview, 'Philosophy–Ideology–Politics'. The second Appendix (which comprises the third chapter of the Mexican edition of *Filosofía y marxismo*) was withdrawn from the French edition and is not translated here. The preface that was ultimately published comprises the first two pages of the introductory section of 'To my Latin American Readers' (see note 33 above).

Philosophy and Marxism

INTERVIEWS WITH FERNANDA NAVARRO, 1984–87

For Mauricio Malamud,[1] *to whom I owe my 'Epicurean' encounter with Louis Althusser – the man, his life and his work*

Fernanda Navarro

Preface

The text that follows is presented in the form of an interview. Fernanda Navarro, a young professor of Marxist philosophy, asks me questions to which I respond. I have not given the interview a particular slant by requesting that Fernanda ask me the questions I wanted to hear so that I could give the answers it suited me to give. It was Fernanda herself who chose the questions, and it was she who put the answers in written form.

She had come to see me in Paris during the winter of 1983–84. First we talked for a very long time, so that I had the leisure to explain my positions to her at length; she had a chance to read several of the unpublished manuscripts that I had written over a period stretching from the 1960s to 1978, and stored away in my files; she recorded, on one or two cassettes, a long conversation of ours – and then she returned to Mexico. She left me with a very positive impression of her philosophical discernment.

Of course, Fernanda's intention was to arrive at a better understanding of the reasons for, and subjects of, my philosophical intervention in France from 1970 to 1978. She also wanted to understand, not only the philosophical and political significance of what I had set out to do, but, at the same time, the reasons for the (to some) surprising interest that it had generated in France and the rest of the world, and the motives for the equally lively, sometimes malevolent, and always fierce hostility that it had aroused in many readers, communists first of all.

Yet Fernanda was pursuing another project as well: she hoped to publish, in the form of an interview, a short text for the use of students at the University of Michoacán. Hence she wanted simple, clear explanations, and, let us say, a brief text *for non-specialists.*

Two months ago, she sent me a seventy-page 'interview' in Spanish. Overall, I found this text to be pertinent and on the mark. Not long after I began reading it, I came to the conclusion that it was so good that it should be earmarked for a purpose other than the one she had in mind. I wrote to her straight away to recommend that she put a very few details to rights, and, especially, to suggest that she turn the interview into a short book. The book could, I thought, be published by my friend Orfila, the director of the publishing firm Siglo XXI in Mexico City, first in Spanish and then in Portuguese, for a readership of philosophy students and political activists in Latin America (Brazilians included), and exclusively for that readership. I reserve the right to publish this text in France at the appropriate time.

L. A.
July 1986

I
A PHILOSOPHY FOR MARXISM: 'THE LINE OF DEMOCRITUS'

You have, throughout your work, shown a marked interest in philosophy and its relation to politics. Could we begin our interview by talking about that?

Certainly. This interest was not restricted to the theoretical level, since, beginning in the late 1940s, I was both a philosopher and a political activist. Part of the reason for this lay in the historical circumstances that it was my lot to live through: the Second World War, Stalinism, the international peace movement, the Stockholm Appeal. This was in the days when only the United States had the atom bomb; we had to avoid a Third World War *at all costs.* I used to spend as much as ten hours a day doing political work.

What you say reminds me of what you wrote in the Introduction to For Marx *about the postwar years. Let me quote you:*

> History: it had stolen our youth with the Popular Front and the Spanish Civil War, and in the War as such it had imprinted in us the terrible education of deeds. It surprised us just as we entered the world, and turned us students of bourgeois or petty-bourgeois origin into men advised of the existence of classes, of their struggles and aims. From the evidence it forced on us we drew the only possible conclusion, and rallied to the political organization of the working class, the Communist Party ... we had to measure up to our choice and take the consequences....
>
> In our philosophical memory it remains the period of intellectuals in arms, hunting out error from all its hiding-places; of the philosophers we were, without writings of our own, but making politics of all writing, and slicing up the world with a single blade, arts, literatures, philosophies, sciences, with the pitiless demarcation of class....
>
> [Later] we were able to see that there were limits to the use of the class criterion, and that we had been made to treat science, a status claimed by every page of Marx, as merely the first-comer among ideologies. We had to retreat, and, in semi-disarray, return to first principles.[2]

I wanted to intervene in France in the French Communist Party, which I joined in 1948, in order to struggle against triumphant Stalinism and its disastrous effects on my Party's politics. At the time, I had no choice: if I had intervened publicly in the *politics* of the Party, which refused to publish even my philosophical writings (on Marx), deemed heretical and dangerous, I would have been, at least until 1970, immediately expelled, marginalized and left powerless to influence the Party at all. So there remained only one way for me to intervene politically in the Party: by way of *pure theory* – that is, *philosophy*.

Against the background of this dissidence, your critique bore on certain basic concepts that helped to sustain the official positions of the Communist parties. I'm thinking, for example, of dialectical materialism.

Yes, I wanted us to abandon the unthinkable theses of dialectical materialism, or 'diamat'. At the time, they held undisputed sway over all the Western Communist parties, with the exception – a partial exception – of Italy (thanks to Gramsci's colossal effort to criticize and reconstruct Marxist theory).

What was your critique of dialectical materialism based on?

It seemed to me essential that we rid ourselves of monist materialism and its universal dialectical laws; originating with the Soviet Academy of Sciences, this was a harmful metaphysical conception which substituted 'matter' for the Hegelian 'Mind' or 'Absolute Idea'. I considered it aberrant to believe, and to impose the belief, that one could *directly* deduce a science, and even Marxist–Leninist ideology and politics, from a direct application of the putative 'laws' of a supposed dialectic to the sciences and politics. I held that philosophy never intervenes directly, but only by way of ideology.

What, in your view, were the political consequences of this position?

I think that this philosophical imposture took a very heavy toll on the USSR. I do not think it would be any exaggeration to say that Stalin's political strategy and the whole tragedy of Stalinism were, *in part*, based on 'dialectical materialism', a philosophical monstrosity designed to legitimize the regime and serve as its theoretical guarantee – with power imposing itself on intelligence.

Furthermore, it bears pointing out that Marx never used the term 'dialectical materialism', that 'yellow logarithm', as he liked to call theoretical absurdities.

It was Engels who, in particular circumstances, christened Marxist materialism 'dialectical materialism'. Marx regretted his own failure to write twenty pages on the dialectic. All that he is known to have produced on this subject (besides the dialectical play of the concepts of the labour theory of value) is contained in this fine sentence: 'The dialectic, which has usually served the powers-that-be, is also critical and revolutionary.'[3] When the 'laws' of the dialectic are stated, it is conservative (Engels) or apologetic (Stalin). But when it is critical and revolutionary, the dialectic is extremely valuable. In this case, it is not possible to talk about the 'laws' of the dialectic, just as it is not possible to talk about the 'laws' of history.

A truly materialist conception of history implies that we abandon the idea that history is ruled and dominated by laws which it is enough to know and respect in order to triumph over anti-history.

What did your theoretical and philosophical intervention in the Party consist of?

I began looking, in the text of *Capital*, for what Marxist philosophy might well be, so that Marxism could be something other than the 'famous formulas', obscure or all too clear, which were endlessly quoted or recited without generating any real progress or, needless to add, any 'self-criticism'.

Were you able, without great risk, to interpret Marx's 'true' theoretical thought in a party like the one you have described?

Yes, I was, even if the Communist Party was very Stalinist, very hard, because the Party held Marx sacred. I proceeded somewhat – to compare great things with small – as Spinoza did when, in order to criticize the idealist philosophy of Descartes and the Schoolmen, he '*set out from God Himself*'. He began his demonstrations in the *Ethics* with absolute substance, that is, God, thus cornering his adversaries, who could not reject a philosophical intervention that invoked God's omnipotence, since all of them, Descartes included, recognized it as an article of faith and a 'self-evident truth'. For them, it was the fundamental Truth, revealed by men's natural lights.

But, as Descartes too said, 'every philosopher advances masked'.

Precisely. Spinoza simply interpreted this God as an 'atheist'.

What happened when you adopted this strategy?

This strategy worked as I had expected: my Communist adversaries, both in the Party and in non-Communist Marxist circles, were unsparing with their virulent attacks, endlessly renewed, but utterly devoid of theoretical value. These attacks carried no weight – not merely from the standpoint of Marxism, but quite simply from a philosophical standpoint, that is, from the standpoint of authentic thought. It was on this narrow, unique, but fertile path that I first struck out; the result was the one I had been aiming for. I had clearly adopted the only strategy possible at the time: a theoretical strategy that later gave rise (beginning with the Twenty-First and Twenty-Second Party Congresses, and in connection with, for example, the dictatorship of the proletariat) to *directly political* interventions. But now the Party could not expel me, because my directly political interventions were grounded in Marx, whom I interpreted in 'critical and revolutionary' fashion. Marx protected me even in the Party, thanks to his status as the 'sacrosanct Father of our thought'.

They never suspected anything?

I think they did. I know, in any case, that 'they' were terribly suspicious of me, that they kept me on the sidelines and even had me 'spied on' by students in the Communist Student Association at the École normale supérieure, where I taught; they were intrigued by the danger incarnated in this strange academic philosopher who dared to offer a different version of the formation of Marx's thought … along with everything that implied. What is more, they suspected me of being a semi-secret, but very effective inspiration for the Maoist youth movement in France, which, in this period, developed in an original and spectacular way.

Marxist philosophy or aleatory materialism?

About your criticisms and questions: did you have an alternative to offer?

Not then, but I do now. I think that 'true' materialism, the materialism best suited to Marxism, is *aleatory materialism*, in the line of Epicurus and Democritus. Let me make it clear that this materialism is not a philosophy which must be elaborated in the form of a system in order to deserve the name 'philosophy'. There is no need to make it over into a system, even if that is not impossible. What is truly decisive about Marxism is that it represents a *position* in philosophy.

When you say 'system', do you mean a self-enclosed totality, in which everything is thought out in advance and nothing can be challenged without capsizing the whole?

Yes. But I want to emphasize that what constitutes a philosophy is not its demonstrative discourse or its discourse of legitimation. What defines it is its position (Greek *thezis*) on the philosophical battlefield (Kant's *Kampfplatz*): for or against such-and-such an existing philosophical position, or support for a new philosophical position.

Could you say something about Democritus and the worlds of Epicurus in order to make your notion of aleatory materialism clearer?

Yes, but first I would like to explain what has motivated my thinking about, precisely, Marxist philosophy over the last few years. I have come round to the idea that it is very difficult to talk about Marxist philosophy, just as it would be difficult to talk about a mathematical philosophy or a philosophy of physics, given that Marx's discovery was basically scientific in nature: it consisted in revealing the functioning of the capitalist system.

To that end, Marx relied on a philosophy – Hegel's – which was arguably not the one which best suited his objective … or made it possible to think further. In any event, one cannot extrapolate from Marx's scientific discoveries to his philosophy. We, for our part, thought that he did not profess the philosophy which was actually contained in his research. This explains what we were doing in attempting to give Marx a philosophy that would make it possible to understand him: the philosophy of *Capital*, that of his economic, political and historical thought.

On this point, I believe that we missed the mark, in some sense, in as much as we failed to give Marx the philosophy that best suited his work. We gave him a philosophy dominated by 'the spirit of the times'; it was a philosophy of Bachelardian and structuralist inspiration, which, even if it accounts for various aspects of Marx's thought, cannot, in my opinion, be called *Marxist* philosophy.

Objectively, this philosophy made it possible to arrive at a coherent vision of Marx's thought. Too many of his texts contradict it, however, for us to be able to regard it as *his* philosophy. Moreover, on the basis of more recent research, such as that Jacques Bidet has published in his excellent *Que faire du* 'Capital'?, we can see that Marx in fact never wholly freed himself of Hegel, even if he shifted to another terrain, that of science, and founded historical materialism on it.

Does that mean that the 'rupture' was never complete?

No, it never was. It was only tendential.

How, precisely, did you come to realize this?

As I have already said, Bidet's research was decisive; it put Marx's work in a new light. Bidet had access to a mass of material, including unpublished manuscripts, that we did not know of twenty years ago; this material is conclusive. A little while ago, Bidet came to see me and we had a long discussion.

What would you say today about Raymond Aron's description of your work as an 'imaginary Marxism'?[4]

I would say that, in a certain sense, Aron was not altogether wrong. We fabricated an 'imaginary' philosophy for Marx, a philosophy that did not exist in his work – if one adheres scrupulously to the letter of his texts.

But, in that case, it could be said that very few authors manage to avoid the 'imaginary', especially when it is a question of something (such as philosophy in Marx's work) which, if it exists, exists only in the latent state.

Perhaps. But, as far as we are concerned, I think that, after this instructive experience, we are faced with a new task: that of determining the type of philosophy which best corresponds to what Marx wrote in *Capital.*

Whatever it turns out to be, it will not be a 'Marxist philosophy'. It will simply be a philosophy that takes its place in the history of philosophy. It will be capable of accounting for the conceptual discoveries that Marx puts to work in *Capital*, but it will not be a Marxist philosophy: it will be a philosophy *for Marxism.*

Had you not begun to develop this idea earlier? In Lenin and Philosophy, *you declared that Marxism was not a new philosophy – at the heart of Marxist theory, you said, is a science – but that it involved, rather, a* new practice *of philosophy that could help to transform philosophy itself.*

That's right.

You had already begun to point out the paradox of Marxist philosophy in a lecture delivered in 1976 at the University of Granada, 'The Transformation of Philosophy'. Marx thought, you said, that producing philosophy as 'philosophy', even in an oppositional form, was a way of entering into the adversary's game, and helping to reinforce bourgeois ideology by validating its form of theoretical expression.

Exactly. It is to risk falling into the grip, in philosophy, of the party of the state, an institution Marx deeply distrusted. As for philosophy, it represents a form of unification of the dominant ideology. Both are caught up in the same mechanism of domination.

Is that not another of the reasons that help to explain why Marx refrained from producing philosophy as such, since, in a way, to produce 'philosophy' would have been tantamount to lapsing into the 'glorification of the existing order of things'?[5]

Bear in mind that when Marx thought about the form of the future state, he evoked a state conceived as a 'non-state' – in a word, a wholly new form which would induce its own disappearance. We can say the same of philosophy: what Marx sought was a 'non-philosophy' whose function of theoretical hegemony would disappear in order to make way for new forms of philosophical existence.

Does that not help us to bring out the paradox of a Marxist philosophy?

The paradox resided in the fact that Marx, who had been trained as a philosopher, refused to write philosophy; nevertheless, he shook all traditional philosophy to its foundations when he wrote the word 'practice' in the Second Thesis on Feuerbach. Thus, in writing *Capital*, a scientific, critical and political work, he *practised* the philosophy he never wrote.

By way of summary of what we have said so far, let us repeat that the task before us today is to work out, not a Marxist philosophy, but a philosophy *for Marxism*. My most recent thinking moves in this direction. I am looking, in the history of philosophy, for the elements that will enable us to account for what Marx thought and the form in which he thought it.

One last clarification: when I say that it is difficult to talk about Marxist philosophy, this should not be understood in a negative sense. There is no reason why every period should have its philosophy; nor do I think that this is what is most urgent or essential. If it's philosophers we want, we have Plato, Descartes, Spinoza, Kant, Hegel, and many others; we can utilize their thought in order to think and analyse our own period by 'translating' and updating them.

Do you consider aleatory materialism to be a possible philosophy for Marxism?

Yes, it tends in that direction. Now we can turn back to Democritus and to Epicurus' worlds. Let us recall the main thesis: before the formation of the world, an infinity of atoms were falling parallel to each other in the void. This affirmation has powerful implications: (1) before there was a world, there existed absolutely nothing that was *formed*; and, at the same time, (2) all the elements of the world already existed in isolation, from all eternity, before any world ever was.

This implies that before the formation of the world, there was no meaning, neither cause nor end nor reason nor unreason. This is the negation of all teleology, whether rational, moral, political, or aesthetic. I would add that this materialism is the materialism, not of a subject (whether God or the proletariat), but of a process – without a subject – which dominates the order of its development, with no assignable end.

This non-anteriority of Meaning is one of Epicurus' basic theses, by virtue of which he stands opposed to both Plato and Aristotle.

Yes. Now the clinamen supervenes: an infinitesimal declination that occurs no one knows where, or when, or how. The important thing is that the clinamen causes an atom to 'swerve' in the course of its fall in the void, inducing an *encounter* with the atom next to it. . . and, from encounter to encounter – every time these encounters are lasting rather than ephemeral – a world is born.

Are we to conclude that the origin of every world or reality, of every necessity or meaning, is due to an aleatory swerve?

Absolutely. Epicurus postulates that the aleatory swerve, not Reason or the first Cause, is at the origin of the world. It must be understood, however, that the encounter creates nothing of the reality of the world, but *endows the atoms themselves with their reality*, which, without swerve and encounter, would be nothing but *abstract* elements lacking all consistency and existence. It is only once the world has been constituted that the reign of reason, necessity and meaning is established.

Can we think of any later philosophy that adopted these theses, rejecting the question of the Origin?

Heidegger comes to mind. Although he is neither an Epicurean nor an atomist, there is an analogous tendency in his thought. It is common knowledge that he rejects all question of the Origin, or of the Cause and End of the world. But we find in Heidegger a long series of developments revolving around the expression *es gibt* – 'there is', 'this is what is given' – which converge with Epicurus' inspiration. '*There is* world and matter, *there are* people . . . .' A philosophy of the *es gibt*, of the 'this is what is given', makes short shrift of all the classical questions about the Origin, and so on. And it 'opens on to' a prospect that restores a kind of contingent transcendentality of the world, into which we are 'thrown', and of the meaning of the world, which in turn points to the opening up of Being, the original urge of Being, its 'destining', beyond which there is nothing to seek or to think. Thus the world is a 'gift' that we have been given.

A gift, it might be added, that we have neither chosen nor asked for, but which opens itself up to us in all its facticity and contingency.

Yes, but instead of thinking contingency as a modality of necessity, or an exception to it, we must think necessity as the becoming-necessary of the encounter of contingencies.

My intention, here, is to insist on the existence of a materialist tradition that has not been recognized by the history of philosophy. That of Democritus, Epicurus, Machiavelli, Hobbes, Rousseau (the Rousseau of the second *Discourse*), Marx and Heidegger, together with the categories that they defended: the void, the limit, the margin, the absence of a centre, the displacement of the centre to the margin (and vice versa), and freedom. A materialism of the encounter, of contingency – in sum, of *the aleatory*, which is opposed even to the materialisms that have been recognized as such, including that commonly attributed to Marx, Engels and Lenin, which, like every other materialism of the rationalist tradition, is a materialism of necessity and teleology, that is, a disguised form of idealism.

It is clearly because it represented a danger that the philosophical tradition has interpreted it and deflected it towards an *idealism of freedom*: if Epicurus' atoms, raining down in the void parallel to each other, encounter one another, it is so that we will recognize – in the swerve produced by the clinamen – the existence of human freedom in the world of necessity itself.

Could one say, then, that this philosophy, inasmuch as it rejects all notion of origin, takes as its point of departure … nothingness [le néant]*?*

Yes, precisely. It is a philosophy of the void which not only *says* that the void pre-exists the atoms which fall in it, but also creates *the philosophical void* [*fait le vide philosophique*] in order to endow itself with existence: a philosophy which, rather than setting out from the famous 'philosophical problems', begins by eliminating them and by refusing to endow itself with 'an object' ('philosophy has no object') in order to start from nothingness. We have then the primacy of nothingness over all form, the primacy of absence (there is no Origin) over presence. Is there a more radical critique of all philosophy, with its pretension to utter the truth about things?

But then how, precisely, would you describe the position of aleatory materialism*?*

On this subject, we can say that aleatory materialism postulates the primacy of materiality over everything else, including the aleatory. Materiality can be simply matter, but it is not necessarily brute matter. This materiality can differ quite sharply from the matter of the physicist or chemist, or of the worker who transforms metal or the land. It may be the materiality of an experimental set-up. Let me carry things to an extreme: it may be a mere trace, the materiality of the gesture which leaves a trace and is indiscernible from the trace that it leaves on the wall of a cave or a sheet of paper. Things go a very long way: Derrida has shown that the primacy of the trace (of writing) is to be found even in the phoneme produced by the speaking voice. The primacy of materiality is universal. This does not mean that the primacy of the infrastructure (mistakenly conceived as the sum of the material productive forces plus raw materials) is determinant in the last instance. The universality of this last notion is absurd unless it is brought into relation with the relations of production. 'It all depends', Marx writes in a passage of the *Contribution to the Critique of Political Economy* about whether the logically prior forms also come first historically. *It all depends*: an aleatory, not a dialectical phrase.

Let us essay a translation: anything can be determinant 'in the last instance', which is to say that anything can *dominate*. That is what Marx said about politics in Athens and religion in Rome, in an implicit theory of the displacement of the dominant instance (something which Balibar and I attempted to theorize in *Reading Capital*). But, even in the superstructure, what is determinant is also its materiality. That is why I was so interested in bringing out the real materiality of every superstructure and every ideology … as I showed with respect to the Ideological State Apparatuses (ISAs). This is where the concept of the 'last instance' is to be sought, the displacement of materiality, which is always determinant 'in the last instance' in every concrete conjuncture.

The two histories

If, with your concept of 'aleatory materialism' in mind, we ask what the nature of an historical event is, do we not have to analyse it as the coexistence of histories that overdetermine each other?

We can say that there are two types of history, two histories: to start with, the History of the traditional historians, ethnologists, sociologists and anthropologists who can talk about 'laws' of History because they consider only the accomplished fact of past history. History, in this case, presents itself as a wholly static object all of whose determinations can be studied like those of a physical object; it is an object that is dead because it is past. One might ask how else historians could react in the face of an accomplished, unalterable, petrified history from which one can draw determinant, deterministic statistics? It is here that we find the source of the spontaneous ideology of the vulgar historians and sociologists, not to speak of the economists.

But is it possible to conceive of a different type of history?

Yes. There exists another word in German, *Geschichte*, which designates not accomplished history, but history *in the present* [*au présent*], doubtless determined in large part, yet only in part, by the already accomplished past; for a history which is present, which is living, is also open to a future that is uncertain, unforeseeable, not yet accomplished, and therefore *aleatory*. Living history obeys only a constant (not a law): the constant of class struggle. Marx did not use the term 'constant', which I have taken from Lévi-Strauss, but an expression of genius: 'tendential law', capable of inflecting (but not contradicting) *the primary tendential law*, which means that a tendency does not possess the form or figure of a linear law, but that it can bifurcate under the impact of an encounter with another tendency, and so on *ad infinitum*. At each intersection the tendency can take a path that is unforeseeable because it is *aleatory*.

Could we sum this up by saying that present history is always that of a singular, aleatory conjuncture?

Yes; and it is necessary to bear in mind that 'conjuncture' means 'conjunction', that is, an aleatory encounter of elements – in part, existing elements, but also unforeseeable elements. Every conjuncture is a singular case, as are all historical individualities, as is everything that exists.

That is why Popper, Lord Popper, never understood anything about the history of Marxism or psychoanalysis, for their objects belong not to accomplished history but to *Geschichte*, to living history, which is made of, and wells up out of, aleatory tendencies and the unconscious. This is a history whose forms have nothing to do with the determinism of physical laws.

It follows from this that what culminates in materialism, which is as old as the hills – the primacy of the friends of the Earth over the friends of the Forms, according to Plato – is *aleatory* materialism, required to think the openness of the world towards the event, the as-yet-unimaginable, and also all living practice, politics included.

... towards the event?

Wittgenstein says it superbly in the *Tractatus*: *die Welt ist alles, was der Fall ist*, a superb sentence that is, however, hard to translate. We might try to render it as follows: 'the world is everything that happens'; or, more literally, 'the world is everything that befalls us' [*tombe dessus*]. There exists yet another translation, which has been proposed by Russell's school: 'the world is everything that is *the case*' ['the world is what the case is'].

This superb sentence *says everything*, for, in this world, there exists nothing but cases, situations, things that befall us without warning. The thesis that there exist only cases – that is to say, singular individuals wholly distinct from one another – is the basic thesis of nominalism.

Did Marx not say that nominalism was the antechamber of materialism?[6]

Precisely; and I would go still further. I would say that it is not merely the antechamber of materialism, but materialism itself.

Certain ethnologists have made a striking observation: that in the most primitive of observable societies, those of the Australian Aborigines or African Pygmies, nominalist philosophy seems to hold sway in person – not only at the level of thought, that is, of language, but also in practice, in reality. Conclusive recent studies have shown that, for these societies, there exist only singular entities, and each singularity, each particularity, is designated by a word that is equally singular. Thus the world consists exclusively of singular, unique objects, each with its own specific name and singular properties. 'Here and now', which, ultimately, cannot be named, but only pointed to, because words themselves are abstractions – we would have to be able to speak without words, that is, to show. This indicates the primacy of the gesture over the word, of the material trace over the sign.

This 'pointing', which appears as early as the Sophists, in Cratylus and Protagoras ...

Of course; it can be said that philosophical nominalism is already to be found in Homer, Hesiod, the Sophists, and atomists such as Democritus and Epicurus, although it did not really begin to be elaborated in a systematic way until the Middle Ages, by theologians whose greatest representatives are Duns Scotus and William of Occam.

One last comment on the question of the historical event. Arguably, neither Marx nor Engels ever came close to proposing a theory of history, in the sense of the unforeseen, unique, aleatory historical event; nor did either of them propose a theory of political practice. I am referring to the political-ideological-social practice of political activists, mass movements and, when they exist, their organizations, a practice which does not have concepts at its disposal, let alone a coherent theory that would make thinking it possible. Lenin, Gramsci and Mao thought it only partially. The one man to have thought the theory of political history, of political practice *in the present*, was Machiavelli. There is a tremendous gap waiting to be closed here. It is of decisive importance and, once again, points us to philosophy.

II
PHILOSOPHY–IDEOLOGY–POLITICS

Could you explain why you have put such emphasis on the triad philosophy–ideology–politics throughout you work?

I think it would be appropriate to begin my answer by discussing my conception of 'philosophy', of its emergence and function. Historically, philosophy emerged, in a sense, from religion, from which it inherited remarkable questions which were then converted into the great philosophical themes, albeit with different approaches and answers: the questions, for example, of the origin, end, or destiny of man, history and the world.

I nevertheless maintain that philosophy as such, philosophy in the strict sense, was constituted with the constitution of the first science, mathematics. This was no accident, since the constitution of mathematics marked, precisely, the transition from the empirical to the theoretical state. From this moment on, people began to reason in a different way about different objects: abstract objects.

Do you hold that philosophy could not have come into existence if a science had not existed first?

I do not think it could have, because philosophy took something of inestimable value from science: the model of rational abstraction that is indispensable to it.

In fact, philosophy came into being when mythological and religious ways of reasoning, moral exhortation and political or poetic eloquence were abandoned in favour of the forms of theoretical reasoning that are constitutive of science. In short, philosophy cannot appear unless there first exists a purely rational discourse, the model for which is to be found in the sciences.

What other characteristics have impressed its specificity upon philosophy over the course of its development?

Traditional philosophy assigned itself the irreplaceable historical task of speaking the Truth about everything: about the first causes and first principles of everything in existence, hence about everything that is knowable; about the ultimate purpose or destiny of man and the world. Hence it set itself up as the 'Science' of the totality, capable not only of providing the highest and most indubitable knowledge, but also of possessing Truth itself. This Truth is logos, origin, meaning.... Once the originary identity between *logos* and speech, between Truth and Discourse, has been posited, there exists, in this world, only one means of making Truth known: the discourse-form. For this reason, philosophy is absolutely incapable of foregoing its own discourse, which is the very presence of Truth as *logos*.

As for the composition/constitution of a philosophical system, there exist rigorous connections between all its theoretical elements, for example, its theses (or philosophical propositions) and categories. Could you explain what these are, and what their function is?

Thezis means 'position' in Greek. That is why a thesis calls forth its antithesis. As for categories, which are the most general concepts, the illustrations that come to mind are 'substance' and 'subject'. The category of 'subject' is of special interest. Between the fourteenth and eighteenth centuries, one finds, above all, the category of 'subject' used to account for a considerable number of ideologies and the corresponding practices. This category arose on the basis of juridical ideology and commodity relations, in which each individual is the *legal subject* of his juridical capacities as an owner of property, and so on. The same category invades the realm of philosophy with Descartes (the 'subject' of the 'I think'), and, later, that of moral ideology with Kant (the subject of 'moral consciousness'). It had long since invaded the political realm with the 'political subject' of the social contract. This demonstrates one of the theses that we defend: philosophy 'works on' categories capable of unifying the encounter of the ideologies and the corresponding practices.

Philosophy: a battlefield

And the functioning of philosophy?

Without claiming to be exhaustive, I maintain that every philosophy reproduces within itself, in one way or another, the conflict in which it finds itself compromised and caught up in the outside world. Every philosophy bears within itself the spectre of its opposite: idealism contains the spectre of materialism, and vice versa.

You have often pointed out that Kant calls philosophy a 'battlefield' [Kampfplatz].

Yes. One of the goals of philosophy is to wage theoretical battle. That is why we can say that every thesis is always, by its very nature, an antithesis. A thesis is only ever put forward in opposition to another thesis, or in defence of a new one.

While we're on the subject of this theoretical battle, do you maintain that the philosophical field is divided into two great blocs or contending positions, materialism and idealism?

No. I think that, in any philosophy, one finds idealist and materialist elements, with one of the two tendencies dominating the other in a given philosophy. In other words, there is no radical, cut-and-dried division because, in philosophies described as idealist, we can come across materialist elements, and vice versa. What is certain is that no absolutely pure philosophy exists. What exists are tendencies.

Can you cite a philosopher to illustrate what you say?

Pascal is an interesting, because paradoxical, instance. By way of the religious problems that he raises, epistemological problems also appear, problems of the theory of the history of the sciences and a theory of social relations, so that we may affirm that he exhibits profoundly materialist features. I was surprised to see, rereading Pascal over the last few years, that, without realizing it, I had already borrowed a few philosophical ideas from him: the whole theory of ideology, of misrecognition and recognition, is to be found in Pascal. When I asked myself where this encounter with him began, I suddenly realized that the only book that I had read in the five years I was forced to spend in a German prisoner-of-war camp was Pascal's *Pensées*. In the interim, I had completely forgotten this.[7]

Pascal has written surprising things about the history of the sciences. He was a great mathematician and a great physicist; he invented the adding machine; finally, he worked out a whole theory of the history of science.

We see here what you said a moment ago: every philosophy bears its own antagonist within itself.

Of course. Moreover, contradiction in philosophy is not contradiction between A and non-A, or between Yes and No. It is tendential. Hence it is traversed by tendencies. In reality, every philosophy is only the realization – more or less complete – of one of the two antagonistic tendencies, the idealist tendency and the materialist tendency. Outside each philosophy, what is realized is not the tendency, but the 'antagonistic contradiction' between the two tendencies.

How do you explain this?

This has to do with the very nature of philosophical war. When a philosophy sets out to occupy its adversary's positions, it is crucial that it 'capture' at least some of the enemy 'troops', that is to say, that it besiege its adversary's philosophical arguments. If one means to beat the enemy, one has first to know him, so that one can then take possession of not only his arms, troops and territory, but, *above all*, his arguments – for it is with their help that the great victories will be won.

I am reminded of a line from Goethe: 'He who would know the enemy must go into the enemy's territory.'[8]

That's right. Thus it is that every philosophy has to carry its defeated enemy within it in order to be able to constitute itself as a new philosophy. It can then parry all objections and attacks in advance, because it has already installed itself inside its enemy's *dispositive* and works on it, thereby modifying it, in order to carry out the task of absorbing and dominating its adversary. So it is that every philosophy of the idealist tendency necessarily contains materialist arguments, and vice versa. I repeat: there is no absolute purity. Even 'Marxian' materialist philosophy cannot claim to be exclusively 'materialist', because, if it were, it would have given up the fight, and abandoned, in advance, the idea of conquering the positions occupied by idealism.

What you say recalls Hobbes's Leviathan, *the state of perpetual war.*

Yet this 'philosophical war' is not quite 'the war of all against all' in the seventeenth-century England discussed by Hobbes. It is a war not *between individuals*, but between philosophical conceptions, and therefore between the philosophical strategies that, in great political and cultural conjunctures, battle for philosophical hegemony in this or that country or continent, or, ultimately – now that the world has practically become one big economic totality – across the globe.

Is this related to your latest definition of philosophy as 'class struggle in theory'?

Yes, as a theoretical form assumed by class struggle. But you have left out a crucial component of the definition: 'in the last instance'.

This 'in the last instance' must not be forgotten, for I have never said that philosophy was purely and simply class struggle in theory. The reservation 'in the last instance' is there to indicate that that there are things in philosophy besides class struggle in theory. But it also indicates that philosophy does indeed represent class positions in theory, that is to say, in the relations it maintains with the most theoretical forms of the human practices and, through them, the most concrete forms of the human practices, class struggle included.... And I have shown that, in philosophy, class struggle takes the form of contradictions between theses and antitheses, between positions of the idealist tendency and others of the materialist tendency.

There is an example in the history of philosophy which proves that philosophy is, 'in the last instance', class struggle in theory. Take Kant's terms, which I have already cited: philosophy is a battlefield. We see Kant setting out to construct a philosophy that is not polemical, not in a state of struggle. When Kant draws up the project of replacing the perpetual battle between philosophies with a 'perpetual peace', he does not evoke class struggle, yet he clearly recognizes the polemical nature, the agonistic nature, of any philosophy. In setting himself the goal of attaining a conflict-free philosophy, in perpetual peace, he recognizes – in the form of a denegation – the existence of a struggle in philosophy.

One last remark: in connection with the conflicts that philosophy has provoked in the course of its history, there appear *margins* or zones that can escape unequivocal determination by class struggle. Examples: certain areas of reflection on linguistics, epistemology, art, the religious sentiment, customs, folklore, and so on. This is to say that, within philosophy, there exist islands or 'interstices'.

The 'philosophy of the philosophers' and materialist philosophy

To conclude on this subject, could you sum up the specific features that distinguish these two philosophical positions or tendencies?

Certainly. But when people say 'philosophy', they always mean traditional philosophy of the idealist tendency, the 'philosophy of the philosophers'. This time, I shall take the materialist position in philosophy as my point of reference.

To talk about 'materialism' is to broach one of the most sensitive subjects in philosophy. The term 'materialism' belongs to the history of our philosophy, which was born in Greece, under Plato's patronage and within his general problematic. It is in Plato that we find the primary, fundamental distinction between the 'friends of the Forms' and the 'friends of the Earth'. Both terms in this pair are posited as essential to its constitution, in which each term commands the other.

Thus there exist friends of the Earth only because there exist friends of the Forms; and this distinction and this opposition are the work of the philosopher who inaugurates our philosophical history and considers himself a 'friend of the Forms' opposed to the 'friends of the Earth', among whom he ranges the empiricists, sceptics, sensualists and historicists. It should nevertheless be pointed out that, in the pair of opposites idealism/materialism, idealism – inasmuch as it is the dominant tendency in all of Western philosophy – has become the basis on which the pair itself is founded and constructed.

When we set out from what Heidegger says about the domination of logocentrism over all of Western philosophy, this is not hard to explain: one can readily see that, every time it is a question of *pronounced materialism* in the history of our philosophy, the term 'materialism' reproduces as, so to speak, its negation and mirror opposite, the term 'idealism'. Heidegger would say that idealism, just like materialism, obeys the 'principle of reason', that is, the principle according to which everything that exists, whether ideal [*idéel*] or material, is subject to the question of the *reason for its existence*.[9]

I would therefore say that, in the philosophical tradition, the evocation of materialism is the index of an exigency, a sign that idealism has to be rejected – yet without breaking free, without being able to break free, of the speculary pair idealism/materialism; hence it is an index, but, at the same time, a trap, because one does not break free of idealism by simply negating it, stating the opposite of idealism, or 'standing it on its head'. We must therefore treat the term 'materialism' with suspicion: the word does not give us the thing, and, on closer inspection, most materialisms turn out to be inverted idealisms. Examples: the materialisms of the Enlightenment, as well as a few passages in Engels.

What other features might be said to characterize idealism considered as the opposite pole required by materialism?

We can recognize idealism, I think, by the fact that it is haunted by a single question which divides into two, since the principle of reason bears not only on *the origin*, but also on *the end*: indeed, the Origin always, and very naturally, refers to the End. We can go further still: the question of the Origin is a question that arises on the basis of the question of the End. Anticipating itself, the End (the meaning of the world, the meaning of its history, the ultimate purpose of the world and history) projects itself back on to and into the question of the Origin. The question of the Origin of anything whatsoever is always posed as a function of what one imagines to be its end. The question of the 'radical origin of things' (Leibniz)[10] is always posed as a function of what one imagines to be their final destination, their End, whether it is a question of the Ends of Providence or of Utopia.

Have any philosophies escaped the idealism–materialism pair?

I would say that *if* certain philosophies escape this materialism–idealism pair, they can be recognized by the fact that they escape, or attempt to escape, questions of origin and end, that is, in the final analysis, the question of the End or Ends of the world and human history. These philosophies are 'interesting', for, in avoiding the trap, they express the exigency to abandon idealism and move towards what may be called (if you like) materialism, thus distinguishing themselves, I repeat, from every philosophy of Origin – whether it is a matter of Being, the Subject, Meaning or *Telos* – since they hold that these themes fall to religion and morality, but not to philosophy.

There are not many of these non-apologetic, truly non-religious philosophies in the history of philosophy: among the great philosophers, I can see only Epicurus, Spinoza, Marx, when he is well understood, Nietzsche and – Heidegger.

Refusing the radical origin as the philosophical bank of emission means that one also has to refuse the currency emitted by this bank in order to elaborate other categories, such as those of the dialectic.

I know that Spinoza is one of the philosophers whom you most admire – for, among other things, his contributions to the materialist position. I would like to ask you if you think that he escapes the temptation of Truth?

Yes, absolutely. Spinoza speaks, clinically, of the 'true', not Truth. He held that 'the true is the index of itself and indicates the false'. It is the index of itself not as presence but as product, in a double sense:

(1) as the result of the labour of a process that discovers it, and (2) as proving itself in its very production.

With this immanent conception of Truth, then, Spinoza leaves the problem of the criterion of Truth to one side.

What is more, he rejects the questions of the Origin and the Subject which sustain theories of knowledge.

What other distinctive features might a materialist philosophy be said to display?

To begin with, it does not claim to be autonomous or to ground its own origin and its own power. Nor does it consider itself to be a science, and still less the Science of sciences. In this sense it is opposed to all positivism. In particular, it should be pointed out that it renounces the idea that it possesses the Truth.

Philosophy of a materialist tendency recognizes the existence of objective external reality, as well as its independence of the subject who perceives or knows this reality. It recognizes that being or the real exists and is anterior to its discovery, to the fact of being thought or known. In this connection, it is sometimes asked how we can be certain that philosophy is not the theoretical delirium of a social class in quest of a guarantee or rhetorical ornaments. Many amateur theoreticians have, in all that they have produced over the centuries, fashioned a philosophy out of their individual fantasies, delusions or subjective preferences – or, simply, out of their desire to theorize.

Can we not say, precisely, that the materialist position marks a radical turn from the philosophies of representation that continue the speculary tradition of idealism, according to which we know only the ideas of things, not the things themselves?

One consequence follows from what we have said: materialist philosophies affirm the primacy of practice over theory. Practice, which is utterly foreign to the *logos*, is not Truth and is not reducible to – does not realize itself in – speech or seeing. Practice is a process of transformation which is always subject to its own conditions of existence and produces, not the Truth, but, rather, 'truths', or *some* truth [*de la vérité*]: the truth, let us say, of results or of knowledge, all within the field of its own conditions of existence. And while practice has agents, it nevertheless does not have a subject as the transcendental or ontological origin of its intention or project; nor does it have a Goal as the truth of its process. It is *a process without a subject* or Goal (taking 'subject' to mean an ahistorical element).

Thus practice shakes traditional philosophy to its foundations and enables us to begin to clarify what philosophy is, since practice is also rooted in the possibility of changing the world.

The irruption of practice is a denunciation of philosophy produced as 'philosophy'. It categorically affirms – in the face of philosophy's claim to embrace the entire set of social practices and ideas, to 'see the whole', as Plato said, in order to establish its dominion over these same practices – it categorically affirms, in the face of philosophy's claim that *it has no outside*, that *philosophy does indeed have an outside*; more precisely, that it exists through and for this outside. This outside, which philosophy likes to imagine that it has brought under the sway of Truth, is practice, the social practices.

We have to grasp the radical nature of this critique in order to perceive its consequences. It flies in the face of the *logos*, that is, the representation of a supreme something called 'the Truth'.

If the term 'Truth' is taken in its philosophical sense, from Plato to Hegel, and confronted with practice – a process without a subject or Goal, according to Marx – then it must be affirmed that there is no Truth of practice.

Practice is not a substitute for Truth for the purposes of an unshakeable philosophy; on the contrary, it is what shakes philosophy to its foundations; it is that other thing – whether in the form of the 'variable cause'[11] of matter or in that of class struggle – which philosophy has never been able to master. It is that other thing which alone makes it possible not merely to shake philosophy to its foundations, but also to begin to see clearly just what philosophy is.

You said a moment ago that practice enables philosophy to acknowledge that it has an outside.

Yes. Hegel's remark is well known: self-consciousness has a back, but doesn't know it. This remark finds an echo in François Mauriac's confession that, as a child, he didn't think grown-ups had behinds.

The irruption of practice attacks philosophy from behind. We shall see how.

To have an outside is the same thing, it will be objected, as to have a behind. But having a 'behind' means having an outside that one doesn't expect to. And philosophy doesn't expect to.

Has philosophy not brought the totality of what exists within the compass of its thought? Even mud, said Socrates; even the slave, said Aristotle; even the accumulation of wealth at one pole, said Hegel, and dire poverty at the other.

From that point of view, everything is indeed contained within philosophy.

Where, we might ask, is the exterior space? Does the real world, the material world, not exist for all philosophies, even idealist philosophies? Why, then, are we levelling these groundless accusations against philosophy? In order to bring all practices within the compass of its thought, and in order to impose itself on them with the objective of announcing its Truth to them, philosophy cheats: when it assimilates them and reworks them in accordance with its own philosophical form, it hardly does so with scrupulous respect for the reality – the particular nature – of such social practices and ideas. Quite the contrary: in order to affirm its power of truth over them, philosophy must first subject them to a veritable transformation. How else can it adjust them all to, and think them all under, the unity of one and the same Truth? The 'philosophers of philosophy' who set out to master the world by means of thought have always exercised the violence of the concept, of the *Begriff*, of 'seizure' [*de la mainmise*]. They assert their power by bringing under the sway of the law of Truth (their truth) all the social practices of men, who continue to toil and to dwell in darkness.

This perspective is not foreign to some of our contemporaries.

Not, at any rate, to those who seek, and, as a matter of course, find the archetype of power [*puissance*] in philosophy, the model of all power [*pouvoir*]. They write the equation knowledge = power, declaring – modern, cultivated anarchists that they are – that violence, tyranny and state despotism are all Plato's fault. In the same way, it used to be said, not so very long ago, that the Revolution was all Rousseau's fault.

The best way to reply to them is to go further than they do into the nature of philosophy, always through the scandalous breach opened up by practice. This is where Marx's influence is, perhaps, most profoundly felt.

Moreover, it must be borne in mind that power is not 'power for power's sake', not even in politics; it is nothing but what one makes of it, that is, what it produces as its result. And if the philosopher is indeed 'the man who sees the whole', he sees it only for the purpose of putting it in order, that is, of imposing a *determinate order* on the elements of the whole.

A final difference from idealism is Marx's concept of 'unity'. It must not be supposed that there exists only one model of unity: the unity of a Substance, an Essence or an act, confused notions that are present in both mechanistic materialism and the idealism of consciousness. Marx's unity is not the simple unity of a totality. The unity of which Marxism speaks is not the simple development of a unique essence or an originary, simple essence. It is the unity of complexity itself, which the mode of organization and articulation of complexity converts into unity. The complex whole has the unity of a structure articulated in dominance.

To conclude on this point, I would like to remind you of the ingenious illustration of the two tendencies that you once provided by drawing a humorous comparison with the passengers on a train.

Yes, I said that the idealist philosopher is a man who, when he catches a train, knows from the outset the station he will be leaving from and the one he will be arriving at; he knows the beginning [*origine*] and end of his route, just as he knows the origin and destiny of man, history and the world.

The materialist philosopher, in contrast, is a man who always catches 'a moving train', like the hero of an American Western. A train passes by in front of him: he can let it pass [*passer*] and nothing will happen [*se passe*] between him and the train; but he can also catch it as it moves. This philosopher knows neither Origin nor First

Principle nor destination. He boards the moving train and settles into an available seat or strolls through the carriages, chatting with the travellers. He witnesses, without having been able to predict it, everything that occurs in an unforeseen, *aleatory* way, gathering an infinite amount of information and making an infinite number of observations, as much of the train itself as of the passengers and the countryside which, through the window, he sees rolling by. In short, he records *sequences* [*séquences*] *of aleatory encounters*, not, like the idealist philosopher, ordered successions [*conséquences*][12] deduced from an Origin that is the foundation of all Meaning, or from an absolute First Principle or Cause.

Of course, our philosopher can conduct *experiments* on the consecutions [*consécutions*] of aleatory sequences that he has been able to observe, and can (like Hume) work out laws of consecution, 'customary' laws or *constants*, that is, structured theoretical figures. These experiments will lead him to deduce universal *laws* for each type of experiment, depending on the type of entities that served as its object: that is how the natural sciences proceed. Here we again encounter the term and function of 'universality'.

But what transpires when it is not a question of objects which repeat themselves indefinitely and on which experiments can be repeated and rerun by the scientific community from one end of the world to the other? (See Popper: 'A scientific experiment deserves the name when it can be indefinitely repeated under the same experimental conditions'.) Here the materialist philosopher-traveller, who is attentive to 'singular' cases, cannot state 'laws' about them, since such cases are singular/concrete/factual and are therefore not repeated, because they are unique. What he *can* do, as has been shown by Lévi-Strauss in connection with the cosmic myths of primitive societies, is to single out '*general constants*'[13] among the encounters he has observed, the 'variations' of which are capable of accounting for the singularity of the cases under consideration, and thus produce knowledge of the 'clinical' sort as well as ideological, political and social effects. Here we again find not the universality of laws (of the physical, mathematical or logical sort), but the *generality* of the *constants* which, by their variation, enable us to apprehend what is true of such-and-such a case.

The question of the functions of philosophy also arises here. Which of its functions do you consider the most important?

I will mention just a few. For example, that of serving as a guarantee or basis for the defence of certain theses that the philosopher needs in order to reflect on scientific discoveries or some other kind of event.

Another function of philosophy consists in tracing 'lines of demarcation' between the scientific and the ideological in order to free scientific practice of the ideological domination that impedes its progress.

Again, philosophy may be likened to a laboratory in which the ensemble of ideological elements are unified. In the past, religion played this unifying role; even earlier, the myths of primitive societies did. Religion contented itself with grand (ideological) Ideas such as the existence of God or the creation of the world; it used them to order all human activities and the corresponding ideologies, with a view to constituting the unified ideology that the classes in power needed to ensure their domination. There is, however, a limit: the dominant philosophy goes as far as it can in its role of unifier of the elements of ideology and the diverse ideologies, but it cannot 'leap over its time', as Hegel said, or 'transcend its class condition', as Marx said.

Philosophy fulfils another function in the political realm. Traditionally, it has played an apologetic, reactionary or revolutionary role with regard to the dominant political system, whether it has done so 'masked' or openly.

This connection to politics has been obvious since Plato – both at the theoretical level, in The Republic, *and at the practical level, when he agreed to become the counsellor of the tyrant of Syracuse.*

That's a good example. I think it is important to point out that, even when these philosophies adopted an apologetic stance *vis-à-vis* the authorities [*le pouvoir*], they attributed the dominant position, a position situated above everything else, to themselves, on the pretext that they were the guardians of the right arguments for upholding authority. The complicity involved here could be direct, but in the philosophical tradition, philosophy presented itself as the guardian of

Truth – until Marx, who allows us to put philosophy in its proper place. As such, it thought that the real *power*, in some sense, belonged to it: the power of *knowledge*.

Does philosophy act directly in the real world?

It may seem that philosophy inhabits a separate, remote world. Yet it acts, in a very special way: *at a distance*. It acts, by way of the ideologies, on real, concrete practices – for example, on cultural practices such as the sciences, politics, the arts and even psychoanalysis. And, to the extent that it transforms the ideologies, which reflect the practices even while orientating them in a certain direction, these practices can be transformed in their turn, depending on the variations or revolutions in social relations. Philosophical theses do indeed produce many different effects on social practices.

Here we must emphasize the fact that *antagonisms* (I do not say 'contradictions', because I am suspicious of this category, which is used every which way) *are inevitable*. If there exist philosophies that oppose each other in antagonistic fashion, it is because antagonistic class practices exist – fortunately.

The last few questions will serve as our transition to the problem of philosophy's relation to ideology. The connection you are making contradicts the traditional conception of philosophy as a self-contained, autonomous world standing above reality. Could you please say something more about this relationship between philosophy and ideology?

This is a subject on which I have been working for a long time, with an eye to elaborating a theory of ideology. But we ought first to explain what we mean by 'ideology'.

We can do so by directly citing a few of the definitions of it that appear in your texts.

- *'Ideology is necessarily a distortive representation of reality.' 'It is the imaginary representation that men make of their real conditions of existence.'*
- *'Ideology is a system of unified ideas that act on men's consciousness.'*
- *'Ideology performs a social function: that of ensuring the cohesion of the members of a society.'*

I would like to add two clarifications. First, man is so constituted that no human action is possible without language and thought. Consequently, there can be no human practice without a system of ideas (I would prefer to say a system of *notions* inscribed in words; this system thus constitutes the ideology of the corresponding practice). Second, I insist on the fact that an ideology is a *system of notions* only to the extent that it refers to a system of *social relations*. It is not a question of an idea produced by an individual imagination, but of a system of notions that can be projected socially, a projection that can constitute a corpus of socially established notions. Ideology begins only at this point. Beyond it lies the realm of the imaginary or of purely individual experience. One must, then, always refer to a social reality which is singular, unique and factual.

But could you explain how the 'consciousness' of a concrete individual can be 'dominated' by an ideological notion or a system of ideological notions?

I could begin by responding that this mechanism operates whenever a consciousness 'recognizes' these ideological notions to be 'true'. But how does this recognition come about? We already know that it is not the mere presence of the true which causes it to be perceived as true. There is a paradox here. It is as if, when I believe in a notion (or a system of notions), I were not the one who recognizes it and, confronted by it, could say: 'That's it, there it is, and it's true.' On the contrary, it is 'as if', when I believe in an idea, it were the idea that dominated me and obliged me to recognize its existence and truth, through its presence. It is 'as if' – the roles having been reversed – it were the idea that interpellated me, in person, and obliged me to recognize its truth. This is how the ideas that make up an ideology impose themselves violently, abruptly, on the 'free consciousness' of men: *by interpellating* individuals in such a way that they find themselves compelled 'freely' to recognize that these ideas are *true* – *compelled* to constitute themselves as 'free' 'subjects' who are capable of recognizing the true wherever it is present, and of *saying* so, inwardly or outwardly, in the very form and content of the ideas constitutive of the ideology in question.

That is the basic mechanism of ideological practice, the precise mechanism that transforms individuals into subjects. Individuals are always-already subjects, that is to say, always-already-subject to an ideology.

It follows from what you have just said that man is by nature an ideological being.

Absolutely, an ideological animal. I think that ideology has a trans-historical character, that it has always existed and always will exist. Its 'content' may change, but *its function never will.* If we go back to the beginning of time, we can see that man has always lived under the sway of ideological social relations.

So much for ideology 'in general', then. As early as 1970, however, you drew a distinction here, affirming that particular ideologies plainly do have a history, even if it is determined, in the last instance, by class struggle.

Granted; but I continued to maintain that ideology in general has no history. The theory of ideology concerns itself with that which is the hardest to understand and explain in any society: society's self-consciousness, the idea it forges of itself and the world. This is not a set of ideas about the world, but a clear representation of the world of ideas as a social product.

I am reminded of something that Robert Fossaert[14] *once said to you on this point. Since the split in the international Communist movement (1961–70), the Chinese Cultural Revolution and the crisis of May 1968, it has become obvious that the ideological question has a certain autonomy and specificity. These events very clearly exposed the contradiction – or system of contradictions – of Marxism or the various Marxisms.*

Indeed. Since then, it has become even harder to imagine that particular, regional ideologies have no history, whatever form they may have – religious, moral, juridical or political.

Finally, let me point out that it is not a question of observing society in so far as it produces or organizes, but, rather, in so far as it represents itself and its world, real or imaginary.

What can you tell us about the form of existence of ideology, the form in which it is materialized?

When we observe the social existence of ideologies, we see that they are inseparable from the institutions by means of which they are manifested, with their codes, languages, customs, rites and ceremonies.

We can affirm that it is in institutions such as the Church, School system, Family, Political Parties, Associations of Doctors or Lawyers, and so on, that the practical ideologies encounter their conditions and material forms of existence, their material support, or, more precisely, their material forms, since this corpus of ideas is inseparable from this system of institutions.

Can we say that the ideological apparatuses are a creation of the dominant class?

No. They existed earlier. What happens is that, under cover of the various social functions that objectively serve the purpose of social unity, these ideological apparatuses are invested and unified by the dominant ideology.

I would like to add a word about the dual nature of ideology. In reality, no ideology is purely arbitrary. It is always an index of real problems, albeit cloaked in a form of misrecognition and so necessarily illusory.

You have spoken of the 'ideological subject'. What, precisely, do you mean?

I mean the subject considered as an effect of structures that precede and found its existence – considered, that is, as an individual subjected or determined by ideological social relations.

It is a fact that social reproduction is not realized exclusively on the basis of the reproduction of labour, but, rather, presupposes the fundamental intervention of the ideological. Let us take an example: a worker who goes to his workplace has already travelled a long road through the social conditions – individual or collective – that induce him to come, voluntarily or involuntarily, and offer his services in exchange for the purchase of his labour-power: time, energy, concentration, and so on. And although the material means of reproducing labour-power is wages, they do not suffice, as is well known. From his school years on, the worker has been 'formed' to conform to certain social norms that regulate behaviour: punctuality, efficiency, obedience, responsibility, family love and *recognition of all forms of authority*.

This formation presupposes subjection to the dominant ideology. In other words, he is a subject structurally subjected to the dominant – or non-dominant – ideology; that is to say, to a society's hegemonic or subaltern norms and values.

Of course, the structure of subjection pre-exists the subject. When he is born, the conditions, institutions and apparatuses that will subject him already exist.

Precisely. There emerges a special relationship between ideology and the individual. It is established through the mechanism of interpellation, the functioning of which subjects the individual to ideology, assigning him a social role that he recognizes as *his*. What is more, he cannot fail to accept this role.

The efficacy of his acceptance of this role is guaranteed by the mode in which the constitution of the subject as a social being operates. If he is to succeed in identifying with himself, the subject needs – in order to be constituted – to identify with an 'other' who is his peer [*semblable*]; he recognizes himself as existing through the existence of the other and through his identification with him. It would seem that ideology here functions as the image of the 'other', an image that has been brought into conformity, socially and familially [*conformé socialement et familialement*], with what the family/society expects of every individual who comes into the world, beginning in infancy. The child assumes this prefigured image as the only possible way he can exist as a social subject. This is what confers his individuality upon him. The individual/subject demands that he be recognized as an individuality and a unity, as a 'someone'. But the 'one' (the subject) must be recognized by the 'other'. It seems that one has a psychosocial need to identify with the 'other' in order to recognize oneself as existing.

Thus, in practice, individuals accomplish the roles and tasks that have been assigned them by the social image of the look-alike [*semblable*] with which they have identified, and on the basis of which the process of their constitution as social subjects has been initiated. The reproduction of the social relations of production is guaranteed in this way.

What has been said so far paves the way for an important theoretical advance, both because this approach to the question of individual behaviour permeates the unconscious (which Freud left in the neutrality of ideological impartiality) with politics, and also because it takes us beyond psychologistic-individualistic explanations of history. But does it not presuppose a determinism which treats the individual as an effect of the already existing structures that found his existence?

That is why one of the central concerns of our theory is somewhat to reduce the theoretical gap between the determining and the determined.

Using the whole set of your theoretical instruments, can we think the transformation of subjects not only at the level of self-consciousness, but also at that of the consciousness of reality and the need to transform it?

Yes. Otherwise there would be no change, and people would never take positions that challenge and oppose that which is established, that which is dominant. There would be no 'revolutionary subjects'. But a subject is always an ideological subject. His ideology may change, shifting from the dominant ideology to a revolutionary ideology, but there will always be ideology, because ideology is the condition for the existence of individuals.

Why is it indispensable that the ideologies, taken together, receive their unity and orientation from philosophy, under the domination of categories such as truth?

To understand this, it is necessary, in Marx's perspective, to bring into play what I shall call the political form of the existence of ideologies in the ensemble of social practices. It is necessary to bring class struggle and the concept of the 'dominant ideology' into play.

As we have known since Machiavelli, in order for the power of the dominant class to endure, this class must transform its power from one based on violence to one based on consent. By means of the free consent of its subjects, it has to obtain the obedience that it could neither attain nor maintain by force alone.

It holds violence in reserve, as a final resort. This is one of the objectives accomplished by the system – the contradictory system – of the ideologies.

Does the class that takes power immediately forge its own ideology, and does it succeed in imposing it as the dominant ideology?

No. Historical experience shows that it takes time – sometimes a long time – to do so. We have only to consider the case of the bourgeoisie, which needed five hundred years, from the fourteenth century to the nineteenth, to accomplish this. But we need to bear something else in mind here. It is not simply a question of fabricating a dominant ideology by decree because one is needed, nor simply of constituting one in the course of a long history of class struggle. A dominant ideology must be constructed on the basis of what already exists, starting out from the elements and regions of existing ideology and the legacy of a diverse and contradictory past, while passing through the surprises represented by the events that constantly surge up in science and politics. Amid the class struggle and its contradictions, it is a question of constituting an ideology to overcome all these contradictions, an ideology unified around the essential interests of the dominant class for the purpose of securing what Gramsci called its *hegemony*.

Let us return to the subject of the relation between philosophy, ideology and politics.

If we understand the reality of the dominant ideology in this way, we can grasp the characteristic function of philosophy. Philosophy is neither a gratuitous operation nor a speculative activity. The great philosophers had a very different conception of their mission. They knew that they were responding to the great practical political questions: how is one to orientate oneself in thought and politics? What should one do? What direction should one take? They even knew that these political questions were historical. They might have believed that they were eternal questions, but they knew that these questions were posed by the vital interests of the society on whose behalf they thought.

It seems to me – this is what Marx enables us to grasp – that it is impossible to understand the determinant task of philosophy except, first and foremost, in relation to the central question of hegemony, of the constitution of the dominant ideology.

In sum, the task which philosophy is assigned and delegated by the class struggle is that of helping to unify the ideologies in a dominant ideology, guardian of the Truth.

How does philosophy help to perform this task?

Precisely by proposing to think the theoretical conditions of possibility for the resolution of existing contradictions, and thus for the unification of the social practices and their ideology. This involves abstract labour, a labour of pure thought, pure theorization.

In carrying out the task of unifying the diversity of the practices and their ideologies – which it experiences as an internal necessity, although this task is assigned it by the great class conflicts and historical events – what does philosophy do? It produces a whole array of categories that serve to think and situate the different social practices under the ideologies. Philosophy produces a general problematic: that is, a manner of posing, and therefore resolving, any problem that may arise. Lastly, philosophy produces theoretical schemas or figures that serve as a means of overcoming contradiction, and as links for connecting the various elements of ideology. Moreover, it guarantees the Truth of this order, stated in a form that offers all the guarantees of a rational discourse.

It follows from all this that philosophy does not stand outside the world or outside historical conflicts or events.

Even in its most abstract form, that of the works of the great philosophers, philosophy is situated somewhere in the vicinity of the ideologies, as a kind of theoretical laboratory in which the fundamentally political problem of ideological hegemony – that is, of the constitution of the dominant ideology – is experimentally put to the test, in the abstract. The work accomplished by the most abstract philosophers does not remain a dead letter: what philosophy has received from the class struggle as a demand, it gives back to it in the form of systems of thought which then work on the ideologies in order to transform and unify them.

Just as we can empirically observe the conditions of existence historically imposed on philosophy, so we can empirically observe philosophy's effects on the ideologies and social practices.

Could you cite a historical example?

Seventeenth-century French rationalism and Enlightenment philosophy, in which the results of the work of philosophical elaboration passed into ideology and the social practices. These two phases of bourgeois philosophy are two constitutive moments of bourgeois ideology as a dominant ideology. It was constituted as a dominant ideology amid a struggle, in which philosophy played its role as theoretical cement for the unity of this ideology.

We are witnessing another case today, under the influence of Anglo-Saxon imperialism. A displacement of domination is underway. What dominates is no longer the theoretical vapidity of the ideologies of human rights, nor even bourgeois juridico-moral ideology, but – this shift began as early as 1850 – a neo-positivist, logicist, mathematized ideology of Anglo-Saxon origin, laced with social biologism, pragmatism and behaviourism. From this standpoint, the truly dominant ideologies in actual practice (I do not mean dialectical materialism) are quite similar in the USSR and the United States.

In the present ideological conjuncture, our main task is to constitute the kernel of an authentic materialist ideology and of a philosophy that is correct,[a] accurate [*juste*, *correct*], in order to facilitate the emergence of a progressive ideology.

a 'Correct' should be distinguished from 'true'. Fundamentally, the attribute 'true' implies a relationship to theory and concerns scientific knowledge. As for the Truth, it is a religious and ideological myth whose function is to guarantee the established order. That which is 'correct' or 'accurate' [*juste ou correct*] concerns a relationship to practice. The theses comprising the philosophical corpus do not admit of any scientific demonstration or proof, but call for rational justifications of a special type. They may therefore be called 'accurate' or 'correct' [*juste*] (in the sense not of justice – which is a moral category – but of 'being well adjusted', a practical category that indicates the adequacy of means to ends). We can therefore say that that which is 'correct', because it refers to action, also refers to the definition of any 'correct' or 'accurate' strategy or line in whatever camp. [This note was added by Althusser. The last sentence is garbled; the basic meaning seems to be that 'correctness' is a category that applies to all practice, whatever its political colouring.]

Notes

1 See pp. 209–14 and note 1 on p. 247 above.

2 *FM* 21–2.

3 See p. 18 and note 24 on p. 152 above.

4 See p. 211 and note 3 on p. 248 above.

5 See p. 45 note 63 on p. 155 above.

6 See *MECW* 4: 127.

7 See Althusser, *Journal de captivité. Stalag XA, 1940–1945*, Paris, 1992.

8 *Wer den Feind will verstehen, muss in Feindes Lande gehen.* Turgenev's adaptation of a couplet by Goethe that Lenin cites in *Materialism and Empirio-Criticism*, *LCW* 14: 317. [*Trans.*]

9 See p. 170 and note 11 on p. 204 above.

10 See p. 174 and note 11 on p. 204 above.

11 Plato, *Timaeus* 48a–b. [*Trans.*]

12 Compare the review of *Capital* by I. I. Kaufman approvingly cited by Marx, *C1* 101–2. Kaufman says that Marx is interested in 'precise analysis of the series of successions, of the sequences and links within which different stages of development present themselves'. [*Trans.*] See also August-Antoine Cournot, *Exposition de la théorie des chances et des probabilités*, Paris, 1843. [*Trans.*]

13 Compare 'OMT' 9: 'Spinoza … discovers generic and not "general" constants.' [*Trans.*]

14 A sociologist whose work on ideology was influenced by Althusser's. He is the author of the multi-volume *La Société*. [*Trans.*]

Portrait of the Materialist Philosopher

The man's age doesn't matter. He can be very old or very young. The important thing is that he doesn't know where he is, and wants to go somewhere. That's why he always catches a moving train, the way they do in American Westerns. Without knowing where he comes from (origin) or where he's going (goal). And he gets off somewhere along the way, in a four-horse town with a ridiculous railway station in the middle of it.

Saloon, beer, whisky. 'Where d'ya hail from, bud?' 'From a long ways off.' 'Where ya headed?' 'Dunno!' 'Might have some work for ya.' 'Okay.'

And so our friend Nikos goes to work. He's a Greek by birth who has immigrated to the USA like so many others before him, and he doesn't have a penny in his pockets. He works hard and, a year later, marries the prettiest girl in town. He scrapes together a little stake and buys the first cattle in his herd. Thanks to his intelligence and knack [*Einsicht*] for picking out young livestock (horses, cattle), he ends up with the best bunch of animals around – after ten years of hard work.

The best bunch of animals = the best bunch of categories and concepts. He competes with the other landowners, but peacefully. Everyone admits that he's the best and that his categories and concepts (his herd) are the best. His reputation spreads throughout the West, and then the whole country.

From time to time, he catches the moving train in order to see, talk, listen – like Gorbachev in the streets of Moscow. Besides, one can catch the train wherever one happens to be!

More popular than anyone else, he could be elected to the White House, although he started out from nothing. But no, he'd rather travel, go out and walk the streets; that's how one comes to understand the true philosophy, the one that people have in their heads and that is always contradictory.

This is when he reads the Hindus and the Chinese (Zen), as well as Machiavelli, Spinoza, Kant, Hegel, Kierkegaard, Cavaillès, Canguilhem, Vuillemin, Heidegger, Derrida, Deleuze, and so on. Thus, without having intended to, he becomes a quasi-professional materialist philosopher – not that horror, a *dialectical* materialist, but an aleatory materialist.

He attains the level of classical wisdom, Spinoza's third kind of 'knowledge', Nietzsche's superman, and an understanding of the eternal return: viz., that everything is repeated and exists only through differential repetition. Now he can engage in discussions with the great idealists. He not only understands them, but also explains the reasons for their theses to them! The others sometimes come round to his views with great bitterness, but, after all,

Amicus Plato, magis amica Veritas!

Index

Algeria 71, 72, 104
alienation 42, 64–67, 136
Althusser, Louis
  marriage 164–5
  PCF and 245–6, 253–6
  political project of 243
  For Marx 211, 253; *The Future Lasts a Long Time* 164; 'Ideology ad Ideological State Apparatuses' 99, 138, 240, 241–2, 263; *Lenin and Philosophy* 231, 240, 258; *Reading Capital* (with Balibar) 196, 240, 263; *The Spontaneous Philosophy of the Scientists* 221
Anderson, Perry 140
Aristotle 93, 169, 175, 177, 192, 225, 260, 276
Aron, Raymond 35, 211, 258
Artaud, Antonin 196

Babbage, Charles 84
Babeuf, Gracchus 34
Bachelard, Gaston 221
Balibar, Étienne 43n, 202, 263
base and superstucture
  Gramsci on 140–1
  Marx on 55–6
Baudelaire, Charles 230, 232–3
Berlinguer, Enrico 112
Bertrand, Mireille 32n
Bettelheim, Charles 199n
Bidet, Jacques 257–8
Big Bang 195
Blanqui, Auguste 34, 86
Boccara, Paul 123
Boddaert, François 208
Borgia, Cesare 172, 193
Bossuet, Jacques-Bénigne 83
bourgeoisie 201–2
Brecht, Bertolt 33
Breton, André 221
  on elephants 193
Brunschvicg, Leon 119

Cabet, Étienne 19

Camon, Ferdinando 219
Canguilhem, Georges 193, 291
capitalism
  as aleatoric in origin 197
  transition from feudalism 201–2
Carnot, Nicolas Léonard Sadi 84, 107
Cavaillès, Jean 291
Char, René 220, 230
Charles I 180
Chartism 18–9, 26
Chile 112
China 8, 282
Christianity 127
clinamen ('swerve') 168–70, 260–2 – *see also* encounter
commodity fetishism 134
Commune – *see* Paris Commune
Communism 37–8, 49, 93, 212–4
Communist Party
Gramsci on 147
  in France (PCF) 10, 35n, 71, 74, 119, 147, 212–3, 238, 243, 245–6, 253–6
    abandons dictatorship of the proletariat 85–6
  in Italy (PCI) 112, 119, 139–149, 254
  self analysis of 9
  in USSR (CPSU) 8
Conry, Yvette 194n
Cornu, Auguste 26
Cournot , Antoine Augustin 193
critique 17–8
Croce, Benedetto 35, 139, 140, 146, 176
Cromwell, Oliver 180
CRS (*Compagnie républicaine de sécurité*) 73–6, 80, 101, 102, 103, 111
Cultural Revolution 8, 90, 196, 282
culture versus politics 146, 149–50

d'Estaing, Valéry Giscard 81
Darwin, Charles 194
De Gaulle, Charles 72–4, 77
Debray, Régis 219
Deleuze, Gilles 189, 291
Della Volpe, Galvano 42
Democritus 190, 192, 256, 260, 261, 265
Derrida, Jacques 167, 178, 189, 191, 215, 231, 262, 291
Descartes, René 176, 177, 178, 191, 225, 255, 268
dialectical materialism ('diamat') 253–4
dialectics 254–5
dictatorship of proletariat 69, 85–95, 144, 256
Dreyfus affair 71
Duménil, Gérard 7
Duns Scotus 266

education 146
encounter [the swerve, *das Vorgefundene*, *la prise*] 146, 167–9, 171–4, 189–90, 193, 238, 260–1
  in *Capital* 197–9
  in early Althusser 196
Engels, Friedrich 31, 66, 68, 217, 272
  Marx and 26–7

on state 120
Communist Manifesto (with Marx) 12, 30, 47, 89; *Condition of the Working-Class in England* 197; *The German Ideology* (with Marx) 29–30, 37, 136, 210; *The Holy Family* (with Marx) 29; 'The Principles of Communism' 200n
Epicurus 167, 168–9, 175, 176–7, 187, 190, 191, 195, 218, 256, 260, 261, 265, 273
epistemological break 27, 29
Eurocommunism 8, 68–9
exploitation 121

fear 180
fetishism 126–35, 136
Feuerbach, Ludwig 64–6, 137
Capital and 126
on elephants 193n
force 108–10, 124, 183
Gramsci on 140–1, 143, 145–7, 150
Fossaert, Robert 282
French revolution 187, 201
Freud, Sigmund 231, 285
on Nietzsche 226
on Schopenhauer 226–7
Friedrich-Wilhelm IV 64
Furet, François 236–7

Gentile, Giovanni 139, 140, 146
Germany 112
God 176–7
Goethe, Johan Wolfgang 270
Goldschmidt, Victor 186
Gorbachev, Mikhail Sergeyevich 291
Gotha Programme 50–54
Gramsci , Antonio 70, 78, 136–7, 173, 228, 230, 239, 286
on hegemony 138–50, 241
on state 99, 125
Grimaud, Maurice 80, 104
Grotius, Hugo 62
Guéroult, Martial 210

Hegel, Georg Wilhelm Friedrich 175, 188, 193, 229, 257–8, 275, 276, 279, 291
on law 61–2
as Marx's horizon 34–5, 42–3
on state 63
hegemony 138–50, 286
Heidegger, Martin 167, 168, 175, 177, 189, 190, 191, 219, 220, 228, 229, 233, 237, 240, 261, 273, 291
on logocentrism 272
materialism and 170–1, 216–7
Heraclitus 189
Hesiod 265
Hinduism 291
'historic compromise' 112
Hobbes, Thomas 62, 167, 168, 179–83, 184, 188, 261, 270
Hölderlin, Friedrich 232–3
Homer 265
humanism 57–8, 127
Hume, David 278
Husserl, Edmund 119, 219

idealism 216–7, 221, 222–5, 268–80
versus materalism 268–80
ideology 135, 137, 269, 279–84
as transhistorical 282–4
imperialism 288
India 38
International Working Men's League 31
interpellation 241, 281–2

Julius II 193

Kant, Immanuel 63, 195, 221, 225, 231, 257, 268, 291
Kautsky, Karl 21–5
Kierkegaard, Soren 291
Krushchev, Nikita 151
Kugelmann, Ludwig 40n

Lacan, Jacques 213
Lafargue, Paul 36
language 231
law 194–5
Lecourt, Dominique 189n, 194n, 221
Lefebvre, Jean-Pierre 43n
Leibniz, Gottfried Wilhelm 217–8
Lenin, V.I. 47, 48
dictatorship of the proletariat and 86–9, 91, 92
on destruction of state 114–7
Kautsky and 22–5
Sverdlov lecture 81–2, 100, 125
Materialism and Empirio-Criticism 244
Lévi-Strauss, Claude 210, 264, 278
liberation theology 228, 230
Locke, John 62–3, 184
Lockheed scandal 78
Lucretius 167, 169, 190, 191, 192
Lyautey, Louis Hubert Gonzalves 103, 183

Macherey, Pierre 222
Machiavelli, Niccolò 46, 140, 167, 168, 171–9, 186, 192–3, 198, 285, 291
machines 105–8
Malamud, Mauricio 208–14, 215, 226, 227, 228, 229, 232, 238, 243, 251
Malebranche, Nicolas 167
Mao Tse Tung 8, 13, 92, 256
Mardashvili, Merab 1–6
Marx, Karl 167, 168, 195, 218, 261, 273, 279
on communism 37–8
concept of unity 277
dictatorship of the proletariat and 89, 92, 94–5
Engels and 26–7
epistemological break 27, 29
Hegel and 134, 210–1, 257–8
idealism of 37–9
ideology and 135, 137–8
as journalist 30–1
letter to Weydemeyer 19–20
limits of 117–8, 135–9
as medium of proletariat 18
omissions of 98–9, 210

philosophy and 257–9
on science 14–5
on state 63–4, 67–8, 78, 96–9, 183
versus totalizing 15–6
1844 Manuscripts 27–8, 67–8; *Capital* 12–3, 16, 31, 38–46, 126–7, 131, 196–7, 197–9, 210–1, 255; *Capital Vol. 3* 95–6. 148; *The Civil War in France* 32, 49–50; *Communist Manifesto* (with Engels) 12, 30, 37, 89; *Contribution to the Critique of Political Economy* 41, 45, 132, 263; *Contribution to the Critique of Hegel's Philosophy of Law* 67; *Critique of the Gotha Programme* 31–2, 37, 50–4, 130, 212; *The Eighteenth Brumaire* 67, 98, 137; *The German Ideology* (with Engels) 29–30, 37, 136, 210; *The Holy Family* (with Engels) 29; *Notes on Wagner* 37; *On the Jewish Question* 67–8; *The Poverty of Philosophy* 29, 98, 135; Preface to *A Contribution to the Critique of Political Economy* ('*1859 Preface*') 20, 37–8, 41n, 47–8, 54–61, 89, 136, 146; *Theses on Feuerbach* 29, 210, 239–40
materialism
aleatory 192, 195–6, 256–66, 278, 291
in Heidegger 170–1
idealism and 216, 221, 222–5, 268–80
as ideology 288
non-teleological 167–8, 188–90, 199, 262
Mauriac, François 275
Mauroy, Pierre 165
May 1968 70, 103–4, 125, 213, 282
Mersenne, Marin 180
Michels, Charles 71
Mitterand, François 165
mode of production
Balibar on 202
as ideological 198, 200
monsters 93
Montesquieu, Charles-Louis-de-Secondat 187
Mosca, Gaetano 139, 141
Moses 179
Musil, Robert 232

National Front 238
Navarro, Fernanda 164, 208, 209, 214–47, 251–2
Nietzsche, Friedrich 189, 196, 217, 218, 219, 220, 226–8, 231, 232, 233, 235–6, 237, 273
on Plato 225
nominalism 265

Occam, William of 266
Osier, Jean-Pierre 16n

Paris Commune 49–50, 115, 125
Pascal, Blaise 175, 269
PCF – *see* Communist Party, in France

Pétain, Henri-Philippe 71–3, 119
Philosophy
origins of 266–7
as petit-bourgeois enterprise 290–1
role of 287
Physiocrats 130, 134
Plato 169, 175, 216, 240, 260, 271–2, 275, 276
Plekhanov, Georgi Valentinovich 136
Po valley 198
politics 150
Popper, Karl 264, 278
practice 259, 274–5, 277
Proudhon, Pierre Joseph 29, 34
psychoanalysis 231
public services 120–3
pyramids 120

Raymond, Pierre 222–4
religion 64–5, 279
reproduction 95–9, 123–6, 199–200
Reynal, Orfila 239, 243, 247, 252
Ricardo, David 34–5
Robinson Crusoe 127, 129, 131
Rousseau, Jean-Jacques 63, 167, 169, 191, 195 , 261, 277
'[Discourse on] the Origin of Languages' 183–8
Rousseau, Henri 'Le Douanier' 184
Russian revolution 112, 142

Sartre, Jean-Paul 219, 220, 245
Saussure, Ferdinand de 210
Schopenhauer, Arthur 226–7
Second International 59
show trials 8
Smith, Adam 34
Soboul, Albert 201n
Socrates 276
Sophists 265
Spinoza, Baruch 168, 176–9, 187, 195, 218, 226, 255, 273–4, 291
Sraffa, Piero 36, 40, 59
Stalinism 253–4
state 67–71
as apparatus/machine 81–5, 99–110
destruction of 114–8
Gramsci on 125
as groups of armed men 103
Hobbes on 183
as instrument 68–70
law and 106–7
Lenin on 81–2
Marx on 183
personnel of 111–4
as separate from class struggle 70–81, 119–20
special nature of 100–6, 123–6
Stirner, Max 175
structuralism 243
substance 235–6
superstructure 55–6, 59–61

ten-hour day 76–7
tennis 215
Third International 8–9
Tillon, Charles 72

Timbaud, Jean-Pierre 71
Togliatti, Palmiro 139

unconscious 231, 285
USSR 212, 254
split with China 8, 282

violence 90–91
  force and 108–9, 124
void 174–6, 202, 262
Vuillemin, Jules 291

Weber, Max 101
Weitling, Wilhelm 19
Weydemeyer, Joseph 19–20
Wittgenstein, Ludwig 190, 265

Zen 291